T0247860

Praise for *Wiseguys and the White House*

"Eric Dezenhall treads new literary ground with this book. The writing is sharp and agile, and the insights are well earned. Read it, and you might find yourself surprised by the fine line between the underworld and the upperworld in American history. You might even be disturbed. But most of all, in Dezenhall's hands, you will be highly entertained by this fresh, bracing exposé of the dark side of American politics."

—T. J. English, *New York Times* best-selling author of
Havana Nocturne and *The Last Kilo*

"*Wiseguys and the White House* is an eye-opening, authoritative, remarkably detailed exposé of the interplay between organized crime and our presidents, shockingly revealing how close we have come to Mob rule."

—Ronald Kessler, *New York Times* bestselling author of
The Secrets of the FBI and *The First Family Detail*

"Mobsters and presidents? The ties aren't just in pulp fiction. Eric Dezenhall tracks down the startling deals and deceptions that both sides might prefer to keep secret—from FDR to JFK to Trump."

—Susan Page, *New York Times* bestselling author of
Madam Speaker

"A cautionary tale about the mob's role in American presidencies that has the considerable virtue of being true."

—Laurence Leamer, *New York Times* bestselling author of
The Kennedy Men

"Impeccably sourced and brilliantly written, Dezenhall provides a tour de force of the shadowy hypocritical world where mobsters and our apex political leaders have intersected over generations. Eye popping revelations in shocking detail jump off the page in every chapter."

—Richard Ben-Veniste, Watergate special prosecutor, author
The Emperor's New Clothes

"Strange bedfellows doesn't begin to tell the story of *Wiseguys and the White House*. This is a fast-paced and fascinating look at a dark side of American history, a political primer that isn't part of Poly-Sci 101. Goodfellas, it turns out, have ALWAYS been bedfellows."

—George Anastasia, author of *Gotti's Rules*

"In this fascinating and wholly original book, Eric Dezenhall excavates the long and troubling history of the Mafia's octopus-like reach into that most storied of America's residences, the White House—and vice versa. With painstaking research, keen intelligence, and acute analysis, Dezenhall illuminates the mutually beneficial relationship between presidents and gangsters that has helped to define the modern era.

—Corey Mead, author of *The Hidden History of the White House*

"*Wiseguys and the White House* is a remarkable work of investigative journalism which not only uncovers the multitude of mob fingerprints left all over the Oval Office, but in the telling of that story gives us a compelling, factual, inside history of the real gangsters who reigned from the end of prohibition into the twenty-first century. Eric Dezenhall is a superior and witty writer."

—Paul Dickson, author of *The Rise of the G.I. Army 1940–941:
The Forgotten Story of How America Forged a Powerful Army
Before Pearl Harbor*

"Equal parts entertaining and informative . . . One of the country's true experts on the mob, Eric does a masterful job of penetrating both the code of Omertà and the secrets of the state in writing this revealing book."

—James Bamford, bestselling author of *The Puzzle Palace,
Body of Secrets*, and *SpyFail*

Wiseguys

AND

THE WHITE HOUSE

Also by Eric Dezenhall

Best of Enemies: The Last Great Spy Story of the Cold War
(with Gus Russo)

Money Wanders

The Devil Himself

*Damage Control: Why Everything You Know
About Crisis Management Is Wrong*
(with John Weber)

*Glass Jaw: A Manifesto for Defending Fragile Reputations
in an Age of Instant Scandal*

Wiseguys

AND

THE WHITE HOUSE

GANGSTERS, PRESIDENTS, AND
THE DEALS THEY MADE

Eric Dezenhall

HARPER
An Imprint of HarperCollins*Publishers*

HarperCollins books may be purchased for educational, business, or sales promotional use. For information, please email the Special Markets Department at SPsales@harpercollins.com.

FIRST EDITION

Designed by Nancy Singer

Library of Congress Cataloging-in-Publication Data has been applied for.

ISBN 978-0-06-339061-4

24 25 26 27 28 LBC 5 4 3 2 1

For Lincoln, Jayme, and Oliver, my little enforcers

During the writing of this book, people important to me from different facets of my life departed, and they were in my thoughts as I tried to make sense of the way things work in our small and strange pocket of the galaxy. I don't have many answers. Perhaps they now do. I will deeply miss signing this book for Danielle Ben-Veniste, Gerald Bernstein, Jessica Fetui Corotan, Michael Ochsman, Tracy Ochsman, Judith Schilling, and Fred Squires.

I am the sheep, wishing to return to the sheepfold. If you were thoroughly acquainted with the nature of my offenses, I should appear to you much less guilty and still worthy to discharge the duties of a good citizen.

—Jean Lafitte, pirate and privateer, in a letter to
Governor William Claiborne of Louisiana

If I could only live to see it, to be there with you. What I wouldn't give for twenty more years! Here we are, protected, free to make our profits without Kefauver, the goddamn Justice Department, and the F.B.I. ninety miles away, in partnership with a friendly government. Ninety miles! It's nothing! Just one small step, looking for a man who wants to be President of the United States, and having the cash to make it possible. Michael, we're bigger than U.S. Steel.

—Hyman Roth, *The Godfather, Part II*

The Mafia exists in the American imagination because we want it to exist.

—Pete Hamill

Contents

Wiseguys

AND

THE WHITE HOUSE

1

Piker Ryan's List

CENTURIES OF POLS AND GANGSTERS

Organized crime will put a man in the White House someday, and he won't even know it until they hand him the bill.

—NYPD organized crime expert Ralph Salerno

On a hot summer day in the early 1980s, I followed two women I worked with in the communications office of the White House out to the South Lawn for a media opportunity with President Ronald Reagan. I was in my early twenties, and my role that day was routine and minor, ensuring I got the contact information for the media in attendance for potential follow-up.

One of the women, Sue, asked me to remind her where I was from. I answered, "Cherry Hill, New Jersey."

"Isn't that Mafia?" she asked.

Her question made sense. My hometown had been in the news lately because of a violent mob war. The long-standing Philadelphia–South Jersey "Docile Don," Angelo Bruno, had been killed in front of his house and photographed, very dead, in the passenger seat of his car, his bloody mouth wide open in a mask of shock. This ignited a power struggle involving a Mafia old guard, "Young Turks," pro-drug and anti-drug gangsters, and two New York City Mafia families with interests in the region. Bruno had been a savvy operator: Someone close to him told me that when the don wanted to meet with his associates, he would check into Cherry Hill Hospital complaining of chest pain, then get a room in the maternity ward near crying babies to hold sensitive meetings. All of this was to avoid surveillance.

My hometown had received particular attention because it was the headquarters of the "Cherry Hill Gambinos," Giovanni (John), Giuseppe (Joe), and Rosario (Sal) Gambino, cousins of the late Don Carlo Gambino and partners with Bruno. Authorities alleged these Gambinos were under scrutiny because they were kingpins in the "Pizza Connection" heroin ring, where drugs were distributed through a network of pizza parlors. Put differently, Cherry Hill was considered by law enforcement to be the headquarters of heroin importation and distribution in the United States. This warranted a mention in a report prepared by Reagan's President's Commission on Organized Crime Report. Bruno's legacy as an anti-drug boss was being questioned because while his men were said not to traffic in drugs, which was fabled to be "the rule" in the Mafia, at the very least, he had been in business with men who did. At most, he had been their partners. *The Sopranos'* boss, Johnny Sack, once said, "For God's sake, we bend more rules than the Catholic Church!"

The Gambinos' headquarters was Valentino's nightclub, down the street from my high school, a five-minute walk from my house. The brothers' adjacent homes, essentially a compound, were close by. One of them was emblazoned with a stained glass *G*. Al Martino, who played the Frank Sinatra–like figure, Johnny Fontaine, in *The Godfather,* lived around the corner from me in a house with a horseshoe drive-way and brick arches that mimicked Roman aqueducts. The Latin Casino Theater Restaurant, across the street from the Garden State Park Racetrack, had also been around the corner and had been Sinatra's go-to venue in the Philadelphia area. Then there was the Sans Souci Restaurant, now long gone, which had been the supper club where Bruno had been known to induct or "make" members into his family.

In the 1980s, denizens of the area turned the local mob war into a spectator sport, betting on one faction or another, bragging about any attenuated personal link to "the boys" (*My aunt sat next to Skinny Joey's barber in high school!*"). You could be a solid citizen in my community and be acquainted with or related to someone from the racket world. My family had been in the region since the early 1900s, and we had and knew our share of characters going back to Prohibition. Most of us were law-abiding and boring. I was an undersized, straight-arrow kid focused on schoolwork, tennis, and student government. If I was a badass, then Mister Rogers was John Gotti.

When Sue, my boss, asked about my hometown, a few other colleagues perked up at the word "Mafia." I defended Cherry Hill with the usual rhetoric about gangsters being a tiny fraction of the population.

"You couldn't bring up Muhammad Ali? He lived in Cherry Hill," I said. "So does the Flyers' goalie Bernie Parent. Keith Richards stayed in Cherry Hill for a month in rehab."

Nobody cared; they didn't want to hear about the teachers, doctors, and lawyers; they wanted to hear about the new boss, the maniacal Nicodemo "Little Nicky" Scarfo, Philip "Chicken Man" Testa (who had just been blown up by a nail bomb under his front porch, memorialized in a just-released Bruce Springsteen song), Philip "Crazy Phil" Leonetti, Anthony "Tony Bananas" Caponigro (recently found dead in the trunk of a car with $100 bills stuffed in various orifices after having been tortured for plotting against Bruno), Raymond "Long John" Martorano (a Cherry Hill resident, reportedly a methamphetamine kingpin), the pint-sized Harry "the Hunchback" Riccobene, who was making a play for the throne, and my late neighbor, the 750-pound Sylvan "Cherry Hill Fats" Scolnick who before his death had been driven around in the back of a mail truck, which provided him a bit more breathing room as he expanded like Violet Beauregard in *Willy Wonka and the Chocolate Factory*.

Then another woman in our White House retinue—I'll call her Jane—said something that shocked me: "You know, the mob killed President Kennedy." The others nodded as if this were a known fact. I couldn't believe what I had just heard.

Before I had a chance to respond, President Reagan came out from the side doors of the Oval Office next to the Rose Garden and began his photo op with a visiting group. He was wearing a light, summer-weight suit. His cheeks were rosy, and his thick chestnut (not black) hair was swept back, showing grayer than conveyed on television.

When the session was done, I responded to my colleague's JFK comment by asking Jane if she was serious. She said she was, as if everybody had known that the mob killed JFK.

"Have you ever *met* these guys?" I asked.

"No," the group said.

"Well, if you ever did, you wouldn't be impressed with their capacity to kill a president and get away with it for decades.

"The real power," I added, "is in that room twenty feet away from us." The sun reflected off the thick bulletproof glass of the three rear windows of the Oval Office.

I understood where my colleagues' notions about organized crime came from. Literature and cinema assign extraordinary talents to gangsters. A new generation of rappers has emerged with names like Capone, Corleone, Gambino, and Gotti somewhere in their monikers, conveying that "Mafia" means cool and sexily dangerous. Online discussion groups are replete with keyboard warriors angrily tagging those who cooperate with the government as "rats," as if they are so in-the-mob that they, too, have been betrayed and must pursue *la vendetta*. Much of what we have come to learn about American organized crime is better than the truth. Crime novelist Mickey Spillane wrote in *Kiss Me, Deadly*:

> The bastards knew everything. What they didn't know they could find out and when they did the blood ran. The Organization. The syndicate. The Mafia. It was filthy, rotten right through but the iron glove it wore was so heavy and so sharp it could work with incredible, terrible efficiency.

I failed to persuade any of the White House aides of my position. They interpreted my skepticism of mob involvement in the JFK assassination as a twisted defense to frame gangsters in a more harmless light. The term "spin doctor" had just come into vogue to describe our line of work, and I suppose they thought I was plying my nascent trade. Nevertheless, the conversation has stayed with me for forty years because

I believed that my colleagues' *lack* of familiarity with organized crime informed their assessment of its role in the most notorious murder in modern history.

Over time, I saw that the reverse was also true: I would hear acquaintances talking about White House intrigue as if presidents could dispatch CIA ninjas to unleash massive conspiracies of violence under cover of darkness without detection. This, too, didn't resemble what my experience had come to be in the ensuing years. While I have never been a big player in presidential politics, or organized crime, I had seen enough to believe that both could do bad things but were constrained by certain limitations, such as the laws of physics and probability.

PERHAPS THEODORE ROOSEVELT WAS THE FIRST PRESIDENT TO VOICE AN opinion about the Mafia. In 1890, New Orleans police chief David Hennessy was murdered. On his deathbed, he claimed that Italians were responsible, saying, "The Sicilians have done for me," perhaps using an ethnic slur. There had been a conflict involving two local Italian crime clans, sometimes called the first Mafia families in the United States. Hennessy had been suspected of being more sympathetic to one group over the other. More than two hundred Italians were arrested without probable cause. Nine were tried for the Hennessy murder and either acquitted or cut loose after a mistrial. They were widely assumed to be Mafiosi. A vigilante party raided the prison and lynched eleven men. Roosevelt, who had been serving as a presidential appointee on the U.S. Civil Service Commission, voiced support for the killings, proclaiming them "a rather good thing." It is considered the largest mass lynching in U.S. history and introduced Americans to organized crime using the exotic word "Mafia." The *New York Times* referred to the murdered Italians as "sneaking and cowardly Sicilians, the descendants of bandits and assassins."

Here, the American underworld ethic about not killing law enforcement officers began. It had nothing to do with morality and everything to do with consequences. After all, New Orleans was where the Mafia in the United States and the consequences of killing cops—in the form of public outrage and severe retaliation—first collided with the broader culture. It was no accident that this was a time when there was an uptick in immigration—there is a reference in the *Congressional Record* to one immigration wave as an "indigestible mass"—so the specter of dangerous foreigners was a ripe narrative.

"DO YOU THINK I'M A GANGSTER?"

I shared these anecdotes with my friend and editor Sean Desmond over breakfast at the Mayflower Hotel in Washington, D.C., where FBI director J. Edgar Hoover had once dined daily. Sean thought it might be worth exploring the myths and realities associated with the mob and the White House, which this book is about. I told him that I had found comparatively little out there in the way of books focusing on organized crime *and* presidential politics and no recent compendium just on this subject.

Specifically, I wanted to know how mobsters used American leaders. How did presidents and their proxies use mobsters? How much of what we've heard about the mob and presidents is true? How much is the kind of lunacy that jams up discussions on Reddit and gives meaning to the lives of people wearing pajamas in their basements who believe they know how notorious events went down?

Because there have been connections between presidents and organized crime, were all exchanges equally corrupt? Were any justified? In some cases, gangsters provided services to help politicians advance. In other cases, they were brought aboard to help confront lethal enemies to national security and civil rights, the kind of threats that are often scoffed at these days by enlightened intellectuals. As we shall see, the Franklin Roosevelt administration's partnership with racketeers during World War II was done because of national security, not personal or political enrichment. Something similar may be said of the Kennedy administration's relentless, if feckless, attempts to kill Cuban leader Fidel Castro. In these affairs, we can debate whether the instrument chosen was commensurate with the threats, but the threats from foreign and domestic saboteurs, not to mention racist hate groups, were real.

This is a study of organized crime in presidencies and presidential pursuits. In this book, we will: learn about Franklin Delano Roosevelt's no-holds-barred campaign to rid the East Coast of Nazi U-boats and sabotage during World War II, and then find resources in Sicily to help plan for the Allied invasion; see how Harry Truman's roots in a mobbed-up Kansas City political machine stayed with him throughout his career and how he helped racketeers despite his reputation for honesty and straight talk; trace how Joseph P. Kennedy co-opted the mob to help his son get elected and how the Kennedy brothers were running an assassination program involving mobsters to kill Cuba's Castro; watch how Lyndon Johnson, fresh off his civil rights victory, saw it nearly evaporate when three civil rights workers vanished in Mississippi and the role the Mafia played in resolving the situation; witness Richard Nixon poach the labor movement from the Democrats by commuting Teamsters boss Jimmy Hoffa's prison sentence and cozying up to his successor, events that led up to Hoffa's infamous disappearance; see how Ronald Reagan's career was recharged by his agent Lew Wasserman, whose show business conglomerate MCA used the services of organized crime to expand its empire; evaluate the long-standing business ties between New York racketeers and real estate developer Donald Trump; and be enlightened about the colorful connections of Joe Biden's ancestors and how a mob-connected union heavy helped him out early in his career.

The modus operandi of politics and gangland is very nuanced and layered. In the absence of mob summits in the East Room, what are the networks and portals between gangland and the White House? And has the mob been a significant cog in the engine of capitalism and democracy and, if so, to what degree?

Understanding how layering and nuance work requires us to differentiate myth from reality. Mob financial kingpin Meyer Lansky denied ever saying, "We're bigger than U.S. Steel" (a line made more famous by his *Godfather II* avatar Hyman Roth). In private records, he wrote, "To say more would be glorifying the same liars that say I said we are richer than U.S. Steel . . . Whom did I say it to?"

The very nature of both organized crime and politics is minimizing risk and maximizing gain. As consigliere Tom Hagen told Don Vito Corleone at his daughter's wedding at the beginning of *The Godfather*, "Senator Cauly apologized for not coming personally. He said you'd understand." This line rings true. It's not easy to get to the truth when writing about people who lie a lot, but I will try, nevertheless.

This brings us to the question of how this book will define "organized crime," "the mob," "gangsters," or "the rackets," words I will use interchangeably. It's an essential exercise because Gambino family boss Paul Castellano angrily asked chicken mogul Frank Perdue if he thought he was some gangster after Perdue requested Castellano's services to ensure labor peace, precisely what the gangster delivered. Because Castellano *was* a gangster, he just didn't think he was.

For this book, at the nucleus of "organized crime" is La Cosa Nostra (LCN),* the once-powerful Italian American collection of criminal gangs accelerating activities such as illegal gambling, bootlegging, labor corruption, loan sharking, narcotics, extortion, and protection. When it comes to presidents and crime, much has been made of alleged criminal mischief associated with Bill and Hillary Clinton in Arkansas, not to mention Hunter Biden's legal troubles. Still, these are not examples of mob involvement as defined in this book. (Although Clinton's brother Roger tried to get the president to pardon my townsman Rosario Gambino in exchange for a $50,000 Rolex. Bill wisely refused.)

There were rabbit holes I chose not to go down. For example, there is a theory that the Watergate scandal was partly motivated by a desire to cover up the existence of a prostitution ring allegedly operated by a Washington, D.C., mob figure. There has been a great deal of litigation surrounding this subject. I didn't even want to come close to speculating about different figures, some of whom are living, when I had nothing dispositive of value to add.

Discussions of organized crime inevitably raise the question of ethnicity and criminality. Organized crime parallels the history of immigration combined with human nature, not ethnic or religious heritage per se. At America's founding, much of the Scots Irish and English behavior toward the Native Americans—the swindles, the violence, the willful spreading of disease upon those who didn't knuckle under—could be characterized

---

* The FBI refers to the Italian Mafia as La Cosa Nostra, which translates into the nonsensical "the Our Thing." FBI records use the acronym LCN, which is why I shall.

as organized crime. At the beginning of the twentieth century in New York, the Jewish gangs exceeded the power of the Italians. The Irish were in the mix, too. This changed quickly.

Italian Americans suffered from two misfortunes when it came to public opinion. First, the Italians had an organizational system that went back to Europe that was used as a template for navigating the indignities of immigration in the United States. Irish, Jewish, Asian, and Black racketeers had no commensurate cultural precedent. Today, other crime groups, primarily the Russians, are as lethal and sophisticated as LCN ever was but not as attractive to American popular culture. A ranking Justice Department official once explained (not for attribution) why there was such a focus on Italian organized crime:

> The Mafia was small and handy. The feeling was the American people would buy it with its family relations and blood oaths a lot quicker than they could understand the complex syndicate. You must remember, we wanted to get public support behind the drive on crime.

Second, Italians were tarnished by a media and entertainment culture that coincided with the rise of LCN and portrayed organized crime as being unique to Italians. Many believe that the RICO (Racketeer Influenced and Corrupt Organizations) Act was cutely named for the iconic mob boss character Rico Bandello in the 1931 film *Little Caesar*. There is something cooler about a crime boss name Rico than one named Sol or Colin. It is more sinister to portray a swarthy band of marauders from a specific alien land descending upon our clean nation than it is to recognize a diverse, loosely affiliated confederacy of capitalist miscreants—which is what the mob is. But look at what happens in online chat rooms when someone dares to suggest there were powerful non-Italian gangsters: The trolls are unleashed.

Nor were Italians helped by America's history of anti-Catholic bias, including entire political parties established to oppose the greatly feared global reach of the Vatican. Nevertheless, "the Mafia" has become a catch-all metaphor for powerful, sinister forces we don't understand, not to mention a dark brand of take-no-shit masculinity. While LCN never really protected the communities in which it operated in any meaningful way, they did provide psychic rewards with the notion that hardscrabble bandits were sticking it to America's overlords.

In 1980, the U.S. Census Bureau estimated an Italian American population of twelve million. The number of LCN members and affiliates amounted to a few thousand. Still, powerful non-Italians emerged in organized crime, such as union boss Jimmy Hoffa (German Irish), mob venture capitalist Meyer Lansky (Jewish), and the Chicago Outfit's political strategists Murray Humphreys (Welsh) and Gus Alex (Greek). One former federal rackets investigator lamented to me the gross underestimation of these personalities and fetishization of the Italian American mob. Still, LCN is at the core of how organized crime will be covered in this book.

GANGSTERS VS. RACKETEERS

Discussions of the mob are often accompanied by a wink as if it's all mischief, but we cannot forget that the enterprise is built on the foundation of violence. The thing people believe differentiates mobsters from others is the notion that they are "tough." Toughness can be an admirable quality; *what these men possess that most of us do not is the instinctive will to violence.* We all have violence in our toolboxes, but most must reach far to find it. With gangsters, the sharp objects are right up top.

Years ago, I spoke with a former LCN member who testified against his old associates. He had committed two dozen murders. I asked him how he dealt with the emotional effects of having murdered another human being, let alone dozens. "Tony" had a Philadelphia accent and a unique pronunciation of my first name.

Tony said, "Urk, tell me somethin' 'bout your job you don't like?"

I said, "I don't like traveling and being away from my family."

He responded flatly, "I didn't like killin' people."

I believed him. Tony was an enterprise criminal, someone who killed when given an order during business or if someone "interrupted the flow of money," as a member of mob land once put it. I didn't sense he was interested in hurting anyone who fell outside those categories. He was a murderer but not a homicidal maniac. Murder fulfilled no emotional need for him. Tony was someone for whom murder was an implement in his Swiss Army knife. He was more racketeer than gangster.

Contrast this with a stone gangster I once had the misfortune to speak with. Harold "Kayo" Konigsberg was pushing ninety at the time. He had been in prison for murder throughout my entire life. *Life* magazine had labeled him "the most dangerous uncaged killer on the East Coast." As old as he was, he was terrifying, unlike Tony, who was in his sixties when we met. Without provocation, Konigsberg would identify a personal slight in a harmless comment I would make—and I try hard not to annoy homicidal mobsters.

Konigsberg had contacted me because I had written a historical novel, *The Devil Himself,* where Meyer Lansky was a leading character based on his naval intelligence work during World War II, which we will discuss in the next chapter. Konigsberg had hoped I would write about him. I mentioned that I had written about Lansky because of his involvement in a historical event, knew his family, and had access to his private papers. Was I suggesting that Lansky was a historical figure and *he wasn't*? Konigsberg exploded.

Konigsberg hadn't threatened violence directly, but he made belittling remarks and referenced the power he had in his heyday. He told me that "Meyer made me a member!" One wonders what Lansky had made Konigsberg a member of since Lansky, like Konigsberg, was Jewish and ineligible for (and uninterested in) LCN membership. The Jewish racketeers had no initiation rituals besides perhaps circumcision. Konigsberg said, "We controlled presidents." He tried to insert himself into the domestic anti-Nazi action in the lead-up to World War II without realizing that I might be skeptical about Lansky tapping a twelve-year-old for assignments. I decided my best move was to feign awe and get out of his life as soon as possible. I heard he died a few months later, having terrorized his Florida nursing home. I was greatly relieved.

ONE OF MY POINTS OF CONTENTION WITH MUCH OF THE HISTORY AND true crime I've read is the absence of human qualities in many of the players. I've always believed that basic impulses motivate people and institutions, not "issues" and "strategies" per se. We know, for example, when we study history, that there was a battle at a specific place and time, but what's harder to understand is what the players on each side *felt* about what they did. Mobsters specifically have become one-dimensional figures in much of true crime, ruthless and smirking villains playing a complex long game, controlling the elements while they outfox their enemies. Political and intelligence operatives are often assigned the same omnipotence.

I bought into the pop-culture portrayals of mob types for a long time, probably because I had an immature need to believe that some of the characters I had encountered were exotic (and perhaps, through osmosis, this somehow made me exotic, too). As a child, I remember my father stopping into a small office in Camden to say hello to someone he knew. I loitered in an outer office and wandered into a small room on the side where men were counting money and stuffing it in a bag they handed to an elderly woman. Afterward, I asked my dad why they would let an old lady carry that much money around in a paper bag. He assured me she wouldn't be touched because "everybody knows whose money that is." It only took me another thirty years to realize he believed these fantasies, too: Mobsters got robbed plenty, albeit by idiots. The boys had probably been using the woman because she appeared to be an unlikely mob courier.

Also, as a little kid, I remember being in a New Jersey diner with my uncle, and he introduced me to a dapper man he called "Pussy." When the man walked away, I shyly asked my uncle, "Do people make fun of that man because of his name?" My uncle looked down at me with raised eyebrows and said, "No." Years later, I learned that this man was Anthony "Little Pussy" Russo and that he had a brother named John "Big Pussy" Russo, and they were part of the New Jersey faction of the Genovese family. I felt a twinge of insider swagger when *The Sopranos* first aired and a significant character was called "Big Pussy."*

Presidents and mobsters fill a need in our culture. If we know what makes them tick, we'll learn more about what makes America tick. But this psychic need obscures something more interesting. It's fun to find out the peccadilloes of iconic figures, good and evil. Nevertheless, when we learn that the famous and notorious can be as petty, weak, hypocritical,

---

* They had been cat burglars in their youths, thus the feline reference to "pussy cats."

and careless as the rest, we balk because it betrays our need to escape into an alternative world.

While we're on human nature, an exchange in the film *The Silence of the Lambs* has always resonated with me when considering the nature of criminals. Homicidal cannibal Hannibal Lecter asks FBI agent Clarice Starling what she believes motivates Buffalo Bill, the killer she is pursuing. She answers that he kills women. Lecter becomes annoyed and tells her Buffalo Bill's murder is "incidental" and says:

> First principles, Clarice. Simplicity. Read Marcus Aurelius. Of each particular thing, ask: What is it, in itself, what is its nature . . . ?

In this book, I will follow Lecter's lead and suggest what may have motivated the players based on the many things we know about them. To cite one example, we'll see how Richard Nixon's foray into Watergate says more about his frame of mind than it does the external threats he faced.

AMERICAN RACKETEERING PREDATES "THE MOB"

The essential goal of organized crime's interactions with politicians is to make what they do permissible. In this, gangsters compete with the government, which ultimately wants to do the same thing, ideally toward more noble ends. Wrote William Howard Moore in his analysis of the 1950s Kefauver Senate Rackets hearings: "If the government substitutes regulatory legislation for prohibition of gambling, the narcotics traffic, and perhaps prostitution . . . a large segment of organized crime *as crime* disappears." One level down from passing legislation is to corrupt policy-makers so that vice peddlers can get what they want. Said self-styled philosopher of the democratic way, one Alphonse Gabriel Capone:

> There is one thing that is worse than a crook and that's a crooked man in a big political job. A man who pretends he's enforcing the law and is really making dough out of somebody breaking it— a self-respecting hoodlum doesn't have any use for that kind of fellow—he buys them like he'd buy any other article necessary for his trade, but he hates them in his heart.

There were corrupting influences in American politics long before the mob as we know it. The term "mob" first referred to political machines, not criminal gangs. It's been said that America's settlers were organized criminals because of the ultimatum they presented to American Indians: "Nice tribe you've got there; would be a shame to see something happen to it . . . maybe if you gave us your land, we could work something out." It's hard to argue with this characterization. Then, of course, the Indians were made enemies and laws were passed favoring white Europeans.

The essayist James Truslow Adams summed up the American criminal spirit like this:

> Lawlessness has been and is one of the most distinctive American traits. . . . It is impossible to blame the situation on "foreigners." The overwhelming mass of them were law-abiding in their own lands. If they become lawless here it must be largely due to the American atmosphere and conditions. There seems to be plenty of evidence to prove that the immigrants were made lawless by America, rather than America made lawless by them.

There were grifters in the presidential ambit going way back. Aaron Burr, Thomas Jefferson's former vice president, had the wiseguy spirit. Burr played an important role in catalyzing the Tammany Hall political machine in his effort to help Jefferson win the presidency. In addition to being a pretty good pistol shot, having not satisfied his appetite for risk after killing Alexander Hamilton in a duel, Burr set his sights on founding a new colony within the borders of the young nation's latest acquisition, the Louisiana Territory. In partnership with the slippery general James Wilkinson as his muscle, Burr led an expedition to scout out the new land he intended to reign over. There were reports that Burr had conveyed to Wilkinson via secret letter that he had received the necessary funding to make his big move.

Wilkinson shrewdly decided that given a choice of backing a Burr on the downslope or the United States of America on the rise, he'd go with the U.S.A. The general alerted President Jefferson, who, furious, sent the troops to get Burr. They caught him in Mobile, Alabama. Ever the smartass, Burr's defense was anchored in the argument that he hadn't launched an "overt" military offensive and that he was only hanging around the Louisiana Territory. Among the things that accrued to Burr's favor was that Wilkinson had forged the coded letter in which Burr allegedly told the general that he secured the funds to go and start his new colony.

Burr was acquitted, but he was not a man who could leave well enough alone; he went overseas to pitch France and the United States' once-and-future enemy, the British, on backing him to take over territories of the American Southwest where he could rule his own country. No sale. Burr returned to the United States, where he settled on Staten Island, the future home of mobster Salvatore "Sammy the Bull" Gravano and the boss he set up for murder, Paul Castellano. At seventy-seven—seriously old for that era—Burr married the much younger Eliza Jumel, whom he had led to believe he was richer than he was. When Jumel learned the truth, she dumped Burr after a few months of marriage. Jumel had her choice of attorneys, but in a feat of colonial chutzpah, she hired Alexander Hamilton, Jr., the son of the man her estranged husband killed.

Declaration of Independence signatory John Hancock financed smuggling raids. Other Declaration signers—Robert Morris and James Wilson—were involved with land fraud schemes. During the James Buchanan administration, his secretary of war, John Floyd, aided his friends in forming a syndicate to buy cheap land, knowing it would be sold to the government at a profit to build military facilities. This is a similar scam to the one featured on *The Sopranos,* where Tony and his associates bought dilapidated houses in Newark that would ultimately be purchased by the Housing and Urban Development Department. And while legal in the southern United States, if slavery hadn't been the ultimate criminal enterprise, it would be hard to think of a worse one in American history.

In 1869, robber barons Jay Gould and Jim Fisk tried to corner the gold market. The pair got to President Ulysses S. Grant's brother-in-law and had him lobby the president not to sell gold, which he had planned to do as part of a plan to stimulate the economy. Gould and Fisk would hold on to their gold and then sell when it became scarce to make a big score. Grant became suspicious of why his brother-in-law suddenly cared so much about gold policy and eventually found a letter from his (Grant's) sister to Grant's wife discussing . . . gold policy. The jig was up. Grant realized it was a scam and decided to put more gold on the market. It wasn't much of a setback for Gould, who quickly recovered and got even richer. Fisk was shot and killed a few years later in a fight over a showgirl.

During Grant's second term, alcohol producers known as the Whiskey Ring conspired to bribe revenue and Treasury agents so that they didn't have to pay taxes to the government. There were 238 indictments and 100 convictions. One of those acquitted was Grant's assistant Orville Babcock. Grant testified at his trial. Other significant scandals involving what today would be considered racketeering resulted in other resignations in Grant's cabinet.

A group known as the Ohio Gang surrounded President Warren G. Harding and tainted his presidency. Among the gang's members were Secretary of the Interior Albert Fall and Attorney General Harry Daugherty. Fall allowed oilman cronies to drill on federal lands in exchange for cash bribes and no-interest loans in what became known as the Teapot Dome scandal (so named for the Wyoming location of one field). Fall was the first-ever member of a presidential cabinet to go to prison.

Attorney General Daugherty was investigated for involvement in Teapot Dome but was found not to have engaged in provable wrongdoing. It hadn't helped Daugherty's reputation that he was known for strutting around Washington telling people that President Harding didn't make a move without consulting him. Harding's successor, Calvin Coolidge, nevertheless asked for the attorney general's resignation. A Daugherty aide, Ohio Gang member Jess Smith, committed suicide when he was suspected of complicity in Teapot Dome. Daugherty was later indicted and tried for allegedly taking money during World War I while he was a custodian for "alien property." The scheme involved the sale of assets of the American Metal Company. He went on trial twice. The first jury was deadlocked, but Daugherty was acquitted in the second trial.

SERVICES RENDERED

What do politicians and gangsters want from each other in the first place? The short answer is power and money, but for an origin story, it's worth looking at how the dynamics of twentieth-century gangsterism had their roots in the nineteenth century during the Gilded Age. The big cities had a "political machine" system, the most famous being that of William "Boss" Tweed's of Tammany Hall in New York City.

With waves of immigrants coming from Europe and needing social services, political bosses saw an opportunity. Given that the United States is a republic, and a republic requires votes to elect leaders, who better to get those votes from than millions of people in desperate need of essential services and who have no idea where to go to get them? The political machine bosses said, "If you vote for these particular people, we can get you the services you need—food, shelter, medical care." These political machines often did provide these services, but something less benevolent lurked beneath the surface. Wrote historian Richard Zacks, "The organization divided the city down to the door frames of the poorest shanty."

To get people to vote the "right" way, the machines used gangs to motivate the populace. New York had criminal gangs with names like the Plug Uglies, Hudson Dusters, Shirt Tails, Bowery Boys, Whyos, Roach Guards, and the Five Points Gang. The Dead Rabbits were refreshingly progressive, allowing women to join. One, Hellcat Maggie, filed her teeth into sharp fangs.

In the mid-1800s, the gangs perfected the art of recruiting and mobilizing "repeaters," citizens who were so civic-minded that they couldn't help from going back to vote. For a fee, these crews would inspire their neighbors to partake in the democratic process. The repeaters were, of course, compensated, as were those who staffed the polls. What might happen when, perchance, an honest citizen questioned the zealous electoral commitment of his peers? That voter likely wouldn't leave the polling location with both ears. There is rich symbolism in America's original macabre writer, Edgar Allan Poe, likely dying because a Baltimore political machine's brute squad plied him with alcohol while holding him captive to induce him to vote for their candidate. This practice was known as cooping.

Once the machine politicians were elected, the bosses' friends would be awarded lucrative contracts for essential goods and services such as roads, schools, hospitals, and waste disposal. The bosses would get a kickback, a secret payment from whoever won the contract. The public would benefit somewhat, but the bosses profited on a larger scale.

The Gophers Gang, one of the mobs that served as muscle for political machines

Ethnic identity was a significant component of the machine-gang alliance, with newer Americans trying to gain ground from the more established groups. One would think that recent immigrants in the mid-1800s would have some empathy for enslaved people being subjugated against their will, mainly in the southern United States. Nope. Many immigrants in New York were delighted that there were people out there who were suffering more than they were and rioted to ensure that Blacks remained enslaved when a draft was being considered for federal troops to march south and liberate them. Wrote Herbert Asbury in his famous study, *The Gangs of New York*:

> At every election gangs employed by the rival factions rioted at the polling places, smashing ballot boxes, slugging honest citizens who attempted to exercise the right of franchise, themselves voting early and often, and incidentally acquiring a contempt for the police and constituted authority. . . . The climax of the purely political rioting was reached in 1856, when Fernando Wood was elected to a second term as Mayor. . . . But he had the staunch support of all the lower

strata of society, especially the saloon and gambling-house keepers, whose loyalty he had assured by preventing the enforcement of a Sunday closing law passed in 1855.

Wood won reelection because his gangsters were better at beating up his opponent's gangsters.* Where were the New York police during the carnage? Mayor Wood had given them Election Day off, which was nice. Wood won the election by 10,000 votes, the exact number his opponent claimed comprised "repeaters" and other Gotham phantoms doing their civic duty.

Political shifts based on the encroachment of potentially new Americans would be seen again decades later with the advent of Prohibition. Wrote crime historian T. J. English:

> The organizational structure of the New York underworld was in many ways a precursor of professional baseball. The tenant neighborhood street gangs represented the minor leagues, where an enterprising hoodlum could establish a reputation and "show his stuff." If a gangster distinguished himself at the street level, he advanced to the majors. He became a mobster, which was a position more connected to the levers of political and economic power. If the mobster was really good, he got to play for Tammany Hall, the New York Yankees of the underworld.

The germ of politics and gangsterism oozed out of a Lower Manhattan neighborhood known as the Five Points. The preeminent gangster of the era was Paul Kelly, born Paolo Antonio Vaccarelli in Italy in 1876. Kelly adopted an Irish name in an attempt at simpatico with the predominantly Irish masters of Tammany Hall. It wasn't that Kelly necessarily thought he could fool Tammany; it was a hustle, a gesture of tribal respect and submissiveness that belied a capacity for strategic violence. It was in the cauldron of the Five Points in the late 1800s that Tammany overlords reached when rhetoric alone failed to inspire political fealty.

---

* Sometimes the warring gangsters would just make deals with each other and *pretend* they had been in conflict.

Kelly was a step up in the evolution of the various gangs that domi-nated the Five Points. Multilingual and well-dressed, he aimed higher than his origins, learning about music, literature, and theater. Nevertheless, Kelly was a champion boxer who, despite his diminutive size (a bit over five feet), had been famous for punching above his weight—and winning.

Kelly's rivals were heavyweights. One of them, Monk Eastman, was a knuckle-dragger who ran a primarily Jewish crew even though Eastman likely was not Jewish. There was much ethnic confusion in those days, with characters like Kelly and Eastman navigating the world of identity as they best saw fit given the tides of the ghetto. Likely, Eastman cultivated Jewish gangsters less out of faith than because Jews at the turn of the century were comparatively new to the country.

Eventually, Kelly and Eastman's power waned. It wasn't that good had triumphed over evil; evil had just gotten smarter, not to mention better dressed. A new, savvier generation of political service-provider rose, the most successful one headed by a Five Points graduate named Salvatore Lucania, later known as Charles "Lucky" Luciano.

In 1905, Kelly was ambushed by a rival gang at his headquarters. He was shot but survived. Kelly leveraged his political capital to avoid being charged with anything related to the ensuing gunfight. He decided it was better to remain alive and prosperous than powerful and soon dead, so he focused on the growing business of labor racketeering while keeping a lower profile. This is a pattern we will see again: A ragtag band is there first; a more streetwise crew with muscle pushes the natives out and grows the racket; once the racket is established, a younger and more energetic group comes in, and what they lack in muscle they make up for in money because they can *buy* muscle with the protection of the law. Eventually, even powerful gang lords got muscled out by racketeers who could adapt to changing political and cultural climates. Put differently, being a badass only got you so far.

Monk Eastman went in a different direction. When World War I broke out, Eastman enlisted. At his mandatory physical, a doctor took note of his body riddled with knife wounds and bullet scars and inquired about the wars in which he had earned them. Eastman brushed off the observation, saying truthfully that the wars had just been local affairs. The anxious physician decided against pressing the matter. Eastman served honorably.

After the war, Eastman returned to gangster life. Not everybody was thrilled to have him back. Loyalty in gangland is a thing Hollywood made up; it rarely happens in the streets. He got into a fight with a Prohibition agent who shot him dead. Eastman's underlings may have tipped off the agent. Eastman was buried with military honors. Kelly died of natural causes in 1936 after a prosperous but quiet life as a "labor consultant," recognizing the folly of becoming famous as the primo gangster.

We will see yet another pattern applied as we look at the mob and the presidents. The gangsters and mob-adjacent figures who made concerted efforts to achieve surface respectability (and had a little luck) fared better than those who remained stone gangsters.

The Monk Eastmans and Paul Kellys would eventually be replaced by the suave but equally sinister Arnold Rothsteins (who played a role in the fixing of the 1919 World Series without a drop of blood being shed) and Lucky Lucianos and Meyer Lanskys, who became the architects of the rackets that reigned for the remainder of the twentieth century.

WHEN RACKETEERS STARTED WORKING WITH LABOR, THE MUSCLE-FOR-hire template used in politics took off. The phenomenon was at its most brutal in the early 1900s. The fear of disrupting the flow of commerce was the most lucrative racket the mob ever had. Company owners in urban manufacturing centers would pay gang members to "convince" laborers to do their jobs peacefully. These gangsters—called *shtarkers*, Yiddish for tough guys—also had unions as clients and would threaten companies with shutdowns if they were not paid "consulting fees." Arnold Rothstein once ignited a war against a garment company while secretly backing both management and labor, incentivizing the conflict and making more money as it wore on. The mob has a talent for providing solutions to problems they invented. A give-and-take between business and labor remains today, even though the tools of persuasion have changed.

In the early days, *shtarkers* knew it wouldn't be easy to threaten corporate chiefs because they had a lot of money and influence with the government. If the gangsters went to the workers to foment a revolution, however, it became a messier problem that the businesspeople simply wanted to tamp down as soon as possible. This is how and why labor racketeers infiltrated the unions to a much greater degree than they ever got inside companies. They gnawed at the personnel tree from the ground up.

To offer an example of the kind of services gang gentry provided in the late nineteenth and early twentieth centuries, we can turn to a list that made its way around Manhattan:

Punching $2
Both eyes blacked 4
Nose and jaw broke 10
Jacked out (knocked out with a blackjack) 15
Ear chawed off 15
Leg or arm broke 19
Shot in leg 25
Stab 25
*Doing the big job [murder] 100 and up**

This list has been attributed to a member of the Whyos named Piker Ryan, who may or may not have existed. Nevertheless, a *New York Evening Post* article from 1909 reporting rampant gang activity displayed a similar menu that they linked to Tammany Hall boss Big Tim Sullivan, who did indeed exist. Among the other services these gangs perfected was the pre-Teamsters art of horse poisoning, which could sabotage commerce and infuriate Fifth Avenue's swells, who would be forced to walk to the theater.

As preposterous as the elusive Piker Ryan's list may seem now, it contains a principle that lasts to this day, which is that politics, business, and crime are all transactional: *Services are rendered by all parties for some fee, even if that fee doesn't come in the form of a sack of cash.* As we shall see, in all the cases in this book, however far-removed powerful politicians may have been from contemporary Whyos, somebody did something for somebody else and got paid for it. Somehow.

Or, as social critic Walter Lippmann put it, "The underworld performs

---

* In almost all cases where I quote from historical documents, I do so without alteration. On a few occasions there were misspellings that I corrected. In other cases, I left misspellings or poor grammar alone.

The elusive Piker Ryan

many services that respectable members of society call for." American corporate interests have been no slouches in mobilizing tough characters, whether the robber barons hiring strikebreakers or more modern companies using racketeers as "consultants" to keep the peace with labor.

THE BIG BANG

Prohibition was the catalyst that brought politicians and mobsters together in a way that catapulted American organized crime into the modern phenomenon that it became. When the Volstead Act went into effect in January 1920, gangs and politicians took serious notice. The gangsters knew that since people who obeyed the law wouldn't be manufacturing liquor, they had a big opportunity. The law wouldn't stop people from wanting to drink, and criminals, by definition, weren't too hung up about breaking the law.

The temperance movement, which was to become the first iteration of American feminism, was rooted in the legitimate concern that alcoholism was destroying families. The problem was about who took the blame. The subtext of much of the activism was that unclean immigrants—with a heavy initial focus on the Irish—had brought the scourge to the republic. How quickly middle America forgot that there had been beer on the

Mayflower and that the passengers probably landed at Plymouth Rock because they ran out of beer, which had been considered a safe alternative to unclean water.

African Americans, as always, took a hit as fears abounded that drinking would lead to a rise in unleashed Black power, which translated into violence against the white majority. Germans took a heavy blow because German immigrants had found success in the American brewing industry. These sentiments became more intense as Germany's aggression in Europe took center stage, eventually leading to the U.S. entry into World War I.

Crooked politicians also recognized an opportunity when they saw one. They knew that many of their constituents didn't want Prohibition and that mobsters would pay big money for assistance in subverting the law. Prohibition took organized crime from being a loose collection of back-alley gamblers, extortionists, and pimps to industrial manufacturers with professional distribution channels. Smaller operators couldn't afford to bribe the authorities as easily as organized criminals. Gangsters also had the cash to manufacture quality alcohol, which allowed them to compete with backwoods moonshiners and basement rotgut cooks. For this to work smoothly, they needed local governments not to interfere. It was an easy sell because politicians viewed alcohol as a harmless vice. All gangsters wanted from politicians was: Tell your cops not to bother us, and we'll keep paying you.

Where people drank, they also wanted to play. One of the most popular forms of play was gambling. The criminal gangs extended their graft from the drinking business to gambling. They paid politicians and local authorities to . . . do nothing. As Jack Nicholson's Jake Gittes responded when asked what he had done as a police officer in *Chinatown*: "As little as possible."

One of the shrewdest political machine beneficiaries of Prohibition was Atlantic City's Enoch "Nucky" Johnson,* nominally Atlantic County Treasurer, but also a prominent regional racketeer with interests in gambling, prostitution, protection, banking, and, of course, bootlegging. A

---

* In HBO's *Boardwalk Empire* his character was portrayed by Steve Buscemi and called Nucky Thompson.

Republican, Johnson had power that reached throughout the state of New Jersey. He also became a national gangland mediator, hosting mob conferences, including a fabled one in 1929 where bootlegging conflicts were discussed. At the height of his power, he earned today's equivalent of millions of dollars per year until he was convicted of income tax evasion.

Obscene gangland violence and the Great Depression brought an end to Prohibition. Nonetheless, mobsters still wanted the same things from politicians as they did before Prohibition, including contracts for public works, "no show" jobs, judges who respected "loyalty" and cash more than they did the law, and pliable juries. The difference was that now these things were needed on a much grander scale.

One of the pioneers in political corruption was Frank Costello, the successor to Lucky Luciano, the latter considered the founder of modern organized crime. When Costello took control after Luciano's deportation, he replaced many Irish Tammany bosses with Italians like himself. So powerful was Costello that wiretaps picked up New York judges calling to thank him for their appointments. In the meantime, mob bosses like Joseph Bonanno maintained offices in venues such as the Abraham Lincoln Political Club in Brooklyn. Costello was to learn that there were limits to the respectability his power could buy.

There is a long tradition of so-called legitimate people using hoodlums to do their bidding to keep a degree of distance between higher and lower. As we shall see in the Ronald Reagan chapter, the Annenberg family, now esteemed philanthropists, is an example. In the section on Lyndon Johnson, we will explore the FBI's recruitment of one of the most violent mobsters in American history to help solve the Ku Klux Klan murders of civil rights activists in Mississippi. In addition, who is considered legitimate is often a function of where one happens to be standing in the great food chain of life when history is written. In the ancient Middle East, Judea had the Sicarii, knife-wielding assassins who used violence to torment the Roman Empire. The rabbis and other Jewish leaders were said to have abhorred the Sicarii on principle, but how can we ever know? After all, "leaders" are never a monolith: A New York rabbi and judge reached out to Meyer Lansky to make life difficult for Nazi sympathizers in the lead-up to World War II—in the same spirit that General Andrew Jackson reached out to pirate Jean Lafitte to help defeat the British in the Battle of

Pirate Jean Lafitte
*Courtesy of the Rosenberg Library,
Galveston, Texas*

New Orleans during the War of 1812. Today, "Sicario," a modern adaptation of "Sicarii," have a whiff of glamour to the degree that blockbuster movies are made about them in the drug world, not the Levant.

WHY THIS BOOK *NOW*?

I hope to accomplish three things: first, deliver *new information*; second, provide fresh *insight* into my subject matter—how the relationship between mobsters and presidential politics worked and how it didn't; and third, *organize* what is now known into a through line that hasn't been done before, or at least not in this way.

There are a few reasons why *Wiseguys and the White House* came together now, after years of tinkering with the concept. First is Donald Trump, who, according to Trump chronicler Wayne Barrett, "went out of his way not to avoid" interactions with racketeers "but to increase them." At this writing, the world of presidential politics and organized crime have grotesquely converged with Trump facing multiple indictments brought under the RICO Act, which was created to prosecute the Mafia (RICO will be further explored), and famously leveraged by former federal prosecutor Rudolph Giuliani to attack LCN.* Giuliani is also under a RICO indictment for attempting to overturn the 2020 election in Georgia. Said one LCN defense lawyer upon his indictment, "The wheel of karma is about to crush him."

Trump was the first U.S. president to admit to openly knowing and dealing with mobsters. He referred to them as "very nice people" on the air to talk show host David Letterman, among others in the public domain. Said Trump in a 2004 speech about why he hadn't wanted to do a reality show:

> I don't want to have cameras all over my office, dealing with contractors, politicians, mobsters and everyone else I have to deal with in my business. You know, mobsters don't like, as they are talking to me, having cameras all over the room. It would play well on television, but it doesn't play well with them.

Trump's publicly (and recently) documented dealings have helped establish how the "legitimate" world interacts with organized crime. At the same time, Trump has also been known to deny mob ties, as only Trump can do. In addition to being a New York and Atlantic City developer where bumping up against organized crime is unavoidable, Trump emboldened a wave of aggressive investigative reporting on a president and organized crime.

Second, the mob is now a husk of what it had been. Accordingly, enough time has passed and so many key players are now deceased that law enforcement organizations have been more generous with the documents they are willing to redact, declassify, allow journalists to review, and publish. This means that the friends, families, and associates of colorful characters have been willing to share more, now that doing so puts no one in danger. The biggest surprise I have encountered writing about gangsters, historical figures, and those who knew them is how the profoundly human drive to talk overrides discretion.

---

* Giuliani claimed that it was his idea to use RICO to go after the New York mob, a claim that has been sharply challenged by others involved in the prosecutions, including the man who drafted the law.

Somewhere within us is the desire to feel significant and a part of the times we live in.

Mobsters and their families have also been willing to share their experiences and misadventures now that statutes of limitations have passed and some key players aren't around anymore to be prosecuted. Among these things are the private records and diaries of Meyer Lansky, one of the American mob's visionaries, made available to me by my friend Cynthia Duncan, the granddaughter of Thelma (Teddy) and Meyer Lansky. These records are noteworthy for their insight into the mind of a mob leader whom one biographer gushed "ran America." To the extent that this book has a Greek chorus reminding us about the realities of mob power, it is the periodic voice of Meyer Lansky.

First-rate journalists in the mob space, such as George Anastasia, Scott Burnstein, Jerry Capeci, Scott Deitche, T. J. English, Larry Gragg, Alex Hortis, Dan Moldea, J. Michael Niotta, Selwyn Raab, Gus Russo, and others have done work from which much can be learned. The Mob Museum in Las Vegas has also synthesized artifacts from the underworld's heyday.

A surge of conspiratorial thinking in our culture also motivated me to explore the role of gangsters in top-level politics. Americans are justified in believing that bad things have happened in government and crime, and, yes, some of these things can rightly be called conspiracies. Nevertheless, while conspiracies exist, magic does not, and sometimes things work more messily than our minds convince us they do. CIA officer Paul Redmond summarized it nicely when asked about the potential complicity of the intelligence community in the 9/11 attacks: "I spent a career in the CIA trying to orchestrate plots, wasn't that good at it, and certainly couldn't carry off 9/11. Nor could the real pros I had the pleasure to work with."

I have also learned things from my experiences, research, and reporting that finally seemed relevant as this book became focused. As a kid who grew up where I did, and as an author writing about organized crime, I've seen some of the workaday realities of this way of life without being a part of it. The same is true, having once worked in the White House. These experiences have given me a modest ability to demystify these subjects. After all, mob bosses have been known to coach Little League, and political aides have been known to talk too loudly in Georgetown bars. On occasions when I purport to know what mobsters were thinking, it is based on either things they said and wrote or what people close to them conveyed they believed.

I won't pull punches about reaching conclusions informed by personal experiences, often at odds with mythology. Some of these insights will come from my forty-year crisis management career, where I have been involved with people and institutions accused of doing terrible things. These experiences have given me some sense of how power, light and dark, works—and doesn't. After all, there is a difference between knowledge and belief, and it is belief that dominates the American understanding of racketeering.

Woody Allen once said, "The Mafia spends very little on office supplies." Accordingly, there are some obstacles to writing about organized crime. For one thing, gangsters are not famous for their recordkeeping. Law enforcement sources and the work of other journalists are helpful but imperfect. We will see these gaps and contradictions most intensely in the chapter on JFK and the mob, especially regarding the assassination attempts against Cuban leader Fidel Castro.

Another challenge is that gangsters often distort the truth about their importance. They enjoy telling others how things really "went down" and like to argue that they are no different than legitimate people in business and politics. (Meyer Lansky's nephew, Mark Lansky, heard the "we're no different" rationalization directly from his uncle.) After all, mobsters tried to boost their internal prestige after the Kennedy assassination by dubiously claiming responsibility.

A hurdle for mob chroniclers is that organized crime has become far more than a sociological phenomenon; it is now a belief system with acolytes ascribing anything murky that occurs to the Mafia, much in the same way the CIA has become a proxy that explains a broad range of troubling events that don't bring a neat emotional resolution. Actor Alan Arkin once wrote that belief systems are "wish lists . . . things you'd like to be true." Having written about the crime and spy worlds, I have become wary of the fervor with which people have made the world of gangland and intelligence into "paracosms," fantasy worlds such as *Star Wars* or *Game of Thrones*. I never underestimate the role that the sheer desire to be perceived as a player in a significant event motivates what people will falsely claim, sometimes so often that it becomes a core part of their identity. The rumors about J. Edgar Hoover being blackmailed by LCN because of his alleged gay lifestyle are a case in point and will be discussed in the final chapter.

So passionate are adherents to these belief systems that they dismiss as agents of crime syndicates or the clandestine services anyone that doesn't subscribe to their conclusions or data. Don DeLillo summarized this mindset in *Libra*: "[History] is the sum total of the things they aren't telling us."

Nor should we forget that the mafia-spy-publishing-entertainment phenomenon is a huge business, and this enterprise is catalyzed by what Italian historians have called *dietrologia*, or "behind-ology," the idea that vast, calculating, and evil forces are *behind* whatever events make the world go round. Still, sometimes there really are dark maneuvers in our republic: Wrote Thomas Hunt in *Informer*, an academic journal about organized crime:

> Secret negotiations between the intelligence community, the underworld, and anti-Castro Cubans resulted in a loose alliance among those groups that continued at least through the Kennedy, Johnson and Nixon administrations.

There is no practical way to quantify the degree to which a president was mob-impacted, but it's hard to wade through so much information about a subject like this and not emerge with some impressions. Accordingly, I came up with a flexible scale of the mob-impacted presidents examined in this book using determinants such as:

- Intimacy or personal involvement and awareness of mob complicity;
- The selfishness of the president's motivation;
- The degree to which the president's career benefited from mob intervention;

- The justifiability of the infraction committed by the president or on his behalf;
- The extent to which there was a direct transaction provably involved;
- Public harm;
- How the public would feel if they were fully aware; and
- Redemptive actions.

My grading scale is as follows:

5 Wouldn't have been president without mob
4 Career significantly affected by mob
3 Mob involvement relevant to aspects of presidency
2 Mob links are not very impactful
1 Tangential mob links at best

This book is more than an anthology of different presidents and their discrete adventures with the mob. I have sought to tie together what these shady deals had in common across presidencies and how we look at an ongoing phenomenon rather than a series of stand-alone encounters. I don't believe the presidential canard about cover-ups not working or being worse than the crime. Cover-ups have been known to succeed.

Wherever possible, I have included quotations from the players in these events that put their spin on what happened and why. I also try to make sense of what the interactions between presidents (and their agents) and malefactors teach us about how power works, has worked, should work, and may function as we move into a time vastly different from the days when the mob brazenly strode through the civic life of the United States.

2

Franklin D. Roosevelt

BLACK TOM AND "THE DEVIL HIMSELF"

> If a Chief of Police makes a deal with the leading
> gangsters and the deal results in no more hold-ups,
> that Chief of Police will be called a great man—
> but if the gangsters do not live up to their word the
> Chief of Police will go to jail.
>
> —Franklin Delano Roosevelt

The boss wanted these eight goons dead. They had been sent over to hurt his people. There had been others before them who had already made back-alley connections in New York. He wanted them all dead to send a message to others who might be coming to play rough.

The boss with the bloodlust wasn't a crime lord. He was President Franklin D. Roosevelt, who didn't care how his enemies were dealt with as long as they were. Permanently.

The miscreants were eight Nazi saboteurs who had traveled to the United States via U-boat in April 1942 to conduct terror operations. They were primarily focused on military manufacturing locations, but Jewish-owned businesses and institutions were also targeted. FDR was not trifling with this crew and was to get the outcome he wanted, mostly.

Hanging, Old West style, was his preference. Roosevelt's death wish for the saboteurs aimed to execute them immediately.

Hitler had vowed, "We will always strike first! We will always deal the first blow!" Weeks after Pearl Harbor, the führer added: "America's war with Japan made us free to act" and "now we shall see what our U-boats may achieve." Admiral Karl Dönitz, the Nazi naval chief, said:

> Our U-boats are operating close inshore along the coast of the United States of America so that bathers and sometimes entire coastal cities are witnesses to the drama of war, whose visual climaxes are constituted by the red glorioles of blazing tankers.

He wasn't kidding. Hitler's U-boats had been destroying military and cargo ships in the Atlantic at a great clip in what was known as "the happy time" for the Nazis; such was their destructive success. In 1940 and 1941 alone, they had sunk 282 Allied ships carrying 1.5 million tons of cargo. That number spiked in early 1942, with 500 Allied vessels sunk in ten months. U-boats had also been spotted in the Hudson River and off Long Island. The attacks occurred as far north as the St. Lawrence River and south as the Brazilian coast. A declassified intelligence report identified U-boat attacks "within sight of New York City." It was widely known that these attacks were occurring. Still, press censorship had been effective and formal reporting in the press on the events at sea was limited, even with the occasional charred body washing ashore. The few stories that made it into the American press occurred only after incidents had been mentioned in media overseas. There had even been stories about ships being blown up and sinking as vacationers watched from shore on their beach towels.

"The Battle of the Atlantic," as the U-boat war was called, was to become the most protracted engagement of World War II. Prime Minister Winston Churchill said, "The only thing that ever really frightened me during the war was the U-boat peril . . . the U-boat attack was our worst evil. It would have been wise for the Germans to stake all upon it."

ON FEBRUARY 9, 1942, THE LARGEST CRUISE SHIP IN THE WORLD, FRANCE'S *Normandie*, caught fire at Pier 88 in New York City and capsized. Nazi sabotage was widely suspected. Roosevelt shared Churchill's fear of the

"U-boat peril," telling the public a few weeks after the *Normandie* fire, "We have most certainly suffered losses from Hitler's U-boats in the Atlantic as well as from the Japanese in the Pacific—and we shall suffer more of them before the turn of the tide."

With its French owners afraid to sail the *Normandie* back to Europe, the U.S. Coast Guard boarded the ship after the Pearl Harbor attack and repurposed it for American military transport as the SS *Lafayette*. It never got to sea with its ten thousand troops bound for Europe. It would have been an attractive target given that it had recently broken the speed record for transatlantic crossing.

Roosevelt had been angling for war with the Nazis for some time, but public opinion and political challenges obstructed him. Among other things, World War I had not been a naval war for the United States, so Americans were operating with an antique perspective on maritime warfare and needed the equipment to conduct it. By the time World War II started, the military was ill-prepared to a degree that would strike contemporary Americans with disbelief.

After the Japanese bombed Pearl Harbor, the war was finally on. Roosevelt needed to be aggressive and creative, especially since U.S. early warning systems had failed so badly. However, what is reported so little is that the Germans accelerated their attacks on American shipping on the Atlantic coast in the immediate aftermath of the Japanese attack. Germany was trying to dissuade America from entering the war and to disable U.S. capabilities if the country decided to engage.

FDR had discreetly authorized FBI chief J. Edgar Hoover to collect information on German sympathizers within U.S. borders and had his agents infiltrate the German American Bund, a pro-German collective. FDR was also aware of the broader context of isolationist political sentiment and how it correlated with potential vulnerabilities in America's defenses. Much of his thinking can be summarized as a desire to make life within U.S. borders as inhospitable to Nazi sympathizers as possible. Events weren't making things easy. Eventually, the U.S. government would turn to the Mafia.

Father Charles Coughlin had been broadcasting pro-German sermons on his weekly nationwide radio program. An initial supporter of FDR, Coughlin had turned toward isolationism. One-quarter of the U.S. population listened to his broadcasts. When war broke out in Europe in

1939, Coughlin urged Americans to travel to Washington to demand that the United States remain neutral, which the Roosevelt administration viewed as a provocation of civil war.

The attorney general suspended Coughlin from circulating his newspaper, *Social Justice*. After the attack on Pearl Harbor, sentiment turned against Coughlin and, using intermediaries, FDR conveyed to Coughlin that the Justice Department would pull back on its prosecutorial intentions under the Espionage Act *if* he stopped broadcasting. Coughlin complied, but millions of Americans still agreed with him.

Among those who shared Coughlin's views was aviation pioneer Charles Lindbergh. Not only had Lindbergh embraced isolationist views, but he had also traveled to Germany to inspect Hitler's air force. He was sufficiently impressed that he aided German propaganda by overstating the might of its air force to dampen the enthusiasm for war among the Nazis' would-be foes. In public speeches, Lindbergh criticized Roosevelt, the Jews, and the British for agitating for war. He had even made plans to move to Germany before the war.

German American Bund Rally in New York *National Archives*

Roosevelt hit back hard through a relentless PR campaign characterizing Lindbergh as a Nazi stooge, but he knew that plenty of people in America agreed with the aviator. FDR wanted Lindbergh and those who supported him to pay the price, including being harassed wherever possible. After the attack on Pearl Harbor, Lindbergh's isolationist views retreated.

Regarding intrigue and skullduggery, Roosevelt wanted to know everything. No delegation, layers, or firewalls for him. He has understandably gone down in history as a humane and liberal wartime leader who deeply cared about the underprivileged and was a grandfatherly figure during perilous times. However, another side of the man has received comparatively little attention: He was a ruthless risk-taker willing to try almost anything. Despite a chin-scratching debate about how far FDR might be ready to go to defeat America's enemies, his son indicated that his father would have certainly used atomic weapons if he had access to them. Secretary of State Henry Stimson wrote, "At no time from 1941 to 1945, did I ever hear it suggested by the President, or by any other responsible member of the government, that atomic energy should not be used in the war."

So why not gangsters?

The enterprise became known in the U.S. Navy as Operation Underworld or "the ferret squad."

Before we see how FDR unsheathed New York's racketeers as a secret weapon, it helps to understand the key players and how they ended up in the unique positions they did—in the same state where FDR had been elected governor twice.

LUCIANO, LANSKY, AND AMERICANIZATION OF THE NEW YORK MOB

Roosevelt was aware of the rackets, both as the governor of the rough-and-tumble state of New York and from his experience running for president for the first time in 1932, where his opponent was another New York governor, Al Smith. Charles "Lucky" Luciano, Frank Costello, and Meyer Lansky attended the Democratic National Convention in Chicago that year.* They

---

* Lansky aide Moe Sedway had also been active in FDR's latter campaigns, primarily in fundraising.

accompanied the Tammany Hall delegation of New York City political tradesmen, specifically Albert Marinelli, the Second Assembly District leader. Luciano had operated a trucking company for Marinelli during Prohibition. He valued this relationship because it gave him access to vote counting in Marinelli's district, plus behind-the-scenes input into the seating of grand jurors. Gangland journalist Nick Pileggi wrote that Luciano had sent gunmen to visit Marinelli's predecessor, Harry C. Perry, to urge him to step down in Marinelli's favor, which is precisely what happened.

Luciano was born Salvatore Lucania in Lercera Friddi, Sicily, in 1897. His immigrant family lived in extreme poverty in Manhattan's Lower East Side. He rolled with what remained of the soulless Five Points Gang and juggled menial jobs with robbing pushcart peddlers and trafficking narcotics, the latter for which he had been arrested. To the consternation of some of his partners, Luciano never wholly lost his attraction to the drug business.

Luciano stood five feet ten inches and had thick black hair and pockmarked skin in his youth. Contrary to popular belief, he was not called "Lucky" because of his good fortune. His real surname, Lucania, was pronounced Luck-AN-ya, thus the nickname Charlie Lucky. In one of the more reliable versions of the origin story, a teenage Luciano attempted to shake down a younger, much smaller Jewish boy, Maier Suchowljansky, who told the Sicilian, "Take your protection money and shove it up your ass!" Said Luciano:

> I was about a head taller than this midget, but he looked up at me without blinkin' an eye, with nothin' but guts showin' in his face, and he said, "Fuck you!" Well, I started to laugh. . . . Next to Benny Siegel, Meyer Lansky was the toughest guy, pound for pound, I ever knew in my whole life.

The two hoods bonded immediately, and just as Salvatore Lucania of Lercara Friddi, Sicily, morphed himself into Charlie Lucky Luciano, Maier Suchowljansky of Grodno, Poland, became Meyer Lansky of the United States of America, who listed his birthday as July 4. With friends Francesco Castiglia (Frank Costello) and Benjamin "Bugsy" Siegel, they were to come to dominate the New York underworld for decades. While there were other big gangsters, it was these four men who together embodied the industrialization (Luciano and Lansky), the politicization (Costello), and the brutality and warped glamour (Siegel) of the twentieth-century rackets.

Luciano and Lansky were especially close and were described as more like brothers. Luciano was calculating and charismatic. Lansky was reserved, cunning, with a brain like a Hewlett-Packard calculator and a deep understanding of human nature. They finished each other's sentences. Under the tutelage of gambler Arnold Rothstein, who had been raised in an upwardly mobile family but, for reason of his bent character, aspired to be a hoodlum, the boys expanded their horizons, engineered bigger deals, and stopped dressing like pickpockets.

It hadn't always been easy on the way up. In October 1929, as the Luciano-Lansky crew began to contemplate taking on an older generation of gangsters, Luciano was thrown into a car and beaten within an inch of his life, the right side of his face slashed with a knife. His nerves were severed, and Luciano was later found wandering a beach on Staten Island. There are conflicting stories about what had happened. We know that Luciano had a droopy right eye from his injuries for the remainder of his life, which gave him a menacing look along with his roughened skin. Still, despite suggestions that this was an intra-gang rivalry, Luciano said later in life that the police beat him because they wanted information on the whereabouts of gangster Jack "Legs" Diamond.

Luciano had a challenge on the Italian side of the gangland balance sheet. Two old-time Sicilian bosses, Giuseppe "Joe the Boss" Masseria and Salvatore Maranzano, vied for control over the New York Cosa Nostra. The Jewish racketeers were also powerful, but the Italians had a system going back to Sicily that the Jews lacked. The Italians were succeeding at importing it to America. Both Sicilian "Mustache Petes"* recognized they needed Luciano and his expanding gang to prosper.

The power struggle that followed has been framed as a generational "creative differences" conflict where the principles of diversification and Americanization were at stake. These forces were by-products more than they were causes. The real causes were the same ones as most power

---

* "Mustache Pete" was a lightly derogatory term for older mobsters like Maranzano and Masseria, who were in their forties, a good deal older than Luciano and Lansky's crew.

Giuseppe "Joe the Boss" Masseria

struggles: One party wanted more, and the other party didn't want to give it to them.

Luciano and Lansky, despite their youth—Lansky was in his late twenties and Luciano in his early thirties when the conflict was raging—had no intention of being subordinate to Maranzano and Masseria for long. They knew, however, that they had to move carefully and not signal their intentions. Luciano pretended he saw each man as his mentor and embraced their methodologies.

Luciano's gang also made inroads into legitimate businesses, establishing what became known as the "mob tax": If, say, a delicatessen wanted to remain in business, it paid the mob a monthly fee, which was eventually passed on to the consumer. (A study of Chicago racketeering under Al Capone showed that the price of corned beef went up by 30 cents a pound—no small amount—in the late 1920s and early 1930s.)

The bosses had wanted to keep the rackets in the manner of the old order: Italian gangsters could deal with Jewish and Irish ones provided they were clearly subordinate to the Italians. Luciano was a capitalist and an equal opportunity criminal; he wanted to partner with anybody who knew how to make money and played along with the Mafia rituals to appease a significant segment of his base that longed to be a part of something. In this sense, even the rackets were a meta-racket—getting people to swear oaths and pledge silence ("omertà") and loyalty, even though these rules were broken as much as they were upheld.

Luciano recognized the long-term futility of tribalism and ethnic hierarchy. Why go to war when everybody can make money? Maranzano and Masseria were sacrificing financial opportunities for tribal dominance. How do you grow an enterprise when your stance concerns ego-driven recognition rather than cash-driven collaboration? And why would politicians want to do business with an enterprise that identified itself as committed aliens when this was melting-pot America? Luciano didn't want to expand the Mafia; he tried to organize crime—or at least things that were currently crimes.

First, Luciano would lead the pudgy Masseria to believe he was his loyal servant and heir apparent. Luciano set up lunch with Masseria at an Italian restaurant in Coney Island, Brooklyn. The two men played cards. Nature summoned Charlie Lucky, who excused himself to go to the bathroom. Once he was safely out of harm's way, four of Luciano's men entered the restaurant and killed Masseria. A gruesome photo depicted Joe the Boss, bloody on the ground, with the ace of spades clutched in his hand. The playing card was a nice touch, but no one knows who put it there for effect. Luciano predictably expressed shock and sadness at finding his boss in such a state.

Now Maranzano. Luciano and Costello, savvy corruptors, wondered how an American public official might react to an immigrant who expected to have his ring kissed, only to be regaled with tales of the Roman Empire, which Salvatore Maranzano had evidently not been informed ended some time ago. Maranzano betrayed his mindset by crowning himself king of Cosa Nostra and inviting underlings to praise him. Luciano embraced Maranzano to his face while laughing with Lansky, Costello, and Siegel about what an ass he was behind his back.

Summoning Julius Caesar, Maranzano proclaimed himself Boss of Bosses and fêted himself before a superficially united Cosa Nostra at an upstate New York jubilee. He failed to realize how no one enjoys celebrating a singular man's greatness except for that singular man. Maranzano prattled on about how they were just like the Romans. Luciano didn't know much about the Roman Empire, nor did he care; he fed his boss some bullshit about feeling like Mark Antony and continued to make

Joe the Boss, after an awkward lunch with Luciano *Bettmann Archive via Getty Images*

his plans with a growing group of converts that felt little but resentment toward their host.

In September 1931, Maranzano was at his Park Avenue offices when several agents of the Internal Revenue Service arrived asking to inspect his records. They were Meyer Lansky's men who attacked Maranzano with knives. If he had wanted to be like Caesar, he indeed was feeling it now. The fake agents shot him when the wounded boss went for his gun. One of the killers was almost certainly the devout freckle-faced Samuel "Red" Levine, who wouldn't kill on the Sabbath, not even for Lansky. With Maranzano out of the way and Lansky's counsel, Luciano refined the modern Commission of New York's Five Families and did away with the concept of Boss of Bosses. Still, Luciano dominated the rackets in New York where he lived under the name Charles Ross in a suite at the Waldorf Astoria.

Once the new management was in control, they turned their attention to politics. After all, they would need political cover if their rackets were to prosper and remain protected. Wrote Lansky in his private diaries:

> Charlie was influenced in politics by Al Marinelli. He played on Charlie's sympathy that it was an Italian cause that he owed it to the Italian people to help organize the people to get in back of Al to be the first Italian Tammany leader of a district. Al was right.

It was time for the Italians to have a leader they were entitled to it. Their population called for more representation.

Journalist Nick Pileggi confirmed that this trend continued, writing in *New York* magazine:

> During a Tammany Hall fight in 1941, Frank Costello dispatched gunmen to Tammany clubs around the city to help elect Costello henchmen as district leaders. Within a year, Costello's men made up the majority of Tammany's governing board.

During the 1932 Democratic convention, Marinelli signaled that he would not support FDR for president because, as New York governor, Roosevelt had endorsed a crackdown on the rackets. Marinelli didn't use those terms, characterizing his decision under a nobler banner. In 1931, Governor Roosevelt initiated what became known as the Seabury Investigations, examining corruption in New York City, named after Judge Samuel Seabury, who reported to the legislature. During the probe, a witness was found murdered, and a Tammany-affiliated New York Supreme Court justice, Joseph Force Crater, famously vanished forever. Among other things, the investigation determined that many court officers were under the thumb of Tammany Hall. The effort resulted in a cleansing of the court system, arrests and indictments of Tammany operatives, and the resignation of New York City's mayor.

Roosevelt wanted the support of the mobbed-up Tammany but was concerned about attacks in the general election for being soft on crime at best and in league with crooks at worst. FDR countered Marinelli's challenge by deftly declaring that he had not been presented with sufficient proof that gangsters had corrupted Tammany. In other words, Roosevelt maintained his disdain for Tammany but claimed to admire some of the exceptional individuals within the system. Satisfied with this rhetoric, Marinelli backed Roosevelt with the encouragement of Luciano, Costello, and Lansky. "I don't say we elected Roosevelt, but we gave him a pretty good push," Luciano later remarked.

Roosevelt, ever the slippery operator, secured the nomination but wanted to send a message to his now broadened electorate that just because he was from New York, it didn't mean he was a tool of organized crime. Simultaneously, he then winked at investigators to keep looking for political corruption and racket activity in his home state.

It had been a smart move. A sheriff in New York City who earned $12,000 per year had cobbled together an investment portfolio worth $400,000, evidence of brilliant investing prowess during the Great Depression or staggering graft. Author James Cockayne reported in his study of corruption:

> A judge with a half-million dollars in savings had been granted a loan to support 34 "relatives" found to be in his care. Against the backdrop of Depression New York, with a collapsing private sector, 25 percent unemployment and imploding tax revenues, this was shocking profligacy and nepotism.

Roosevelt knew he couldn't look the other way at these outrages in the general election.

Luciano said of Roosevelt's betrayal, "He done exactly what I would've done in the same position. He was no different than me . . . we was both shitass double crossers, no matter how you look at it."*

The misadventure in the 1932 election was a lesson in the hazards of dabbling in politics. While Luciano appeared philosophical about having been snookered by FDR, his partner, Lansky, felt burned and lost much of his enthusiasm for getting directly involved with national political plays where the odds weren't in his favor.†

SPYMASTER IN CHIEF

From an early age, Franklin D. Roosevelt had a love of intrigue. When he fell for a young woman during college, Roosevelt deployed a coding system he had conjured in his youth to record musings about her so that his roommates

---

* Vincent "The Chin" Gigante, an eventual Luciano successor, had been known to point to the White House on the television news and tell his family, "See that? That's the real organized crime."

† As we will see in the Truman chapter, FDR would prove to be no dummy in navigating the underworld, especially as it involved organized labor.

wouldn't catch on. Another youthful idea that captured his fancy was developing a naval reserve comprised of private yachts, a notion that wouldn't come to fruition until World War II. As the youngest-ever assistant secretary of the navy during World War I, the object of his most significant interest was the Office of Naval Intelligence, which author Joseph Persico described as "the closest equivalent to an American central intelligence agency."

Roosevelt had a particular obsession with sabotage and fire. According to historians at Springwood, his Hyde Park estate, who spent an afternoon with my son and me on a private tour, as Roosevelt gained strength during his recovery from polio, he would roll himself out of bed and onto the floor and use his upper body strength to drag himself down an immense hall to the front staircase and out the front door. He would have to pass beneath one of the larger nautical paintings adorning the wall above the stairs. Nautical themes remain throughout the house, including a large wooden ship steering wheel mounted on a stone wall. Also on display was an "ice yacht" FDR used to skim the surface of the Hudson River during cold winters.

Sometimes, when he wanted to mix up his fire-safety routine, Roosevelt would drag himself to the elevator, lowering the lift to the first floor via pulleys. (When I returned home, I tried to crawl a fraction of Roosevelt's distance and gave up.) Much of his fear was informed in his boyhood by having seen his aunt Laura running out of a house on fire from having used an oil lamp. Ships and fire inhabited much of FDR's mental real estate, so one can imagine his preoccupation with what had happened to the *Normandie*.

Roosevelt's management style was "bureaucratic anarchy," but not without strategy. He led subordinates to believe they oversaw an individual portfolio—and they did, kind of. Famous for wanting loyal people reporting directly to him, FDR would retain those inside and outside that bureaucracy who would brief him personally. If this approach seems unwieldy, that's because it was.

Roosevelt's point man on wartime intelligence in the conflict's early stages was a close friend and fellow aristocrat, Vincent Astor. Roosevelt was eight years older than Astor, who referred to the president's half brother James as "Uncle Rosey." When Astor's father, John Jacob Astor IV, perished on the *Titanic*, he left his son with one of the greatest fortunes on Earth, most of it invested in New York real estate.

The president and Astor were obsessive sailors who became reacquainted when Roosevelt was assistant secretary of the navy during World War I. Given the emergence of German submarines, they conspired to find a way to mobilize recreational boaters into a volunteer force. Astor loaned the navy one of his own yachts and pressured wealthy friends to do the same. Their rich kid brainstorming eventually became the naval reserve.

The event that brought Astor and FDR closest was the 1921 polio attack that left Roosevelt disabled. The Astor estate near Roosevelt's included a heated indoor pool that the future president used for physical therapy. Astor was one of the few people Roosevelt was comfortable letting see him in his condition. Later, Roosevelt set sail annually on Astor's massive yacht, *Nourmahal*, which had a crew of forty-two. He retreated to this ship after anarchist Giuseppe Zangara attempted to assassinate him in Miami while still president-elect. Roosevelt had not been hit, but Chicago mayor Anton Cermak was killed. Astor had been in the car following Roosevelt.

In the 1930s, Astor* was a founding member of an informal club

FDR's friend and secret intelligence adviser, Vincent Astor
New York Times

---

* In a strange parallel, President Woodrow Wilson's chief intelligence adviser during World War I was another American aristocrat, Franklin Polk, a descendant of President James Polk.

of uber-elites that advised FDR on worldwide intelligence developments known as "The Room." These men, who included Kermit Roosevelt (Theodore Roosevelt's son), publisher Nelson Doubleday, banker Winthrop Aldridge, and diplomat David Bruce, met to share updates on what they were hearing from their contacts around the world at one of Astor's town houses at 34 East Sixty-Second Street in Manhattan. Given current events, it didn't hurt that these men were anglophiles, and one of the men in touch with this circle was William Stephenson, the head of British Intelligence during World War II. Stephenson met with Astor and others in the high-end St. Regis Hotel, which Astor owned. FDR loved the intrigue, but he loved it even more if it was delivered to him by men who shared his background—and FDR knew all The Room's members mainly through Groton, Harvard, or the New York social scene.

On March 19, 1941, FDR placed Astor in charge of defense intelligence for the New York metropolitan area. Wrote Persico of Astor: "So comfortable was he in his association with FDR that he used White House stationery when communicating with the President. He enjoyed Roosevelt's trust to the extent that he occasionally went ahead with his schemes and told FDR later."

Astor personally investigated crew lists, cargo rosters, and materials being shipped. Astor was also in direct contact with the FBI's J. Edgar Hoover, who sometimes communicated with him and FDR through the president's assistant, Grace Tully. Astor was at the scene of the *Normandie* fire after it broke out. Wrote Astor to Roosevelt: "I do know the facts for I arrived aboard within ten minutes of the outbreak of the fire and remained there or in the immediate vicinity for most of the period up to the time she capsized twelve hours later."

There was every reason at the time to believe the *Normandie* fire had resulted from sabotage because it would have been a colossal troop transport vessel powerful enough to outrun U-boats. Sabotage was also suspected given what had happened during the lead-up to the *first* world war, which requires highlighting because it informed what FDR would do in the second. On the evening of July 16, 1916, a massive explosion occurred at the munitions depot on Black Tom Island in Jersey City to the immediate west of Liberty Island in New York Harbor. The explosion, one of the most enormous nonnuclear explosions in history, killed four people and could be felt as far away as Philadelphia and Maryland. Shrapnel hit the Statue of Liberty, and windows shattered throughout Manhattan. Millions of pounds of small arms and dynamite were being held on Black Tom for shipment to France, England, and Russia. Strangely, Black Tom is rarely mentioned in discussions of World War I, nor are the other two hundred incidents of domestic terror and sabotage that occurred within the United States by a constellation of German agents before and during the conflict. These included forty-three unexplained factory explosions or fires. About $500 million (today's dollars) of damage was done, and there was no question that the Germans, with whom we would soon be at war, were responsible. Germany later paid the United States reparations.

There had been other catalysts for FDR's concerns about violence within U.S. borders. In 1919 Franklin and Eleanor Roosevelt had been living across the street from Attorney General A. Mitchell Palmer when an anarchist bombed his house. Palmer hadn't been injured, but the bomber blew himself up. Roosevelt had been walking past the Palmer house minutes before the explosion and likely would have been killed if it had gone off then. The incident left an impression. When the Second World War came around and the U-boat menace arose in the New York area, dealing

Attorney General Palmer's house after anarchists detonated a bomb in 1919
Library of Congress

harshly with Nazi infiltration close to home was a subject about which the president brooked no debate.

German penetration into the United States pre–World War I had been so deep that Roosevelt used the Black Tom sabotage to help explain his justification for the internment of Japanese Americans during World War II, stating, "We don't want any more Black Toms."

Vincent Astor's role as FDR's chief intelligence adviser was not to last, at least not officially. A rival leaked his role to the *New York Journal-American*. Astor used his influence to have the story killed in future editions, but the damage had been done. FDR couldn't have his top personal spy publicized in the press. The president shifted Astor to another role, ostensibly involving supplying the navy with fishing boats for a purpose that was never officially confirmed. However, Astor was promoted to captain and received multiple citations for his service. The mission of one of Lucky Luciano's deputies, Joseph "Socks" Lanza, was to use fishermen along the Atlantic coast to report unusual developments to the navy. This idea is close to the one FDR had concocted while he was with the Navy Department during World War I.

Two years after his area controller position had officially ended, correspondence from Astor to the FBI indicated that Astor was "at the moment on active sea duty with the United States Navy and we do not expect him back for some time." Another item of correspondence to Hoover indicated that Astor "was given a Navy Commendation Ribbon for Meritorious Performance of Duty, in connection of his handling of the so-called 'fishing fleet.'" In the world of Washington intrigue, sometimes the people who do not have an official portfolio have greater freedom to operate in the shadows than those who do. Wrote historian Jeffery Dorwart, "For Astor the war meant antisubmarine and convoy duty in the headquarters of the Eastern Sea Frontier."

THE COMMANDER

John Franklin Carter, Astor's replacement, was a onetime journalist who had covered FDR favorably. Carter was the likely culprit gunning for Astor, having mentioned to Sumner Welles, undersecretary of state, that U.S. intelligence capabilities were "pretty well loused up and floundering around. There might be a use for a small and informal intelligence unit operating out of the White House without any bullshit." This was the group that

Carter had been refining as Astor was getting his feet wet. Carter noted, "The overall condition was attached to the operation by President Roosevelt that it should be entirely secret and would be promptly disavowed in the event of publicity." Part of this secrecy can be attributed to a sensitive aspect of Carter's work: hunting down fifth columnists within the country.

Carter quickly demonstrated his value, determining that the Germans likely could tap telephone conversations between New York and Switzerland, Sweden, Spain, Portugal, and Vichy France. Given that there had been 108 merchant vessels sunk in March 1942 alone, this made it likely that a loyal German agent in America was somehow conveying information to the Nazis. Carter established an alternative and circuitous manner of making overseas contacts, but the problems on the Atlantic coast remained. In addition to the ongoing U-boat attacks, U.S. intelligence was getting reports that the Nazis were testing a capability to fire rockets from platforms attached to U-boats into American cities.

It was eventually determined that the *Normandie* fire was an accident involving acetylene torches interacting with kapok fiber insulation. Still, at the time, it was interpreted to be another Black Tom act of sabotage to both destroy munitions and dissuade the United States from entering the war. Given that the United States was home to the world's second-largest Italian population, there were suspicions that perhaps Mussolini sympathizers might be responsible. In fact, a presidential proclamation had declared six hundred thousand Italian Americans as "enemy aliens" (a small number were placed in internment camps). There were also fears that Italian gangland bootleggers would begin running fuel to enemy submarines.

Activity on the New York docks was strategically important because they were transfer stations for wartime matériel under the Lend-Lease Act to be delivered by convoys worldwide, not to mention domestic goods destined for the American heartland. In addition, U.S. strategists established early on that one of the most important ways the Allies would prevail would be to out-manufacture the Axis. To accomplish this, the most active port in the world—New York—had to be protected so that food, clothing, and manufacturing materials could reach their destinations.

The docks were unique in another way, too: They were the nexus of the U.S. Navy and organized crime.

KNOWN BY FRIENDS AS "RAD" BECAUSE OF HIS MIDDLE NAME, COMMANDER Charles Radcliffe Haffenden was an extrovert who had been in various businesses, including manufacturing and advertising. He was a risk-taking Damon Runyan character with Tammany Hall connections who once said, "I'll talk to anybody, a priest, a bank manager, a gangster, the devil himself. . . . This is a war. American lives are at stake. It's not a college game where we have to look up the rule book every minute." British prime minister Winston Churchill said something similar: If the devil was in a fight with Adolf Hitler, "I should feel constrained, at least, to make a favorable reference to the Devil in the House of Commons."

The navy first tried to see what inroads it could make, talking directly to the men on the docks. It went poorly. These were hard men with work to do, and they had neither the time nor the inclination to talk to anyone from the government. Frank Hogan, the Manhattan district attorney, likely had been the first to suggest approaching the mob. Hogan had been elected, the irony of ironies, with the help of the Democratic Tammany machine, which didn't make a significant move without a nod from Frank Costello, Luciano and Lansky's business partner who had taken over Luciano's organization upon his imprisonment for compulsory prostitution in 1936. New York County district attorney Thomas E. Dewey had prosecuted Luciano during a controversial trial featuring dubious testimony by prostitutes who had been coached. While Luciano saw prostitutes, it is questionable that someone of his stature was personally involved with supervising houses of ill repute. Among the indignities discussed in open court were Luciano's alleged problems with venereal disease and impotence, which likely served more to humiliate the boss than to convict him. Luciano was given a walloping sentence of thirty to fifty years.

Haffenden was an active Tammany affiliate, and the first mobster approached was the waterfront Luciano family boss "Socks" Lanza. When an investigative report on the program was undertaken years later, it made clear that Hogan had been on board with gangland cooperation: "I told Captain MacFall [navy district intelligence officer] there was nothing in the office the Navy could not have, and I instructed Mr. Gurfein [Assistant D.A. Murray Gurfein] to make available information in our possession, and which might come into our possession, that appeared to have a bearing on the matter."

The Captain MacFall in question was Haffenden's boss and the top man at the navy overseeing what became known as Operation Underworld. Roscoe MacFall looked precisely as you would want a battleship commander to look. In his sixties and sporting a pencil-thin white mustache, he had planned to retire to his home in La Jolla, California, when Hitler's romp through Europe scuttled all that. As disciplined as Haffenden was hip-shot, MacFall was nevertheless unafraid of risk. If for no other reason, he was highly motivated because two of the battleships he had commanded, *California* and *West Virginia*, had been destroyed at Pearl Harbor.

MacFall was much more than a figurehead leader. He may have been a more significant player in American military history than will ever be confirmed. In addition to his operational role, he was also the man who turned out to be personally coordinating the coastal fishing boat fleets with none other than Vincent Astor. If there was a conduit between the mob and the president of the United States, that great lover of the detail of naval intrigue, the pathway would have been through MacFall and Astor to FDR. Said MacFall of his Astor operation:

> Some of the larger fishing fleets had their own ship-to-ship and ship-to-shore telephones, including codes used to guide the other ships of the fleet to places where the catch was good. Utilizing these ships and their equipment, and installing similar telephonic equipment on fishing ships that did not themselves install such equipment. Naval Intelligence worked out a confidential, cooperative arrangement and code with them as part of the submarine lookout system.

Next, Haffenden approached the waterfront chief, Socks Lanza, the preeminent mob figure on the docks because he controlled the Fulton Fish Market, the entry point for a sizable percentage of the fish consumed in the eastern United States. Said one chronicler of the waterfront, "Not a scallop moved through the place that Lanza did not profit from." Given the perishable nature of fish, the delivery and shipping process had to move quickly—no payment, no delivery, which was the principle that gave Lanza so much leverage. Lanza was a heavyset, flat-faced hood who wasn't called Socks because of any penchant for stylish footwear; he resolved waterfront conflicts by socking recalcitrant employees straight in the mouth, occasionally with a sharp-scaled fish.

Among the rackets that took place under Lanza's watch some involved outright theft. Whoever's goods were stolen would be approached by a Lanza mobster who would express regret upon hearing about the theft. The thug would assure the victim he could get the merchandise back for a fee. For an additional fee, the kindly Lanza representative could arrange for the Fulton Fish Market Watchman and Patrol Association to keep an eye on the future shipment of goods.

Haffenden was aware of these rackets; whatever he may have felt about them privately, they weren't his concern. He wanted Lanza to keep open eyes on the docks. Haffenden also knew that Lanza had a network of fishermen out at sea who needed to be brought into the program. The navy believed that Hitler's U-boats were being refueled off the coast by someone sympathetic to his cause, and Haffenden wanted to disrupt it.

Despite his gruff demeanor, Lanza was willing to listen but had a few concerns. One was that the subtext of Operation Underworld, or informally "the ferret squad" (because the combination of gangsters and naval operatives wanted to ferret out spies), was snitching. Snitching was risky, regardless of on whose behalf it was taking place. Haffenden understood. Next, Lanza asked Haffenden if he could help with an indictment he was under. Haffenden said he would see what he could do. Finally, Lanza said that he was inclined to help. Still, any program would be more effective with the blessing of the big boss, Luciano.* In order to get to Luciano, somebody bigger than Lanza was needed, and that man was Luciano's closest confidant, Meyer Lansky.

Lansky, willing to leave his business and his family behind to fight the Nazis, had tried to enlist in the army. He had taken pains to become an American citizen in 1928—Luciano never had, which was to become a significant problem for him later—and chose July 4 as his official birthdate because he had no records of his real one. If he was declined for combat, Lansky said he was willing to do menial tasks such as "machinist, lathe shaper or drill press," experiences he legitimately had. He was rejected for the service because of his age, forty, and his diminutive stature, five-four.

---

* Another version of this story has Lansky suggesting that Luciano be recruited.

Lansky's Certificate of Naturalization   *Author's Private Collection*

Still, he was determined to serve. He wanted to fight the Nazis, the latest iteration of the Jew-haters who had forced his family out of Eastern Europe. He wanted to be a real American.

Lansky got some practice tormenting troublesome Germans when 1938 New York Judge Nathan Perlman enlisted him to break up pro-Nazi German American Bund rallies, an order he gave to a band of enforcers enthusiastically and repeatedly. Perlman's only request was that Lansky's men not kill anyone. We'll never know how closely that directive was followed. Jewish gangsters replicated similar activities in New Jersey, Chicago, and elsewhere. It didn't help that American Nazis eventually couldn't hold meetings in the United States without risking hospitalization. A shift in public opinion eventually diminished the presence of American Nazis.

Lansky hadn't been the only mobster who wanted to fight for America. Other Jewish racketeers were eager to take on Nazis. Cleveland's Moe Dalitz became a captain in the army. A Lansky deputy, Doc Stacher, also joined the army. The lethal Dave Berman of Minneapolis tried to enlist, was rejected, and joined the Canadian army under a fake name. Italian mobsters took pains to demonstrate their loyalty to America, not Italy. Even the psychopathic Albert Anastasia,* who had falsely claimed to have started the *Normandie* fire to help his friend Luciano, enlisted. By all accounts, he served honorably, as did Venero "Benny Eggs" Mangano of the Genovese family, who fought as a tail gunner in the United States Army Air Corps and won the Distinguished Flying Cross and an Air Medal with four oak leaf clusters and three battle stars. Matty "the Horse" Ianniello, also of the Genovese, won the Purple Heart and Bronze Star for his service in the Pacific theater.

Bugsy Siegel had a different notion of how he would help America: He wanted to kill Axis leaders Hitler and Mussolini. While there's no credible evidence that he ever got close to Hitler, one of his many girlfriends (Siegel was married with two daughters) was an Italian countess who knew Mussolini. Siegel had once seen Nazi propaganda minister Joseph Goebbels and Luftwaffe chief Hermann Göring at a restaurant in Rome. Siegel wanted to kill them then and there, but the countess thought that might be rude and, ever sensitive to charges that he was crazy, backed Siegel off, to his eternal regret. He also had bigger challenges closer to home, dodging murder indictments, hunting down snitches and competitors, building his Los Angeles rackets, contemplating Las Vegas gambling adventures, and having violent fights with his mistress Virginia Hill.

At a meeting at the Longchamps restaurant in Manhattan, Lansky, Haffenden, and prosecutor Murray Gurfein,† whom the district attorney's office had designated as its representative to the navy, discussed the Luciano situation. When he heard Haffenden's pitch, Lansky responded, "It's patriotism. I'll do it." In later testimony Lansky said, "Submarines. Submarines, that was mainly what they were fearful of." Lansky shared the navy's concern that some of the Italians on the docks might be loyal to Mussolini, but the imprisoned Luciano's involvement would help. Given the dictator's crackdown on Cosa Nostra in Italy, Lansky also felt the

---

* Some believe Anastasia enlisted to avoid prosecution as some of his rackets were under siege, but given that he remained in the United States, that theory doesn't quite work.

† Thirty years later, Gurfein was to serve as the judge on the Pentagon Papers case.

Mafia in the United States and Sicily might be motivated to assist. When Mussolini rose to power, the *New York Times* declared in a headline:

THE MAFIA IS DEAD; A NEW SICILY IS BORN
Mussolini's War Against the Secret Society
Rids the Island of an Evil Many Centuries Old

Had the Mafia had its own newspaper, its headline would have answered: *OH REALLY?* Not only was the Mafia not dead, but it would play a supporting role in Mussolini's downfall. It was difficult to dislodge the Mafia because it was less an organization than a steady manifestation of the basest instincts of human nature: greed, lust, sloth, pleasure, and wrath, to name a few.

Lansky mentioned that Luciano was imprisoned far away and it would make the operation go more smoothly if he could be moved closer, a request ultimately granted. We will see this theme again: mobsters seeking to escape jail in gradations. On May 15, 1942, Lansky and attorney Moses Polakoff met a surprised Luciano, who had been moved to Great Meadow, a closer and better-appointed New York State prison, without knowing why.

After starting out at Sing-Sing upon his conviction, Luciano was taken to the Clinton Correctional Facility in Dannemora, New York, close to the Canadian border. Because of its coldness and distance from civilization, it became known as "Siberia." The prison had been chosen for a few reasons. One was that the government didn't like crime bosses and enjoyed making them miserable for revenge and to send a message to would-be wiseguys that the government would be relentless. Second, they didn't want Luciano running his empire from behind bars, which he could only accomplish if his associates could visit on a regular basis. Luciano was isolated, and it was hard for a mob boss to run his rackets from prison. He had loyal colleagues, but none were so dedicated that they wanted to get caught in a blizzard visiting him and risk the government's wrath.

Luciano was lukewarm on the navy program and said he would help, provided his participation remained secret. He didn't want his underworld cronies to think he was cooperating with the government. Luciano also knew he could someday be facing deportation and "was fearful of bodily harm," said Lansky. After all, one of the Allies' main enemies was Luciano's former Italian countrymen, who might someday be his hosts.

The first order of business was to get Luciano out of Siberia. He began cooperating once he was moved to the more hospitable climate at Great Meadow. The mob's next task was to get union cards for Haffenden's men to work among the other dock laborers as truck drivers, stevedores, seafood workers, and fishermen. Defense manufacturers and hotels and restaurants also employed them. Lanza recruited Ben Espy, a gangster friend, to accompany him on a "fishing trip" from Maine to North Carolina to spread the word about keeping eyes open for Nazi U-boats, saboteurs, and anyone who might aid them. "It came to the point where the Navy was putting intelligence officers on fishing boats through the union to monitor better what was happening in the water. Cooperation with organized crime helped to get ONI [Office of Naval Intelligence] a greater level of access to sources of information throughout the city," said naval historian Matthew Cheser.

There was a less subtle message from the Lanza/Espy visit: If you side with the Germans, you'll either deal with the U.S. government or us, and we both know how to deal with people who betray us. Lanza returned to Haffenden the names of key fishermen who might be especially useful. We do not know whether Vincent Astor's reassignment into the navy-fishing nexus included direct interactions with Lanza and Espy. Still, it is difficult to imagine that Astor was uninvolved with this effort, given the specific tasks he had been assigned.

Matériel needed to make its way through the ports, and any obstreperousness from the workforce would have to wait. There were exceptions. Among the other services the mob provided was ensuring labor peace by quashing strikes. When Haffenden's men expressed concern about an impending visit from West Coast Longshoremen boss, the socialist Harry Bridges, Lanza assured them he would take care of it, which Lanza did by beating the hell out of Bridges. This may not have been Haffenden's first choice of negotiation tactic, but it worked.

One of the ferret squad's principal assets was a psychopath named John "Cockeye" Dunn, so named because of one eye perpetually focused elsewhere, perhaps searching for someone to kill. Dunn was the top watchdog on the waterfront tasked with ensuring safety and keeping labor peace. He knew the necessary names and faces. Anyone who didn't look familiar was beaten, dunked in the river, or escorted off the docks and given a lesson on the hazards of trespassing. He kept an eye out for "men that may lend themselves to sabotage, or leakage of information," according to Lansky. "He also got friends along the waterfront in the bar rooms. If any of the crews got drunk, and they would talk something that you would feel is subversive, to report him, or whomever he pleased on that, to assist him on that."*

Lansky helped Haffenden create a network of spies at hotels through the mob's unions. If, for example, a bartender was to see something unusual, word would find its way back to Lansky. A similar system was in place involving fishing boats in the region. If U-boats or other strange activities were detected, word would be passed to Luciano's waterfront chief, Lanza, and back to Haffenden.

The Hotel Astor, where navy and underworld operatives met to discuss waterfront spying and security operations   *Library of Congress*

---

* Dunn was executed in the electric chair after the war for murder.

So secret was Operation Underworld that there was concern about others in naval intelligence finding out that the military was in bed with the mob. Haffenden had to seek out a hideaway office to meet with his gangland contacts. In addition, the mob figures were concerned about being seen going into government offices. Their fears were well-founded because there was ample reason to believe that district attorney Hogan had Haffenden's offices in the Third Naval District wiretapped and bugged.

Haffenden and Lansky, no fools, thought it would have been far less conspicuous for gangsters to be seen entering and leaving a hotel where they might have been having lunch or some other kind of assignation acceptable to gangland. Haffenden landed upon the Hotel Astor on Times Square for his hideaway lair, a popular hotel built by none other than the Astor family. Vincent Astor managed much of the family's extensive Manhattan real estate holdings, although, unsurprisingly, there is no documentation proving that Astor offered up the family property. Nevertheless, this was where Haffenden usually met with Lansky, Lanza, and other associates as needed.

VISITORS FROM THE DEPTHS

According to naval intelligence officers, a fisherman in Lanza's crew first reported the unusual sighting at Amagansett, Long Island, to the Lanza-Lansky network. In the wee hours of June 13, 1942, a U-boat surfaced off the coast of Amagansett, and four Nazi spies rowed ashore. They possessed a deadly cache of dynamite, fuses, and detailed plans to blow up aluminum plants,* chemical plants, canals, bridges, railways, and Jewish-owned places of business. While not incredibly well planned, the objective was to destroy or disrupt the United States' capability for wartime manufacturing. Shortly after landing, the saboteurs attempted to bribe a young coast guard member who promptly reported the visitors. A twin team of four men came ashore a few days later near Jacksonville, Florida, with similar equipment and plans. The Florida team made their way to the Midwest to await sabotage orders.

---

*   The aluminum plants were targeted in order to disrupt airplane production, which was thought to be of especially great strategic purpose.

There are conflicting accounts about the intelligence that led to the capture of the spies with parties that run the gamut from gangsters to G-men. If Hoover was to be believed—and what he told FDR—was that the FBI single-handedly cracked the case. Hoover left out of his briefing that Haffenden's navy team had gotten to Amagansett first and let loose the ferret squad of mobsters and other spies to see what they could find in the city. Hoover also didn't tell the president that the lead Long Island Nazi, George Dasch, eventually turned himself in rather than be hunted down. Dasch had once lived in the United States, hadn't been the most committed of Nazis, and he claimed he had not planned to carry out the sabotage mission from the get-go.

We also cannot be sure whether Dasch received "encouragement" to turn himself in from characters he may have run into in the city. He may have just chickened out on his own; it's easy to be a terrorist from four thousand miles away but much more complicated when you arrive at the place of murder and mayhem and must do it. It's possible, therefore, that Dasch realized he was in deep trouble and it was better to cut his losses while he had the chance. It must have been quite a shock to have been discovered immediately upon coming ashore at Amagansett.

Dasch gave the FBI information about the possible whereabouts of the other saboteurs. Lansky, however, claimed that the networks he helped establish in hotels, restaurants, and bars—including the retention of German-speaking servers—led the authorities to the rest of the men. At least three of the other spies had once been waiters in the United States and spoke English. They also had convened at hotels and restaurants in New York City.

Lansky specifically said he had been approached by the brother of a local fisherman who had seen U-boats off the coast of Long Island and spotted men rowing ashore in darkness. Lansky transmitted the information to Haffenden, who then contacted the New York office of the FBI, which Dasch had also done. Lansky's account is plausible, but the evidence that Dasch had turned himself in to try to catch a break with the FBI is more likely.

All the players had strong incentives to lie: Hoover wanted the FBI to be the hero; Haffenden needed to show that the navy controlled the coast; Dasch was desperate to demonstrate that he was and had always been a double agent sympathetic to the Red, White, and Blue, not a Nazi spy; and Lansky wanted to reinforce the mob's value to the effort.

Nevertheless, what were the chances that Hoover would keep a record of any gangland sleuthing achievements regarding the spies? Slim to none, especially since his position was that the Mafia didn't exist. Dasch said, "The FBI's interest was to let the Nazis think that a vigilant United States had nipped the sabotage mission in the bud and that it would be useless to waste any more men and time on similar missions against such an alert country."

Hoover biographer Beverly Gage wrote, "As Hoover told it, FBI ingenuity, efficiency and scientific prowess alone accounted for the saboteurs' capture." With a flair for the rat-a-tat-tat dramatic, Hoover took to the radio airwaves and barked: "In foiling this diabolical scheme, the agents of the FBI have again proven more than a match for Hitler's trained hirelings in the field of counterespionage."

Roosevelt was brutal in his demand that the spies be humiliated and executed. He told his attorney general Francis Biddle, "Let's make real money out of them. Sell the rights to Barnum and Bailey for a million and a half—the rights to take them around in lion cages at so much a head." By most accounts, FDR personally managed the media relations associated with the handling of the saboteurs. He queried one of his assistants, "Should they be shot or hanged?" He later sent a memo to Biddle stating, "I do not see how they can offer any adequate defense . . . it seems to me that the death penalty is almost obligatory."

Biddle argued that the men had not yet committed any sabotage, but Roosevelt wanted them executed. When informed that he couldn't unilaterally demand this, the president forbade them to be tried by a civil court and said, "I want one thing clearly understood, Francis: I won't give them up . . . I won't hand them over to any United States Marshal armed with a writ of habeas corpus. Understand!" Newspaper editorials echoed Roosevelt's position with bold headlines declaring, "Let's Shoot the Gang!"

Nor was getting the spies to "flip" and become double agents an option. Wrote Joseph Persico, "Turning the eight captured Germans never entered FDR's head." Indeed, Roosevelt felt the pressure to ward off sabotage acutely and publicly alluded to being willing to deal with gangsters.

Attorneys for the saboteurs rapidly made a case before the Supreme

Court that being tried by a military court with a jury of generals was unconstitutional. The justices rejected their claim. Roosevelt invoked the Articles of War so that the men could be tried by a military jury rather than a civil one. The Civil War was the last time such a saboteur trial was held.

ON EXECUTION DAY, AUGUST 8, 1942, ROOSEVELT WAS IN A GREAT MOOD, entertaining guests at the presidential retreat, Shangri-La, now known as Camp David. He was waiting for word that the saboteurs had been electrocuted. One of his guests asked the president if he had any qualms about the executions, and he said his only regret was that they would not be hanged.

Only Dasch and associate Ernest Burger were spared execution at the attorney general's recommendation because of their cooperation. According to witnesses, the other condemned spies had been stunned that their executions were happening, having been under the impression that they still had other options. The executions began alphabetically at noon and were completed shortly after one o'clock. As he waited, FDR cracked jokes about the spies being cooked like veal. Their bodies were buried in a Washington, D.C., field. Dasch and Burger figured out the fates of their comrades when they were returned to their cells and found their comrades' cells empty. The two men were eventually deported to Germany. No other known attempt was ever made by the Nazis to bring its saboteurs to American shores.

Roosevelt could not have been more open about his "whatever it takes" approach to hunting down Nazi sympathizers and saboteurs. The navy was especially sensitive to Roosevelt's priorities given the president's affection for, if not obsession with, this military branch.

Wrote Lansky in his private notes:

I was approached to enlist Luciano's services. I understood the feelings of Italians [and] it was really needed to convince Italians that their duty was first to help U.S. and that it would be helping Italy when the war was over . . . I was very happy to handle the contract. I knew it was necessary to watch the docks and what was going on with Italian fishermen. I convinced Charlie, Frank and many others that this was their country.

OPERATION HUSKY

As the war progressed, it looked increasingly likely that there would be a European invasion and that Sicily might be the point of entry. Allied leadership believed it would be important to have the support of Italian Americans in the attack. President Roosevelt sent British prime minister Winston Churchill a telegram saying: "In view of the friendly feeling toward Americans entertained by a great number of citizens of Italy and in consideration of the large number of citizens of the United States who are of Italian descent, it is my opinion that our military problem will be made less difficult by giving to the Allied Military Government as much of our American character as possible."

In other words, the United States would make a concerted effort to involve Italian Americans in conquering Sicily.

On May 23, 1943, Haffenden was placed in charge of intelligence-gathering for the Italy-Sicily region. By this point, the navy's ferret squad contingent consisted of 150 intelligence officers, many Italian Americans, so Haffenden's initial crew had expanded and could tend to the domestic front. Among his many tactics was to seek information about the country's terrain and locate possible Sicilian Mafia resources with which the American military could connect. Lanza and Luciano's other Sicilian contacts shook loose potential assets. Lansky brought them to the Hotel Astor for Haffenden to vet along with Lieutenant Anthony Marsloe, of Italian heritage,* who spoke Sicilian dialects.

The U.S. top military leaders, the Joint Staff Planners (JSP), had been presented with an invasion plan, which included the following language: "Establishment of contact and communications with the leaders of separatist nuclei, disaffected workers, and clandestine radical groups, e.g., the Mafia, and giving them every possible aid."

General George Marshall and the Joint Chiefs approved the broader

---

* Marsloe's family name had been Marzullo. Not only did Italian Americans in Sicily help break the language barrier, but it was important for the military to acknowledge that it viewed Italian Americans as *real* Americans, given FDR's earlier characterization of them as "enemy aliens." Another star of the Italian campaign was Max Corvo of the Office of Strategic Services, the precursor to the CIA.

document, Special Military Plan for Psychological Warfare in Sicily. In plain English, this was permission for the military to work with the Mafia in the United States and Sicily. It was then passed on to the commander of the North African theater, General Dwight D. Eisenhower, and eventually to the man who would directly lead the invasion with American forces, General George S. Patton, Jr.

With the navy in New York showing Sicilian immigrants' photos and postcards, they could provide information about the region's beaches, roads, and mountain passages. Lansky later described navy officers sharing maps with the Sicilian immigrants who compared them to their memories of villages, beaches, and waterways. The Sicilians were also asked for contacts who could interact with Sicilian bosses Calogero Vizzini and Giuseppe Genco Russo. The Germans had been known to use Sicilian labor for planting mines, but once U.S. forces came ashore, they were either alerted to the minefields by their new friends or were told that the devices had either been swiftly dug up or defused.

The invasion of Sicily was an essential inroad into Europe and an opportunity to defeat Germany's ally, Italy. The weather conditions were not ideal, leading the Axis to believe an invasion was unlikely. The Americans and British went ahead anyway. The Italian army was weak, and the Germans accepted that they would have to do the heavy lifting in the fight.

The invasion of Sicily by British general Sir Bernard Montgomery and American general Patton began on July 9, 1943. Twenty-five hundred sea vessels carried 181,000 men from the two armies to the rocky island. It was code-named Operation Husky.

In one of the more intrepid Husky adventures, Lieutenant Paul Alfieri "made contact with a mafioso 'cousin' of Luciano." Sicilian gangsters led Alfieri and his team to the Axis naval headquarters, where he cracked a safe and "discovered priceless operational intelligence: the order of battle and location of Italian and German naval forces for the Mediterranean; a radio code book and minefield maps." He had similar success on the Italian mainland at Salerno. Alfieri was taught his safecracking skills by a mob-linked crook in New York. He later was awarded the Legion of Merit for his intelligence work in Sicily and on the Italian mainland.

It took slightly over one month, but the Allies prevailed in Sicily at the price of twenty-five thousand casualties. Said Haffenden in a later interview, "The greater part of the intelligence developed in the Sicilian campaign was directly responsible to the number of Sicilians that emanated from the Charlie 'Lucky' contact." Lansky later said that Luciano's name was used like "magic" in the Sicilian villages, an overstatement.

WHAT DID THE PRESIDENT KNOW?

FDR personal operatives didn't end with Vincent Astor. Syndicated columnist and broadcaster Walter Winchell also played an extraordinary role during World War II. Winchell, who had significant gangland sources, wanted to join Naval Intelligence but had been rejected by the Third Naval District, the very same one that was running Operation Underworld. Winchell found other ways to join the war effort. He was FDR's most influential mouthpiece agitating for war with Germany and supported it once it began. His biographer, Neal Gabler, wrote that he "had virtually become part of the Roosevelt team."

FDR directly recruited Winchell, who met with him in the White House multiple times. Upon their first meeting, the president told the broadcaster to keep him posted if he heard anything he thought Roosevelt should know about, adding, "That's an order!" Winchell maintained contact with White House press secretary Steve Early and was pleased to transmit the anti-Axis propaganda the administration wanted in the public domain. Winchell's role was concerning to more traditional journalists. Wrote Gabler, "Walter was seen as simply a firebrand who had no cogent political philosophy save blind support of the President and J. Edgar Hoover."

In the lead-up to the war, Winchell threw journalistic sunlight on the German American Bund, which had been brazenly promoting Nazi interests in the United States—from their base in the Yorkville section of the Upper East Side of Manhattan. Their leader was the Munich-born Fritz Kuhn, who enjoyed whipping up German and anti-Semitic sentiment at events including a significant Nazi extravaganza with twenty thousand attendees at Madison Square Garden, where he hoped to be positioned as the American Hitler. He referred to the president as "Frank D. Rosenfeld" at the event playing to his anti-Semitic base.

Winchell was also a neighbor in the Majestic, a high-end apartment tower on Central Park West, of none other than Meyer Lansky. The journalist had been known to receive tips about the locations of Bund meetings and transmit them to Lansky, who would then send in his troops to break up the gatherings violently. Winchell then gleefully covered news of Nazi sympathizers getting pummeled. It's likely the two men, who were Jewish Americans supportive of the war effort, didn't need an official sanction to help the cause.

Said Lansky: "Walter Winchell phoned to thank me for busting up that meeting and I told him he had nothing to thank me for because I was doing what had to be done anyway. I also told him he had given me the wrong address: We had found the right address on our own."

The Jewish gangsters soon moved on to another cause: supporting Jewish revolutionaries fighting to establish the modern state of Israel.

The Majestic Apartments on Central Park West. Three big players in the war effort happened to live there and were friendly: Walter Winchell, Meyer Lansky, and Frank Costello. Winchell tipped Lansky off to Bund rally locations.
Courtesy of King of Hearts

According to Luellen Smiley, daughter of Ben Siegel's business partner Allen Smiley, the two men began raising money for the fighting force known as the Haganah. Other reports support her story. Initially, Siegel was skeptical when hearing about the warrior Jews of the Middle East. Reuvin Dafni, a Haganah representative, had been contacted by a man identifying himself simply as "Smiley," asking for a meeting. He agreed. As Dafni waited at a Los Angeles meeting place, two bodyguards entered silently and said nothing. Moments later, a man entered whom Dafni assumed was a movie star. The handsome tough introduced himself as Ben Siegel and told Dafni to start talking. Dafni said:

> I told him my story, how the Haganah was raising money to buy weapons with which to fight. When I finished, Siegel asked, "You mean to tell me Jews are fighting?" Yes, I replied. Then Siegel, who was sitting across the table, leaned forward till his nose was almost touching mine. "You mean fighting, as in killing?" Yes, I answered. Siegel leaned back, looked at me for a moment and said, "OK, I'm with you."

By the time of America's entry into the war, the Bund had lost a great deal of steam and was likely exhausted from having the stuffing beaten out of them. Manhattan, of course, was not the ideal choice for a Nazi political base. In addition to being a bigot, Bund boss Kuhn was also a thief. He was charged with and convicted of embezzlement, having spent a fortune of Bund funds on his mistress. He was deported and quickly found that Nazi Germany wasn't as delightful a destination as he had hoped; he wanted to return to his now-beloved America, which was a no-go. After the Allied victory, he was imprisoned in Dachau and prosecuted under German de-Nazification laws. He remained angry with Walter Winchell for his anti-Nazi columns and for helping Jewish mobsters sabotage his rallies. Kuhn, in exile, sent Winchell a nasty letter reading, "Tell Herr Vinchell, I will lift to piss on his grafe [sic]," meaning "live to piss on his grave." Kuhn died in obscurity in 1951. Winchell lived until 1972.

When the fire on the *Normandie* was later ruled an accident, Winchell, ever the agitator, didn't buy it, stating, "If no one was to blame, all they had to find was who pushed her over." At one point, he even suggested that Luciano should be given a medal for helping to secure the docks, which caused great heartache for Thomas Dewey, the man who prosecuted him and later commuted his sentence—and Hoover, who didn't want a mob boss getting credit for anything.

Operation Underworld would have been an awkward subject for Winchell or FDR to broach directly with each other. Still, one wonders how often in American history an operative like Winchell had been in direct contact with the president of the United States and a leading mobster discussing the same subject toward the same ends. There is enough data about Operation Underworld to overlay it with what we know about FDR's priorities and personal interests to speculate about his awareness of the gangland campaign responsibly:

1. Roosevelt was personally obsessed with the minutia of espionage.
2. He was particularly focused on naval vulnerability, especially after Pearl Harbor, where one of the ships he launched as assistant secretary of the navy was destroyed. Churchill shared FDR's preoccupation with maritime espionage.
3. Sabotage became a key focus around New York because of FDR's awareness of the World War I munitions explosion at Black Tom Island and related incidents. This mindset intensified after the *Normandie* fire, which for some time was suspected of being caused by sabotage.
4. The president appointed his intimate friend Vincent Astor as his espionage consigliere and then had him focus not only on the New York area but maritime operations specifically. They were in constant personal contact.
5. Astor worked closely with the top officer with supervisory responsibility for Operation Underworld.
6. An Astor family hotel was used as the hideaway office for the ferret squad.
7. Even when Astor left his formal role as FDR's top espionage adviser, he took on maritime responsibilities that dovetailed precisely with the activities of the ferret squad and mob figures conducting surveillance in and around coastal New York.
8. The Nazi saboteurs were captured in the specific region where the ferret squad was operational. Roosevelt took a personal supervisory interest in their capture, punishment, and media coverage.

9. FDR had been governor of New York and was aware of the mob's capabilities. Luciano, Lansky, and Costello's participation at the 1932 Democratic convention could not have gone unnoticed, especially since they had played a key role in backing FDR's opponent for a time.

10. Journalist Walter Winchell, who was close to both Lansky and Roosevelt, was an active propagandist for the activities of both men.

11. A memo prepared during the Herlands Commission investigation into mob involvement in securing the New York waterfront specifically referenced FDR's interest: "In the latter part of 1941, the security of the Port of New York was a matter of great significance, not only to the Commandant of the Third Naval District but to the Secretary of the Navy, and *the President of the United States*." [author's emphasis]

Given the aggregate of these factors, it would defy the basic tenets of logic if FDR was not aware of—or even encouraged—Operation Underworld.

MOB INVOLVEMENT IN CONTEXT

Operation Underworld has been polarizing for mob scholars who fall along two extremes. One point of view cynically asserts that the program was a sham, a stunt whereby racketeers faked patriotism to get Charlie Luciano sprung from prison. Luciano himself may have played a role in spreading this rumor out of concern that his gangland allies would see him as having been a government cooperator. Waterfront mobster Albert Anastasia even bragged that he had lit the fire to drive the government into the arms of Luciano for assistance—as if this would have been the logical response given that FDR had issued a proclamation allowing Italian Americans to be imprisoned as "enemy aliens" if they fell under the suspicions of the FBI. A dubious biography of Luciano has Luciano himself making similar claims along with giving himself credit for winning the war. These, too, are unlikely given his documented self-effacing statements in the wake of constant prosecution and surveillance.

Respected organized crime reporter Selwyn Raab doesn't believe Luciano and Lansky did much of anything. The opposite pole is a hagiography that has Luciano storming the shores of Sicily with Patton's Seventh Army waving a flag emblazoned with the letter *L* to alert his countrymen that a native son had returned to liberate them from the fascists. Yes, Luciano going to Sicily had been proposed but was swiftly dismissed.

There's another—and more practical—way to look at Operation Underworld: Desperation in wartime calls for experimentation. Americans had been losing a staggering amount of matériel, and sailors were being boiled alive when torpedoes hit ships—five hundred merchant ships and five thousand merchant seamen and U.S. sailors by accounts. General George C. Marshall summarized, "The losses of submarines off our Atlantic seaboard and in the Caribbean now threaten our entire war effort." According to naval historian Michael Gannon:

> The U-boat assault on merchant shipping in United States home waters and the Caribbean during World War II constituted a greater strategic setback for the Allied war effort than did the defeat at Pearl Harbor . . . the loss of nearly 400 hulls and cargoes strewn across the sands of the U.S. Navy's Eastern Gulf and Caribbean Sea frontiers threatened both to sever Great Britain's lifeline and to cripple American war industries.

Also, the U.S. Navy was severely outnumbered. They had only one hundred rickety airplanes and troops had been training with flour bags instead of artillery. In the autumn of 1941, before the United States was officially at war, FDR secretly okayed the navy to accompany merchant ships and "shoot on sight" vessels hostile to Allied shipping in a secret war. The military had to do *something* else.

The navy had been scrambling. Roosevelt, too. Like General Andrew Jackson long before his summoning the help of the pirate Lafitte, Haffenden reached out for a weapon and found one in Lansky, Lanza, and Luciano. The mob need not have saved the republic to have participated in the war effort and added value. It likely had a chilling effect on the Third Reich's efforts to penetrate the New York waterfront. There is ample evidence of Jewish mobsters harassing and injuring Nazi sympathizers in New York and New Jersey, making the environment inhospitable to the enemy. Any Nazi tiptoeing into Manhattan and encountering gangsters would be highly motivated to turn around. German operatives looking for assets on the docks would have a similar reaction. We've seen evidence here from military and intelligence officers that contacts in Sicily obtained through mob connections provided Patton's army with information that aided Operation Husky.

Hoover attributed the lack of enemy penetration to the work of his team. Lansky concluded that once his group got involved, "nothing went wrong in the port of New York. No sabotage, no strikes, no ships delayed . . . no suspicious characters were allowed anywhere near the loading docks." On this, Lansky and the FBI agree; the bureau stated: "Although many allegations of sabotage were investigated by the FBI during World War II, not one instance was found of enemy-inspired sabotage." Detractors say the sabotage wouldn't have happened anyway, which is reckless given what the country had been facing. Concluded Lansky in his interview with the Herlands Commission investigating Dewey's role in pardoning Luciano, "I feel that it was a great precaution."

It was better to have the mob with America than not. The main point is not whether the cooperation of gangsters was essential or worthless; it is that the highest level of government approached a cohort of the population that was considered the lowest, in the same way that the power elites of an earlier time in New York sought out gangsters to check off items on Piker Ryan's list—from a distance.

LUCIANO RECEIVED THE SENTENCE COMMUTATION THAT HE HAD HOPED for, partially: He was freed but was deported to Italy. While Lansky was studying American history to become a naturalized citizen, Luciano laughed it off and dismissed it as one of Lansky's intellectual indulgences. It was a severe miscalculation.

On December 5, 1946, the New York State Parole Board agreed to commute Luciano's sentence as an "undesirable alien." On January 3, 1946, New York's Governor Dewey formally commuted Luciano's sentence, along with those of other foreigners. Had Luciano gotten his American citizenship, he could have asserted his rights and requested to remain in America. However, he had made no effort to become a citizen, emboldening the government to deport him.

Dewey's statement to the New York legislature read, in part: "Luciano is deportable to Italy. Upon entry of the United States into the war, Luciano's aid was sought by the armed services in inducing others to provide information concerning possible enemy attack. It appears that he cooperated in such effort though the actual value of the information procured is not clear. His record in prison is reported as wholly satisfactory."

Some cried foul and believed Luciano's commutation was a dirty deal, but the truth is that it wasn't as exotic as it may have seemed. FDR had commuted the prison sentences of 151 aliens, primarily for narcotics offenses, expressly for deportation. As Governor Roosevelt once said, "Every effort should be made to rid the country of the criminal element."

A CAPER WITHIN A CAPER

The first rule of spycraft is "trust no one"—for a good reason: We should never assume that because one is on the "same team" in theory, every player is united toward the same end. In the case of Operation Underworld, the naval players worked sufficiently well together. This was not the case for others in the wartime government bureaucracy. To this end, a bizarre sideshow never fully explained emerged during Operation Underworld.

The Office of Strategic Services (OSS), the precursor to the CIA, and the Federal Bureau of Narcotics (FBN) tried to smear Dewey as having been bribed by Luciano for his freedom. These charges made it into some media and circulated through the political and intelligence worlds. Both government bodies made efforts to declare the ferret squad a fiction. One possibility for this might be a little-known cloak-and-dagger scheme within Operation Underworld to experiment on people with a truth serum that might be used on U-boat sailors. A low-level mobster, August DeGrazia, was allegedly used as a test subject, a precursor to the CIA's later MKUltra drug/mind control experiments. It didn't work.

The characterizations of FBN agent George White and OSS chief William "Wild Bill" Donovan were filled with denials and doublespeak aimed at Luciano's service and Dewey's involvement. Donovan told an FBN supervisor that "Charlie Luciano was not used by the Office of Strategic Services in any way whatever in any capacity and he made the further statement that the OSS would not have used this man under any circumstances." This isn't very likely. We know that naval intelligence worked with Luciano. Donovan may have been exercising the doctrine of plausible deniability (lying) or playing a game of bureaucratic Three-card Monte, deliberately muddling the players.

George White had served in the OSS in the New York area beginning in 1942, the year Operation Underworld got its footing. It must be more than a coincidence that he also eventually served as an investigator *and* an interview subject for the Senate's Kefauver Committee to investigate organized crime (which will be addressed in the following chapter). White testified that the FBN played no role in anything like Operation Underworld and that Luciano had no value to the wartime effort. But why would he care so much about Luciano if the FBN had nothing to do with the secret program? Regarding work with the Kefauver Committee, according to an analysis in *Intelligence and National Security*, White and a colleague, Charles Siragusa: "influenced the selection of individuals for hearings, manufactured data, testified as experts, and used each other as sources. In short, these two FBN agents partially controlled the information process; equally important, they also knew about the Navy project."

Furthermore, a naval officer, John Hanley, testified to a separate commission investigating Operation Underworld in New York that White had even been among those who had visited Luciano in prison. Indeed, a recently discovered (and partially burned) memo belonging to Commander Haffenden lists Hanley as a "Squad #4" member of the ferret squad.[*] Additional documentation indicated that Hanley served with naval intelligence in 1942 and 1943 and would have been able to know about visits to Luciano.

Why the vigorous campaign to discredit the secret drug-testing campaign? A possible explanation is that to admit Operation Underworld was real would be to admit that whatever was done under its cloak was real—things like two government agencies experimenting with dangerous narcotics on civilians. Lansky claimed to have never heard of White or DeGrazia, which is likely true because if FBN and OSS had executed such a program, they would have wanted to keep the circle as small as possible. The question then becomes: What were Luciano and White talking about during prison visits, and what, if anything, did they do for each other?

---

[*]   On the actual document, he is listed as "J. Hanly."

All we know is that a budget for some experimentation was approved for Donovan and that there was no known successful effort to use narcotics as a truth serum on U-boat sailors. If there had been a program to experiment on civilians, successful or not, then the cover-up was successful because it never went public in an explosive manner, as had happened with the Tuskegee syphilis experiments on African Americans in the 1940s (exposed in 1972) and CIA's MKUltra and Operation Midnight Climax (involving experimenting on San Francisco brothel patrons with hallucinogens) experiments in the 1950s (revealed in 1975), which also involved George White and famed CIA counterintelligence chief James Jesus Angleton. CIA chief Richard Helms destroyed the Agency's MKUltra files decades later.*

AFTERMATH OF OPERATION UNDERWORLD

After years of postwar gossip about Operation Underworld, which tended toward the craven and cinematic, Judge William B. Herlands, New York State commissioner of investigation, was assigned to study what happened. Dewey had pushed for the inquiry, partly motivated by clearing his name from the FBN/OSS smear accusing him of having been compromised into commuting Luciano's sentence.

Part of the problem with the tall tales about Operation Underworld was their wild inconsistency. Haffenden had confirmed on-the-record aspects of the program in postwar news reports. MacFall, being the first-rate intelligence officer he was, claimed that no program had involved Luciano. All genuine clandestine operatives understand that there are excellent reasons for silence and deception, not the least of which is to protect certain spying assets. The time for transparency and soul-searching is *after* the enemy has been destroyed and informants and operatives are long out of harm's way.

The study was undertaken in January 1954 and completed in September. There were fifty-seven witnesses and more than 2,800 pages

---

*   There have been credible reports that Boston mobster Whitey Bulger and Unabomber Theodore Kaczynski were among those experimented upon under the MKUltra umbrella.

of testimony. The ferret squad had been operational from March 7, 1942, to May 1, 1944, and involved seventy-two naval officers and eighty-two enlisted men and other assets deployed opportunistically. The report was technically made public in 1976, but the full version has never been easily accessible. Herlands died in 1969 and Dewey in 1971; Dewey's family did not consent to allow the report summary to be released until after his death. They waited until 1976 to give that consent. Concluded Herlands: "Over and beyond any precise rating is the crystal-clear fact that Luciano and his associates and contacts during a period when 'the outcome of the war appeared extremely grave' were responsible for a wide range of services which were considered 'useful to the Navy.'"

The slam-dunk confirmation of the program's existence came from Rear Admiral Carl F. Espe of the Department of the Navy at the Pentagon: "We are advised that contacts were made with Luciano thereafter and that his influence on other criminal sources resulted in their cooperation with Naval intelligence which was considered useful to the Navy."

Espe, to his further credit, was the most honest player in the Herlands document, admitting the reason why the navy had kept the ferret squad quiet for so long: "Just where imaginative and irresponsible publicists would stop in their search for spicy bits for the public palate is hard to guess. That there is potential for embarrassment to the Navy public relations-wise is apparent."

One of the losers in the navy-mob partnership was Commander Haffenden. He had volunteered for a risky mission that could—and did—destroy him. His motive had only been to protect the Eastern Seaboard and transatlantic cargo from Nazi attack. Haffenden's widow, for the Herlands record, said, "The Navy didn't want any part of 'Lucky' Luciano or any underworld character having been connected to the Navy."

Later in the war, Haffenden was sent to the South Pacific, where he participated in the Battle of Iwo Jima. He won the Purple Heart. He was severely injured in battle and was listed as being 100 percent disabled.

After the war, Haffenden was named the head of the Marine and Aviation Commission for New York. There were rumors that the appointment came courtesy of Frank Costello. This scheme was deemed plausible when witnesses reported having seen Haffenden playing golf with the mob boss despite having denied knowing him. This was probably discovered because there were federal investigators gathering information in the event the navy man had to be discredited if he spoke up about Operation Underworld, which he later did during the Kefauver Senate hearings on organized crime.

His testimony didn't go well. Haffenden waffled between attempting to show that the program was effective enough to be warranted and not so effective that the senators had anything to worry about aiding and abetting gangland activity. He had little ammunition to defend himself because the navy had authorized the destruction of its Luciano files long before. Haffenden claimed to have kept no records, which was likely true. He almost certainly perjured himself when he denied arranging for mobsters to visit Luciano in prison, saying, "I had nothing to do with arranging people going to prison. That was done by Mr. Hogan's [district attorney] office."

Haffenden was fired from the Marine and Aviation Commission, his termination letter delivered by a New York policeman. Haffenden's health had been deteriorating, and he declined sharply after his exit from the commission and even more after his testimony at the Kefauver hearings. He died shortly thereafter. His last job was as a salesman of Dictaphones, a precursor to the tape recorder.

The only thing that could have been worse for Haffenden than Operation Underworld failing was its success. After all, he had gotten the United States of America in bed with the Mafia, and no one was interested in hearing that the American victory over Nazi Germany was due to anything besides a vigorously fought military campaign by tough

Navy Commander Charles R. Haffenden

leaders like "Old Blood and Guts" Patton. The Allies would have indeed conquered Sicily without the mob, but did anybody want to parse every aspect of how this victory had been achieved? Haffenden had succeeded in an endeavor that suddenly didn't look very good, and now the government had to decide how to frame the program.

Haffenden's fate is one we would see again in American politics: The guy who did the dirty work ended up paying a more significant price than those at the top who ordered it. It should be lost on no one that there is a similar principle at work in LCN: The hitman becomes marked for death because he knows how the deed went down, so now must be eliminated. This happened to Salvatore "Sally Bugs" Briguglio, the primary suspect as the triggerman in labor leader Jimmy Hoffa's murder. The lesson? When the government or the mob comes calling, don't be so quick to take a risk under the false promise of upward mobility because no deed, good or bad, goes unpunished. Even Socks Lanza wasn't spared prison. He went to jail for labor racketeering before the war was over and was released in 1950.

A former government official characterized the "dirty little secret of Operation Underworld" as being:

> that the United States Government *needed* Meyer Lansky and organized crime to force an industrial peace and a policing of sabotage on the wharves and in the warehouses. The government turned to him because hiring thugs was what government and business had been doing for a long time to contract workers, and because it could conceive little other choice in the system at hand.

LUCKY, LATER

Luciano, with the support of Dewey, the man who prosecuted him, settled in Italy but became restless. Luciano traveled to Havana, an unwise decision because his partying made the gossip columns, likely with a tipoff from subordinate and rival Vito Genovese, provoking American law enforcement who thought that they had gotten rid of him. One report had singer Frank Sinatra flying from the United States to meet Luciano and a planeload of female "fans." Later, Sinatra played down his encounter with Luciano as a fleeting salutation; however, when Luciano was arrested in

Rome a few years later, his address book contained Sinatra's private home address in Los Angeles.

When Harry Anslinger, the head of the Federal Bureau of Narcotics, heard Luciano was in Havana, he was furious. He suspected Luciano was looking to establish a fresh toehold near the United States for an international narcotics network. At the very least, Cuba had been of interest to Luciano because the mob's ownership of resorts there was *legal*: Once illegally obtained cash arrived on Cuban shores in suitcases, the friendly government was pleased to have the investment, and the mob was able to do in the Caribbean what it couldn't easily do in the United States: go straight.

Anslinger first noticed LCN as a national phenomenon because he knew that narcotics trafficking required inter-regional coordination, usually involving LCN players. While Anslinger didn't have much proof of what Luciano was up to, he didn't need it. He went to President Harry Truman, who immediately halted a shipment of medical supplies to Cuba on the premise that Luciano might seize them for illegal purposes—and didn't resume shipping until Luciano was deported to Italy in February 1947.

As popular as Luciano was among his fellow mobsters, the money they were making legally was even more popular. In fact, after the war both the American LCN and Mafia in Italy enjoyed an unprecedented boom and resurgence, respectively. No one, not even Lansky, was likely distraught to wave goodbye. Luciano told a reporter, "If I'm going to have trouble on this side, I'll go back to Italy. I just want to be nice and quiet. I don't want to be kicked around like this for no reason."

Despite the legends of Luciano's power extending beyond the war, this misrepresents what occurred. It is challenging for Mafia chieftains to maintain power from prison or overseas, especially with a frothing pack of murderers thinking of nothing else besides taking their place. Not even Lansky, Luciano's most trusted business partner, had visited him in his six years in prison (prior to Operation Underworld). Yes, Luciano was respected, and he was paid tribute in Havana. But all the while, his old friends were slowly making their plans, being careful not to make sudden moves that would betray a level of ambition that would be threatening to the other gang chiefs.

From the moment he set foot back in Italy, Luciano was in trouble. In addition to being a criminal, he was rightly suspected of being an Allied operative against Italy's Axis power. He was arrested immediately for smuggling $57,000 in cash into the country. He was nicked for illegally importing a car, banned from entering Rome. While he received the occasional visit from old friends from New York, they weren't eager to be seen with him, so most of his guests were lower-level hoods who wanted to be photographed posing as players. Luciano said he'd give anything to smell and taste hot corned beef from a New York deli again.

According to Luciano mobster Angelo "Gyp" DeCarlo, those looking into Luciano's welfare "found out . . . [Luciano] owed grocery bills, everything. . . . When he left to go over . . . [t]hey cut him off and gave him ten thousand dollars. . . . Then after that he got on the pad for two a month; after that, just before he died, he was getting three."

Luciano was monitored constantly by multiple government authorities including the Ufficio Stranieri (Italian immigration), Interpol, U.S. narcotics agents, the United Immigration and Naturalization Service (INS), U.S. Naval Intelligence, and Italian police, to name a few. This doesn't include unrelenting media surveillance. (If you think it's easy to operate with all this scrutiny, just try it.) None could find evidence that Luciano was involved in running any rackets. Luciano invested in legitimate businesses, including medical supplies. Most of his investments lost money (few mobsters are good at legitimate business). He was widely suspected of running an international heroin trafficking empire, although no one could ever confirm the association.*

The less Luciano was doing, the more his chroniclers were convinced his seeming retirement was proof that he was clever about concealing his power. One Italian government agent reluctantly admitted that the only thing they could prove Luciano was up to was helping fund the reconstruction of a church in nearby San Sebastiano that had been destroyed in the eruption of Mount Vesuvius. Wrote historian Tim Newark, "It was a case of yet another law enforcement agency magnifying Luciano's reputation to suit his own purpose."

The invisible narcotics empire has been explained away as evidence of Luciano's supernatural sleight of hand. It's conceivable that, at most,

---

* Even Lucky Luciano didn't believe in the Mafia's prohibition on drugs. Not only had he been caught selling heroin to a federal agent in 1923, but he also immediately led the authorities to a larger shipment in order to dodge a jail sentence.

Lucky Luciano and Bambi,
retired in Naples *AP Photo*

he facilitated a few meetings, got a little finder's fee, and returned to his modest flat at via Tasso 484 in Naples that he shared with his girlfriend, dancer Igea Lissoni, who broke his heart when she died of cancer in 1959. It's also possible that Luciano did nothing at all besides stroll down the street smiling archly with his miniature pinscher Bambi while law enforcement authorities of the 1950s continued chasing the Lucky Luciano of the 1930s, who had ceased to exist years before.

So besieged was Luciano that he once wrote to his nemesis, Governor Thomas Dewey, and urged him to investigate him and his ongoing tormentor, anti-narcotics czar Harry Anslinger. In a neatly handwritten letter, Luciano wrote:

> I wish you would take some interest in this matter, because I never gave it a thought in going into the dope business, direct or indirect, and if it wasn't so I wouldn't be writing to you. . . . If you don't believe me I make the sujestion [sic] and that is to have the Attorney General appoint one investigator to investigate the Narcotics Division there and all the European Interpol, including me. . . . If you don't want to do it for me, please do it for yourself, that you didn't let out of jail an international dope smugler [sic].

Luciano did receive the occasional dividend from his New York rackets, but it wasn't serious money, nor did he have a power base to protest his circumstances. His old friends were increasingly dying or getting prosecuted, which curtailed their generosity, lamenting his lost America: "Just six months, that's all I want, three months in New York and three months in Miami. Then they could bury me. I'd still be there if it wasn't for that son of a bitch Tom Dewey. He framed me . . . and that's the God's truth. I never took a dime from a woman in my life, let alone a prostitute."

Luciano attempted to write a screenplay based on his life. He suffered the fate of most would-be screenwriters: Producers were unimpressed, both by his skills and his take on his life story, which was that of a modest gambler who had been framed by a crooked prosecutor, a storyline that precisely no one would find interesting or believe. What about his murderous purge of the old-time Cosa Nostra bosses? What about the bootlegging wars and his repeated arrests for narcotics trafficking? Luciano spent his remaining years as a gangster without a gang.

In January 1962, he went to the Naples airport and waited to meet producer Martin Gosch to discuss doing a film about his life. When the men stepped out of the airport and made their way to Luciano's gray Alfa Romeo, the forlorn ex-mob boss slumped against Gosch, collapsed, and died. The last photograph of Luciano ever taken was of him, lifeless, being gawked at on the ground by police and airport authorities as an attendant approached to cover up his body. Three years after his death an FBI memo put his remaining years into a sobering context: "Over the years, there have been many allegations that Luciano continued to be the 'Mafia boss' of the United States, directing criminal activities from his place in exile. Information developed during the past several years indicates that these allegations generally have been overstatements."

BOTH PARTIES RECEIVED SOMETHING VALUABLE IN THE WARTIME DEAL between the navy and the mob. The navy got extra security on the docks and intelligence before the Sicilian invasion. Roosevelt's ruthless prosecution of the war effort got the support of a kind that bypassed the obstacles of congressional approval. Luciano won his freedom and the opportunity to reaffirm some participation in his rackets. Law enforcement turned a blind eye to Luciano managing his operations anew from his digs from Great Meadow, a prison closer to New York.

Lansky remained proud of his wartime service but wasn't convinced all of the outcomes of the conflict were good. In a letter to a friend, he betrayed his feelings about who ended up in charge of America: "Remember ever since the end of the second World War our World Policy was and is in the hands of the oil interests and the industrialists." In a coda that is hard to imagine, years later, Lansky received an invitation to Dwight D. Eisenhower's inauguration. His son, Paul, attended West Point* and later served in Vietnam in the employ of the CIA, according to one family member.

His roommate's father was a military friend of the president-elect. Meyer Lansky was honored but declined the invitation, not wanting to embarrass his son or draw attention. Said Lansky, "That certainly made me smile. But I sent thanks and regrets again. Big public things just aren't my style."

What was referred to in Lansky's obituary as a "never-confirmed story" about teaming with Naval Intelligence is now an irrefutable fact. Lansky's role in the war effort remained unknown for decades and the likelihood of the White House's awareness of or involvement in Operation Underworld has been practically nonexistent despite the exhaustive recounting of President Roosevelt's leadership during World War II.

---

* There is a widely circulated myth that Senator Kefauver supported Paul Lansky's application to West Point, the implication being that Meyer "got to" him. No such thing happened. Paul's support came from a New York congressman and, in fact, Kefauver unfairly implied at a hearing that there may have been something untoward about Paul's application. There hadn't been; Paul Lansky was accepted to West Point on his own merits.

3

Harry Truman

RAGE FOR THE MACHINE

> I had to let a former saloon keeper and murderer,
> a friend of the Big Boss, steal about $10,000 from
> the general revenues of the County . . . to keep the
> crooks from getting a million or more. . . . I could
> have had $1,500,000. I haven't $150. Am I a fool
> or an ethical giant? I don't know.
>
> —Harry Truman, in his diary

When we think of Harry Truman, we think of a feisty midwesterner who brooked no nonsense, ended World War II by dropping atomic bombs on Japan, and fired General Douglas MacArthur for forgetting who was boss. The last thing that comes to mind is men with smashed noses wearing fedoras and carrying tommy guns. Yet Truman's origins, however corruption-resistant he may have been personally, were perhaps more grounded in the rackets than any other president.

The "Big Boss" about whom Truman spoke was his mentor, Tom Pendergast, the Kansas City political machine leader responsible for his early rise. Even Harry Truman's most affectionate biographers don't dispute that his early career was rooted in Kansas City's all-powerful Pendergast machine. Still, they have been less inclined to explore how tightly linked this machine was to La Cosa Nostra. Pendergast was the "ruling spirit" behind organized crime in that city—and organized crime was booming with illegal gambling, bootlegging, prostitution, labor racketeering, and even narcotics. Pendergast's cops even protected Pendergast's rackets.

Truman had met Pendergast through the machine boss's nephew. As the future president struggled to find his professional footing after the failure of a menswear business, Pendergast stepped in and found Truman a job as a "judge." This was a municipal administrative position, not a judicial one (Truman was not an attorney).

Pendergast hadn't taken Truman's prospects seriously until his preferred candidates decided not to run for the U.S. Senate in Missouri in 1934. He pushed Truman forward by default. Truman won big. Still, even after making it to the Senate, Truman wasn't taken seriously, and he was known in some circles as "the Senator from Pendergast." The *Chicago Tribune* was even more vivid, opining that the nation was "faced with the grinning skeleton of Truman the bankrupt, Truman the pliant tool of Boss Pendergast in looting Kansas City's county government, Truman the yesman and apologist in the Senate for political gangsters." Pendergast openly attended Truman's swearing-in in the Senate chamber.

Pendergast was a notorious self-dealer who shamelessly awarded contracts to companies he owned or controlled. Truman was perfectly aware of exactly who his sponsor was, writing in reflective diaries: "I am obligated to the Big Boss, a man of his word; but he gives it very seldom and usually on a sure thing. . . . He in times past owned a bawdy house, a saloon and

Truman mentor, Kansas City machine boss, Tom Pendergast (right)
AP Photo

gambling establishment, was raised in that environment but he's all man. I wonder who is worth more in the eyes of the Lord?"

Pendergast passed his orders on small slips of paper he wrote on with red ink. This was either considered very discreet in that day and age, or his power was so great that he wasn't concerned about the evidence being used against him. If not for being a degenerate gambler, Pendergast would have become obscenely wealthy. While friendly and engaging, he didn't hesitate to use extreme violence to enforce his political will. Yet he was capable of discretion and met with Truman face-to-face only several times during their entire relationship.

Nor was Kansas City a gangland backwater; instead, the hometown Cosa Nostra had been innovators in gangland-political partnerships. Said Pendergast: "Well, the rich men have their clubs where they can gamble and have a good time. Would you deny the poor man an equal right. Ours is a fine, clean and well-ordered town."

Pendergast partnered with Kansas City's LCN boss, John Lazia, whom Treasury Secretary Henry Morgenthau called "the Al Capone of Kansas City." In fact, according to the FBI's Bill Roemer, "The Kansas City mob is a subsidiary of the Chicago mob. Every LCN family west of Chicago belongs to Chicago . . . the Outfit takes a hunk of their income and oversees their activity." Pendergast and Lazia had attended the famed 1929 Atlantic City conference of mobsters, which included marquee names like Al Capone, Lucky Luciano, and Meyer Lansky. Pendergast had been seen with Luciano and Costello in visits to New York.

Argued FBI agent William Ouseley, who spent his career prosecuting the Kansas City mob: "In the beginning the politician was the master, the hoodlum his servant. As time passed the roles would be reversed, the politician becoming the servant on the payroll of the underworld at its beck and call."

Ouseley characterized the political machine as "a homegrown criminal organization that became part of the La Cosa Nostra syndicate." The Kansas City LCN's influence over the Democratic political machine in the region was not restricted to being an early to mid-twentieth-century phenomenon. The Civella family—Nick Civella headed the Democratic Club in Kansas City's North Side—ruled the city's LCN until the mid-1990s and were influential in Las Vegas into the 1980s. (They were major

players in the Nick Pileggi book and Martin Scorsese film *Casino*.) In the
Reagan era, Teamsters boss Roy Williams was convicted of bribery and had
admitted that his power base had been the Kansas City LCN.

Lazia was a short, charismatic man who wore rimless glasses that gave
him a professorial look that offset how he made his living. Lazia controlled
gambling and liquor during Prohibition. Among the things in Lazia's
portfolio was personnel input into the local police department. In 1932,
the Missouri Supreme Court granted control of the Kansas City Police
Department to City Hall—in other words, Pendergast and Lazia. Before
this, the city's police were governed by the state. Truman biographer David
McCullough shared the story of a federal investigator from Washington,
D.C., calling the Kansas City Police Department to inquire about Lazia
only to find the mobster himself answering the telephone. Wrote Truman
and Pendergast historian Robert Ferrell:

> Lazia recruited new officers, hiring sixty recently released convicts
> from Leavenworth for second careers in law enforcement. An es-
> timate had it that 10 percent of police officers possessed criminal
> records. The next year Lazia helped Charles "Pretty Boy" Floyd
> obtain an assistant in attempting the release of a fellow gangster
> under custody, resulting in the so-called Union Station Massacre
> conducted in broad daylight in the station's parking lot, which
> killed four law-enforcement officers and the prisoner. Lazia assisted
> the would-be liberators in escaping the city.

So influential was Lazia that when a prominent local woman was kidnapped, Lazia sent out word of his disapproval. She was freed unharmed a
day later. This was the same Lazia who kidnapped his rival's lieutenants on
the day of a particular policy vote. Nevertheless, Lazia was unique among
American mob bosses because he was a popular public figure who openly
attended civic meetings.

In 1927, Kansas City beat Chicago in murders, with 16 people murdered per 100,000 people, compared to 13.3 for its more notorious rival.
On the evening of July 10, 1934, Lazia was blasted with eight rounds
from a machine gun outside the Park Central Hotel. As he lay dying, he
gasped to a doctor, "Why to me, Johnny Lazia, who has been a friend to

everybody . . . if anything happens, notify Mr. Pendergast . . . my best friend, and tell him I love him." Michael "Jimmy Needles" LaCapra, a gangland rival, was murdered shortly after in retaliation.

A few factors eventually converged to Pendergast's peril. The federal government in the form of the Internal Revenue Service, the Treasury Department, and Narcotics Bureau had noticed the unfettered gallop of organized crime in Kansas City along with its political corruption, the two chief malefactors being Sicilian mob moss Charles "Charlie the Wop" Carrollo and, of course, Pendergast himself. The boss's gambling had finally caught up to him, acutely affecting his finances. In 1939, he was convicted of income tax evasion and was sent to prison in Leavenworth. Facing prosecution, the treasurer of multiple Pendergast businesses committed suicide. Carrollo, also serving a sentence in Leavenworth, was caught running a black-market operation within prison walls and transferred to Alcatraz. After prison, Pendergast lived quietly in ill health and died in 1945. Vice President Truman openly attended his funeral.

Deceptively professorial Kansas City LCN boss John Lazia openly attended civic meetings.
Courtesy of the Kansas City Museum and the Kansas City Star

TRUMAN RISES, REMAINS LOYAL TO RACKETS

Despite Pendergast's high-profile troubles, Truman was reelected to the Senate in 1940. President Roosevelt was aware of his future vice president's roots, having told U.S. attorney Maurice Milligan, "I told Harry Truman the other day that he better get away from that crowd out there."

Truman's ability to accommodate corruption from the political machine that spawned him didn't always transfer onto the national scene. Truman shed much of his Pendergast baggage and became known to many Americans when he chaired the Special Committee to Investigate the National Defense Program. By most accounts, Truman was an aggressive investigator who could ferret out abuses associated with military contracts during the lead-up and prosecution of World War II. Said Truman, who had once run a small business, the current system of awarding contracts "make[s] the big men bigger and let[s] the little men go out of business or starve to death." The oversight was a success resulting in defense contracts being centralized under the War Production Board. Washington reporters named Truman one of the best public servants in 1944, no doubt contributing to what would happen next in his career.

There had been a paradoxical benefit to Truman's intimate acquaintance with mob-style corruption from his Kansas City machine days, namely his understanding of the dynamics of dirty contracts and public officials: Wrote Pendergast expert Ferrell of Truman: "The experience with Pendergast made him far more understanding than the ordinary elected official. . . . Still, working with one of the nation's greatest political bosses, cooperating when convenient, balancing Pendergast's requests with the public interest when such was called for, proved of immense importance to the senator."

Unlike other politicians who were known to grab cash for themselves, Truman—the humble farm boy, haberdasher, and World War I field artillery captain—deservedly had a reputation for being clean-cut, a square of squares. While Truman had not lived his post-presidency life with the spartan finances commonly believed, there has never been credible evidence that he ever accepted a bribe. This didn't mean Truman hadn't been aware of what the Pendergast machine was all about and provide assistance. There had reportedly been occasions where the votes in Kansas City exceeded the number of registered voters.

Harry Truman became the surprise choice as the vice presidential candidate in 1944 as he had practically no relationship with the man who headed the ticket, Franklin Delano Roosevelt. When FDR decided to drop his vice president, Henry Wallace, from the 1944 ticket because he was too liberal and close to the labor movement, big-city machines—also close to labor and the rackets—swung into action to make sure someone friendly to their interests was selected. Truman earned the backing of political bosses with mob connections in Chicago, St. Louis, Jersey City, and the Bronx.

In the behind-the-scenes negotiations to name a VP candidate, one of Truman's most forceful advocates was Sidney Hillman, chief of the Amalgamated Clothing Workers of America. Hillman, who had once been imprisoned for taking part in the Russian Revolution, was well-acquainted with lethal labor racketeers such as murder impresario Louis "Lepke" Buchalter. Hillman resembled a college professor and "kept eclectic company," which included days with Lepke and "evenings with Felix Frankfurter of the Harvard Law School."

Hillman, who had served on FDR's war board for employment, walked a fine line between cooperating with labor gangsters and pushing back against their infiltrations. Regardless, the Amalgamated was very mob-influenced, having once given Lepke a $25,000 bonus for "resolving" a strike in the union's favor.* Hillman paid Lepke $350 per week to keep clothing companies and troublesome laborers in line. Lucky Luciano received $50 per week from Lepke as tribute. Hillman also used Lepke and his gang to execute work stoppages when called upon. According to Lepke biographer Paul Kavieff: "Hillman's dealings with Lepke proceeded through stages from resistance to détente to criminal cooperation. At first, Hillman was reported to have attempted to have Lepke and his partner, Gurrah Shapiro, killed, but the job was botched."

---

*   Lepke was considered the head of Murder, Inc., the alleged killing arm of New York's five Cosa Nostra families. According to legend, contract killers waited for orders at Midnight Rose Candy Store in Brooklyn. This is a distortion of what took place. Buchalter's gang was actually a brute squad for the garment industry rackets where some of its members took on freelance assignments for other mobs. How big could the garment rackets be? In 1960, 95 percent of the clothing worn by people in the United States was made in the garment district.

Pulitzer Prize–winning syndicated columnist Westbrook Pegler opined that Hillman had been behind the murder of independent trucker Joseph Rosen, which Lepke's gang had carried out. Lepke was ultimately executed for the murder and became the only mob boss to die in the electric chair. Pegler concluded that after Lepke (who had been in hiding for years) finally turned himself in to J. Edgar Hoover, FDR wouldn't hand the gangster over to the state of New York to protect Hillman. This hadn't been niceness on FDR's part; it was fear. Kavieff concluded that New York prosecutor Dewey, a Republican, "could link Lepke to Hillman and create a corruption scandal surrounding the Democrats that could hang over the party in the 1944 elections." Even the Socialist Party leader thought Hillman's relationship with Lepke was problematic: "I think that was very fortunate for Mr. Hillman that Mr. Lepke went to the electric chair without talking more than he did."

So, here we had a union official who was, at the same time, very close to President Roosevelt (and part of his wartime advisory) and a mobster best known as the leader of a pack of murderers.

Hillman had been so close to FDR that it prompted the anti-Roosevelt meme "clear it with Sidney" to make the rounds in political circles. There were political consequences. Roosevelt, who pioneered the presidential use of public opinion polls, learned that many voters saw the president's ties to

Labor leader Sidney Hillman was close to FDR, Harry Truman, and lethal mob boss Louis "Lepke" Buchalter.
Library of Congress

labor as being corrupt. This corruption wasn't only because of the influence of organized crime but because many workers felt the FDR-labor alliance was an inside game that didn't benefit them.

In a secret meeting with Truman, Hillman informed him that labor would likely back him for Roosevelt's VP if Wallace went down. Organized crime scholars have observed that given Truman's history with the rackets in Missouri, the broader American mob would be likely to catch a break with him in office. Truman eventually emerged as the choice, but his selection was a surprise to everyone outside of the backrooms where the deal was made. Hillman maintained a relationship with Truman out of necessity, but the relationship was frosty compared with the one he had with FDR. Hillman found Truman to be a disappointment.

Not everyone was thrilled with the choice of Truman on the ticket with FDR. Congresswoman Clare Booth Luce of Connecticut (wife of Time, Inc., chief Henry Luce) had been targeted by Hillman's political action committee for defeat and tagged Truman's beloved wife as "Payroll Bess" for being one of the highest-paid employees in the Senate. Truman's niece had been on the Senate dole, too. This stung Truman, who had much more to be concerned about in his career background than this.

While those in Roosevelt's inner circle knew the president hadn't been well, he had been president for so long that he had an aura of invincibility about him in the eyes of outsiders. On the afternoon of April 12, 1945, Truman was having a drink with House Speaker Sam Rayburn when he received a call to return to the White House as soon as possible. Lyndon Johnson enjoyed telling the story about what Rayburn told Truman when he got the call. Even though neither man had been told officially that Roosevelt had died, both men had a horrible feeling. Rayburn said, "Harry, I think this is the last time I'm going to be calling you Harry so let me say this: When you go down to the White House, people are going to tell you for the first time in your life that you're the smartest man who ever lived. I just want to be the first to tell you that we both know you ain't."

Soon after rising to the presidency, Truman pardoned fifteen operatives in the Pendergast organization. He terminated the U.S. attorney who had prosecuted his old boss and investigated voting irregularities involving organized crime. Treasury Secretary Henry Morgenthau and Treasury officer Elmer Irey, who had also played roles in the Pendergast prosecution, were on the chopping block. Wrote Jonathan Marshall: "Instead of asserting his independence from the political machines that helped elect him, as Roosevelt had, or as Jack Kennedy did after the 1960 election, President Truman loyally began paying back their favors."

DEWEY TIPTOES, TRUMAN WINS

In one of the stranger twists in the peculiar dance between politicians and organized crime, Truman came up against Lucky Luciano's nemesis Thomas Dewey, the Republican nominee in the 1948 presidential election. Dewey ran an oddly passive campaign, pulling his punches when it came to hitting Truman with the crony-and-crime baggage he had previously suffered. Had Dewey feared being hit with his own vulnerability on this score?

It is not outrageous to speculate that Dewey may have played cute in prosecuting Luciano for the compulsory prostitution that landed him a prison sentence of thirty to fifty years. Much has been written about the case, but the critical theory is that Dewey had coached the witnesses against Luciano into making false charges. Not to defend the mobster's career choice, but it would have been highly unusual for someone of Luciano's rank to have been directly supervising a prostitution ring and for the sex workers to know him as well as they had claimed under oath.

A factor that may have complicated matters was J. Edgar Hoover's resentment of Dewey's crime-buster headline-grabbing, which the FBI director believed was his domain alone. Hoover was well-known for doing favors for the presidents who kept him on the job. Might Dewey have been concerned that if he ran too hard against Truman, positioning himself as America's super-cop, Hoover would have done some digging that could have been problematic for the Republican nominee?

Dewey had cause for concern. Walter Winchell had once reported that $250,000 had been paid to certain public officials for Luciano's commutation ($4.25 million today). Later, Senator Estes Kefauver, who investigated the rackets, attempted to find evidence but came up with nothing. A big payoff like this was unlikely. That kind of money wasn't that easy for the mob to come up with in those days, especially when considered against the funds Luciano received from his associates at his send-off under heavily policed conditions—$400 in cash and $2,500 in traveler's checks from

Frank Costello. (For his deportment, Luciano was allowed visitors' ship passes for three members of his family, who turned out to be Meyer Lansky, Frank Costello, and Albert Anastasia.)

Suppose the line of thinking about what may have been gnawing at Dewey has any merit. In that case, just as Harry Truman had become president through an extraordinary chain of events originating with organized crime, Dewey may *not* have become president for reasons pivoting on organized crime.

To be sure, the heat during those years had been on Dewey, who had hoped the Luciano escapade was behind him. The Associated Press had reported, "The U.S. Navy department has disclaimed any connection with Luciano and has said that if any naval officer figured in the case he did so on his own responsibility." Treasury agents told the media that they all "categorically denied that Luciano had furnished any information or given any service of value whatsoever," which turned out to be false.

Dewey was soon charged with not cooperating with the Kefauver Committee investigating organized crime and looking into why he had commuted Luciano's sentence in 1947. Dewey, who was conveniently on vacation somewhere in the Pacific when Kefauver came to New York, had been defensive about why he, the famed rackets-buster, had freed the mob boss. He once passed it off as a "routine parole board suggestion." Another time, according to one news report, "Dewey has said that it was state policy to release prisoners who could be deported in order to save maintenance costs after they had served what the state considered sufficient time."

We will never know for sure why Dewey was so restrained during the 1948 campaign—perhaps it was simple overconfidence—but he famously lost by a razor-thin margin, which led to the famous newspaper headline that Truman proudly held aloft, claiming, "DEWEY DEFEATS TRUMAN."

There may have been another factor somewhere in the recesses of Dewey's mind. Dewey had not been aware when he successfully prosecuted Luciano in 1936 that Luciano had saved his life the year before. Dewey's initial target had been the maniacal Dutch Schultz (Arthur Flegenheimer), but Schultz and his gang had been killed in October 1935. Schultz had become an acute crisis for Luciano and the rest of the New York rackets when he proposed Dewey's murder. Luciano and Lansky thought this was sheer lunacy. The rackets had been an on-and-off priority for the New

York authorities. However, killing a prosecutor with big political ambitions would likely bring down the full heat of local law enforcement and the feds. Schultz said he would kill Dewey despite the no-go from other mob leaders. He even had colleagues out scouting, including the lethal Albert Anastasia, who had taken a stroll past Dewey's house pushing a baby carriage loaded with artillery. Luciano was furious when he found out; the other bosses were, too. The contract on Schultz was set.

Schultz and his three top men were murdered in the Palace Chop House in Newark in October 1935. Protecting Dewey hadn't been Luciano's only motive for killing Schultz: New York's mob leaders wanted Schultz's lucrative numbers racket for themselves, so they knocked off the whole administration of the Schultz mob. Dewey didn't know that he had been the primary catalyst for the murder until Brooklyn hitman Abe Reles turned state's evidence in 1940 and named the two members of his gang who carried out the hit.

It would be a stretch to say that Dewey might have wanted to show Luciano his gratitude by commuting his sentence, as his critics suggested. Nevertheless, did he really want to answer questions about his methods in Luciano's prosecution *and* what he may or may not have known about Dutch Schultz being eliminated to save his life?

SHOWBIZ SOCIALISTS COME TO THE MOB'S RESCUE. KIND OF.

The Cold War came about during the Truman presidency, and, while racketeers didn't orchestrate the Red Scare, they fanned the flames. Nowhere was this truer than in show business.

Movie studios in the late 1940s and 1950s were terrified of Communist infiltration. In recent years it has become fashionable to write off the Red Scare as irrational right-wing viciousness—and much of it was. Nevertheless, there *were* Communists in Hollywood, and at the outset of the Cold War the studio bosses weren't sure how big a problem they had. There was also an unspoken subtext: Many in the American Socialist movement were Jewish, and so were the largely Jewish (and immigrant) studio heads. The movie bosses wanted so badly to be seen as American to the core that they invented a white picket fence heartland version of the United States that has come to exist primarily in our imaginations.

Despite the reputation Hollywood has today for being run by liberals, the old studio chiefs were very conservative, MGM's Louis B. Mayer had been chairman of the California Republican Party.

Enter the labor unions and a racket was born. As the studios faced strikes from unions like the IATSE (International Alliance of Theatrical Stage Employees), the Alliance of Motion Picture and Television Producers decided to bring in a big gun—actually, a gunman, the Chicago Outfit's Johnny Rosselli. Rosselli's thugs roughed up strikers and "encouraged" labor leaders to reach an accommodation with the studios. At the same time this was happening, Rosselli and his cohorts were seizing control of IATSE.

Meanwhile, the *Hollywood Reporter*'s owner, Billy Wilkerson—later the business partner of mobster Bugsy Siegel and the syndicate that built the Flamingo Hotel in Las Vegas—and other media began tarring uncooperative labor groups and leaders as being in league with Communists. Painting unruly unions with a bright red brush had a mitigating effect on how hard they were willing to push in their negotiations with the studios. It likely had a prophylactic effect on potential trouble with Hoover's FBI and meddlesome legislators like Wisconsin senator Joseph McCarthy and his attack dog staff man, the young attorney Roy Cohn. Despite his Jewish origins, Cohn had become greatly feared for his delight in targeting Jews with Socialist leanings, which could have made matters worse for show business big shots. He had famously prosecuted nuclear spies Ethel and Julius Rosenberg.

For his work with McCarthy's Senate Permanent Subcommittee on Investigations, Cohn recruited the son of a hotel mogul, David Schine, whose family had a financial arrangement with mob bookmaker Frank Erickson in an illegal gambling operation at Miami Beach's Roney Plaza. Schine became best known for drafting overwrought and inaccurate anti-Communist propaganda and being exposed for having used his McCarthy contacts to seek exemption from being drafted by the U.S. Army. This scandal contributed to McCarthy's political demise.

One thing that hastened McCarthy's fate was his morphine addiction. During his investigations, Bureau of Narcotics chief Harry Anslinger—an unsung enemy of organized crime—discovered McCarthy's addiction. A devout anti-Communist, Anslinger, who associated drug addiction with Communism, became concerned about the risk this posed to the movement to stop the Red Menace. He confronted McCarthy, who had no intention

Anti-Communist senator
Joseph McCarthy and aide,
attorney Roy Cohn
*Bettmann Archive via Getty
Images*

of addressing his habit. Wrote a historian in the *Pennsylvania Magazine of History and Biography* (Anslinger was a Pennsylvania native):

> Realizing the power McCarthy wielded and the potential for public scandal that Anslinger feared would embarrass the country, Anslinger agreed not to force McCarthy into hospitalization or to expose him. Instead, Anslinger secured a pledge from him not to go to the pushers; in return, McCarthy would be supplied with all the drugs he needed. Anslinger was uncomfortable with the arrangement but rationalized his action on the premise that he was acting out of loyalty to his country.

McCarthy's addiction could have proved awkward had he been designated to hunt down the mob instead of the rival who got the job, Senator Kefauver of Tennessee. Nevertheless, in the Anslinger-McCarthy subplot, we have a government official working against his ostensible mission in the service of a larger cause. Like Hoover, Anslinger picked his battles; the big one was the Reds. Unlike Hoover, who was more focused on Communists than racketeers, Anslinger made life miserable for Mafia drug traffickers.

Wrote Jonathan Marshall in his study on corruption:

> Movie producers also encouraged the Los Angeles Police Department's notorious Red Squad as it beat up strikers and union

leaders while protecting racketeers from Chicago and New York. During a Hollywood strike in 1937, provoked by widespread wage cuts, the Red Squad handed out pistol permits to gangsters imported by the studios and IATSE to crush labor militants.

There were more formal mechanisms for gangsters to raise the specter of Communism to their benefit. In 1950, a group of anti-Communist business and political leaders formed the Committee on the Present Danger (CPD) to influence the Truman administration and the general public on the dangers posed by the Soviet Union and its agents domestically and abroad. At the core of CPD was a document known as NSC 68, a treatise on the intentions of the Soviets and recommendations to counter Soviet aggression for Harry Truman to initiate a massive arms buildup, among other initiatives. The defense budget under Truman tripled.

Among the CPD's original members were Harvard president James Conant; tire mogul Leonard Firestone; future Supreme Court Justice Arthur Goldberg; William J. Donovan, founder of the Office of Strategic Services, precursor to the CIA; journalist Edward R. Murrow; "father of the atomic bomb" J. Robert Oppenheimer; and movie mogul Samuel Goldwyn, who was a major fundraiser. At the California state level, a particular name on the committee was somewhat less esteemed: Sam Genis, an often-accused crook and an associate of Meyer Lansky's network of gamblers. Genis and Goldwyn had something besides the CPD in common—a more than passing association with the Outfit's Johnny Rosselli. The CPD was no fleeting propaganda stunt. It reached the height of its influence during the Reagan years and exists with a China-focused mission to this day.

There were other efforts by mob-connected figures to demonstrate their revulsion toward Communism based on personal sentiments and the fear of being lumped in with alien figures. Schenley's liquor mogul, Lewis Rosenstiel, who had graduated from bootlegging to legitimate manufacturing and distribution, was a case in point. Rosenstiel was a member of the American Jewish League Against Communism, which provided dirt on Communist sympathizers to McCarthy and Roy Cohn, who later became Rosenstiel's attorney. Rosenstiel also bought twenty-five thousand copies of Hoover's book, *Masters of Deceit*, about the Communist threat and provided for generous distribution. In 1965, the businessman donated $1 million to Hoover's foundation and retained as a lobbyist Hoover's aide Louis Nichols. Nichols had been Congressman Richard Nixon's FBI liaison when he was making his bones on likely spy (and convicted perjurer) Alger Hiss.

Meyer Lansky, too, was famously anti-Communist, which is no surprise given the existential threats facing his Cuban empire from Soviet-backed Fidel Castro in the 1950s. He assured his mob compadres that he had things under control and that whoever might succeed Batista could be guaranteed a healthy cut of the profits. Nevertheless, given that he was the mob's portfolio manager in Havana, he had to be cagey in speaking about what was happening. Any overtures Lansky may have made to Castro were heartily rebuffed, which may have been why he put a $1 million murder contract on him. To American authorities, Lansky told a different story.

Lansky was a student of history, among other things (he had secretly retained tutors in different subjects and particularly devoured economics texts that he kept his entire life). As Castro gained power, Lansky's attorney Joseph Varon suggested his client speak with the U.S. government to provide intelligence about what was happening in Cuba. In an interview, Lansky told the FBI, "The time [is] ripe for communists to entrench themselves . . . and the entire government will soon be communistic." And he named names. The FBI agent who interviewed Lansky said, "He ran past us the names of the people that he felt might be involved in the Communist or Red group trying to take over." After all, it must be remembered that Castro had once been considered a garden-variety radical but not a Communist.

Nevertheless, Lansky admitted to family and friends that he had underestimated the threat that Castro's revolution posed, something he reportedly also shared with producers of *The Godfather, Part II*, who included it in their portrayal of Lansky as Hyman Roth. He told his nephew, Mark Lansky, that in late 1958 he and his wife, Teddy, had the furniture from their South Florida home packed and shipped to Havana because they planned to settle there permanently.

Cuba fell to Castro, and Lansky, however prescient his insights on the Communist threat had been, lost his legitimate fortune there. Or, as the man himself said, "I crapped out." Whatever mob efforts to eliminate Castro took place after Havana fell, they didn't involve Lansky. People close to Lansky and his partner Vincent "Jimmy Blue Eyes" Alo said they knew the Cuban game was over in 1959 if for no other reason than Lansky fell gravely ill with a heart ailment and a bleeding ulcer. Approaching sixty, his heart trouble left him hospitalized in an oxygen tent for one month. One family member said he was in no position to lead a war against a Soviet-backed strongman.

While Castro was schmoozing Khrushchev, who eventually put nuclear missiles in Cuba, Hoover was chasing Communist threats, real and imagined. The FBI identified Soviet agents in the United States who were making headway on obtaining nuclear secrets. Still, Hoover also sent dirt on schoolteachers with liberal leanings to their school board employers. Meanwhile, the Mafia was building Las Vegas using funds obtained violently from the back alleys of America with little federal scrutiny.

As we shall see in the chapter on Richard Nixon, the intersection among the presidency, Communism, and the rackets didn't end there.

HARRY TRUMAN UNDERSTOOD EARLY IN HIS CAREER THAT ORGANIZED crime and machine politics were tragic, if unavoidable, aspects of public life. Whereas Roosevelt's navy made a deal with the mob on an episodic basis, Truman's accommodation of gangsters was chronic. He didn't like it, but from the beginning of his career, he saw no way around it. Given that he likely received no secret payoffs for his permissiveness, Truman could reconcile the devil's bargain in his mind. Political advancement had been compensation enough. After all, a farm boy and haberdasher eventually became the leader of the free world—and a consequential one.

Consistent with his forthright nature, Harry Truman recorded the compromises he made in his diary as if it were a moral ledger. He once checked himself into the Pickwick Hotel in Kansas City to read history books and reflect on his choices in what became known as the Pickwick Papers. In one entry, Truman referenced looking the other way at one corrupt exchange "to satisfy my ideal associate and keep the crooks from getting a million or more out of the bond issue."

The diaries were an extension of Truman's blunt personality, which belied a man who balanced conscience with pragmatism. Truman must have reasoned that if he was transparent about accommodating crooks and explained why he had to do it, his soul would be as pure as it could be. Still, he once huffed that he was tired of being seen as "Pendergast's office boy."

Tellingly, Truman did nothing substantial to cover up the things he did to advance; he just did them with a "whattaya gonna do?" outlook.

THE PAROLE SCANDAL

One of the more noteworthy mob-tinged scandals of the Truman era involved Chicago Outfit leaders who were tried and convicted of infiltrating IATSE and extorting Hollywood studios through strikes. The Outfit expanded the scheme by siphoning off union funds through corrupt insiders.

A rotund former pimp named Willie Bioff originated the scheme while serving as an IATSE official and recruited Chicago mobsters, including bosses Frank Nitti and Paul Ricca and Outfit emissary to Hollywood and Las Vegas, Johnny Rosselli. When Bioff received a federal indictment, he quickly agreed to turn state's evidence against bigger game. Nitti, a severe claustrophobe terrified of prison, committed suicide after being indicted while Ricca, Rosselli, and others were convicted. They went to jail in 1944.

Years later, Bioff changed his name and moved to Arizona, where he befriended Senator Barry Goldwater. One day, he noticed unusual wire protruding from his vehicle. Figuring that the authorities were after him again, he called his lawyer, who told him to immediately bring the eaves-dropping device to him. It exploded when Bioff returned to the car, leaving him in pieces. The crime has never been solved, but the vengeful Outfit is the rightful suspect.

As we saw with Luciano in New York, the Chicago boys wanted to move their top man, Ricca, closer to home so they could conduct business, and they worked to get him sprung. While the mob is known for violence, it's not as if they are incapable of subtlety. A favorite play is trying to bring a mob partner "closer to his family." Then once he's closer, they pitch, "What's the big deal about letting the old guy work from home?"

Outfit political fixer Murray Humphreys and rising star Anthony "Joe Batters" Accardo concocted a plan to spring Ricca. They retained a Missouri attorney and political operative named Paul Dillon, who had served as Harry Truman's U.S. Senate campaign chief. Among his other

Willie Bioff
Bettmann Archive via Getty Images

What's left of Willie Bioff (under blanket) after he started his car
Bettmann Archive via Getty Images

credentials, Dillon had represented Tom Pendergast and his mob partner, John Lazia. The objective: Get Ricca transferred from a federal prison in Georgia to Leavenworth, Kansas, which was much closer to Chicago.

In Gus Russo's history of the Chicago Outfit, he reported on the successful maneuver: "It may never be known exactly whom Dillon leaned on, but buried in documents discovered years later among the Bureau of Prison's files is a memo noting that Tom Clark would like the subjects transferred to Leavenworth."

Clark was President Truman's attorney general. Dillon had been known to drop in on Truman when he visited the nation's capital, but no one had a formal record of what they talked about.

Humphreys and Accardo began visiting Ricca regularly, and within the next few years, Ricca's legal fate improved. He could settle IRS violations for a fraction of what he owed. Later, the mail fraud charges against Ricca and others involved in the IATSE schemes disappeared.

Now it was time for the parole board. Dillon paid a visit to the federal board's chief. Against the recommendation of the judge who presided over the case, the board paroled Ricca and several Outfit coconspirators.

Subsequent investigative reports concluded that the paroles occurred as part of a deal whereby the Outfit bosses supported Democratic candidates in the 1946 elections. Reported author Jonathan Marshall, "In the 1948 election—just a year after the parole decision—the Cook County political machine helped deliver Illinois to President Truman by a margin of less than 34,000 votes."

A congressional probe into the parole scandal followed, concluding, "The syndicate has given the most shocking demonstration of political clout in the history of the republic." Nevertheless, no proof turned up connecting Truman to the scheme.

YOU PEOPLE

As Truman's second term got underway and the Marshall Plan began rebuilding Europe, the focus was no longer on foreign scoundrels and big defense contractors squeezing the federal government. Congress always needs villains to excoriate, so characters closer to home began drawing the first hints of scrutiny, especially after an uptick in the news reporting on big city crime in 1949. The likeness of Luciano's successor, Frank Costello, appeared on the cover of *Newsweek* magazine, followed immediately by a *Time* cover of Costello against the backdrop of an avalanche of slot machine coins. In South Florida, the New York mob openly operated casinos run by Meyer Lansky and Jimmy Alo, who bought off the local police. Then there was the legitimization of the rackets through legal and quasi-legal ownership of Las Vegas casinos. This enterprise received its share of media attention when its spiritual leader, Bugsy Siegel, went down in a fusillade of bullets in 1947.

Local crime commissions had been formed, but according to some—not the FBI's Hoover—there was a nationwide network of criminals, primarily but not exclusively Italian, that merited scrutiny. If such a thing existed, local authorities couldn't deal effectively with a national syndicate. Nor did it help that so many of the names of the alleged criminal big shots were Italian and Jewish and were sure to provoke a big "I told you so" in the heartland. One way to catapult the idea of a sinister cabal of ethnic gangsters into the public consciousness would be through televised hearings, and a particular U.S. senator thought he was just the man for the job.

Democratic Tennessee senator Estes Kefauver pushed for hearings

Senator Estes Kefauver
(right) with President
Harry Truman (left) and
Democratic presidential
nominee Adlai Stevenson
AP Photo

on the rackets, having seen how Truman had made a national name for himself by holding hearings on corruption in defense contracting. Given his racket baggage, Truman wasn't thrilled about Kefauver's plans. The president tried to slow things down by pulling together crime prevention groups under the direction of Attorney General J. Howard McGrath. Truman even agreed to personally address a conference of U.S. attorneys where he tossed out obligatory tough-on-crime rhetoric. Hoover shared Truman's position that a Senate inquiry was not worthwhile. Columnist Jack Anderson wrote that the FBI made a "frantic attempt to block the investigation." What if the hearings brought up the Pendergast-Lazia machine and how Hoover didn't think the rackets were a big deal?

And then a stroke of bad luck for Truman: On the evening of April 6, 1950, current Kansas City mob boss Charles Binaggio and his torpedo Charles Gargotta were on the way to meet with associates in the political machine. Binaggio had been making aggressive plays to control the local police department, as had his predecessors. This and other power maneuvers put Binaggio in conflict with Pendergast. Binaggio (a mentor of later Kansas City kingpin Nick Civella) believed that President Truman had encouraged a federal grand jury probe of the mobster's affairs at the behest of Pendergast. Binaggio and Gargotta were shot to death *in the local Democratic club* and, in a flourish proving that truth is stranger than fiction, Gargotta's body was photographed face up, his head in a pool of blood beneath a giant photo of President Harry Truman.

The Kefauver hearings were on.

There was some question over whose committee would handle the hearings, but finally, Truman's vice president, Alben Barkley, cast the tie-breaking vote that authorized the Special Committee to Investigate Organized Crime in Interstate Commerce. After some jockeying in the Senate, Kefauver emerged as the man who would try to use his hearings as a springboard to the White House with the encouragement of Philip Graham, publisher of the *Washington Post*.

Kefauver's rival for chief mob buster? Senator Joseph McCarthy of Wisconsin, who moved on to the Communist menace, perhaps the most remarkable stroke of luck the mob ever had. The Democrat Kefauver had outmaneuvered the Republican McCarthy, but it was McCarthy's efforts that captured the resources of the FBI. Wrote one analyst after his defeat:

Kansas City mobster Charles Gargotta, dead in the Democratic Club in front of a photo of President Truman *AP Photo/Kansas City Star*

"McCarthy lumbered off in the direction of the State Department. The following month he announced the discovery of a large but imprecise number of Communists making foreign policy for the Democrats."

If the postwar villain void came down to Commies or crooks, however, it would have to be crooks for the moment.*

Kefauver held hearings in fourteen major cities nationwide in 1950 and 1951, interviewed six hundred witnesses, and created television's first blockbuster. The ratings were double that of the World Series. There is a myth that Cleveland Syndicate boss Moe Dalitz snapped at Kefauver when asked if he had been a bootlegger. Dalitz allegedly answered, "If you people wouldn't have drunk it, I wouldn't have bootlegged it." He was, as always in public, much more respectful. The Dalitz myth likely stemmed from something Al Capone had said decades before: "When I sell liquor, it's called bootlegging; when my patrons serve it on Lake Shore Drive, it's called hospitality." Nevertheless, the Dalitz legend belied a more profound truth: There was much hypocrisy at work in the American temperament.

Kefauver's questioning was intense, and the lights were hot and bright. The most notorious highlight was the testimony of Luciano (later Genovese) boss Frank Costello. The man who had not committed an act of violence for decades, and who was used to the bowing and scraping of supplicants, began to panic. He had not taken refuge under the Fifth Amendment (as was his right) because he believed he could charm these senators sitting on a raised platform behind thick wooden desks that served as barriers between the high and the low.

Costello complained about the heat in the room. Attorneys requested that the camera feed be killed. Why would the senators comply? After all, the sweating had been the whole objective. The committee refused but agreed that the cameras would focus on Costello's hands, which were wringing with tension. The performance betrayed not a kingmaker but a very scared hoodlum who was way out of his element. He had attempted to shape-shift from the shadows onto the public stage and crashed hard. Cave dwelling doesn't look good under bright lights. TV is a different racket.

---

* Kefauver followed up his hearings about organized crime with a new villain: comic books. This form of mass entertainment was apparently corrupting American youth along with gangsters and Communists.

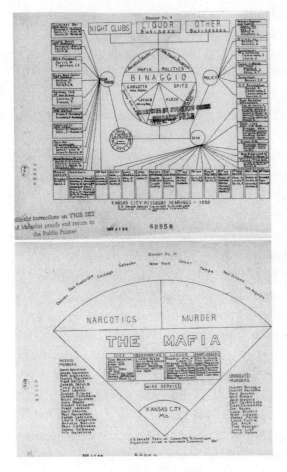

Charts used by
Kefauver to diagram
the Kansas City LCN
National Archives

What had Costello been thinking, having been so unprepared? Like many powerful men, Costello overestimated the extent to which his power in one world would convey to another. Ask anyone who has ever testified under oath or been deposed what it's like. It's not a job interview; it's a firing squad where the questions aren't questions but rather accusations tinged with contempt. You begin to doubt yourself and wonder if, when you uttered your name, you might have been lying. This is especially true in a congressional hearing, which is not a fact-finding exercise but a public burning of a heretic.

After watching the hearing, Costello's associate Joe Adonis muttered, "What a sucker." Adonis had exercised his Fifth Amendment rights against self-incrimination. Noted Lansky of his friend Costello not long after his death (in private notes), "He was a vain man . . . he grew to like acting the part of a leader" and scoffed, "Frank at one time didn't think that people in our endeavors should be involved in politics."

There had been no upside to Costello's testimony. Pleading the Fifth never *looks* good, but that's not its purpose. Its purpose is to protect a target *legally*, not improve his image. When Senator Charles Tobey of New Hampshire asked if he had ever done anything for his country, a humiliated Costello responded in a croaking voice,* "Paid my tax." Costello served over a year in prison for playing cute with Kefauver. Wrote Lansky:

> His reason for being in contemp [*sic*] with the Senate Committee was not to embarrass the politicians. When things got too hot . . . and all the politicians broke bread with him, their excuse was that they feared his power or underworld influence. Show me one incident where a politician was physically harmed through Frank's doings but they sure harmed him and never hesitated to take a loan from him.

Another hearing highlight was the late Bugsy Siegel's brassy girlfriend, Virginia Hill, who, like Costello, clearly wasn't thinking strategically when she showed up wearing a $5,000 mink stole. She was so angry at a question that she responded in typical foulmouthed bravado, "You bastards, I hope a goddamn atom bomb falls on every goddamn one of you!"

It got even better—or worse, depending on what one was hoping for. Her testimony and attendant media coverage were so colorful that a widely circulated urban legend made it into multiple organized crime books and articles. Supposedly, when Kefauver had asked why mob associate Joe Epstein of Chicago had entrusted her with so much money, she answered, "I'll tell you why. Because I'm the best cock sucker in town!" Kefauver was

---

* Costello's raspy voice was due to having throat surgery related to removing a growth. His voice became such a sensation after the hearings that it began to be identified with racketeering to the point where Marlon Brando based Don Vito Corleone's sandpaper vocals on Costello's.

Bugsy's baby, Virginia Hill, under oath
Courtesy Everett Collection

said to have frantically demanded order. People across America were covering their children's ears, and housewives were fainting at Hill's vulgarity. The problem is that there is no record of this ever happening, including in the congressional transcripts. What did happen, however, was that Hill became a target of the IRS because she admitted to receiving a fortune over the years from male admirers, all of which went unreported to the government. The mink stole didn't help.

As the hearings dominated the airwaves, the advertising agency Young & Rubicam took out a full page stating, "With staggering impact, the telecasts of the Kefauver investigation have brought a shocked awakening to millions of Americans," adding, "What's happened to our ideals of right and wrong. . . . What's happened to our principles of honesty and morality?" Something monumental is happening in the culture when advertising agencies become our moral tutors. No dummies, Madison Avenue recognized early that the Mafia would be hot.

The spectacle didn't end here. One of Kefauver's informal advisers was the newspaper columnist Lee Mortimer, who had made headlines not long before by being punched out by Frank Sinatra, who claimed Mortimer had called him by an ethnic slur. Mortimer was known for his flashy prose that portrayed the Mafia as a centralized and monolithic corporation with a Mr. Big and functionaries loyally carrying out his orders.

He had no compunction about associating the mob with everything from Communism to a "swishy homosexual" cabal infiltrating show business.*

The relationship between Kefauver and Mortimer soured over personality issues and an inability to agree upon whether the mob was a sinister criminal corporation or a diffuse and opportunistic collection of crooks. Kefauver also didn't want Mortimer on staff, and they began criticizing each other in public forums. Kefauver had been right to assume that given Mortimer's penchant for purple prose, it would have been ill-advised to invite him inside the official tent.

Hoover initially tried to steer clear of the Kefauver hearings. He had seen it as a greater risk to testify than not testify. He knew he would have had to face questions about why he hadn't done more about the mob. After the better part of a year, Hoover decided that his absence would be conspicuous, and he went before the committee and maintained his long-standing position that the alleged mobsters being interviewed represented a local phenomenon and that local law enforcement had simply been failing at their jobs: "All too frequently in the past few years there has been too much 'buck passing' to the Federal government . . . The Federal government can never be a satisfactory substitute for local self-government in the enforcement field."

Hoover could not, in good conscience, spend taxpayer dollars chasing local hoods when he was best employed chasing bank robbers stealing the public's hard-earned savings and Communists who had been infiltrating the very fabric of American society looking for nuclear secrets. Hoover had, after all, just arrested atomic spies Julius and Ethel Rosenberg, and the Soviets had recently tested their first nuclear bomb.

Hoover's great innovation had been advancements in forensic evidence, and this capability lent itself better to catching bank robbers and spies than it did racketeers. LCN knew they weren't Hoover's priority. Said the Chicago Outfit's Chuckie English in the early 1960s (picked up on an FBI bug): "The FBI will be like it was five years ago. They won't be around no more. They're gonna investigate them fair play for Cuba's. They call that

---

* Despite the slur, the New York mob did, in fact, become the driving force in the gay nightclub business.

more detrimental than us guys. They'll say these local problems at home, let the local police handle it."

While Hoover may have been misguided in his assessment of the Mafia, he never tried to hide his operating philosophy. As he told the Kefauver Committee: "I am very much opposed to any expansion of the Federal Bureau of Investigation. I think it is too big today. We have had to take on additional duties and responsibilities . . . because of the international security."

Kefauver's inquiry concluded, "The committee found it difficult to obtain reliable data concerning the extent of Mafia operation, the nature of Mafia organization, and the way it presently operates." There was a reason for this that Hoover understood before others: The Mafia was not a centralized organization but dozens of cooperatives that formed schemes on the fly. This presented a very different challenge from tracking banknotes or a spy's fingerprints on packages left at dead drops. This didn't stop Kefauver from winging it by tagging the Mafia at one point in the hearings as "a secret international government-within-a-government" headed by Lucky Luciano from his overseas base like a Bond villain from S.P.E.C.T.R.E. As we shall see, Kefauver was way off the mark on this account.

THE RACKETS HEARINGS HAD SINGLE-HANDEDLY MADE KEFAUVER A household name. The senator was often seen wearing his coonskin hat, the trademark of his fellow Tennessean Davy Crockett. Wasn't it great that those dark, un-American, big-city gangsters could be chased out of this good clean country of ours by a gangly, bespectacled frontiersman?

When Kefauver confronted Lansky during a recess at his hearings about gambling, Lansky reminded him that he was known to enjoy gambling himself. Kefauver admitted, "I do. But I don't want you people to control it."

You people. Lansky huffed in his diary that "Kefauver's state is known to have open gambling."

Nor was Kefauver so pure that he couldn't be persuaded to pull his punches. When his hearings came to Chicago, he was approached by Outfit attorney Sidney Korshak. Korshak presented the senator with photographs taken with an infrared camera of him in action with a woman not his wife. This would have been problematic for a man with Kefauver's love of purist posturing. Kefauver decided against making the hearings public and interviewing Outfit leaders on camera.

TRUMAN-ERA DEMAND FOR VILLAINS

On March 12, 1951, Kefauver, looking as if Norman Rockwell had painted him, appeared on the cover of *Time* magazine, gazing past a masked black octopus wielding a pistol and dripping with cash, sexy women, dice, and booze. (In addition to gambling, Kefauver also liked booze and women, once overheard loudly barking after a campaign rally about how he needed to leave, adding, "I gotta fuck!") Truman knew he couldn't ignore the rackets altogether and, not long after Kefauver's magazine cover, he signed legislation that taxed sports gambling, wiping out a vast majority of the racing books in Nevada.

The race was on for America's biggest villain. Was it that squat, bald Soviet Communist Nikita Khrushchev with his deadly missiles and pinko minions infiltrating American entertainment, government, and academia? Or was it Italians and Jewish men with dark hair, black fedoras, and nicknames like Scarface, Momo, Bugsy, the Lord High Executioner, Kid Twist, Charlie the Blade, Tick Tock, Joe Bananas, the Snake, and Ice Pick Willie? It was difficult for the subtext here not to register more broadly. Was it any accident that Ian Fleming's James Bond had villains with names like Goldfinger, Stromberg, Max Zorin, Blofeld, Kronsteen, Dr. Mortner, Dr. Kaufman, Davidov, not to mention Scaramanga and Largo?

As the FBI's Hoover and Joe McCarthy placed their bets on Communists, Kefauver went all in on gangsters. He challenged Truman in the 1952 New Hampshire primary—and beat him. Truman was exhausted. His popularity was at a low of 22 percent, unemployment was rising, the war in Korea was dragging on at what was widely considered a "stalemate," and scandals relating to cronyism were dogging the president. *Time* magazine reported on "influence peddlers," saying: "The finest specimens claim Missouri as their habitat, have at least a nodding acquaintance with Harry Truman, a much chummier relationship with his aides and advisers, and can buzz in and out of the White House at will. They also have a fondness for crisp currency."

Truman could not have relished going head-to-head with a one-note racket-buster like Kefauver. Truman dropped out of the election, stating, "I have served my country long, and I think effectively and honestly." Kefauver lost the nomination to Governor Adlai Stevenson of Illinois but was selected for vice president on the Democratic ticket in 1956. Eisenhower defeated the Stevenson-Kefauver ticket that year. Kefauver never went any further in his career, his organized crime hearings being his primary legacy.

The hearings were not the death blow for organized crime that Kefauver had hoped, but they had succeeded in making him a star for a period. Gangsters were becoming stars, too.

THE ROAD TO APALACHIN

The Kefauver hearings happened during Truman's time in office but served as the precursor to the gangland bomb that would go off during the Eisenhower era. The watershed event that would be seared in the public and FBI's consciousness came in 1957 when sixty-two Cosa Nostra mobsters were caught and arrested at a conclave in rural Apalachin, New York.

Apalachin validated the paranoia woven into the fabric of the American psyche—that there was, in fact, a cabal of evil-doing aliens with strange customs plotting against us somewhere deep in the woods. There are flimsy conspiracy theories about Apalachin being a setup orchestrated by Costello, Lansky, and Luciano. Still, there is little reason to believe that these men would take such a risk knowing how the fallout might boomerang on them. It is almost certain that New York State trooper Edgar Croswell's ongoing detective work and observant eye were the main reasons for the bust. This is validated by trooper reports, and a source once affiliated with the Magaddino family, in whose territory the Apalachin meeting occurred, confirmed for me that the New York State police had indeed foiled the conclave.

Apalachin was also a jubilee for Senator John McClellan of Arkansas whose own 1957 hearings had been underway for months. The McClellan hearings included Senator John F. Kennedy of Massachusetts and Robert F. Kennedy as chief counsel where RFK demonstrated precisely how the Teamsters could strangle commerce in and around New York City because they "have an obligation to gangsters and hoodlums because they would not have achieved their position of power unless they had made a deal." Wrote the *New York Times* upon the hearings' launch, "James R. Hoffa of the Teamsters Union was accused today of aiming for a position where he could throttle the Eastern Seaboard and part of the Midwest [with work stoppages]."

Bobby Kennedy took Apalachin to validate his laser-focused hatred of gangsters, especially since one-third of those arrested identified themselves as being in the labor field. The convening gangsters had a combined 153 arrests, including 18 for homicide. This proved to RFK that the FBI was out of its depth: "The FBI didn't know anything, really, about these people who were the major gangsters in the United States."

The younger Kennedy seethed when handsome John "Johnny Dio" Dioguardi testified, wearing an expensive suit, gold cuff links, and a silk handkerchief, and a young woman in the audience sighed, "He's beautiful." Dio was somewhat less beautiful after the hearing when a photographer captured him snarling with a cigarette dangling from the side of his lips after punching a photographer. This became the enduring image of the McClellan hearings. Indeed, scholars have written that the popularity of labor unions was at its zenith in 1957 and began dropping thereafter. The McClellan hearings changed all that, transferring the association of labor with Communists to the Mafia. The unions never recovered.

Stated Lansky in his private records about these hearings: "McClellan's State—Hot Springs had open gambling just across the street of the Hotel that McClellan was a guest. . . . It was not run by Italians. That made it OK."

He couldn't hide his bitterness in another entry: "Arkansas had gambling going when its Saintly Senator was investigating it everywhere else."

The broad judicial question stemming from Apalachin concerned whether it had been illegal for a bunch of guys who happened to be criminals to go to a barbecue. A ruling by Judge Irving Kaufman (who had condemned Ethel and Julius Rosenberg to death) concluded that it was improper for the Apalachin mobsters to coordinate pleading the Fifth Amendment related to investigations of the conference.

Nathan Lewin had been a clerk to Judge J. Edward Lumbard of the Second Circuit Court of Appeals, which struck down Kaufman's ruling. Lewin was among the attorneys who wrote Lumbard's brief, which, in layperson's terms, meant that the mobsters were not violating the law when

Johnny Dio decks a reporter
at the McClellan hearings.
Bettmann Archive via Getty Images

they took the Fifth as it related to Apalachin. Later, Lewin encountered Kaufman in a courthouse elevator. The judge demanded of the young lawyer, "You're Lewin?"

Lewin nodded.

"You have ruined me!" Kaufman said and exited the elevator. Presumably Kaufman felt that his ruling had been of great legal significance and that Lewin's role in drafting its rejection would somehow impede his judicial future, a conclusion that still leaves the now eighty-seven-year-old Lewin shaking his head. Lumbard's ruling further deepened the debate about what kind of organizing constituted a crime.

Apalachin had been the first provable modern incident of LCN crossing state lines to meet. It was also of symbolic cultural interest so profound that J. Edgar Hoover, a pop-culture icon himself, could no longer ignore a nationwide network of criminals, however loose their affiliation. In a post-Apalachin analysis prepared by a subordinate, the FBI director was starkly told: "The truth of the matter is, the available evidence makes it impossible to deny logically the existence of a criminal organization, known as the Mafia, which for generations has plagued the law-abiding citizens of Sicily, Italy, and the United States."

A prominent agent at FBI headquarters, William Sullivan, said, "Apalachin hit the FBI like a bomb. The meeting proved beyond any doubt that organized crime existed on a massive scale in this country." Hoover's response was to make public the Top Hoodlum Program, where the FBI would increase surveillance of Mafiosi and specific mobsters would be

The upstate New York home of Joseph Barbara, where the 1957 LCN conference was held—and disrupted   *Photo by Frank Castoral/New York Daily News via Getty Images*

named and shamed. Some journalists have reported that the Top Hoodlum Program was only established after Apalachin; it had existed since 1953, but after Apalachin, Hoover realized he needed to raise its profile.

About two dozen Apalachin gangsters were indicted on weak charges of having tried to cover up the conclave, but despite convictions, the cases were thrown out on appeal. In today's parlance, we would say that the Apalachin bust "went viral" and has remained a key moment in any discussion of mob history.*

The purpose of the Apalachin meeting has long been debated, but we know a few things. First, national mob meetings had been held periodically for decades. In other words, the conclave was not as unique as it was made out to be. Second, a lot was going on in mob land then, including power plays in New York City. Vito Genovese had recently deposed Frank Costello after an assassination attempt. A young hood named Vincent "The Chin" Gigante shot him in the lobby of his apartment building, the Majestic on Central Park West, on the night of May 2, 1957. The shot grazed Costello's head, drew blood, and Costello got the message and

---

* The conference is mentioned in *Goodfellas*, is depicted dramatically in *Analyze This*, and is the subject of the recent *Mob Town*.

retired. He lived another decade and a half in reduced circumstances as the psychopathic Genovese took over. Costello failed to recognize the shooter when the latter was tried for murder. Gigante was acquitted, and Costello lived on to regale chroniclers about stories from the old days. Gigante later thanked Costello for his memory lapse.

Apalachin also came on the heels of Albert Anastasia's fatal encounter in a barbershop at the hands of either his deputy Carlo Gambino (with Genovese's likely complicity) or another internal cabal. Then there were tensions surrounding investments in Havana (more families wanted in, and there were rumblings about Cuban radicals trying to overthrow the mob-friendly regime) and policy differences over narcotics.

Hilariously, New York boss Joe Bonanno, whose family trafficked heavily in drugs, was to say later that if the conference had gone forward the gang leaders would have upheld their long "tradition" of opposition to the drug trade. The drug business, of course, had never been about morality and always about risk. Risks associated with drugs varied at different times, and the same mobsters who once trafficked—most famously the Genovese's Gigante—later declared it too risky. Finally, Genovese, whose ego had no limits, was looking to be lauded as the alpha boss of Cosa Nostra, something he felt was long overdue.*

By happenstance, I was to eventually obtain an unusual personal insight into Apalachin. My grandfather was in (legitimate) business with a man I'll call "Uncle Vince." The men used to sit in our backyard and talk and sip anisette. I remember, as a very small boy, them handing me a tiny glass of clear liquid and asking me to taste "the water," which, of course, was the anisette that I promptly spit out to their amusement. Many years later, I learned that Uncle Vince had been one of the heads of the Philadelphia–Southern New Jersey Cosa Nostra and had attended Apalachin. In fact, Uncle Vince had driven to the meeting in a black Chrysler Imperial with Vito Genovese and had been placed in the same police car after their arrest.

I was told that Uncle Vince and Genovese had been mortified by their arrest, Genovese because he had put LCN in harm's way by coordinating the meeting. Both men were ashamed and disgraced by being publicly

---

* Contrary to popular opinion, there was no position of "boss of bosses" by this time, but there was a sense of "first among equals," as there is in most endeavors.

labeled as gangsters, which affected their families. Uncle Vince saw himself as a businessman, had been involved almost exclusively in gambling, and was well-liked in the community. He was not known to be violent and had been expanding into more legitimate holdings. Apalachin introduced shame into Uncle Vince's realm where there hadn't been before.

Given his nature, it's hard to imagine that Genovese had the same preoccupation with being seen as a legitimate businessman by his peers. He was more concerned about how Apalachin made him look like a *half-assed* gangster than he was looking like a gangster. There were hard feelings toward Genovese among his associates, which emboldened his enemies to plot against him. Chicago's Sam Giancana was furious, having offered to hold the meeting in his region where rural police were safely on the Outfit's pad. While the details are disputed, we do know that on the heels of Apalachin, a small-time criminal was able to link Genovese to a narcotics deal that put the boss in prison for the rest of his life.

OF ALL THE PRESIDENTS WITH LINKS, DIRECT AND INDIRECT, TO ORGA-nized crime, the give-and-take between Harry Truman and the rackets represented the best marriage. Truman got himself a wildly successful career with mob help, and the mob got itself a president with very little interest in going after them, not to mention a few specific bonuses on the way, mainly in the form of the Outfit parole deal, the continued emphasis on catching Communists, and the defanged Tom Dewey.

Said U.S. Attorney Milligan, who prosecuted Tom Pendergast: "Harry S Truman's career, without the help of Boss Pendergast, would have ended far short of the White House. . . . When the Senator became Vice-President in 1944, the political stock of the renascent Pendergast machine boomed, but it was nothing compared with the golden opportunities that came on Mr. Truman's succession to the Presidency."

Evidence has surfaced that Truman may have been capable of the kind of financial sleight of hand Boss Pendergast and John Lazia would have admired. In the half century since his death, the rap on Truman was that he lived on little more than his $112.56-per-month army pension. The recent release of Mrs. (Bess) Truman's financial records suggests that her husband earned more from his post-presidency memoirs than originally believed. His net worth when he left office was more than today's equivalent of

$6 million, mostly from investments in land. Some of the funds for these investments likely came from an untaxed White House expense account that had been misrepresented to the Internal Revenue Service.

A report in *New York* magazine's Intelligencer column stated, "To be as rich today relative to other Americans as Truman was in 1953, a person would have to have a net worth of around $58 million." Truman's poor-mouthing had been a factor in the passage of the Former Presidents Act five years after his presidency ended, which provided lifetime benefits for chief executives after they left office. This boondoggle has led to luxurious perks for former presidents in the form of offices, staff, travel, and security.

Summarized Ouseley, the former Kansas City FBI agent, of Truman: "On the one side he is viewed as the honest public servant, able to rise above the cesspool that surrounded him, unaware of the crimes taking place. On the other side, he is considered no better than those who put him in office, an honest front man protecting the power of thieves, racketeers and murderers."

Political machines and organized crime are distinct entities with mutual interests. The machines want money, votes, and power. Mobsters want public works contracts and lenient treatment from judges, prosecutors, and juries. The interactions between Harry Truman and his agents with players in organized crime were stylistically different from what had taken place with other presidential personalities. While corruption around Truman was extensive, and the man himself benefited politically, there is no hard evidence that he ever accepted anything besides career advancement and perhaps access to a generous fund that pales in comparison to today's presidential perquisites. His attitude toward political and crime bosses was that they were a necessary evil for doing his constituents' business. Nor did Truman make much of an effort to conceal the dirty deals that had happened around him, justifying them because he never took a bribe.

Truman's administration teed things up nicely for organized crime to prosper during the following administration, even though President Dwight Eisenhower was neither friendly nor especially antagonistic toward mobsters, which is why we will skip ahead to the Kennedy era.

4
John F. Kennedy

SHARP PRACTICE AND PLAUSIBLE DENIABILITY

To believe otherwise would have taken the
Kennedy-mob skeleton out of the closet.
—Gus Russo, *Live by the Sword*

It's one of the strangest paradoxes in the annals of organized crime and politics that two of the greatest foes of the rackets were, through both happenstance and design, its biggest enablers and beneficiaries.

John F. Kennedy served on the racket-busting United States Senate Select Committee on Improper Activities in Labor and Management, or the McClellan Committee (aka Rackets Committee). Robert F. Kennedy was the committee's chief counsel. Whereas Kefauver had about fifteen investigators on his staff, McClellan had one hundred. While several things percolated in gangland, the final catalyst for the hearings was the 1957 blinding of journalist Victor Riesel, who had aggressively covered the labor rackets. A mob-connected hood threw sulfuric acid in Riesel's face blinding and scarring him for life.[*] Riesel's witless assailant demanded more money from his gangster

---

[*] Riesel never lost his zeal for reporting on labor. I used to take his calls in the White House media relations office a quarter century after his misfortune.

clients for the attack and was soon found in a Lower East Side gutter with a bullet in his head. Teamsters boss Jimmy Hoffa was less than distraught by the attack on Riesel and was considered a suspect, through layers, of course.

One of the reasons it took so long for the government to act against unions was that labor racketeering wasn't considered sexy. Labor itself was an established legal endeavor, as opposed to things like gambling, prostitution, narcotics, bootlegging, protection rackets, and extortion, which were illegal per se. Much labor-related mischief could be hidden in the workaday realities of conducting business. Said Dan Castleman, former chief of investigations for Manhattan district attorney Robert Morgenthau, "Every industry I've ever seen the mob take control of started with their influence in the union." As the twentieth century rolled on, the violence was mitigated, and gangsters were more adept at achieving their ends using mostly the threat of violence rather than violence itself. A law enforcement report in the 1960s estimated that labor racketeering was a $7 billion per year business, which was equivalent to the earnings of the ten biggest corporations in America.

At his first meeting with Hoffa, McClellan chief counsel Bobby Kennedy asked the union boss about his background and education. While Kennedy may have just been making small talk, Hoffa took it as an insult. A furious Hoffa left his first encounter with Kennedy, barking, "He's a damned spoiled jerk."

There was another factor in RFK's zeal: Up until the McClellan hearings, he was a supporting player in the Kennedy dynasty. His war on the mob was making him a force in his own right. Joe Jr. died a war hero in a plane crash. Jack became a war hero after an attack on his PT boat, a Pulitzer Prize–winning author. And now, U.S. senator Bobby was a dragon slayer. "This is when he blossomed," JFK's friend LeMoyne Billings said.

No figure incurred Bobby Kennedy's wrath more than Hoffa, with whom RFK sparred in the McClellan hearings over allowing gangsters access to the Teamsters' pension fund and wiretapping grand jury proceedings. As attorney general during his brother's presidency (and slightly afterward), RFK was able to boast in 1962 that prosecutions against mobsters rose by 300 percent and convictions rose by 350 percent over the prior year. Among those convictions were big names such as Anthony "Tony Ducks" Corallo, future Lucchese family boss; Carmine "Lilo" Galante, a

Bonanno family leader; John Ormento, a Lucchese narcotics kingpin; and boxing fixers Frank Carbo and Frank "Blinky" Palermo.

And then there was Hoffa. Kennedy's Justice Department successfully prosecuted Hoffa for jury tampering and fraud associated with access to the Teamsters pension fund. Not even Kennedy's fiercest critics doubt the sincerity of RFK's crusade against the mob, which is why the story of the Kennedy brothers' entanglement with organized crime is so hard to comprehend.

But we will try.

THE BOOTLEGGING ORIGIN STORY

We begin the Kennedy-mob saga with the myth that the patriarch, Joseph P. Kennedy, was a mobbed-up bootlegger. The old man was many things, including a crook, but he was not a bootlegger, which is defined as someone who manufactures and distributes a product *illegally*. The bootlegging legend gets to the seedier aspects of Kennedy mythology explored by an increasing number of journalists and storytellers. It stands to reason that if Joe Kennedy was a Prohibition-era bootlegger, then he was also a mobster, so everything rotten alleged about the Kennedys and crime must be accepted as such. The truth is more complicated and more interesting because it gets to a reality that we will see repeated in this book: *The people who knew how to use the mob often fared better than the mobsters themselves.* Joe Kennedy was the quintessential user.

Joe Kennedy's bootlegging is almost always mentioned with a sly smirk, as if it's both inside information and a proven fact. It's something that people desperately want to believe for their own reasons, not the least of which is that it's fun in a "crime pays" sort of way. In one of the more recent and voluminous biographies of Joe Kennedy, David Nasaw concluded: "Not only is there no evidence of Kennedy's being a bootlegger, but it flies in the face of everything we know about him. As an East Coast Boston Irish Catholic Outsider struggling to be allowed inside, he was willing to take financial risks, but not those associated with illegal activities such as bootlegging."

Kennedy was also a man who had many motivated adversaries and had been vigilantly investigated for his confirmation hearings for three high-profile public jobs: Securities and Exchange Commission chairman, Maritime Commission chairman, and ambassador to Great Britain. He was also investigated during the 1950s to serve on four presidential commissions, all of which required background checks. Finally, Nixon's 1960 campaign employed some of the most ruthless opposition researchers and political knife fighters in the game and they couldn't find any credible evidence of bootlegging. Said Nasaw, "It became really clear that all of the stories about his bootlegging were just farcical."

However, it wasn't hard to understand where Kennedy-phobes might have gotten the idea for the bootlegging slander. Joe's father (hence JFK's grandfather), Patrick, had been a saloonkeeper and liquor store owner with an interest in an oil importation business. Biographer Laurence Leamer adds an essential observation that best explains how Joe Kennedy approached moneymaking: "Joe had no interest in risk, leaving that sad concept to entrepreneurs, plungers and business school professors."

Joe Kennedy was able to wangle permits to ship alcohol for "medicinal" purposes to the United States where the liquor was held in storage until December 5, 1933, which happened to be the day that Prohibition

A Boston liquor store owned by JFK's grandfather P. J. Kennedy
City of Boston Archives

ended. All of this was legal since the Volstead Act allowed Americans to store liquor; it only prohibited the "manufacture, sale and transportation of intoxicating liquors."

Shortly before the end of Prohibition, in September 1933, Joe Kennedy traveled overseas to purchase the distribution rights to prestigious U.K. liquor brands such as Dewar's Scotch, Gordon's gin, Ronrico rum, and Haig & Haig scotch, seeking to meet with "the very best people." Kennedy's traveling partner was none other than James "Jimmy" Roosevelt, the sitting president's son, to send a not-so-subtle message about his American business capabilities.*

According to Leamer, Kennedy's investment in this distributorship, which he named Somerset Importers after an exclusive Boston brahmin social club, was $118,000 ($2.7 million today). He sold the company in 1946 for $8.5 million ($129 million today) to a company partly owned by New Jersey mob boss Abner "Longy" Zwillman. Kennedy's massive score did not include whatever profits he had taken during the years of his ownership, which must have been huge because he sold 150,000 cases of Scotch whiskey alone in the first year. Kennedy was the largest Scotch distributor in America. In addition, he had been a major shareholder of publicly traded distilleries where he also made a fortune.

Jimmy Roosevelt made out well, too. He was savvy enough not to become Kennedy's direct partner in Somerset, but he was a partner in an insurance company that made its money protecting transatlantic cargo shipments. It is a lesson in insulation and layering that we will see repeatedly. Nor could it have hurt Joe Kennedy to have the inside track, through FDR's own son, on how the president's efforts to repeal Prohibition were faring because Joe was to be among the repeal's star beneficiaries.

Historian Leamer doesn't rule out the possibility that Kennedy may have partaken in activities that danced along the line of bootlegging. After all, Kennedy may not have stored *all* of his liquor until Prohibition was over and had the resources to deliver liquor from outside U.S. territory to bootleggers off the coast. It would then have been the bootleggers who would be breaking the law by distributing and selling it in America. Still, there is no proof that Kennedy did this—and even if he did, it would

---

* One of Kennedy's partners in another liquor venture was a British politician named Winston Churchill.

demonstrate the deftness that differentiated gangsters from the business-men who knew how to use them and when to drop them.

No one has a greater incentive to dig up dirt than the biographer of a controversial figure, yet Nasaw and others found nothing on bootlegging save Joe Kennedy's possibly supplying liquor for his Harvard reunion during Prohibition. Daniel Okrent, formerly of the *New York Times* and author of a thorough history of Prohibition, reached a similar conclusion about Kennedy. In an interview, Okrent said that skeptics often confront him with comments such as, "You say he wasn't a bootlegger, but my cous-in's next-door neighbor's grandfather's roommate used to buy from him!" These tales become so deeply ingrained in the identities of the tellers of such tales that they are impossible to dislodge.

It's always possible that someone with Kennedy's access to liquor dab-bled in sketchy activities on the side. Still, it's unlikely that a man earning a fortune in legitimate business (banking, movies, real estate) and who was obsessed with respectability would choose to supplement his already huge income in a notoriously violent enterprise involving ethnic groups from whom he wanted to distance himself—remember that the temperance movement heavily blamed the rise in alcoholism to Irish immigrants. Was this a stereotype an enormously wealthy banker and businessman would seek to inflame? Other journalists have found anecdotal reports of boot-legging. Still, there are simply too many dubious characters with too little proof longing to insert themselves into the Kennedy bootlegging narrative to accept these tales as proven fact.

In retirement, Meyer Lansky and Frank Costello claimed to have done business with Joe Kennedy during Prohibition. Lansky told a bi-ographer about a liquor hijacking incident involving Kennedy, but this kind of tale—many of them reporting that so-and-so's uncle personally saw Joe Kennedy on the docks supervising shipments—are doubtful. There is too little support for these legends—just the fish tales told by some combination of people with axes to grind (worn-out mobsters) and those who want to insert themselves into an insider narrative about America's royal family.

The Kennedy bootlegging stories have snowballed over the decades into something resembling the truth because Joe Kennedy being a bootlegger fulfills a deep psychic need. In contemporary times, this phenomenon has come to be called the Mandela effect, named after many people who believe they remember former South African president Nelson Mandela dying in the 1980s when he lived until 2013. These stories are urban legends combined with false memories—anchored in having personal access to inside dope—run amok. Among other things, people take pleasure in trafficking in the Kennedy bootlegging myth because it makes them appear to have special knowledge available to few others about Big Stuff.

AFTER HIS MONEYMAKING GENIUS, PERHAPS JOE KENNEDY'S GREATEST talent was his ability to dwell in the gray, that line between criminality and marginally lawful conduct. For example, by today's standards, Kennedy, the first chairman of the Securities and Exchange Commission, would be an arch-criminal insider trader. At the time he did it, however, such activity was not illegal per se. Said securities attorney C. Evan Stewart, "Kennedy did three things. He traded on inside information, which was unethical, but not illegal then. He sold short, often based on inside information, and participated in stock pools, whereby participants trade up (or down) the stock to influence the general market then dump their holdings and leave the 'suckers' holding the bag, which was not illegal then." It was in this spirit that when Vito Corleone sent his adopted son Tom Hagen to law school, he did so with the stated philosophy that "a lawyer with a briefcase can steal more than a hundred men with guns."

In an interview, playwright David Mamet said, "Success in business comes from blurring the line between fraud and sharp practice." Joe Kennedy was the gold standard for sharp practice. *He was not a bootlegger because he didn't need to be.* Gangsters, on the other hand, needed the income that came from bootlegging because they weren't in Kennedy's position to control banks and movie studios, just extort them. Bootlegging was a way for mobsters to move up in the world from street crime. Bootlegging would have been a way for Kennedy to move way down. Kennedy going into bootlegging would have been like Warren Buffett deciding to rob an armored truck.

In the novel *Solomon Gursky Was Here*, loosely based on the Bronfman family of Seagram's, author Mordechai Richler wrote, "Dig deep enough into the past of a noble family and there is a Bernard at the root. The founder with the dirty fingernails. The killer." Joe Kennedy, who had long-rumored but never proven ties to the Bronfmans, had dirty finger-nails, but not from bootlegging.

THE 1960 ELECTION

Winning the presidency for his son was to be the ultimate validation that Joe Kennedy had not only made it in America but would become the closest thing this country would have to royalty. He succeeded. History has written at great length about the price he paid for this success. What is less well understood is that Joe Kennedy was also a very engaged and protective parent, far more so than the oft-sainted matriarch Rose. More recent studies on the family, including Ted Kennedy's autobiography, have revisited the notion of a cold, distant, and imperious patriarch seeking only to advance his own ambitions. His sons very much shared Joe's ambi-tion rather than simply had it inflicted upon them, and their father wanted to shield them from reality's sharper edges along the way.

What is of interest here is how the patriarch accomplished JFK's rise with the help of organized crime, a peculiar eventuality given the high-profile roles of his sons Jack and Bobby with the Senate Rackets Committee. According to one friend, Joe's "ties to the underworld intersected at a hun-dred points." Kennedy had a controlling ownership of Miami's Hialeah Park Race Track, which was a favorite haunt of mobsters like Meyer Lansky, Jimmy Alo, and Santo Trafficante, Jr., not to mention visiting LCN gentry. Rose Kennedy said Joe went to the track "a couple times a week." Kennedy also gambled at Lansky's illegal "carpet joints" in South Florida, favoring roulette. T. J. English cited Kennedy's likely hidden ownership stake (10 percent) in Las Vegas's Tropicana Hotel and Casino, which also featured investors such as Frank Costello, Carlos Marcello, and Johnny Rosselli.

One of those mob touchpoints was the Kennedy-owned Chicago Merchandise Mart, then considered the largest commercial building in the world. The building is so huge, it had its own zip code. It was also the crown jewel in the Kennedy family's asset portfolio between the mid-1940s and when it was sold in 1998 for $625 million (more than $1 billion in 2023 dollars). It was the last operating business the family owned.

One couldn't work with a major commercial enterprise in Chicago in

Joseph P. Kennedy owned the enormous Chicago Merchandise Mart. He couldn't possibly have operated such a massive facility without some help from the Outfit. *Keith Levit/Shutterstock*

most of the 1900s without union and mob compensation. For a shrewd businessman like Joe Kennedy, reaching an accommodation with organized crime would have been a small price to pay for a smooth-running operation. Given the size and strategic importance of the Merchandise Mart, the Kennedy relationship must have been with someone senior in the Chicago Outfit. That person was likely Curly Humphreys, who was known to maintain strong contacts with Mart management and able to provide the services laid out on Piker Ryan's list.[*]

Bobby Kennedy was particularly hostile to the Chicago gangster who was the most helpful to his brother's campaign a few short years later, baiting him for giggling like a little girl (his exact words) during the McClellan hearings. Patriarch Joe was horrified. Moreover, Joe was able to hold his nose while dealing with the likes of Sam Giancana and knew that hoodlums could be helpful with the labor movement in a national election.

---

[*] Before the labor rackets in Chicago were prosecuted, union rules required that nine workers unload each forklift, and an electrician was paid about $80 to bring a lamp into a warehouse.

RFK's pursuit of organized crime was sincere, but he and JFK were brutal realists who had the capacity for denial and self-exemption when need be. The Kennedy brothers had lived vastly different lives from almost all other politicians. Kennedy-level wealth and influence bought *impunity* and, more important, a congenital absence of a gyroscope that could calibrate cause and effect.* "That degree of wealth creates its own morality," said presidential journalist Hugh Sidey.

A 1957 *Saturday Evening Post* story by Harold H. Martin addressed the Kennedy family's "charismatic authority system": "What was good for JFK was good for the country" and: "They are taught in the cradle or are born already knowing that they must aid each other, side with their friends and fight common enemies even when their friends are wrong and their enemies are right."

By 1960, the Kennedy brothers were middle-aged men who never had to worry about *how* their extraordinary lifestyle had come about. They had been sheltered from the repercussions of how things had gotten done their entire lives. Contrary to the cliché that men like the brothers *think* they can get away with things, they *do*; they have a very different sense of risk than the rest of us. Moreover, after December 1961, they no longer had Joe to talk sense into the boys or smooth things over with gangland because the patriarch had suffered a debilitating stroke, leaving him unable to speak or walk.

When the brothers were going after the rackets, they hadn't considered the downstream consequences for the labor vote in a future presidential bid. They had never had to think this way. Not so Papa Bear; he knew exactly what kind of trouble lay ahead. It wasn't that Joe had any great loyalty to the mob, *it was that he knew racketeers were shot callers for labor.* Around the time the McClellan Committee was forming, Joe and Bobby had a blowout fight, according to sister Jean Kennedy Smith, who described it as "the worst we ever witnessed." JFK's close friend Lem Billings said, "The old man saw this [going after the rackets] as dangerous, not the sort of thing or sort of people to mess around with. He felt Bobby was being awfully naïve."

---

* In a discussion with the author, a close friend of JFK's indicated the president's private fascination with and bewilderment about money and how much people earned because he was self-conscious about being oblivious to the cost of everyday items.

Joe's assessment of Bobby's strategic thinking was validated years later—with more than a little disbelief—when Meyer Lansky privately told his nephew, Mark Lansky, that "Bobby went after the very unions than helped his brother get elected."

Nevertheless, the younger Lansky dismissed as preposterous the notion that the mob had anything to do with JFK's assassination as some form of retaliation. Meyer and his partners had been licking their wounds and knew that their Havana casinos were lost and were focused on quietly seeking out new opportunities, not to mention running for cover from federal subpoenas. As for rumors of CIA involvement in Kennedy's murder, Meyer expressed later in life that it would have been the last thing the agency would do given how worried they were that their Operations Mongoose mischief might come back to bite them in any federal investigation. Any cover-up the CIA may have participated in would have emphasized keeping Mongoose under wraps.

Nathan Lewin was a young attorney in RFK's Justice Department, and he confirms that Kennedy and his team pulled no punches in prosecuting Hoffa. Bobby's convictions were sincere. He also despised Hoffa. For Lewin, his experience at Justice was anchored in sharpening his technical legal skills and he had borne no animosity toward the union leader.

During Hoffa's Nashville federal trial, one of his closest advisers, Ed Partin, discreetly informed the prosecution that Hoffa had been attempting to bribe a juror, having told Partin, "I've got the colored juror in my hip pocket." Prosecutors had to find a way to disqualify the juror without Hoffa finding out why. Lewin arranged for an affidavit from Partin summarizing what he knew about the bribe. Despite his diminutive size, Hoffa could be menacing, albeit not to Lewin. The juror was removed. Hoffa was furious that he hadn't been told why, and only Lewin and the judge knew the affidavit's contents. Still, the trial ended in a hung jury. Hoffa was later convicted by a jury in Chattanooga of bribery and other charges.

LOADING THE DICE

The Chicago Outfit wasn't just another big-city mob family. The Outfit is consistently—and wrongly—characterized as being secondary to New York when there have been persuasive arguments made by both investigative reporters and law enforcement that Chicago was as influential as New York, albeit structured differently. Whereas the New York families were rigid on Cosa Nostra ceremonies, "making" members through rituals including pinpricking or knife-pricking fingers and the burning of cards depicting saints, that type of thing happened in Chicago at the discretion of the boss. In addition, the Outfit had non-Italian executives who held great power for much of the twentieth century, even if they couldn't technically be "made." They included Jews like moneymen Jake "Greasy Thumb" Guzik, Alex Louis Greenberg, lawyer Sidney Korshak, and political fixers, Welshman Murray Humphreys and Greek Gus Alex.

Another thing that makes the Outfit worth flagging is how violent they were. Violence was the solution to almost everything, and the boss during the early 1960s, Sam (Salvatore) "Mooney" Giancana, rose to the top more on murder than genius. Giancana may have been a psychopath according to FBI agents, but he was an opportunistic one. He had been arrested more than fifty times before he was twenty. He had first gone to prison when he was fifteen. Three of these arrests were for murder. One of those cases was dropped when the main witness turned up dead.

In his controversial bestseller *The Dark Side of Camelot*, author Seymour Hersh wrote: "Jack Kennedy and his brother took office knowing that organized crime and [Sam] Giancana helped win the 1960 election. Just what Joe Kennedy promised Giancana in return is not known, but the gangster was convinced he had scored the ultimate coup by backing a presidential winner. The heat would now be off the Chicago syndicate."

The Outfit had already been approached to help Republican nominee Richard Nixon in the election, but like good gangsters, they played both sides to see who came to them with the better deal. Interestingly, Joe Kennedy's campaign to enlist the mob in his son's battle with Nixon didn't begin with Chicago. Gus Russo's work on the likely origins of Joe Kennedy's approach to the Outfit merits flagging, as it presents original detail. Russo reported that Joe Kennedy approached Vincent "Jimmy Blue Eyes" Alo, the New York Genovese capo and longtime partner of Meyer Lansky, a version validated by my own discussions with those in Alo and Lansky's orbit. While Alo and Lansky had their share of experiences with politicians, neither man trusted them. In Lansky's private records, he lamented his friend Frank Costello's vulnerability to being used by

Vincent "Jimmy Blue Eyes" Alo,
Meyer Lansky's business partner and
the first mob figure Joe Kennedy
approached to help his son in the
1960 election. Alo also sent Joe
Kennedy to Frank Sinatra.
Courtesy Carole Russo/Alo Family

politicians: "I warned him sooner or later he would not be able to fulfill all the demands made on him and he will become a bastard to them. That is just what happened. . . . Instead of being looked upon as a savior for all he did for them . . . he suddenly became a gangster."

This was the mindset of distrust with which Alo went into his discussion with Joe Kennedy. There was another likely factor as well: Alo and Lansky were first and foremost gamblers. Gamblers play odds, and neither man thought there was any chance that backing Kennedy would yield a payout.

Alo told Joe Kennedy that he "wasn't in the habit of interfering in elections." Alo thought that Frank Sinatra would be the better emissary to the Outfit. Alo and Sinatra knew each other through a mutual close friend, the William Morris Agency's George Wood. According to Alo's niece, Carole Russo (no relation to author Gus), whom Alo raised like a daughter, Alo had no great affection for Sinatra, believing he was a bully who enjoyed acting like a gangster. It's very possible that Alo was happy to bring two parties he didn't like together and let them take whatever risks they wished. It is also possible that Alo's contact with Joe Kennedy had been through intermediaries.

The rumors about Sinatra's relationships with gangsters are more than pop-culture myth. He loudly bragged about his associations, which were confirmed by law enforcement surveillance. One FBI report (of many) noted, "On Saturday night 6/8/63 REDACTED NAME, SAM GIANCANA, FRANK SINATRA and AVA GARDNER (actress) went to SINATRA'S parents' home in New Jersey." The point here is that while some of the Sinatra stories may be exaggerated—it was common for nightclub performers to know mobsters—they are not old wives' tales like the tales of Joe Kennedy and bootlegging.

According to the singer's daughter, Tina, Sinatra met with Joe Kennedy in Hyannis Port, Massachusetts, where the patriarch told him what he wanted: labor support for JFK in key states. This was problematic because Teamsters boss Hoffa had already endorsed Nixon, understandably loathing the Kennedy brothers after his Senate grilling. Sinatra had arranged a meeting between Joe and Teamsters vice president Harold Gibbons but had been unable to smooth the ruffled feathers of the union's leaders. Sinatra then agreed to approach Chicago Outfit boss, Sam Giancana. FBI records indicate that the Outfit supported Lyndon Johnson before Kennedy was nominated. Once JFK prevailed, a hedging strategy was called for in the general election. And the games began.

Sinatra first proved useful during the West Virginia primary. His friend Paul "Skinny" D'Amato, proprietor of Atlantic City's 500 Club, was dispatched to West Virginia to distribute cash to those who would vote for Kennedy. Joe Kennedy had promised D'Amato* that he would put in a word with his sons so that Genovese mobster Giuseppe "Joe Adonis" Doto would be allowed to return to the United States after his 1956 deportation. It is unlikely that Joe Kennedy ever spoke to Jack and Bobby about this, but regardless, Adonis never returned to America. Kennedy rival Hubert Humphrey had spent $25,000 in West Virginia compared to an estimated $1 million to $2 million by Kennedy.

Sinatra spoke with Giancana on a golf course, away from surveillance. The mobster was all ears and said he would consider helping. Giancana was aware that JFK had been criticizing Eisenhower as ineffective in ridding Communism from Cuba. The Chicago Outfit, which had just lost

---

*   The FBI identified D'Amato as a member of La Cosa Nostra. Some disagree.

Chicago Outfit boss Sam Giancana

legal assets in Havana hotels and casinos, were encouraged by this—or pretended to be. They were snakebit by what they had just lost and wanted to keep their options open.

The next trick would be to arrange a meeting between Joe Kennedy and Giancana. For this task, according to Hersh and research by Gus Russo, Kennedy reached out to a Chicago judge he knew, William J. Tuohy. Tuohy didn't know Giancana and didn't really want to. However, he knew somebody who did, criminal defense attorney Robert McDonnell, who made the arrangements.

The meeting was reportedly in the chambers of a very nervous Judge Tuohy, who didn't participate. McDonnell later reported: "I don't know what deals were cut; I don't know what promises were made. But I can tell you, Mooney [Giancana] had so many assets in place. They could put drivers in every precinct to help out the precinct captains, to get the voters out. And they had the unions absolutely going for Kennedy."*

It may have been more complicated than this. After all, Nixon had the

---

* Joe Kennedy and Sinatra weren't the only ones in the JFK camp with Outfit contacts. Press Secretary Pierre Salinger knew attorney Sidney Korshak and accepted a $10,000 campaign donation from him in 1964 when he ran for the U.S. Senate in California.

support of Jimmy Hoffa and presumably many Teamsters. Nevertheless, this made Giancana's services even more valuable. Anything he could do to sway segments of labor over to Kennedy would be helpful. Outfit brass was not universally thrilled about getting mixed up in presidential politics. Humphreys, the most politically savvy, was against it because he didn't trust Joe Kennedy and was skeptical that the Outfit could have any control in a national race the way they did in local politics. Humphreys was outvoted. He also happened to be very, very right.

Joe Kennedy sitting down with Sam Giancana would have been a very risky proposition given that the latter was the target of multiple investigations, including by Kennedy's own sons. There is ample reason to believe that Joe knew Giancana (and Rosselli from his days in Hollywood), but he would have been careful to keep contact indirect whenever possible. An intermediary would have been well-advised to handle the discussions; after all, it wasn't as if extensive negotiations were necessary. Deals like this are seldom clearly articulated because both parties fear being caught committing a crime and seek wiggle room if a precise outcome is not achieved. Any deal would have been simple and self-evident: *Help my son's campaign however you can, and I'll work on the boys to back off with their investigations.*

In an analysis of the 1960 election, John J. Binder concluded that "it's hard to comprehend how the Outfit, having been attacked by the McClellan Committee, would trust the Kennedys." It's a fair point, but Giancana, a man under heavy fire, may have reasoned that getting a responsible parent to rein in his reckless kids was worth a shot. The mobster may also have reasoned that by helping the Kennedy campaign, he would have fresh dirt on them if he needed it, which could have led to a theoretical and cringeworthy exchange in a hearing such as:

Pretend RFK: Mr. Giancana, do you do awful things like fix elections?

Pretend Giancana: Maybe, punk. I remember that time your dad asked me to send goons to stuff ballots for your brother.

Pretend RFK: I think we'll take a recess now.

There can be little doubt that there were lines of communication between the Kennedys, Sinatra, and the Outfit. The FBI recorded a postelection discussion between someone named "Johnny" (perhaps Rosselli or John Formosa) and Giancana about the Kennedys' easing up on the mob:

> **Johnny:** I said, "Frankie [Sinatra], can I ask one question?" He says, "Johnny, I took Sam's [Giancana] name and wrote it down and told Bobby Kennedy, 'This is my buddy. This is my buddy. This is what I want you to know, Bob.'" . . . Between you and I, Frank saw Joe Kennedy three different times. He called him three times, Joe Kennedy, the father.

Later in the conversation, the FBI tap picks up Giancana:

> **Giancana:** And then the last time I talked to him [Sinatra] was at the hotel in Florida, a month before he left, and he said, "Don't worry about it, if I can't talk to the old man [Joe Kennedy], I'm going to talk to the man [President Kennedy]."

Additional wiretaps picked up John Rosselli and Giancana discussing Sinatra's contacts with Joe Kennedy about Outfit support and contributions to Kennedy's campaign, Giancana lamenting that his assistance hadn't yielded his "money's worth": "In other words, if I even get a speeding ticket, none of these [expletive] would know me."

The FBI took it seriously, noting: "Information has been received indicating that Samuel M. Giancana, a hoodlum figure, has sought to enlist Frank Sinatra to act as an intermediary to intercede on Giancana's behalf with the Attorney General. In this regard, consideration was allegedly given to making such overtures through the father of the Attorney General."

It's unlikely Sinatra talked to Joe Kennedy after this because a week and a half later, the elder Kennedy had a stroke that left him unable to speak. Bobby Kennedy did not relent in the Justice Department's prosecution of the mob, which would have exasperated his dealmaking father.

HELP IN THE OUTFIT'S BACKYARD

Nevertheless, whatever Joe Kennedy couldn't do post-1961 because of his stroke, he did very well in 1960 and before. Jeanne Humphreys, the wife of Outfit political fixer Murray Humphreys, noted in her diary that her husband made lists of union leaders, political and ward bosses with whom he made exhaustive contacts. Of particular interest to Giancana and Humphreys were non-Teamsters labor unions who didn't share Jimmy Hoffa's affinity for Richard Nixon. In addition, the Teamsters were no monolith and Joe Kennedy and the Outfit alike believed that plenty of union members could be persuaded to vote for JFK. Giancana even persuaded the Teamsters to contribute to JFK's campaign from funds secured by its pension.

Historians have made the argument that Kennedy wouldn't have needed the mob's help in Illinois, especially in and around Chicago, because the Democratic machine of Chicago mayor William Daley would have taken care of any challenges. Perhaps, but it's impossible to separate the Outfit from the Daley political machine fully.* Furthermore, in the general election, outside of the Chicago area, Richard Nixon did well in Illinois, a state that was key to Kennedy's win.

Even if mob support hadn't been decisive in Kennedy's victory in Illinois (or other states), Joe Kennedy was not one to let the free market determine his family's fate. Nor does the contention that Illinois wasn't essential for Kennedy to win the election neutralize the campaign's motivation to get all the help it could secure. The initiative didn't have to be an all-or-none proposition any more than mob involvement in Operation Underworld needed to have determined the outcome of the war for it to have been a noteworthy development. At the very least, Joe wanted to put his thumb on the scale. Whether Outfit support was essential to JFK's

---

* An FBI report from October 1963 offers a sense of how influential the Outfit was in Chicago politics during the early 1960s. Unidentified Chicago political leaders met with bosses Anthony Accardo and Paul Ricca and complained that "they had never in their many years of service in Chicago seen a situation" where it was so hard to "fix" political outcomes. They claimed, "they were doing all in their power to continue their functions as they had in years gone by." The report said that the politicos would "do their utmost in the furtherance of GIANCANA'S desires."

Chicago Outfit political fixer
Murray "the Camel" Humphreys
*ST-17644594, Chicago Sun-Times
Collection, Chicago History Museum*

victory or mythologized over time, a little push couldn't have hurt, especially given concerns about labor's drift toward Nixon.

Chicago columnist Mike Royko wrote that voter fraud in Illinois was "obvious." Even JFK friend, journalist Ben Bradlee, assumed Kennedy knew down deep that he had won Illinois through legerdemain. Said Kennedy aide Kenneth O'Donnell, "If Jack had known about some of the phone calls his father made on his behalf to Tammany Hall–type bosses during the 1960 campaign, Jack's hair would have turned white." House Speaker Thomas P. "Tip" O'Neill said something similar about JFK not ever knowing the particulars of what his father had done on his behalf.

On election eve, according to Ben Bradlee, Mayor Daley spoke to JFK on the telephone and said, "Mr. President, with a little bit of luck and the help of a few close friends, you're going to carry Illinois."

The granular mechanics of what exactly the Outfit did will likely never be fully known, but we know the essence of the program. In order to endear themselves to a would-be Kennedy administration hoping for prosecutorial leniency, the Outfit distributed "walking around money" to buy votes during the West Virginia primary and in Illinois in the general election where Nixon, despite winning 93 out of 102 counties, still lost Illinois by 8,800 votes. The Outfit also put pressure on their political and labor contacts to get out the vote in Kennedy's favor.

While the Outfit worked hard for Kennedy in Illinois, contrary to legend, the race didn't come down entirely to this midwestern state. Given that it was a close election across the country, labor likely had a major effect elsewhere, including New Jersey, where Joe Kennedy worked closely with Frank Sinatra to shake loose support in the singer's home state, which JFK won by 0.8 percent. Writes Russo:

> Most pertinent, in the states where the Outfit had a strong union presence, Kennedy squeaked to gossamer-thin victories: in Illinois (+.2%), Michigan (+1%), Missouri (+.6%), and Nevada (+1.3%). These states accounted for a decisive 63 electoral votes, which, if given to Nixon, would have changed the outcome (269 were needed to elect; Kennedy obtained 303).

As we've seen, there is some support for claims that there were Giancana–Kennedy Sr. meetings; however, such meetings would not have been required for there to have been collusion. In these affairs, more things are accomplished by intuitive favor-granting than by negotiated backroom deals and briefcases of cash. If nothing else, Sam Giancana deeply *believed* that he had helped Kennedy win the presidency. According to an internal FBI memorandum:

> During the campaign of John Kennedy in the early 1960s, Giancana made certain representations to the [LCN] commission that Sinatra would be able to have influence behind the scenes in the Kennedy administration. . . . Giancana lost considerable face because of the reliance of the leadership of organized crime on Sinatra's representations and Giancana never forgave Sinatra for this situation.

Other FBI electronic surveillance picked up senior Outfit men talking about how their ward leaders "stole the vote . . . in effect winning the presidential election for Kennedy."

There are a few obstacles analyzing a corrupt arrangement such as the Outfit-Kennedy deal. First, simply because two parties agreed to conspire, it doesn't mean that either party fulfilled their end of the deal. We know for certain that the Kennedy administration did not tread lightly on the mob. In addition, the vast evidence of the Outfit's efforts on Kennedy's behalf is anecdotal, which has value but is less than a guarantee of truth.

It's noteworthy how little investigative reporting there was on all of this until years after President Kennedy's death. Even before the 1960 campaign, there were jokes about buying elections, JFK himself remarking at the 1958 Gridiron Dinner that he had just received a note from his father reading, "Dear Jack—Don't buy a single vote more than necessary—I'll be damned if I am going to pay for a landslide." This nod toward corruption had a Rat Pack groove to it for Kennedy supporters, but there was somebody who wasn't amused, and it would have implications that would ring in the American political system and culture for decades: Richard Nixon.

If Nixon had ever read the FBI files, it would have justified his every paranoid impulse. Read this FBI memo:

Allegations have also been received concerning hoodlum connections of Senator Kennedy . . . no effort is being made to list these allegations in full detail—much of the information being unsubstantiated. In March, 1960, for example, it was reported that Frank Sinatra had purposely cultivated Kennedy's brother-in-law (actor Peter Lawford) and that Sinatra would assist in Kennedy's campaign so that Joe Fischetti [of the Chicago Outfit] and other notorious hoodlums could have an entre to the Senator.

In short, there is enough evidence to support that Joe Kennedy tapped the Outfit and that JFK's campaign received that help. That there was any mob support for JFK at all is reason for concern, but the *degree* of intimacy between Joe Kennedy and the Outfit requires ongoing scrutiny.

NIXON PRIVATELY TOLD PEOPLE HE HAD BEEN ROBBED BY THE KENNEDY machine. He had some external validation, the Republican-leaning *Chicago Tribune* stating, "The election of November 8 was characterized by such gross and palpable fraud as to justify the conclusion that [Nixon] was deprived of victory." Concerned about being seen as a sore loser, Nixon contemplated his next move carefully but was publicly gracious. The morning after the election, he said, "I want Senator Kennedy to know, and I want all of you to know, that if this trend does continue, and he does become our next president, then he will have my wholehearted support."

Nixon told his advisers that he didn't want to trigger a constitutional crisis. Perhaps, but there were other factors at work. For one, Nixon allowed third parties to take steps to challenge the results while he publicly tried to rise above it. Thruston Morton, Republican Party chairman, petitioned for recounts in eleven states. Recounts proceeded, and even the *New York Times* supported the process opining, "It is now imperative that the results in each state be definitively settled by the time the electoral college meets."

Fraud had been discovered in Cook County, Illinois, and a few people ended up going to prison for it. Even J. Edgar Hoover thought that Nixon was the legitimate winner of the election. In late November, the RNC's general counsel floated the idea that the Illinois vote might be reversed. Subsequent recounts showed discrepancies there, but they were not necessarily due to fraud. Regardless, they were not of a margin sufficient to have changed the election results.

The recount only made a difference in one state, Hawaii, which had been awarded to Nixon after having been called for Kennedy. It had been the Democrats that had called for a recount there. Two things brought the broader recount to an end. One was the Hawaii flip from Nixon to Kennedy and the surprise appointment of Bobby Kennedy as attorney general. What were the chances now that Attorney General Robert F. Kennedy was going to investigate voter fraud, which would inevitably lead back to his father and the mob connections that may have given an electoral push to his brother? Even President Eisenhower urged the Republicans to give up the fight. A source familiar with the thinking of Republican leaders at that time said that with RFK's appointment, Nixon knew it was time to end the challenge.

According to G. Robert Blakey, a Kennedy Justice Department official no less, the main services the Outfit provided in Illinois were mobilizing union voters and stealing votes so that JFK would win this critical state. Illegal FBI wiretaps that Blakey was privy to indicated "beyond doubt, in my judgment, that enough votes were stolen—let me repeat that—stolen in Chicago to give Kennedy a sufficient margin that he carried the state of Illinois." And he did, by comparatively few votes. Blakey also said, "Can you say that mob money made a difference? My judgment is yes." Even pro-Kennedy journalist Theodore White expressed his sense that some of what went on in Illinois was dirty.

More reports of 1960 voting fraud have dribbled out in the ensuing decades. For many years, Frank Sinatra kept a handwritten note from Kennedy reading, "Frank—How much can I count on from the boys in Vegas?—JFK." Sam Giancana told the girlfriend he shared with JFK, Judith Campbell Exner, "Listen, honey, if it wasn't for me, [Kennedy] wouldn't . . . be in the White House." Still, Irwin Gellman, who has done extensive analyses of the 1960 election, believes the allegations of mob impact in Illinois were overstated: "While there is a convincing possibility of fraud in the predominantly black wards, there is far less evidence to support claims that the Mafia stole the election."

Whereas the 2020 "stolen election" charges are a lie, a stolen election in 1960 was likely, be it with the help of the mob, the Daley political machine, or Kennedy cash. Nixon scholars have argued that this event so traumatized Nixon and aggravated his already dark psyche that it deepened his obsession with the Kennedys and his commitment to deploying dirty tricks going forward so that he would never lose—at least not like *that*—again.

Nixon decided to give up the fight, live, learn, forgive, and remember. Said Nixon political adviser Len Hall to the defeated candidate: "You know, Dick, a switch of only 14,000 votes and we would have been the heroes, and they would have been the bums." According to Mark Mazo, whose father Earl had been reporting about what he believed to have been the stolen 1960 election, Richard Nixon personally called him and asked him to stop investigating the Kennedy machine's alleged fraud. Nixon told Mazo that given the Cold War, he could not be a party to undermining American democracy at such a critical time. Nixon also called Mazo's boss at the *New York Herald Tribune*, which ceased its coverage. Mazo took Nixon's request at face value, believing that the losing candidate did not want a compromised electoral system as part of his legacy.

If the mob had anticipated leniency from the Kennedys once elected, it had been a bad bet. Bobby went after them harder than ever, a conclusion confirmed by Howard Willens, a Justice Department official who later was a key staff member on the Warren Commission. There were only 49 racket indictments in 1960. The year Bobby became attorney general, there were 121 indictments; in 1962, 350; and 1963, 615.

The boys in Chicago weren't happy with Sinatra's inability to deliver Kennedy prosecutorial leniency, an FBI memo summarizing, "Chicago sources have advised of Giancana's disappointment in Sinatra's apparent inability to get the administration to tone down its efforts in the anti-racketeering field." There were even reports of Giancana wanting to kill Sinatra but tearfully deciding against it because he loved his singing voice; such was the gangster's soft side.

Qualified analysts of diverse ideologies and agendas have run the 1960 election statistics to the moon and back and come to differing conclusions. Regardless, *it is unequivocal that organized crime was a consciously sought-after resource of the highest-level players in American politics.*

KILLING CASTRO

As Communism continued its march around the world, very few expected it to land at the foot of America's bed, specifically off the coast of Florida, in Cuba. The island nation falling to Castro was not a foregone conclusion. The rich kid that he was, there was reason to believe Castro's flirtation with Communism was a rebellious act soon to be shed for the realities of adulthood and the burdens of leadership.

A combination of events paved the way for Castro and Communism, including aggressive American corporations looking for new markets, mob rule over the island's hotels and casinos, and repressive crackdowns on dissent by dictator Fulgencio Batista, who had been in Meyer Lansky's pocket for many years. There was something else: The Soviets had made Castro a better deal, which included protection from the capitalists to the north, who he believed were plundering the nation. President Dwight Eisenhower had become vexed by his inability to dislodge the Communists from Cuba, so his CIA set in motion plans to evaluate toppling Castro before JFK took office.

Under the Kennedys, Operation Mongoose, so named for the ferret that kills snakes, was off and running in 1961 with a budget estimated at $50 million to $150 million (about $500 million to $1.5 billion today). It comprised a portfolio of activities set to undermine and destroy Castro's domination of Cuba and end Communism on the neighboring island once and for all. Some of the anti-Castro plans were more Austin Powers than James Bond. One plan involved spraying Castro's boots with thallium, which would cause his iconic beard to fall out, thereby weakening his charismatic, masculine public image. However, this scheme required

Castro to leave his boots outside a hotel room door for pickup and shining, something the CIA concluded was unlikely. The plan was scrapped.

Another plan involved Castro having an underwater accident while scuba diving, which required knowing when Castro would venture out and then having underwater killers stalk him. A program that was also considered—and rejected—by President Kennedy was Operation Northwoods, a Defense Department/CIA plot to commit "false flag" acts of terrorism within the United States and blame it on Cuba in order to justify a full-scale invasion. At least the Mafia assassination plans, most of which consisted of somebody shooting Castro, made sense.

The Kennedy brothers had not soft-pedaled their desire to see Castro gone. Contrary to their contemporary reputation as liberal peacemakers, they were both hard-line anti-Communists. After running his brother's successful 1952 Senate campaign, Bobby went to work for Senator Joseph McCarthy, hunting Communists. McCarthy had been a Kennedy family friend who had even dated two of the Kennedy sisters. One historian of Bobby's devotion to McCarthy after his death said, "For him the errant senator was a kindred spirit—one engaged, as he was himself, in the struggle against evil."

The Kennedys had been humiliated at the failed April 1961 Bay of Pigs invasion* by Cuban exiles. They blamed CIA covert operations boss Richard Bissell, Jr., for "sitting on his ass and not doing anything about getting rid of Castro and the Castro regime." Said historian Robert Dallek, "After the Bay of Pigs, John Kennedy becomes increasingly skeptical about how to deal with Castro. Bobby Kennedy is, in essence, the point man for trying to find a way to topple Castro."

JFK had spoken of the potential for Castro's surprise removal and Bobby was put in charge of exploring options, having once said his main goal was to "get rid of that bastard Castro." The Kennedy brothers' point man on the Castro assassination program was the CIA's William Harvey. There

---

* In April 1961, Cuban exiles, supported by the CIA, attempted to overthrow the Castro regime in a landing campaign. About one hundred were killed, and twelve hundred were captured at the Bay of Pigs. Even though the Eisenhower administration initiated the effort, Kennedy executed it, and it was an unmitigated disaster.

can be no doubt of Bobby Kennedy's direct involvement in what was coded Task Force W. While it was technically a CIA endeavor, the Kennedys were concerned about it being in the hands of a bureaucracy and wanted it supervised closer to home, in the White House Situation Room located in the southwest corner of the West Wing basement. Wrote Gus Russo of Bobby Kennedy, "Unbeknownst to official Washington or the American people, he had also become, in the wake of the Bay of Pigs, the virtual head of the CIA's counterinsurgency operations, if not of the agency itself."

THE CUTOUT

Robert Maheu had the kind of business where if you wrote about it in a screenplay, it would be nixed for being unrealistic. A former FBI agent, he ran a consulting firm helping powerful clients out with . . . stuff. One of his best clients was the CIA to whom he served as a "cutout," a "front," or intermediary creating a layer between the CIA and whatever clandestine activity it had been undertaking. This is a common CIA practice: setting up a company with a generic name that could interact with parties the Agency didn't want to deal with directly and would give them a degree of deniability.

The whole idea was to look boring, and Maheu looked like every middle-aged guy you would see at a convention in Omaha. Balding with a friendly, doughy face, there was nothing scary about him on the surface. Nevertheless, this was the man the CIA's Sheffield Edwards contacted when it came time to murder the leader of a neighboring nation.

The Mafia wouldn't be summoned only because they were scary guys. Contrary to cinematic portrayals of American CIA assassins awaiting kill orders in an underground lair, veterans of the clandestine services explain that this isn't how it works. On the rare occasions when someone overseas is targeted for assassination, assets *from that country* with a natural political motive are identified and supported. The reason to use gangsters was that if Castro turned up dead, outlaws could be blamed, not the American government, which could spark an international political incident. The thinking was that mobsters maintained assets in Cuba from their gambling concessions and that these assets could be put to work. This was true to some degree. Maheu, who had already met the Outfit's Johnny Rosselli through mutual acquaintances in Las Vegas, approached the glamorous mobster in early September 1960, two months before the election where JFK would be elected president. This was eventually entered into the FBI's records, which read: "As Maheu recalls the conversation, the Support Chief [of the CIA] asked him to contact John Roselli,* an underworld figure with possible gambling contacts in Las Vegas, to determine if he would participate in a plan to 'dispose' of Castro."

They met at the Brown Derby restaurant in Hollywood, where Maheu raised the Castro plot. Maheu never identified his elusive client. Rosselli was intrigued and wanted to hear more. Maheu said his client was willing to pay Rosselli $150,000, but Rosselli turned him down.

A second meeting was held at the Savoy Hilton in New York City a few weeks later. This time, the men were joined by the CIA's James O'Connell, who was identified as a Maheu employee. There was another meeting with Outfit boss Sam Giancana and a man who identified himself as "Joe," an interpreter. "Joe" was really Santo Trafficante, Jr., Tampa's LCN boss who had lost a fortune in Havana. Yet another meeting between CIA officials and Rosselli took place at the Plaza Hotel in New York while Castro attended a conference at the United Nations General Assembly. By this point the mobsters had a good idea who their would-be business partner was: the CIA. They were intrigued. And skeptical. A personal insight into Rosselli and Giancana is helpful to understand the schemes that unfolded to remove Castro from this mortal realm.

FOR A FRESH LOOK AT JOHNNY ROSSELLI I SPOKE TO LUELLEN SMILEY, daughter of Allen Smiley, right-hand man to Bugsy Siegel and later Rosselli. As the suave Rosselli aged, he imparted morsels of reflection to her. Luellen describes Rosselli as "deeply religious" and close to a Los Angeles priest. He had a glow around him, and conversation stopped when the tan, silver-haired Rosselli strode into a restaurant.

"I really loved him," Luellen said. "When he was in LA, I was ordered to dine with Dad and Johnny." There was plenty of speculation about why Rosselli never had a family. Rosselli, Luellen learned, had had a

---

* Rosselli's name has been alternatively spelled with one or two *s*'s. The FBI records it here with one *s*.

vasectomy, not wanting to bring a child into the precarious world in which he operated. Luellen filled the offspring role for Rosselli, and he was very good at playing a paternal and avuncular role in her life, considering he was a very dangerous man.

One day around 1970, when Luellen and Rosselli were waiting in the back seat of a car for Allen Smiley, Rosselli, thin and frail from worry and stress over potential deportation, admitted to having been contracted by the CIA to assassinate Castro. He told Luellen about a time when he had approached Cuban shores in a dinghy where his mission was to deliver poison to operatives who would slip it to Castro. For whatever reason, Rosselli ended up swimming longer than expected, presumably from the dinghy to the beach. Luellen recalls Rosselli laughing when he told the story. He had loved the adventure. Later that night when her father asked her what she had discussed with Uncle Johnny, Allen Smiley went cold in disbelief that Rosselli had told her about his Cuban adventure. He admonished Luellen in no uncertain terms that Rosselli had told her no such story. Ever. That's when she knew it had really happened, something that was confirmed by the news media and the Senate in the immediate years ahead.

Smiley had reason to be a very cautious man: He had been sitting about eighteen inches from Bugsy Siegel on a chintz sofa at his rental home at 810 North Linden Drive in Beverly Hills at 10:45 on June 20, 1947, when gunfire tore through a side window, killing Siegel instantly. A .30 caliber bullet from an army carbine had gone through Smiley's left sleeve. "It went right through his jacket, the bullets. The only reason he was saved is that he acted quickly and dove to the floor," said Luellen. Smiley crouched in an adjacent fireplace until the gunfire stopped and the police arrived.

We cannot overlook persistent stories about the role of Rosselli and Giancana's sidekick, party girl Judith Campbell Exner. Frank Sinatra had introduced Exner to candidate John F. Kennedy and Giancana on separate occasions in Las Vegas in 1960. She became romantically involved with both the candidate and the mob boss around that time. Law enforcement identified her as a high-end sex worker although there is a fine line that separates this trade from being an amply rewarded girlfriend.

Exner has given sharply different accounts of her underworld connections, including admitting having once lied under oath. While we can be confident that she had romantic relationships with both Kennedy and

Judith Campbell Exner, girlfriend of both JFK and Chicago Outfit boss Sam Giancana   *Courtesy: CSU Archives/Everett Collection*

Giancana, her claims of being a courier of cash and top secret correspondence between the two men related to the Castro assassination plot have been rightly contested. Given that a top secret CIA program had already been established for the sole purpose of killing Castro, it defies reason that the president of the United States was personally giving briefcases full of cash—plus helpful murder directions—to an immature and lovestruck woman to hand-deliver to one of the most volatile Mafia leaders in the country.

These scenarios are not only implausible, but they are also senseless given the spy mechanism in place. Besides, even those who believe that the Kennedys engaged in cash-fueled dirty tricks do not believe that JFK was personally stuffing the briefcases. In this case, credulity should only extend to the recklessness of the romantic triangle between the president, the party girl, and the gangster.

The president's relationship with Exner and Giancana wasn't the only problematic one; his relationship with Frank Sinatra, the man who introduced them, was, too. On the home front, Jacqueline Kennedy loathed Sinatra. She wasn't impressed with Hollywood or the whole Rat Pack scene, especially as they related to women. She knew what happened when her husband got together with Sinatra.

Jackie was also aware of Sinatra's mob ties, and, unlike other upper-class women, she didn't find it to be remotely appealing in that bad boy way. She wanted nothing to do with it because she knew that behind the noirish groove of it all, somebody somewhere was getting smashed over the head with a baseball bat.

Then there was the political risk. Among other links, Sinatra was an investor in the Cal-Neva gambling resort in Lake Tahoe. The major off-the-books owner was none other than Sam Giancana, a man Sinatra had claimed publicly he had only known casually. Giancana and his gambling fraternity were under intense investigation by Bobby Kennedy's DOJ, which made the web of connections very challenging to untangle. Complicating matters was that Joe Kennedy may have been another hidden investor in the Cal-Neva through the official owner, his friend Bert "Wingy" Grober. The FBI was certainly looking into it. Sinatra's FBI file contained a memo reading:

> REDACTED advised that he had heard from numerous sources that prior to the last presidential election, Joseph Kennedy (father of John F. Kennedy) had been visited by many gangsters (not identified) who had gambling interests. A deal was made which resulted in Peter Lawford, Frank Sinatra, Dean Martin and others obtaining a lucrative gambling establishment, the Cal-Neva Hotel, at Lake Tahoe, California. Joseph Kennedy was staying at the Cal-Neva at the time of the meeting.

According to Gus Russo, "If Grober was actually a front for Kennedy, and Sinatra was a front for Giancana, then, in essence, Bobby Kennedy's nemesis, Mooney Giancana, was now in partnership with Bobby's father."

Among the things that J. Edgar Hoover had determined was that Giancana and the president had the same girlfriend and that that girlfriend, Exner, had been calling the White House—*and* there were records she called at least seventy times. Hoover told Bobby about this on February 27, 1962, and likely added that Exner had been more than a caller; she had been a *visitor*, something that Bobby surely knew. Nevertheless, it was one thing for Bobby to know. It was another for Hoover to know. Big brother had not been as clever as he thought he had been. Hoover must have been experiencing euphoria when he confronted JFK with this information a few weeks after he spoke with Bobby. Job security.

Hoover eventually happened upon Operation Mongoose when his

agents received a tip from the Las Vegas police that surveillance equipment had been found in the hotel room of comedian Dan Rowan. In the spring of 1961, Rowan was being monitored by intelligence operative Robert Maheu at the behest of Outfit boss Sam Giancana, who believed (rightly) that his girlfriend, Phyllis McGuire, was having an affair with Rowan. Among other things, McGuire complained that her other boyfriend, Giancana, had a second girlfriend in Los Angeles. McGuire was okay with her own cheating, but apparently Giancana's dalliance with Exner was a betrayal. All Hoover knew was that Giancana's L.A. girlfriend had a boyfriend of her own: President John F. Kennedy. This had the makings of a world-class firestorm.

The FBI chief determined that the eavesdropping equipment had been paid for by Maheu whom he knew from the operative's days as an FBI agent. After initial denials, Maheu admitted that he had been hired as a cutout by the CIA to coordinate the assassination of Castro with leaders of the Chicago Outfit. Hoover was incredulous and told RFK what he knew in a May 21, 1961, memo. Bobby Kennedy came clean and admitted the whole plot to Hoover, his nominal subordinate.

There was, of course, another subtext to the discussion about Frank Sinatra: the singer's role in bringing Giancana into the 1960 election conspiracy. We don't know what precisely Joe Kennedy told his sons about the arrangements, but the boys were bright enough to intuit the rough outlines of labor and the electoral environment. Hoover didn't need to state everything he knew about the Kennedys and gangland to make the brothers very, very uncomfortable.

"The potential for a disastrous scandal must have been obvious to Hoover and the Kennedys especially given what the FBI had been hearing about Giancana and Rosselli" considering the Castro assassination plans, wrote Tom and Phil Kuntz, experts on Sinatra's FBI files.

JFK had been scheduled to stay at Sinatra's Palm Springs estate while visiting Southern California but at the last minute decided to spend the night at Bing Crosby's estate. It fell to Kennedy's brother-in-law, Rat Pack actor Peter Lawford, to break the news to Sinatra. Sinatra's reaction was to smash the telephone against the wall and destroy every photo and bit of JFK memorabilia that he had. There were reports that the singer, who had installed a helipad for Marine One, grabbed a sledgehammer and destroyed it. Sinatra denied this, but he also denied a lot of things on the Kennedy-mob front that later turned out to be true.

Sinatra had deeply misread his relationship with Kennedy. For the president, it had been a good-time lark and a way to meet women. For Sinatra, it had been a deep friendship that served as a validation of his seriousness as a cultural figure. To be relegated to the role of court jester was more than Sinatra could bear, especially since he wasn't taken seriously as a gangster, either. Sure, the hoods took photos with him and loved his singing, but Sinatra wanted more from them than that. Whereas with the Kennedys he wanted to rank with their guests like Pablo Casals and Leonard Bernstein, with the Mafia he wanted to be held in the tough guy esteem of a Bugsy Siegel or Joe Adonis.

If nothing else, the thing that pushed Sinatra into a rage was that Bing Crosby, JFK's fresh new host, had been a Nixon-backing Republican. How much did his idolized Kennedys disrespect him?

The decision to drop Sinatra was easy for Kennedy to make. No, the president didn't want to hurt Sinatra—and privately called him later—but, at some level, Kennedy must have known he had been pushing his luck with his sexual affairs, his hoodlum ties, and running a murder scheme in Cuba. If the president hadn't fully appreciated this, his brother, Hoover, and his wife did. It was in this spirit that presidential politicians dealt with the mob: for the most part, very carefully. As reckless as JFK was on the sexual front, when he realized that Sinatra's shadowy ties presented a political problem for him, he cut Sinatra loose.

There were other occasions when RFK and Hoover had to come to a meeting of the minds where JFK's risk-taking was concerned. Their deal came down to this: If Hoover would finally commit to pursuing LCN and drop his investigation of JFK's sexual relationship with high-risk women, including suspected German spy Ellen Rometsch,* RFK would permit Hoover to step up his surveillance of Martin Luther King, Jr., and other suspected civil rights "subversives" whom the FBI director believed

---

* Rometsch was smack dab in the middle of another scandal that surfaced in a Senate investigation of Vice President Johnson's former aide, Bobby Baker. No known records remain related to her deportation. More on Rometsch in the LBJ chapter.

were Communists. Much of this narrative was borne out by subsequent investigations: RFK had Rometsch discreetly deported, and on October 10, 1963, he authorized Hoover to begin wiretapping King's telephones, which eventually expanded to bugging hotel rooms in which King was staying. The *Atlantic* characterized the eavesdropping as "one of the most ignominious acts in modern American history." Why would RFK approve something so odious if he hadn't received something in return?

THROUGHOUT 1961 AND 1962, THE CASTRO MURDER PLOT WAS IN MOTION with Rosselli repeatedly visiting Florida to meet with Cuban exiles and CIA men. Bobby Kennedy also showed up at Florida training camps but there is no evidence that this coincided with Rosselli. Rosselli also spoke with operatives about the prospects of securing casino properties that the Outfit had operated during its Havana heyday. The FBI reported that Giancana had even specified to others the time frame in which Castro would be killed. In September 1961, there had been an apparent attempt on Castro's life at a Havana traffic intersection, but it failed.

There were eight known assassination attempts on Castro as part of Operation Mongoose and its predecessor efforts. The CIA had also developed a deadly pill that could be dropped in liquid and kill whoever drank it. Tampa Cosa Nostra boss Santo Trafficante, Jr., identified someone close to Castro who could slip the poison pill into his morning glass of juice. This person may have been Juan Orta, an administrator in Castro's executive office. This plan fell apart when Orta lost his position.

Another plan involved having Cuban exiles plant botulinum pills into Castro's dinner and drink at a Havana restaurant the leader was known to frequent in early 1961. This effort was said to have failed because the operative on the ground had not been given a satisfactory "go" signal.

As for Rosselli, if nothing else, the man seemed to enjoy being up to his eyeballs in an international caper, zooming on speedboat runs to deliver weapons and poison and practicing stealth landings. Neither he nor any other mobsters accepted a dime for their services.

Nor was the Giancana-Rosselli combine the only LCN resource the CIA tapped. Scranton LCN boss Russell Bufalino and New York's James Plumeri and Salvatore Granello were also asked to participate. The three men held investments in Havana casinos and a racetrack, properties they lost when Castro came to power. The essence of the program—which took place prior to JFK's election—was that the men would be given back $450,000 in cash they had left in Cuba if they could provide the CIA with intelligence that would help depose Castro assuming a successful Bay of Pigs invasion. They ended up providing nothing of value and never recovered their money. Plumeri and Granello were later murdered in New York, but Bufalino remained the boss of his LCN family until his death at age ninety in 1994.

"CIRCUMLOCUTIOUS"

There has been much post-assassination fantasizing about how JFK would have avoided military conflict around the world. Nevertheless, rather than rejecting Eisenhower's subversive plans to take out Castro, Kennedy stepped them up. President Kennedy, upon meeting the CIA's Bill Harvey, light-heartedly inquired whether he was "our James Bond." Sean Connery, he wasn't. Short, heavyset, balding, "froglike," and alcoholic, he was an accomplished spy who always carried a gun from his extensive collection. He was credited with identifying Kim Philby, the high-ranking British intelligence officer, as a KGB "mole." He had also found a way to tap Soviet military telephones via a hidden tunnel into East Germany. Harvey was a risk-taker, but he wasn't crazy. Like Hoover, he recognized there were risks associated with partnering with criminals, but for a time Harvey thought those risks were worth taking.

While the plot against Castro was at its most intense, Bobby Kennedy was investigating the same gangsters who were carrying out his plans. He had even written a book about his mob-busting work, *The Enemy Within*, where he wrote, "If we do not . . . attack organized criminals, with weapons and techniques as effective of their own, they will destroy us." There are a few theories about why he appeared to be working at cross-purposes. One is that Bobby hadn't been briefed in detail about who exactly was doing what regarding Cuba—and to what degree. Lawrence Houston, who had been the CIA's general counsel, later testified that RFK had been unhappy "because at the time he felt he was making a very strong drive to try to get after the Mafia.

William Harvey, a CIA point
man on getting rid of Fidel
Castro. JFK asked him if he
was "our James Bond."
Photo by Garston Wallace Driver

And so his comment was to us that if we were going to get involved with the
Mafia, in the future at any time, to make sure you see me first."

RFK had been told about the CIA collaborating with organized crime,
but we are not certain about how detailed any briefings were. There are,
after all, briefings and then there are *briefings*. Telling someone something
doesn't mean telling them everything. The word operatives used when ex-
plaining what Presidents Eisenhower and Kennedy were told about the
Castro efforts was "circumlocutious."

Decision-makers often demand certain outcomes but get skittish when
they learn about the particulars. This is the ethic the Kennedy brothers
adopted during the 1960 election when they knew their father was up to
something, even though they couldn't detail chapter and verse.

Given that there were different phases of the Castro operation, there
was a timeline element to what the Kennedys knew and the extent to
which they knew about some aspects but not all. There have been reports
that Bobby had initially been unaware that the Chicago Outfit and Tampa
LCN had been employed to kill Castro (until he was told by Hoover),
became angry, and asked that the program be hurried along. But the
quotation from RFK entered into the record of the 1975 Senate Church
Committee report—to investigate abuses by the intelligence community—is
vaguer: When being briefed by the CIA, he said, "I trust that if you ever
try to do business with organized crime again—with gangsters—you will

let the Attorney General know." This falls short of being a direct order to discontinue. Master spy Bill Harvey didn't buy it, later stating for the record, "Robert Kennedy was knowledgeable of the operation which had been devised by the CIA with the collaboration of Rosselli and his cohorts. . . . Kennedy is in an extremely vulnerable position if it were ever publicized that he condoned an operation which involved U.S. Government utilization of hoodlum elements."

While RFK was sincere in his dislike of "hoodlum elements," he was also a man frantic to accomplish the task at hand. According to journalist Michael Dorman, Kennedy had sent an emissary to New Orleans to speak to LCN boss Carlos Marcello about getting the Louisiana delegation to back JFK rather than Lyndon Johnson. Marcello explained that he had already backed Johnson. Kennedy was incensed and never forgave Marcello. Not long after Kennedy was elected, Bobby had Marcello deported to Guatemala where he wandered through the forests in a business suit and eventually found his way back to New Orleans.

Even if RFK had demanded the CIA stop using the mob, it wouldn't be a valid excuse for immunity. After all, the Kennedys had been running an assassination operation. What kind of people did RFK believe that the CIA would use to murder the leader of another country if it were not U.S. troops? Who, with American interests in Havana, might have the incentive to eliminate Castro? The Daughters of the American Revolution? The U.S. military couldn't do it without triggering a war, and the CIA was having mixed results with anti-Castro Cubans as evidenced by the disastrous Bay of Pigs affair. Furthermore, when it came to programs such as Operation Mongoose, it was difficult to tell where Cuban rebels ended and the mob began because they were in the anti-Castro business together.

Interpretations of what the Kennedys knew and did tend to fall along the political lines of the journalist writing on the subject. Kennedy apologists prefer to believe that Operation Mongoose mostly happened behind the brothers' backs and cling to the truth that it had been initiated by the Eisenhower administration. In his book about RFK, former Kennedy administration official and historian Arthur Schlesinger, Jr., wrote:

> The available evidence clearly leads to the conclusion that the Kennedys did not know about the Castro assassination plots before

the Bay of Pigs or about the pursuit of those plots by the CIA after the Bay of Pigs. No one who knew John and Robert Kennedy well believed they would conceivably countenance a program of assassination. . . . I, too, find the idea incredible that these two men, so filled with love of life and so conscious of the ironies of history, could thus deny all the values and purposes that animated their existence.

Then again, Schlesinger had written in a confidential memo: "The character and repute of President Kennedy constitute one of our greatest natural resources. Nothing should be done to jeopardize this invaluable asset. . . . When lies must be told, they should be told by subordinate officials."

RFK even had others send memos to the proverbial file indicating that he had been shocked when he had learned of the plans to use gangsters to kill Castro. Harvey characterized the practice as such: "If this ever comes up in the future, the file would show that on such and such a date, he was advised so and so, and he was no longer chargeable with this."

Harvey and others had tired from the pressure Bobby Kennedy was putting on the covert operatives to dispense with Castro, not to mention the mixed messages he had been sending, which came down to: *We need you to kill this guy but, Heavens to Betsy, please use only the nicest people to do it.* If RFK had demanded that the mob not be used for the Cuban operation, it appears his wishes weren't heeded. Had the CIA disobeyed him or taken his rant as a play for plausible deniability or the Washington wink conveying "just don't get caught?"

Anti-Kennedy writers believe the brothers knew everything and were hypocrites. The preponderance of the evidence shows that the Kennedys were very much aware that an assassination program was underway to depose Castro and to use criminals to do it. RFK likely *was* angry to learn that gangsters were being used. He also supercharged the effort to use Cuban exiles rather than gangsters. Nevertheless, the desire to remove Castro from power took precedence. It was war. Initiating something and permitting it are different things. Nor did RFK need to *like* it to permit it (or at least not stop it). The Kennedys, therefore, moved forward but may have been content not to know every detail or interrogate the CIA too intensely. This is the modality of willful ignorance or, as the Church Committee described it, the doctrine of "plausible deniability": "Evidence before the Committee clearly demonstrates that this concept [plausible deniability], designed to protect the United States and its operatives from the consequences of disclosures, has been expanded to mask decisions of the president and his senior staff members."

In addition to plausible deniability, there is another doctrine of intelligence and political work that isn't written down anywhere: the doctrine of obfuscation. If one studies official documents, there are so many subgroups and initiatives with acronyms that it is nearly impossible to determine who was doing what. *This is precisely the point.* This fog proved effective because here we are, more than sixty years after Operation Mongoose, quibbling about who knew and did what and when.

A MARCH 16, 1962, MEETING IN THE OVAL OFFICE GIVES US A FIRM SENSE of the Kennedy brothers' involvement in the Castro plot. The "Special Group" meeting was attended by JFK, RFK, national security advisor McGeorge Bundy, CIA chief John McCone, military adviser General Maxwell Taylor, Joint Chiefs chair General Lyman Lemnitzer, State Department undersecretary U. Alexis Johnson, Deputy Defense Secretary Roswell Gilpatric, and CIA Operation Mongoose point man Edward Lansdale, who memorialized the meeting in a memo.

During this meeting, attendees discussed an assassination option involving killing Castro at Ernest Hemingway's retreat where his widow Mary still lived. Castro was a Hemingway fan and remained in touch with Mary. Bobby raised "the opportunities offered by the shrine," meaning Hemingway's finca. Lansdale's memo stated that the plan was "worth assessing firmly and pursuing vigorously. If there were grounds for action, the CIA had some valuable assets which might well be committed for such an effort," also noting that "the matter was so delicate and sensitive that it shouldn't be surfaced to the Special Group until we are ready to go, and then not in detail." Said a former CIA director whose name was not cited, "The language of the memo speaks for itself. The only thing Robert Kennedy can be referring to is the assassination of Castro. This paragraph should never have been written."

Indeed, Kennedy and Johnson administration official Joseph Califano, Jr., later said he was shocked that RFK "talked about knocking off Castro. I was stunned. He was talking so openly, and there were other people

Ernest Hemingway's Cuban finca, where there were plans to kill Castro at Bobby Kennedy's direction and with JFK's awareness
Courtesy of Tony Hisgett

in the room." By "knocking off," it was highly unlikely that Bobby was talking about "knocking his block off," as if it were a Georgetown barroom brawl. A CIA Cuban desk official confirmed that someone at the Agency had been designated specifically to interact with gangsters. His code name was Rocky Fiscalini. Sam Halpern of the CIA's Task Force W said: "[Robert Kennedy] was always pushing. No matter what you came up with, no matter what we thought up, wasn't good enough. . . . We went berserk, honestly, trying to satisfy this guy's dreams of what an intelligence service is supposed to do. And we couldn't satisfy him, ever."

Halpern added in a separate interview, "They didn't have any ground rules as far as I knew." Years later, *New York Times* reporter Tad Szulc admitted his surprise in a memorandum-to-file that in a discussion with JFK: "Then, suddenly, Pres leaned forward and asked me 'What would you think if I ordered Castro to be assassinated?'"

Spymaster Harvey told the FBI in 1968 that the operation had been about "direct elimination, assassination": "Robert Kennedy was knowledgeable of the operation which had been devised by the CIA with the collaboration of Rosselli and his cohorts. . . . Kennedy is in an extremely vulnerable position if it were ever publicized that he condoned an operation which involved U.S. Government utilization of hoodlum elements."

The CIA's Helms separately concurred, saying, "There isn't any doubt who was running that effort. It was Bobby Kennedy on behalf of his brother" and "you haven't lived until you've had Bobby Kennedy rampant on your back." Helms also said, "It was made abundantly clear to everyone involved in the operation that the desire was to get rid of the Castro regime and to get rid of Castro. No limitations were put on this injunction."

Senator George Smathers, a JFK friend, said years later that the brothers had been aware of the Mafia component of the Castro elimination plan. On January 4, 1975, Henry Kissinger presciently warned President General Ford that the Castro plots were soon going to be uncovered, which they formally were in a Senate investigation. Kissinger told Ford, as noted in a now declassified "memorandum of conversation": "Helms said all these stories are just the tip of the iceberg. If they come out, blood will flow. For example, Robert Kennedy personally managed the operation on the assassination of Castro." At some point, the anti-Castro efforts continued but without the known assistance of organized crime.

WHAT GOES AROUND . . .

The problem came when the key mob figures in the Castro assassination plot got word that Bobby Kennedy was still coming after them. According to Russo, Giancana and Rosselli decided to "stand down," meaning they kept up the façade of going after Castro while dragging their feet. Knowing how important it was to the Kennedys to get rid of Castro, according to the wife of Outfit strategist Murray Humphreys, Giancana "decided to string them along to get even with them." Florida boss Trafficante, who was supposed to transfer the poison pills that were to be dropped in Castro's drink, claimed he just "flushed them down the toilet."

This is probably not all that Trafficante did. President George H. W. Bush was told that Trafficante knew the jig was up when Havana fell to Castro. The mobster had traded information about the assassination plots with the Cuban dictator in exchange for his looking the other way at his narcotics-running operation in the region. In early 1962, the spy Harvey gave Rosselli other poison pills for use against Castro in addition to fire-arms, explosives, and marine radar. Rosselli assured Harvey that action was being taken, but nothing came of it. FBI and CIA operative Ron Fino, whose father was a New York LCN boss, said that his father informed him that there had been dissent in mob circles about the anti-Castro operations and that, indeed, the key players purposely stalled.

Wrote author James Cockayne in his study *Hidden Power*:

> Many questions have been asked, including by U.S. Congress, about what the Kennedy brothers knew about all these efforts. The answers are highly revealing because they highlight the extent to which Mob and CIA methods converged—and the affinity between organized crime and covert state action more generally. Neither President Eisenhower nor President Kennedy ever gave a documented, explicit directive to assassinate Castro. . . . But both administrations recognized the importance of "plausible deniability" in tackling Castro: achieving the result without the U.S.' role being visible.

Cockayne added that given their oversight of the hearings on organized crime while JFK was in the Senate, "Indeed, both Kennedys were intimately aware of the steps taken by Mob leaders to insulate themselves from knowledge of operational details once they had given a general order for a hit."

Despite the failure of Operation Mongoose, the CIA didn't give up trying to exploit the unique abilities of organized crime. The Agency's Richard Bissell and Richard Helms approached Bill Harvey about developing a program code-named ZR/RIFLE, also known as "Executive Action," which would serve as "a general stand-by capability to carry out assassinations across the Agency's files." One of the problems with this idea is that contrary to fictional portrayals of cool, calculating hit men such as James Grady's Joubert in *Six Days of the Condor*,* most violent people are unstable characters who set their own policies, foreign, domestic, and personal. The CIA had to withdraw one of its assassins from the Congo where he had been sent to kill leader Patrice Lumumba when he proved to be an "unguided missile" with little interest in doing what he was told. Senator

---

*   The movie version was called *Three Days of the Condor*.

George McGovern, who investigated the CIA plots in the 1970s, commented on "the extreme incompetence of the people that were employed to do it [assassinate Castro]. It seems incredible that the most powerful country in the world could be so inept."

If Sam Giancana had been skeptical of the Castro operation initially, had he become a true believer or had he had something else in mind besides getting his casinos back? Based upon what we now know, he had probably been angling for leniency from future prosecutions, not to mention leverage over the government if he needed it. Giancana supported anti-Castro efforts that were not difficult, such as supplying names of potential assets in Cuba and perhaps weapons and safe houses. While there were attempts on Castro's life, it does not appear that Giancana took significant risks—such as dispatching Outfit killers that could be tied to him—to Havana. The evidence shows that any tactical heavy lifting fell to Rosselli. If, by some chance, the program yielded a dividend, that would be great; if it didn't, then maybe the feds would still tread lightly on the mob in the future.

Just because there was an effort to assassinate Castro and that effort involved scary people, it doesn't mean the mob gave it their best. As the 1960s chugged on, so did Rosselli's illegal activities and his vulnerability to prosecution. Giancana and Rosselli knew that the mob was kaput in Havana but wanted to buy themselves a little insurance. Before a Senate hearing, Maheu testified that Giancana had said, "You can't hit an entrenched leader like Castro but all they [the CIA] want from me is some names in Havana, so how can I turn them down?"

Feeling the noose tighten, Rosselli began making noises that if the CIA didn't help him with his immigration problems, he might be forced to talk more about his partnership with the government to kill Castro. At the crux of the blackmail was a new twist: Intelligence reports suggested that when Castro learned of the plots against him, the dictator put his own team together and tried to kill Kennedy. This came to be known as the "turnaround" theory. Given Kennedy's fate, this news story would not look good for the CIA or FBI, which had known about the program. Rosselli began to leak this scenario to prominent columnists, who covered it without attribution.

Initial news reports about the Castro plots began to trickle out in 1967. Columnist Drew Pearson met privately with President Lyndon Johnson

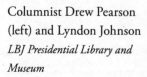

Columnist Drew Pearson
(left) and Lyndon Johnson
*LBJ Presidential Library and
Museum*

and told him about a story he was digging into involving RFK's complicity
in the kill-Castro campaign. Johnson encouraged Pearson to dig deeper,
worried about a challenge from Bobby Kennedy for the Democratic nomination the following year.

Pearson ran a lightly sourced column: "President Johnson is sitting
on a political H-bomb, an unconfirmed report that Sen. Robert Kennedy
may have approved an assassination plot which then possibly backfired
against his late brother."

LBJ himself came to believe that the Castro assassination plots had
come back to harm Kennedy and could have spiraled into a global,
even nuclear, war, which was one reason why he appointed the Warren
Commission to investigate Kennedy's death and pressured investigators
to reach its conclusions swiftly.

Pearson's column went nowhere. Other reporters didn't want to believe
that the martyred president's brother would be involved in an assassination
attempt. In addition, the "turnaround" theory appeared fantastical. LBJ,
nevertheless, prodded the CIA's inspector general to investigate the plot,
which it did in 1967. The report, which indeed implicated the Kennedy
brothers in Operation Mongoose* and related programs, was not declassi-

---

* The report also indicated that Vice President Richard Nixon had not played a
significant developmental role in the Castro assassination plans, as is often alleged.

fied until years later. It stated: "It's likely that at the very moment President Kennedy was shot a CIA officer was meeting with a Cuban agent in Paris and giving him an assassination device for use against Castro."

Wrote journalist and media professor Mark Feldstein, "Between 1962 and 1975, U.S. journalism both concealed and revealed the anti-Castro conspiracies." Moreover, the arrangements between Rosselli and the journalists were unique: "[Rosselli attorney] Edward P. Morgan's innovative strategy was to get the government to back off by threatening to expose its conspiracy to kill Castro—using the news media to deliver his (veiled) threat."

Rosselli wanted to be in a position where he could deny having spoken to a reporter, so, as Feldstein relates, he arranged a farce:

> But Anderson was allowed to pose questions to Rosselli's lawyer [Thomas Wadden], who then repeated them to his client. In turn, Rosselli directed his answers to his attorney, who then echoed them back to the reporter. Thus, Rosselli and Anderson could both truthfully state that they never talked to one another even as the journalist received the first-hand confirmation he needed to produce an accurate column.

The government's fear of being blackmailed by the mob was well-founded. The CIA's general counsel met with Immigration and Naturalization Service boss Raymond Farrell and Rosselli's CIA case officer. The case officer's report of that meeting concluded in safe bureaucratic language: "It was the commissioner's opinion that a good lawyer could keep proceedings in an administrative stage for many years; and in review of Rosselli's age, 66, it is highly [un]likely that he would be deported." "Administrative stage" being another word for deliberate, never-ending foot-dragging.

Similarly, the CIA intervened when the FBI wanted to prosecute Maheu and Giancana for illegally wiretapping entertainer Dan Rowan. The FBI stood down.* The last things Bobby Kennedy needed were disgruntled operatives and mobsters running to the press about why he had been doing business

---

* The FBI had been prolifically—and illegally—wiretapping mobsters, which may have played a role here, too.

with two of the FBI's top prosecution targets, Giancana and Trafficante. Not even JFK's famously protective press could have ignored this.

As for how the broader deal between the Kennedys and the mob went, the Kennedys had won an election and gained assets for the hit on Castro. Giancana got little but heartache. Yes, the Justice Department had declined to prosecute him for the Phyllis McGuire wiretap caper. Still, on the bigger things, the government never stopped hounding him, not even after Giancana was chased to Mexico. Rosselli got somewhat more for his Cuban participation (at least for a few years) given the help he got from the CIA when he faced deportation. The *New York Times* reported, "While Mr. Rosselli tried to use his CIA connections when he got into legal trouble, Mr. Giancana apparently did not."

DAYS BEFORE HE WAS SET TO TESTIFY BEFORE THE CHURCH COMMITTEE, Sam Giancana admitted someone he likely knew into his Oak Park, Illinois, house. He was cooking a dinner of sausage and peppers. When he turned his head toward the stove, his guest placed a muzzle-suppressed .22 pistol to the back of his head and pulled the trigger. Giancana collapsed onto the kitchen floor and his visitor, likely the Outfit's Butch Blasi, shot him multiple times in the mouth and five times below his chin. Some mob experts believe the shots in and around the mouth were a message about talking too much.

When his niece Carole Russo asked Jimmy Alo later in life what she thought had happened to Giancana, he said, "Well, Christ! He went around all over the country sayin' that he put John Kennedy in the White House!" Alo was right: Giancana had been recorded on bugs bragging that his assistance in the 1960 election had provided him influence with the Kennedy administration, which turned out to be a gross misreading of his position.

Just because Giancana thought it was a clever idea to get involved with the 1960 election and Operation Mongoose doesn't mean his Outfit board of directors, in the form of Anthony Accardo and Paul Ricca, had been thrilled with the direction things took. These were street guys who had no qualms about corrupting politicians toward specific ends but were grudgingly aware they were criminals with limited horizons as far as strategic partnerships with the people who were trying to imprison them were concerned. They never liked Johnny Rosselli and his Hollywood-Washington

Mob diplomat Johnny Rosselli was
the main underworld operative in
the assassination plot against Castro.
Castro survived. Rosselli didn't.
Los Angeles Times Photographic Archive,
UCLA Library Special Collections

aspirations, nor were they thrilled about Giancana playing around with
Las Vegas singers.

This ethic very much paralleled Lansky and Alo's reluctance to get
involved with the 1960 election on Kennedy's behalf. These legendary
gangsters preferred narrow, tactical partnerships where the path to profit
was more straightforward, especially if it allowed them to collect dirt on
the politicians in question. For their part, politicians had no trouble working with the mob *provided that the work remained private.*

Giancana's murder has never been solved, but most experts believe
his Outfit colleagues ordered it, the catalysts being his impending testimony and perhaps a suspicion that he had not been sharing the profits of
his Mexican gambling interests. His cooperation with the congressional
inquiries is the likelier explanation because his finances had been sharply
dwindling. The Outfit's chairman, Accardo, understood two things about
Giancana's position. One was that old men facing legal challenges would
do anything to avoid prison. The second is that sooner or later, people who
spend time with the feds can't resist horse trading to protect themselves.
Accardo wasn't about to take that chance.

John Rosselli testified with full immunity about his involvement in
Operation Mongoose before the Church Committee. Months later, he
testified again before the committee in a fishing expedition about possible
mob involvement in the JFK assassination. Senator Church said Rosselli
had not identified any of his mob cohorts.

Rosselli was called back to Washington, but before he could testify again his body was found floating in a fifty-five-gallon oil drum in a Miami bay. He had gone out on a yacht with cohorts who strangled him. His legs had been sawed off so that his body could fit into the drum, which likely wasn't supposed to surface. His abdomen had been sliced open neck to belly, presumably to allow gases to escape so the body wouldn't float to the surface.

As with Giancana's death, Rosselli's death is assumed to have been ordered by Outfit bosses but carried out by Florida's Santo Trafficante. The boys presumably didn't care for his penchant for testifying.

Simply because the CIA didn't appreciate Rosselli leaking allegations that Castro had a "turnaround" plot to kill Kennedy, it doesn't mean they would kill him, especially since his murder took place five years after the initial leaks. Far more likely was that Rosselli's ongoing dance with the government forced his Outfit colleagues to act.

There may be a subtle lesson in the fates of Giancana and Rosselli, namely that the efforts of a few mobsters don't necessarily reflect the agenda of the broader organization. By most accounts, these two men enjoyed playing spy. Just as men like Alo and Lansky had become averse to messing in national politics as they grew older, Outfit bosses disliked their colleagues' furtive meetings with representatives of the U.S. government. After all, avoiding attention from the government had been the modus operandi that had allowed some of the big shots to die of natural causes, free men, in old age. The Giancana and Rosselli murders hadn't been about Operation Mongoose per se; they were about the breadth of what these aging, ailing men could conceivably give up to stay out of prison.

As for the Church Committee, for all its exemplary investigative work, it also validated every 1970s paranoid conspiracy theory that would turn the Kennedy brothers into saints martyred by an assortment of Central Casting Bond villains. The committee concluded that JFK was most likely assassinated due to a conspiracy. Wrote Gus Russo: "The Committee essentially pretended that Jack Kennedy had no idea that Campbell [Judith Exner] was linked to the Mafia, that Kennedy himself was oblivious to the entire milieu. To believe otherwise would have taken the Kennedy-mob skeleton out of the closet."

Gangsters were angry with the Kennedys, but it didn't mean they were going to kill the president, given that the full wrath of the federal government would have descended upon them. Given what they knew about Kennedy's sexual escapades,* they could have just exposed or blackmailed him with none of the risks associated with murder. In fact, a source familiar with one such plan indicated that the mission of the Exner-Giancana-Kennedy trio was to obtain sexual dirt on JFK. According to FBI records: "REDACTED advised that he had heard that LCN [La Cosa Nostra] members had allegedly planned to attack the characters of U.S. Senators Edward and Robert Kennedy, as well as their brother-in-law, Peter Lawford. This was to be accomplished through associates of Frank Sinatra, who were to get the victims in compromising positions with women."

When LBJ heard about what the Kennedys had been up to with their Cuban campaign, he was shocked and said they were running "a damned Murder, Inc., in the Caribbean."

RECKONING

How do we reconcile the Kennedys attacking the mob while leveraging organized crime toward their purposes? Anyone who rises to the top of a field must make devil's bargains. Even those who don't lead nations must do things they don't like—work for bad bosses, handle unsavory people, pick battles, and choke down thorny compromises in relationships. What the Kennedys had been facing was playing out on a grander scale. Or, as JFK had once reconciled, a dad was helping his son. They were, after all, trying to lead the most powerful nation on Earth, and, in doing so, expediency would have to overwhelm ideal options. Mongoose hadn't been RFK's only devil's bargain: He had been both a champion of civil rights and the man who gave the nod to wiretap Martin Luther King, Jr.

As for the brothers' plot against Castro, this was war. While they may have preferred a removal method that didn't involve hoodlums, the Kennedys were realists; they had to use the weapons they had, and they had the Mafia. Cuba became an idée fixe for the Kennedy brothers and the American intelligence apparatus; Castro's continued existence, especially

---

* Lansky, according to his wife, had met JFK in Havana prior to his presidency and arranged for him to meet Cuban women. Kennedy apparently hadn't been interested in gambling.

after JFK's humiliation at the Bay of Pigs, was emasculating on a personal level—*If he's still in power, what kind of man am I if I can't knock him off?* Wrote underworld historian T. J. English: "Even so, Bobby's sometimes obsessive fascination with the Mafia seemed to contain an undercurrent of expiation—as if, by underscoring the fraternal Italian and Sicilian nature of organized crime in America, he was shifting the focus away from others (like his own father) who may have occasionally benefitted from or played a role in the underworld's conspiracy of evil."

"Jimmy Blue Eyes" Alo would have agreed with this analysis. He told his friends and family that RFK went after the mob to preemptively de-claw them lest they ever speak about their father's 1960 solicitation. Alo was so pleased when Bobby was assassinated that he went out and got drunk for the only time in his life.

It would be no surprise if RFK was both enthusiastic about killing Castro and ambivalent once he heard the brutally realistic details about how it would be done and who would do it.

The two Kennedy partnerships with the mob raise different questions about the extent to which the conspiracies grant the brothers moral or political cover. With the 1960 election, Joe Kennedy and his sons were pursuing power and glory. It's hard to justify their electoral mischief under the banner of "the public good."

Operation Mongoose was a different thing altogether. The United States was amid a Cold War with the Soviet Union that could have turned nuclear at any moment. Khrushchev had put atomic weapons in Cuba. Nobody thinks that killing a foreign leader is a nice thing to do, but against the backdrop of a global conflict, it shouldn't be off-limits to raise the question about its justification. Whatever the legality or morality surrounding Operation Mongoose, a national security matter needs to be evaluated with a different lens than an election.

There is an ironic component in the mob's Cuban adventure. It was in Cuba that the mob had hoped to go straight, which, paradoxi-cally, meant to control a foreign government legally. One of the ways Lansky had won Batista's support was to rid mob casinos of cheating. It didn't turn out well for anyone. The mob lost a fortune (Lansky never recovered), the major U.S. politicians involved with Cuba were snakebit, and a cruel Communist dictatorship has governed Cuba for over sixty years.

In 1960, JFK said, "There are two people I'd like to get out. Jimmy Hoffa and Castro." At the time of his death, he had gotten neither. Had his brother not been assassinated, would Bobby Kennedy have continued his attack on organized crime? Of course he would have.

Joe Sr.'s indulgence in mob services in the 1960 election was something Bobby could ignore because he hadn't participated. Operation Mongoose would have required a more potent mind trick because his complicity cannot be denied. Perhaps Bobby's expressed disapproval of mob recruitment took care of the mental contradiction, combined with his enlistment of Cuban exiles, so the campaign could be written off as warfare.

Neither RFK nor JFK had any experience being on the wrong end of the kind of political karma that most people in their line of work had to think about. How can one assess what else one can get away with when one is not even aware of ever having gotten away with anything in the first place? Put differently, the Kennedys opposed *and* leveraged the mob because they could.

During the McClellan hearings, Bobby had an uncharacteristically ill-prepared exchange with a mob figure without evidence to back up his charge. In an FBI memo, Hoover rejoiced in Bobby's pratfall, noting, "This is what happens when the prodigal son gets too far away from home and papa."

Do we forgive the Kennedys because they kept more layers between themselves and the mob and may not have had perfect awareness of what gangsters had done on their behalf? This is exactly what Joe would have wanted: He knew the value of insulation and plausible deniability in the crusade to keep his sons respectable. For whatever good the Kennedy brothers wanted to do, theirs was a world beyond the reach of consequences, one where their father could deal with gangsters for the benefit of his sons but keep those sons far enough removed from the skullduggery. Said Aristotle of the young: "They are high-minded, for they have not yet been humbled by life nor have they experienced the force of necessity."

All of that changed on November 22, 1963. RFK adviser John Seigenthaler "sensed in the months after JFK's assassination that Robert Kennedy seemed haunted as if he was holding something back." RFK biographer Evan Thomas reported that CIA chief John McCone "felt at the time that there was something troubling Kennedy that he was not disclosing." McCone knew something was amiss when he first saw RFK after the assassination, and the attorney general confronted him about whether the CIA had a hand in the murder, which a dumbfounded McCone denied. McCone "began to suspect that Kennedy felt personally guilty about the assassination." These sentiments came into focus in 1975 after the Church hearings revealed the Kennedy brothers' deep involvement in Operation Mongoose.

Sometime after JFK's murder, Bobby reflected, "I found out something I never knew. I found out my world was not the real world." Said Senator McClellan, "When Bob Kennedy left the Department of Justice, the organized program seemed to leave with him, it just seemed to fall apart."

THROUGH THE JFK ASSASSINATION LOOKING GLASS

A conspiracy is everything that ordinary life is not.
—Don DeLillo, *Libra*

I have deliberately avoided slipping into a debate about mob involvement in Kennedy's assassination in this book. Far too much ink has been spilled on this subject; I felt spilling too much more debating the facts would trigger a diversion that would be hard to contain. Nevertheless, I owe the reader an *opinion* on the matter given my subject.

The Kennedy assassination is no longer a historical event: It is a belief system, an American religion.

Authors and Redditors alike are so certain about the talents of the spectral plotters that they've come up with little but seeing dark shapes in trees, theoretical correlations, and puffs of smoke in the shadows since November 22, 1963. And if you don't believe that the Dark Ones are out there working their magic, you must be among their agents, likely compensated by the CIA or Mafia. As the saying on conspiracies goes, "You have to believe it to see it."

I think back to Senator George McGovern's comment about Operation Mongoose and "the extreme incompetence" that defined it. Yet the same coterie of thugs and nimrods who couldn't knock off the head of a banana republic managed to kill the leader of the free world and cover it up perfectly for more than six decades. *The mob that killed Kennedy and blackmailed J. Edgar Hoover into submission is the mob that our culture needed it to be, not the mob that was.*

An example of logical (and factual) silliness is the prominent theory that New Orleans boss Carlos Marcello ordered Kennedy's murder despite his having largely diversified into legitimate real estate holdings by the early 1960s. According to this theory, because Oswald had an uncle, Charles "Dutz" Murret, who had been a bookmaker in New Orleans decades earlier, Marcello (one of the least violent mob bosses on record) must have gotten to Oswald through this channel. Not only is there no proof that Murret ever knew Marcello, but during the time he was a bookmaker, Oswald was four years old. "So, Marcello had such a good memory and such foresight," said Gus Russo, "that he was able to deduce that a low-level bookmaker's toddler nephew might make a great presidential assassin in two decades and set his plan in motion."

My own brush with Marcello assassination lore came when Ed Becker (see Reagan chapter) told me about his discussion with the New Orleans boss. This conversation set off the everlasting rumor that Marcello ordered JFK's murder. I pressed Becker on an earlier allegation he had shared with federal investigators about Marcello suggesting he wanted President Kennedy dead and had intended to make his move. Becker confirmed that Marcello had told him this.

And then I made my mistake: Without thinking through the consequences of my question, I asked Becker earnestly, "Why would Marcello tell *you* this? Or was he just blowing off steam?" The avuncular man, then in his eighties, exploded. He told me that I had no idea what I was talking about and that I had been a baby when his conversation occurred. This was true, but I had never suggested that I had been privy to assassination-plotting when I was an infant.

I apologized for the way I had worded the question but had felt sorrier for having wounded an elderly man whom I liked—even though I thought my question had been reasonable. I reframed the question: "Marcello was a Mafia boss stating his intent to murder the president. He must have trusted you a lot." Becker calmed down and said something about this having been what he wanted Marcello to think and that he saw Becker as being part of their world enough to trust him. I ceased my inquiry, now feeling depressed about the whole exchange because I realized that the man sitting with me had launched an industry because of a need to position himself as a player in a huge historical event. Among Becker's claims was that Marcello had told him in Sicilian that he wanted to "take the stone out of my shoe." The problem is that Marcello was born in Tunisia, not Sicily, and had never spoken Sicilian or Italian, just a variation of Cajun English. It's a great story, though.

Gangster Jimmy "the Weasel" Fratianno was much more realistic about the Kennedy tragedy when speaking with his friend John Rosselli, who was convinced the Cubans had killed Kennedy. Fratianno said: "You know, Johnny, the more of this bullshit I read, the more I'm convinced that we've become scapegoats for every unsolved crime committed in this country. What's this mob the papers are always talking about, for Christ's sake? It's against the fucking rules to kill a cop, so now we're going to kill a president?"

In a discussion between Philadelphia LCN boss Angelo Bruno and ranking LCN members about an incident where a mobster got physical with an FBI agent, Bruno was shaken. The FBI had responded "off the books" with force. Bruno said: "They almost killed him [the hot-tempered hoodlum], the FBI. They don't do that, you know. But they picked up one of his fellows and they crippled him. They said 'this is an example. Now, the next time anybody lays a hand on an FBI man, that's just a warning. There is nothing else we got to tell you.'"

After Kennedy's assassination, a boss in another region, upstate New York's Stefano Magaddino, fearfully said that mobsters shouldn't even joke about the murder: "It's a shame we've been embarrassed before the whole world by allowing the president to be killed in our own territory [the United States]. You can be sure the police spies will be watching carefully to see what we think and say about this."

Wrote one scholar: "Kennedy's death has produced an endless number of plots . . . it has opened up an 'anarchy of possibilities'—

a reflection of the public's mass fears and aspirations and also a constant vehicle for discussing those sentiments."

Or, as Daniel Bell put it, "There is . . . in the American temper, a feeling that 'somewhere,' 'somebody' is pulling all of the complicated strings to which this jumbled world dances."

Also for consideration is the acid blinding of journalist Victor Riesel. In the early 1960s, the mob was still reeling from the McClellan hearings triggered partly by this event. McClellan's committee had almost ten times Kefauver's number of investigators, and the mob was running for cover. If this singular incident triggered such an overwhelming reaction by the federal government, one must imagine what the response of the feds would have been to the murder of the president of the United States in broad daylight.

Intrepid investigative reporter Sandy Smith of the *Chicago Tribune* (and later *Time*) had nailed scoop after scoop about the Chicago Outfit, even infiltrating the wedding of mob leaders' children, but the edict from Chairman Accardo was unequivocal: hands off Smith. The bosses didn't want the heat.

Mark Olshaker, author of the *Mindhunter* book and TV series on killers, told me: "With murders that are done for strategic purposes, you always must ask what was accomplished? Did the wife of the murdered husband collect on his life insurance policy? What would the mob have gained from Kennedy's murder? A ceaseless storm of certain prosecutions, imprisonment, the destruction of their children's lives, and likely death."

To Olshaker's point, the whole idea of enterprise crime is that the payoff exceeds the risk. Killing the president is all risk and no benefit, besides some vague and cinematic conceit about vengeance. Furthermore, as any good crook will explain, committing a crime is one-third of the battle, the other two-thirds being getting away with it. There is no practical chance that the same mob that botched a hit on a Third World dictator suddenly turned into James Bond–like ninjas and killed the most powerful man in the world and kept it perfectly silent for more than six decades—with every ambitious investigative reporter and headline-seeking prosecutor on the hunt for them.

Oswald, on the other hand, was a textbook assassin, said Olshaker, a violent loner of average intelligence and abysmal self-esteem buoyed by grandiose notions of being a historical figure—and seeking a vessel to deliver him to greatness. Said Olshaker:

Oswald thinks he'll find a socialist paradise in Russia then ends up working a menial job at a radio factory in Belarus. Not exactly the dream he had for himself. He attempts suicide, fails. Tries to become a Cuban revolutionary, fails. Gets married, fails, and routinely beats his wife. Gets jobs, fails. Tries to kill General [Edwin] Walker, fails. Tries to have sex with his wife the night before the assassination, she brushes him off. *This* is the guy the Mafia and the CIA is going to pick as their patsy? The guy kept a diary!

Olshaker adds that Oswald, contrary to conspiracy theories, was a very good rifle shot operating in a small space in Dealey Plaza. He quotes a Secret Service agent in Dallas: "That day, Oswald had all the luck, and we had none."

Organized crime had nothing to do with Kennedy's murder. Many mobsters were thrilled with the assassination, of course, and "they talked about it all the time," said FBI agent Bill Roemer, Jr. Hoover may have been slow to prosecute the mob, but after Apalachin, he wasn't asleep at the wheel regarding surveillance. By this time, Hoover knew he had to do something and began illegally wiretapping major mob figures, not for prosecutorial purposes but for intelligence gathering. Illegal FBI wiretaps were operational during the assassination and "listening on a minute-to-minute basis." In addition to comprehensive physical surveillance, the FBI was electronically eavesdropping on its targets in the headquarters of precisely the same Mafiosi suspected of Kennedy's murder. The sheer volume of recordings of top Outfit leaders alone makes one wonder how they got anything secret done.

The feds found nothing indicating that anyone in the mob's orbit had anything to do with the crime. Said Roemer, "Lee Harvey Oswald was the sole shooter . . . there was no conspiracy whatsoever." NYPD organized crime detective Ralph Salerno agreed:

Since that time [the JFK assassination] . . . up to the current day, you have had a large number of high-level members of organized crime [who] . . . have made a deal with the government and testified against their fellows, and were . . . debriefed on all of their knowledge. None of them has ever suggested that they knew of, or even heard of involvement by organized crime in the death of President Kennedy. . . . I listened to thousands of pages of electronic surveillances of organized crime leaders all over the United States. Over 360 volumes.

It wasn't until years later that the mob rumors started because gangland chiefs, having achieved sufficient distance from the tragedy, started bragging about how the big event had unfolded, suggesting they had arranged it. As Philip Roth said, "The big money is in fairy tales." Or, as a JFK author friend told me, "No conspiracy theory, no book contract."

THE WRATH OF THE GOVERNMENT

When working on another book dealing with the Soviet spy world, a former KGB agent asked me if I had heard the theory that the CIA had killed Kennedy. I said I had, even though I thought the CIA theory was even more preposterous than the Mafia one. He asked me if I knew where that theory had come from. I said I didn't know. He palmed my forehead like the Three Stooges and said in a thick Russian accent, "What do you think we were doing in the sixties and seventies? We were running around paying left-wing writers to say it was CIA!" I asked him who he thought killed Kennedy. He said, "We knew who did it! Fucking idiot Oswald!" Then he said slyly, "But there was no money in this."

Other experts had affirmed that Khrushchev was panicked when he learned that Oswald had spent time in the Soviet Union and specifically feared the revelation leading to a world war. The new president, Lyndon Johnson, shared Khrushchev's concern. The driving aim of the administration after that was moving past any examination of the Oswald-Soviet ties that could trigger a world war. This does not mean, however, that there was a conspiracy to murder the president.

Then there is the fever dream that Oswald's killer, Jack Ruby, was a gangland operative other than a loud-talking wannabe looking for his moment to be the ultimate badass. It was the emergence of Ruby that sparked speculation that there was a mob connection to the assassination, said Warren Commission staff member Howard Willens. Willens added that upon investigation "there was no internal dispute" among Commission staff that Ruby was a gangland operative. If Ruby were a mob asset, under the definitions being used, then the very *jabroni* I saw as a kid on the boardwalk with a toothpick hanging out of his mouth and who "knew a guy" was "connected," too. I don't think I knew *anyone* growing up in New Jersey who wasn't one person removed from a mob connection—but this doesn't necessarily mean anything.

The FBI had plenty on Oswald. Still, they were unable to stop him. *Herein lies the real conspiracy—to cover up bureaucratic incompetence, the assassination caper against Castro, and prevent a war with Russia.* The government—the CIA and FBI specifically—had played cute in its *investigation* into Kennedy's murder, according to Willens. Hoover needed cover given that the FBI had had Oswald on their radar and failed to stop him. Given some of Oswald's pre-assassination activities, it would be easy to assume that Oswald was engaging in activities that could *appear* to be tied to the assassination. He had, after all, traveled to the Cuban and Soviet embassies in Mexico City in the weeks prior to the assassination in a deluded attempt to become the Communist James Bond. Nevertheless, it was discovered after Kennedy's murder that Oswald had written to the FBI threatening violence if they didn't stop harassing his wife about Oswald's Communist ties. It is highly unlikely that the mob (or anyone) would employ an operative who openly threatened the FBI prior to undertaking a presidential assassination.

The real conspiracy around the assassination was a damage control exercise by Hoover and the CIA, the latter of which didn't want their Operation Mongoose adventures to surface—and they didn't for a dozen years. The FBI director was aware of the Kennedy brothers' operation to kill Castro and never disclosed it to the

Warren Commission. It would have been a good lead to chase, confirmed Willens, who would have chased it. Willens believes that Hoover's failure to raise this added kindling to conspiracy theories.* Wrote G. Robert Blakey: "If nothing else, the proximity of the period of the Castro plots [Rosselli's last-known meeting with CIA officer William Harvey was in June 1963] to the assassination implied a degree of significance that might have altered the course of the Commission's investigation, if not its ultimate outcome."

The CIA and Bobby Kennedy did not want there to be too deep an exploration of Operation Mongoose, which would not be officially exposed for another dozen years. RFK was so concerned about Mongoose surfacing that he arranged for his friend, former CIA chief Allen Dulles, to serve on the Warren Commission to ensure it didn't enter the discussion—the very same Dulles who conspiracy theorists have outrageously asserted was involved in JFK's assassination. Wrote Michael Isikoff of Yahoo News shortly after the latest batch of JFK assassination documents were released in what is perhaps the best summary: "What emerges from this account is not so much a portrait of CIA officials horror-struck that their role in the president's murder might be exposed but of government bureaucrats scrambling to find details about the accused assassin and cover themselves, no doubt worried that they might be blamed for not paying more attention to him before the murder."

In the meantime, the prison of belief trumps all. Or, as historian William Manchester wrote: "If you put the murdered President of the United States on one side of a scale and that wretched waif Oswald on the other side, it doesn't balance. You want to add something weightier to Oswald. It would invest the President's death with meaning, endowing him with martyrdom. He would have died for something. . . . A conspiracy would, of course, do the job nicely."

---

* Willens added that it was later determined that Hoover had, in fact, quietly disciplined seventeen FBI agents for failing to properly investigate Oswald. Willens also believed that it had been a tactical mistake to have former CIA chief Allen Dulles, who had been involved with Operation Mongoose, serve on the Warren Commission because it unnecessarily aggravated conspiracy theories.

5

Lyndon B. Johnson

THE GRIM REAPER COMES TO THE RESCUE

I know your kind, he said. What's wrong with you
is wrong all the way through you.

—Cormac McCarthy, *Blood Meridian*

Lyndon Johnson's administration let loose one of the most cunning and vicious psychopaths in the annals of organized crime. What might have inspired such a thing for a presidency not associated with gangland? Amazingly, the cause for employing a stone-cold gangster known as "the Grim Reaper" was LBJ's greatest achievement: civil rights.

One of the most significant developments in the history of organized crime was also to occur on LBJ's watch—the first LCN member to publicly acknowledge the organization's existence on national television, Joseph Valachi. There were also sleazy sideshows during the Johnson administration involving the president's personnel, namely the misadventures of his onetime aide, Bobby Baker. Baker's venality reached into many dark corners of the American economy, including brushes with organized crime. We'll first look at Baker, whom JFK had once referred to as "the 101st senator" before we spend time with the Grim Reaper.

SEX, SLEAZE, AND BOBBY BAKER

Shortly after being elected to the Senate in 1948, Lyndon Johnson spoke to a twenty-year-old hustler on the telephone. "Mr. Baker, I understand you know where the bodies are buried in the Senate. I'd appreciate it if you'd come to my office and talk with me."

At the time, Bobby Baker had been a staffer to the Senate leadership, a lubricant in the engine of legislation. Wrote the *Washington Post* in Baker's 2017 obituary, "His vast knowledge of the operations of the Senate and his facility in the art of accommodation—moving pet legislative projects ahead for some senators or helping fulfill the proclivities of others for drink, sex or cash—would make him an invaluable asset to Johnson."

While still a very young Senate aide, the wheeler-dealer assembled a net worth of about $2 million, $20 million today, an impressive but unlikely achievement on an annual salary of $19,600. Baker had bank deposits alone of $1.5 million.

Even though Johnson ostensibly cut ties with Baker after news of his mischief broke, the allegations that poured out were so lurid that the story wouldn't die. Among them was Baker's ownership of the Maryland Carousel Motel where women such as Ellen Rometsch, the suspected German spy, cavorted with politicians and military personnel.

The mob enters the picture at several points. For one, Baker accompanied Vice President Johnson to the February 1963 inauguration of Juan Bosch, the first freely elected president of the Dominican Republic. Among the other VIP attendees were Philadelphia Cosa Nostra boss Angelo Bruno and Edward Levinson, a gambling partner of Meyer Lansky. These men could have been there for only one reason: to scout opportunities for mob-owned hotel casinos.

Baker had also been doing business with men actively watched by the FBI. President Kennedy knew it and had warned LBJ about his friend. Johnson explained that he had not been Baker's boss in a few years. He was being cute: The two men had met or spoken fifty times during this period. JFK shouldn't have been one to talk because he had been concurrently passing the time with Rometsch and Judith Exner, the girlfriend he shared with Outfit gangster Sam Giancana. Nevertheless, a Kennedy is a

Kennedy; there were rules for Kennedys and rules for plebians. JFK was more focused on the risks posed by Baker than by Exner and Giancana, telling Johnson, "I'm very distressed that Bobby Baker has been having conversations with some bad people out at Las Vegas and some bad people over at the Dominican embassy, some bad people down at . . . Miami and I think you ought to get him to resign." Johnson had been given the same warning by his friend J. Edgar Hoover who had illegally placed eavesdropping devices all over Las Vegas.

During this period, mob involvement in Las Vegas was an open secret, but very little had been done to prove that underworld investments were prosecutable crimes. Bobby Kennedy intended to change that. Among the things that DOJ was examining was that Baker "had acted as an intermediary in [sic] behalf of a prominent Las Vegas gambler who had extensive associations with notorious underworld figures." The suspicion was that in addition to advancing mob-run casinos in the Dominican Republic, Baker had been bringing gangland figures such as Ed Levinson into other business deals, such as a vending company he owned called Serv-U. It turned out that Levinson indeed had a financial interest in Serv-U.

All of this was a very big deal because Baker's links were coming to the fore when the Genovese family soldier Joe Valachi announced the Mafia's real name in 1963 on national TV, responding to a question about being a member of a criminal organization by confirming its name, Cosa Nostra. This meant "our thing" or "our family" in English. Valachi pronounced it "cause-uh nostra" in a thick New York accent. He explained there was a boss, a "*sottocapo*," or underboss, "consigliere," or adviser who also adjudicates disputes in a family, "*caporegimes*," or lieutenants, and soldiers. Valachi described his initiation with the Genovese family or "*borgata*" and how the boss "went on to explain that you live by the gun and knife and you die by the gun and knife."

Cosa Nostra. Valachi defined the fraternity of gangsters in a manner so specific that it was impossible to refute—so much so that Attorney General Kennedy called for sophisticated new surveillance methods and laws to support "the legitimate needs of law enforcement for authority, closely circumscribed, to use this means of gathering evidence."

Wrote historian Jonathan Marshall of the impact of the Valachi hearings on the Baker scandal: "Unfortunately for Johnson, these hearings

LBJ aide Bobby Baker wheeled and dealed with miscreants, including mob-connected characters.
AP Photo

highlighted the significance of Baker's ties to front men for the syndicate. FBI bugs revealed that several secret partners of Baker . . . Levinson, his Miami business partner Benjamin Sigelbaum, and Miami investor Jack Cooper—were senior associates of Meyer Lansky and other hoodlums."

One of Baker's other investment partners had ties to Cleveland Syndicate leader Moe Dalitz, who now owned the Desert Inn in Las Vegas. Nor could Baker's association with Levinson be passed off as a fleeting handshake; these men knew each other well and Levinson was unequivocally an associate of the biggest gambling racketeers in the country. The media began reporting on a multimillion-stock fraud involving Baker and Levinson, and Kennedy's DOJ was now looking into it. Additional reporting tied Baker partner Sigelbaum to a massive casino "skimming" operation, alleging that Sigelbaum was a courier delivering cash to Swiss banks and distributing it to mobsters nationwide.

Lyndon Johnson was in such serious trouble over the scandal that specific names were being bandied about in mid-November 1963 to replace him as vice president on the ticket in 1964. Hilariously, even Meyer Lansky was appalled, writing in a journal of the Baker scandal: "the Senate Ethics committee . . . hasn't raised a finger." This is especially amusing because Lansky's widow found Baker's business card in an old wallet soon after her husband died. JFK's secretary told LBJ biographer Robert Caro that "the ammunition to get him off [the ticket] was Bobby Baker." Even Baker's resignation from the Senate did not defuse the tension. The only thing that did was the president's trip to Dallas. After Kennedy was assassinated, national grief consumed both the news and politics, and even the new president's opposing party lost the will to chase the scandal to the doorstep of the Johnson White House. In 1965, LBJ shut down the bugging of LCN figures. FBI Agent William Roemer believed this was because of his concern that Baker's mob ties would again come back to bite Johnson.

The Texan was about to face a new set of challenges.

MISSISSIPPI BURNING

On July 2, 1964, President Lyndon Johnson signed the Civil Rights Act, which was to become the crowning achievement of his presidency and arguably his life. This happened in the wake of a steady stream of violence against African Americans, not to mention a few centuries of savage mistreatment that contradicted the principles the United States was founded upon. The consensus among even historians who have no great love for LBJ is that his political skills, not to mention his southern credentials, made this happen. Given his colossal ambition and his relegation to the shadows during President Kennedy's administration, it was now Johnson's moment.

Johnson's achievement was quickly sabotaged by publicity surrounding the disappearance of three civil rights workers—James Chaney, Andrew Goodman, and Michael Schwerner. The men had gone to Philadelphia, Mississippi, to investigate the burning of the Mount Zion African American church as part of the Mississippi Summer Project. More than one thousand volunteers traveled to the southern state to register Black voters. It was later determined that after a town sheriff had arrested the civil rights workers, he contacted the local Klan and informed them that one of the men, Schwerner, nicknamed "Goatee," was among them. Schwerner had been a death target for the Klan's imperial wizard. Not long after this event, a crew of Klansmen trailed the activists, led by the sheriff, to Rock Cut Road, pulled them over, and executed them.

Hoover initially characterized the disappearances as "a local affair."

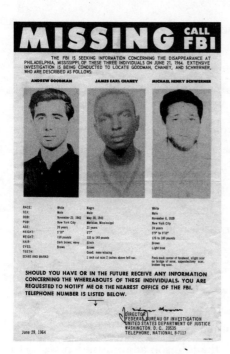

A flyer distributed by the
FBI during the 1964 search
for civil rights workers
missing in Mississippi
Federal Bureau of Investigation

President Johnson, however, was frantic about the disappearance and took personal command of the response. Audiotapes depict a furious Johnson demanding, "Fill up Mississippi with FBI men and infiltrate everything you could!" He then gave the FBI a "standing order" to do what was necessary to solve the case.

Hoover, increasingly concerned about his own political survival in this new era, given his not-so-subtle hostility to the civil rights movement, opened a new case code-named MIBURN for Mississippi Burning and dispatched resources to the southern state. He also went to Jackson and dedicated the opening of an FBI field office.

Hoover and Lyndon Johnson had lived diagonally across the street from each other for many years. They were as close friends as two Machiavellians could possibly be and trusted each other as deeply as one could in such relationships. LBJ even named his dog J Edgar. In Washington, if you're going to take a big risk or cross a line with someone, it pays to do it with someone with whom you have a history.

Hoover personally updated Johnson. Some of these discussions were recorded and preserved.* The briefings got into detail, including the intense heat that burned the activists' car. It turned out that Chaney, Goodman, and Schwerner had been removed from the vehicle before they were killed. It was feared that the fire may have burned up the bodies of the three men completely.

When Johnson queried, his voice filled with anxiety, whether the civil rights workers might have been kidnapped, then taken and held somewhere, Hoover responded, "I would doubt those people down there would give them that much of a break." He also urged the president to not "give the details of the number of agents that we've got" when meeting with Members of Congress. LBJ stressed that Hoover needed to go over and above his usual aggressive tactics and gather intelligence "better than you've got on the communists. They can't open their mouths without you knowing what they said," which Hoover confirmed. The president underscored his mindset, instructing Hoover that, given what needed to be done, "Nobody needs to know it but you."

Complicating matters was that the Johnson administration was getting no help from authorities based in Mississippi. U.S. Senator James Eastland, an opponent of civil rights, waved LBJ off by dismissing the disappearance as a "publicity stunt." Nevertheless, the pressure was so acute that Johnson ordered the Department of Defense to send personnel to Mississippi to scour the woods and fields. Attorney General Robert F. Kennedy consulted former CIA director Allen Dulles (who was very much aware of his agency's earlier efforts to depose Castro in Cuba) on traveling to the state to become an independent observer reporting back to Kennedy.

There was ample political motivation to do something extraordinary to find Chaney, Goodman, and Schwerner and see that justice was done. LBJ and Hoover had known that JFK used mobsters to try to kill Fidel Castro, however feckless that effort proved to be. It should have come as no surprise then that American leaders thought of employing gangsters when confronting a challenge closer to home. The 1960s would become a time when the FBI would go beyond traditional boundaries in areas

---

* LBJ, like JFK before him (and Nixon afterward), had a hidden audiotaping system in the Oval Office.

including the illegal wiretapping of gangsters and "subversives" and using creative methods of intelligence gathering and infiltrations.

What happened next is the subject of division and confusion. Some in the civil rights community have argued that their contacts in the region provided information that cracked the case while popular culture in films such as the 1988 *Mississippi Burning* gave dogged FBI sleuthing the credit. The FBI also prefers this version. Neither group seems keen on discussing the likely role of one of the most vicious gangsters in Cosa Nostra history.

Enter the living embodiment of brute force, the Colombo family's Gregory Scarpa.

666

Scarpa was quite a piece of work. In a world of racketeers—selectively violent enterprise criminals—Scarpa was a bloodthirsty gangster who killed dozens of people, including a young woman suspected of being a snitch. Some estimates report that Scarpa may have killed as many as two hundred people but admitted he "stopped counting after fifty." Standing five feet ten inches and weighing in at 210 pounds, he was known equally for his avuncular smile and his menacing sneer. His headquarters was at Brooklyn's ironically named Wimpy Boys Social Club. There isn't much undercover video footage of Scarpa, but one clip shows the killer, unaware he was being observed, snarling menacingly while working a toothpick across his lips. When Scarpa wanted to speak with his associates, he paged them and identified himself with "666," numerals associated with Satan.

Among his other delights, Scarpa has been suspected of involvement in the murder of his brother for thinking he was a rat. Scarpa was married to three women at the same time and when he found out that a local kid, Larry Mazza, had been sleeping with his youngest wife, not only did he *not* kill him but he also gave him permission to keep up the affair and adopted him like a son, taking him into his gang.

Said Scarpa's former attorney, Louis Diamond: "He killed a lot. He was nuts . . . Greg was an absolutely fearless man who enjoyed killing, and enjoyed vengeance. And enjoyed the subtlety. He would smile at a guy, take him out to dinner, and blow his brains out."

Scarpa had once been hauled before Senator John McClellan's rackets committee in 1971. While the senator may have known Scarpa's reputation as a killer, he would not have known about his status as a confidential informant. On this day, Scarpa was displaying a face different from his Wimpy Boys snarl. In the hearing, he was grinning broadly, prompting McClellan to inquire about why the mobster appeared so jaunty.

"Why are you smiling?" McClellan asked.

"I smile because you, too, have a pleasant smile, Senator," Scarpa answered like a jovial lion playing with a baby antelope before he popped the little creature into his mouth. Scarpa, nevertheless, invoked his Fifth Amendment rights sixty times.

The Colombo family—called Profaci when Scarpa joined—was at that time the most dysfunctional of the New York five families. Upstarts, led by Crazy Joe Gallo, challenged founding father Joseph Profaci by igniting a war in the early 1960s, which still plays out today. Gallo promoted himself as a shooter in the landmark hit on Albert Anastasia (he was probably lying), dubbed "the Lord High Executioner of Murder, Inc." while sitting in a barber's chair at the Park Sheraton hotel in Manhattan in 1957. The crime has never been solved, but the Gallo brothers were dubbed the "barbershop quartet," a reputation they did nothing to knock down. This was one of the mob's most frequently employed devices—taking credit via indirection and playful allusions, whether you did the deeds or not.

The FBI tapped the Colombo Mafia family's most prolific killer, informant Greg Scarpa, to help solve civil rights crimes in Mississippi. Ku Klux Klansmen found him very persuasive.
Danvis Collection/Alamy Stock Photo

Boss Joseph Profaci had run a successful olive oil business, which was used to inform the hybrid *Godfather* character of Don Vito Corleone. The boss was known to be a devout Catholic with a private chapel in his home. Profaci was generous with his church but had a unique take on the Ten Commandments. In the 1950s, a local thief stole a bejeweled crown from the head of a Jesus statue in the Regina Pacis Roman Catholic Church in Brooklyn where the Profacis belonged. Profaci's men hunted down the thief, known as "Bucky," who was found strangled to death with rosary beads soon after. We do not know if the statue of the Savior received His crown back, but we do know that this was the spiritually unique environment into which Greg Scarpa joined the family and became its ace killer.

The stress of the Mafia civil war weakened Profaci, and he died of cancer in 1964. After interim management, leadership finally fell to Joseph Colombo, who later drew a great deal of attention by establishing the Italian American Civil Rights League, which was anchored in the premise that the FBI's war on the mob was a harassment campaign against decent, hardworking Italians. Honorable Italians were horrified by this spectacle, as were not-so-decent ones such as the predominant New York boss, Carlo Gambino, who thought the League was bringing too much attention to a fraternity that operated best in the shadows. Colombo was shot by a Black man (likely chosen to distract attention from LCN) with news media credentials at a League rally at Columbus Circle. The assassin, Jerome Jackson, was killed immediately by a Colombo gunman. Joe Colombo fell into a coma and lingered seven more years. No one believes that Jackson acted without a sponsor, which is widely assumed to have been Gambino hiding behind multiple layers, as he always did.

Scarpa had become an FBI informant on the heels of a hijacking arrest in 1959. Likely, the charges against him were dropped in exchange for him becoming a confidential informant in 1960. He didn't become especially active until 1961, which is significant for a few reasons. First was the breakthrough in the war against organized crime that came with the testimony of Genovese family turncoat Joseph Valachi, who named the Five Families of New York and their leaders and explained the everyday workings of the enterprise.

Not every Kennedy DOJ official believed that Valachi's testimony was the ultimate exercise in transparency. Jack Rosenthal, a public information officer for RFK (and later *New York Times* journalist), wrote the following after reviewing the DOJ report draft on Valachi: "Probably the biggest question of all, which may not be asked literally, but which might well be widely wondered about, is: Why is the administration saying all this now? If it didn't know before, why didn't it, in view of all the hullabaloo about progress against organized crime. If it didn't know before, why didn't it do something?"

Despite the seismic significance of Valachi, he had not been the first major turncoat. He was the first major turncoat *to go on television* with his story. Greg Scarpa was one of the original whales in the snitch department even though nobody knew about it for thirty years. One can debate which does more damage, snitching before the world or snitching behind closed doors, but Scarpa was classified as a "Top Echelon Criminal Informant" in March 1962 and went on the FBI's payroll. Hoover himself, under pressure to crack down on the mob, personally reviewed reports on Scarpa, who began providing information immediately. He never stopped committing crimes, including murders, as he gave up his rivals at a great clip.

Scarpa didn't just betray his gangland rivals; he betrayed his bosses, too. Scarpa had aligned himself with the man who would become the Colombo boss for decades, Carmine Persico. This gave Scarpa a working blueprint for the entire Colombo family, a bonanza for the FBI. In addition, Scarpa kept the FBI abreast of peace negotiations within the warring Colombos, not to mention the players in the Gambino and Genovese families seeking to influence the civil war.

Now, as Lyndon Johnson faced one of the great crises of his presidency, Greg Scarpa was the incarnation of Piker Ryan sent down to Mississippi to deal with America's most acute civil rights problem.

THE DEVIL GOES DOWN TO DIXIE

Before calling on Scarpa immediately after the three activists went missing in 1964, the bureau tried talking to the Mississippians directly. Nevertheless, contrary to the law-and-order reputation of many southerners, this sentiment didn't apply to federal authorities. The FBI was viewed as agents of a government passing judgment and seeking to destroy their way of life via legislation and aggressive enforcement. Very few Mississippians of that era were willing to be helpful to the FBI. A dislike of "rats" wasn't just a New York phenomenon.

The FBI realized the news in Mississippi hadn't been good when the activists' blue Ford station wagon was found. It had been burned. No bodies were discovered. The FBI frantically searched for the bodies for more than a month to no avail. It was time to try something else. Or some*body* else.

In one account, Scarpa flew to Mississippi with his young girlfriend, Linda Schiro, and checked into a motel. There are a few different versions of what happened next. Still, it began with the FBI, knowing whom the key area Klansmen were. Scarpa, supplied with a government-issued handgun, kidnapped a prominent Klansman, "put the gun in his mouth and threatened to 'blow his fucking brains out' if he didn't spill the beans." Beans were spilled.

A related version was shared years after the events by Judge W. O. "Chet" Dillard, a former Mississippi state's attorney, whose research concluded that the Klansman Scarpa kidnapped had also been a local mayor. Scarpa worked him over, but the mayor lied. Scarpa wasn't pleased when the FBI told him he had been snookered, so he paid the official another visit. This time, Scarpa wielded a straight razor, held it between the man's legs, and suggested he would soon be singing falsetto. Having been beaten and had a gun jammed in his mouth, the mayor's memory began clarifying. He shared the location of the earthen dam where the three men's bodies were soon discovered seventeen feet below the surface on August 4, 1964. They had all been shot, but Chaney, the Black man, had also been bludgeoned.

For his work, Scarpa received an envelope filled with cash from an FBI agent. Scarpa then took Schiro on a vacation to Miami Beach, where they upgraded from their Mississippi digs to the Fontainebleau Hotel. His compensation has been estimated at $30,000 in legal documents.

During Scarpa's decades as a snitch, the FBI contracted the work to him because they knew that there were deeds from Piker Ryan's list of services that they could not readily perform themselves. *Mr. Hoover, did your men beat a confession out of any of the suspects? Absolutely not . . .* No, the more pleasant versions of the investigation are that (1) a thorough inspection of potential crime scenes led the FBI to have a strong hunch that *this* was the spot and (2) an informant was simply paid to give up the location of the slain civil rights workers' graves.

In 1967, trials on the 1964 civil rights charges—not murder—resulted in seven convictions, eight not guilty verdicts, and three mistrials. None were tried for murder until four decades later when Edgar Ray Killen was convicted of manslaughter in 2005 at eighty. In the lead-up to the trial, the FBI affirmed its policy of protecting the identity of confidential informants in ongoing investigations. Winning the civil rights era's award for chutzpah, Killen eventually sued the FBI for violating *his* civil rights. Killen's attorney wrote, "The information that Scarpa obtained by use of torture violates Killen's civil rights . . . [his] rights to due process [and] the right to confront witnesses." Counsel Robert Ratliff referenced "typical Mafia-type behavior" and "the use of intimidation of potential witnesses, pistol-whipping actual witnesses, and assaulting other local residents." The suit also claimed that Killen's defense counsel at that time, Clayton Lewis, was also allegedly an FBI informant who provided the FBI with information about defense strategy.

Killen died in prison in 2018 at age ninety-two. In 2016, the Justice Department officially closed the MIBURN case. It stated in its report to the Mississippi attorney general: "There is no written record of this source [who provided the tip on the location of the bodies]. The only FBI agent who knew the source's identity is now deceased." In other words, no mention of the Grim Reaper, Scarpa.

THE FBI WASN'T DONE WITH SCARPA IN MISSISSIPPI. VERNON DAHMER, A Hattiesburg shopkeeper, had allowed his place of business to be used for voter registration. On January 10, 1966, Klansmen in multiple cars carrying firearms and gallons of gasoline ambushed Dahmer at his house and set it ablaze. Dahmer fired his shotgun at the attackers, which allowed his family to escape, but Dahmer didn't survive. The KKK had targeted him for a "Project 3" (arson) and/or "Project 4" (murder) in Klan-speak. The group had been especially offended by Dahmer because he could quickly be taken for being white, an underhanded attack on the purity of the race.

No leads were forthcoming. The Johnson administration was feeling the pressure, and the FBI wasn't getting anywhere, which, again, had led to allegations of Hoover not prioritizing civil rights. President Johnson sent condolences via telegram to the Dahmer family, and the attorney general vowed to take swift action. An internal FBI memo from the Jackson, Mississippi, FBI field office to New York office of Assistant Director John Malone dated January 21, 1966, requested the assistance of "the informant and enough money to cover expenses for hotel room and transportation for the SA [Special Agent], plus two individuals. . . . The informant should leave Monday." The memo referenced that the informant's wife would join him on the trip, consistent with Linda Schiro's version of the events. One of those individuals accompanying Scarpa was an FBI agent who had played a role in Scarpa's informant relationship in New York and picked the mobster up at the airport in Mobile, Alabama. They drove an hour and a half to Hattiesburg.

According to former Mississippi state's attorney Dillard's memoir about his experiences as an official during the civil rights movement, Scarpa and an associate, wearing disguises, arrived at Byrd's Radio and

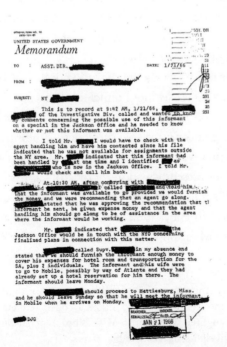

A redacted 1966 FBI memo requesting the assistance of an informant on a "special" assignment related to the murder of Vernon Dahmer in Hattiesburg, Mississippi. That informant was almost surely Greg Scarpa.

Federal Bureau of Investigation

TV Service owned by Klansman Lawrence Byrd. They purchased a TV and indicated they wanted to load it into their car in the rear. According to Dillard, Scarpa beat Byrd "within an inch of his life." A subsequent FBI memo described Byrd as "in a state of semi-shock." One month later, Byrd confessed to his involvement in the Dahmer murder and identified seven other Klansmen as having participated in the arson and killing.

In 1998, the imperial wizard of a Mississippi KKK chapter was convicted of killing Vernon Dahmer. His name was Samuel Bowers, and this had not been his lone atrocity. His White Knights (KKK) group had been responsible for "300 beatings, arsons and bombings," according to one report, and nine murders. He had already served six years in prison for being among the men who had murdered Chaney, Goodman, and Schwerner. An ostentatious racist, Bowers had been operating the Sambo Amusement Company, a vending machine distributor.

Over the years, there has been conflation between the 1964 MIBURN and 1966 Dahmer cases, something that an FBI source recently confirmed. Lawrence Byrd has been identified as an informant in both the MIBURN case and the Dahmer murder, which may be true. However, it is only sometimes apparent in the accounts to which case the testimony is referring. While both cases involve Scarpa as the operative in these versions, sometimes the source has Byrd providing information solving the MIBURN murders, and other times Dahmer.*

One would not expect the FBI to clarify the confusion or acknowledge that it used Scarpa to resolve the Mississippi homicides. Indeed, there is no documentation in FBI files confirming that Scarpa, by name, played a role. The bureau's long-standing policy is to avoid surrendering information about its confidential informants even after their deaths, and understandably so. It's very likely that no one presently working at the FBI has firsthand proof of what Scarpa did or didn't do. Some of the most vivid details of the operation come from Scarpa's girlfriend, Linda Schiro, who testified about having accompanied Scarpa to Mississippi. While Schiro was under oath,

---

* Former FBI agent Anthony Villano, Scarpa's first FBI handler, has yet another version of events where a mob informant he calls "Julio," a coded reference to Scarpa (confirmed by Scarpa's daughter), was sent to Mississippi to persuade witnesses to give up the killer of civil rights activist Medgar Evers.

which gives her some credibility, she may also have reasoned that there was no likely mechanism for her to get caught telling tales given how extraordinarily adept Scarpa had been at playing the feds for decades. Nevertheless, a New York judge presiding over a case involving Scarpa's 1980s-era FBI handler Lin DeVecchio cited Scarpa's involvement in the MIBURN affair. State Supreme Court Justice Gustin Reichbach stated: "That a thug like Scarpa would be employed by the federal government to beat witnesses and threaten them at gunpoint to obtain information regarding the deaths of civil rights workers in the South in the early 1960s is a shocking demonstration of the government's unacceptable willingness to employ criminality to fight crime."

Confirmation from sources such as Scarpa's DeVecchio, the *New York Times'* Selwyn Raab, and, more recently, the late justice Reichbach, affirm Scarpa's likely involvement with locating the three civil rights activists. More recent investigative work renders it nearly certain he was involved in resolving the Dahmer case. A federal law enforcement official familiar with the civil rights era indicated to me on background during the research for this book that he believes it has become increasingly accepted that the FBI deployed Scarpa in the Dahmer affair, but not necessarily MIBURN.

Investigative journalist Ronald Kessler, author of *The Secrets of the FBI*, told me, "It wouldn't be a stretch for the FBI to use a mobster in a high-stakes situation. That's what they do—pressure informants when they can't get information through more conventional channels." Reports years after the murders indicated that a Mississippi highway patrol officer

The burned Ford station wagon the three civil rights workers were driving when they were pulled over by KKK operatives
Federal Bureau of Investigation

named Maynard King played a crucial role in determining the location of the MIBURN victims in 1964. However, this does not preclude Scarpa's involvement, as it's possible that both men were involved in different stages of the operation.

HEARTBURN FOR THE FEDS

Years later, when the Senate Church Committee was about to examine the FBI's and CIA's past activities, Deputy Attorney General Laurence Silberman, under President Gerald Ford, expressed concern about what might surface regarding Hoover's methods in the Mississippi investigations: "Hoover did things which won't stand scrutiny, especially under Johnson."

There can be no question at all that Scarpa had a mind-boggling deal with the FBI abetting him in becoming a multi-decade mass murderer, racketeer, thief, and, simultaneously, an informant. With this reign of terror as background, why would the FBI use Scarpa to help expose racist murderers?

While the FBI files on Scarpa are exhaustive, they do not provide the details of what precisely he, by name, did, if anything, in Mississippi. Nor should we expect details about guns-in-mouths and razors-to-genitals to be memorialized in bureau files, especially since it is publicly known that some of Hoover's most sensitive records were destroyed immediately after his death. We do know that Scarpa was actively informing for the FBI during this period, and the bureau recorded contact with him on June 24, three days after the activists disappeared in 1964, and on July 7, 17, 23, and 30. The bodies were discovered on August 4.

It may well have been true that no evidence gathered in advance of the MIBURN grand jury was done through illegal surveillance. Nevertheless, beating the living daylights out of somebody wasn't exactly "surveillance." While the illegal surveillance couldn't be admitted in court, the bureau could use it to assemble cases and pressure informants and targets discretely.

Attorney General Nicholas Katzenbach was skeptical. Opined DOJ's civil rights chief Burke Marshall, according to the FBI memo: "It is just incredible as to how the Agents were able to find the boys in the location they did based solely upon an intensive search of the area."

FBI Agent Alan Belmont added, helpfully: "He said he was not asking me for an answer but he felt that if this case does go to trial certainly Katzenbach or Marshall ought to be aware of the facts so that they would not be caught by surprise. . . . I did not volunteer any answer."

The Belmont memo later states:

If this matter is pursued by the Department and the question comes up again, it was believed the Bureau under no circumstances should disclose information which we must retain in full and complete confidence. If we have to disclose anything further than what has already been said, the most we could tell Marshall or the Attorney General, whoever it may be, on the basis that it is to be solely for their information alone and is not to be disclosed to anyone else as it does not effect the presentation of the civil rights cases is that *"We were able to secure information leading to the location of the bodies; however the source cannot be disclosed."* [author's italics] Insofar as this suggestion is concerned, the Director indicated that we will consider this again for an answer if we are pressed.

In non-bureaucratic language, the memo could be construed to mean: "Look, we were under severe pressure from the White House, so we imported one of the deadliest Mafioso killers in the country to get a Klan guy to give up the location of the bodies. If we're asked, we're going to say we scoured the woods, came upon a muddy patch and said, 'I got a hunch this is it!'"

Toward the end of the Belmont memo following a redaction, Belmont writes, "This could very well be a 'cute' way of trying to find out who our source may be and I believe that the question of perjury is inconsequential in the overall consideration of the case."

There were more memos of this kind in the MIBURN affair. Other files consistently refused to disclose the methodology of locating the bodies. Given the references to Director Hoover himself, he must have ordered that no inconvenient records be kept, and we can infer that he did not want to put his friend, the president, in political or legal jeopardy by raising the role of Scarpa in the post-Valachi climate. In a memo directly from Hoover, he declined to let specific agents testify before the grand jury and cited that the acting attorney general wanted it this way, too. We can also be confident that Hoover wanted to convey that *he* was responsible for uncovering the bodies of Chaney, Goodman, and Schwerner using the forensic techniques and investigative work that the FBI had become famous for.

By way of comparison, when looking back at the FBI's recordkeeping during World War II, it is hard to find a contemporaneous mention of any possible role that gangland figures may have played in fingering any of the Nazi saboteurs, so it makes sense that Hoover didn't keep (known) records of the Scarpa/MIBURN arrangement. Said Scarpa's protégé, former Mafioso Mazza of Scarpa, "Once he made those deals in Mississippi, he had carte blanche and he was able to do whatever he wanted in the streets and never have to worry about being arrested. Carte blanche."*

SCARPA EVENTUALLY DEVELOPED HIV IN 1986 AFTER RECEIVING A BLOOD transfusion. He had suffered from ulcers (he chewed aspirins all day) and had been hospitalized with internal bleeding. Despite surgery, he continued to lose blood. Our unlikely civil rights hero was racist and did not want to risk accepting blood from Black donors, so he asked his LCN crew to donate. One of them, a bodybuilder, had contracted HIV from a contaminated needle and passed along the virus to Scarpa in a dose of rare karma. HIV eventually killed them both.

Scarpa did not view his misfortune as a sign from the heavens about how he had conducted his life or as an opportunity to reflect or repent. Instead, he told his associates he had cancer, not HIV, and would be pleased to participate in a gang war. In his mind, Scarpa concluded that he had nothing to lose and could blast anyone he desired from the planet. Even after becoming extremely ill—he was visibly withered and gaunt—Scarpa proposed exploiting his illness, suggesting he be brought into a mob meeting. Then, once the targets were relaxed and disarmed by his frail condition, Scarpa would surprise the enemy with a machine gun hidden under a blanket and kill them all. His colleagues thanked Scarpa for his brainstorming but demurred.

---

*   Mazza served time in prison and is now an actor who is a highly articulate analyst on organized crime in the media.

While ill, Scarpa violated his house arrest and set out to resolve a conflict involving his younger son. In the process, rival mobsters shot his eye out. He returned home, poured strong liquor into his eye, and assured everyone he was fine. He was later driven to a hospital, where he was treated and received an eye patch.

By his own admission, Scarpa's latter-day FBI handler, DeVecchio, knew Scarpa was engaging in violence on the streets. Scarpa's violence was so prolific that the FBI began investigating the Scarpa-DeVecchio relationship. Allegations surfaced that DeVecchio had provided Scarpa with FBI intelligence that helped Scarpa kill Colombo rivals during the ongoing civil war. During DeVecchio's subsequent trial for murder, the case was dropped—as it should have been—when an investigative reporter produced evidence that the prosecution's star witness, Linda Schiro, had once told a completely different story about DeVecchio's interaction with a mobster. The reporter had recorded Schiro. DeVecchio has asserted in books and interviews that the government's "deal with the devil" was worth it to take down the larger Cosa Nostra.

The DeVecchio case highlights a similar sequence we saw with Commander Haffenden during Operation Underworld: When the government has a thorny problem, it demands its operative get close to a target. The operative then gets close to the target. Results are achieved, the brass deems the affair to be contaminated, and the operative is accused of getting too deeply involved with the target and is punished.

Imagine Scarpa's leverage in the position where the FBI, under extreme pressure, brought him to Mississippi to torture men to solve a high-profile crime. Then imagine him being interviewed by the press or testifying in open court about his "civil rights work." His arrangement with the feds lasted another thirty years, a lifetime in organized crime. Scarpa was paid an estimated $66,000 for his work while DeVecchio supervised his case. This does not include the criminal fortune Scarpa made as a free man, Teflon from the law.

There is no evidence that LBJ personally knew about the FBI's use of Scarpa to solve the civil rights tragedies. It wouldn't have looked very good if Hoover had to convey, *"Look, Boss, we were really struggling with this one, so we had to bring in a serial killer from Brooklyn to handle it for us."* There is ample evidence, however, that LBJ put intense pressure on

Hoover to solve the crime using any means necessary. Ignorance does not absolve Johnson because it was his relentless demand to get the job done that forced Hoover to reach into the very bottom of his bag of tricks. The more we have learned about Johnson's cunning in his prosecution of the Vietnam War and hardball tactics against civil rights leaders like Martin Luther King, Jr., the less it seems he would have had objections to the likes of Greg Scarpa.

While Scarpa's mobilization was undoubtedly illegal, if there was ever a moral reason to send a gangster to rough somebody up, it would be to hunt down racist murderers. Still, the summer of 1964 remained turbulent: Dozens of civil rights workers were beaten, more than one thousand were arrested, and thirty African American churches and thirty homes were firebombed. For his part, Scarpa got the deal of the century. The Mississippi affair catalyzed a thirty-year underworld reign of terror that is unmatched in impunity in the annals of American racketeering.

While many presidencies used organized crime to oil its gears, no single mobster was as monstrous an individual as Scarpa. He can't be written off only as a product of his environment. The government knew what kind of tool they were getting when they pulled Scarpa from the Piker Ryan toolbox. But a reasonable argument can be made that Greg Scarpa was being used for hunting down monsters that were systematically doing to an innocent race of human beings what Scarpa only did to his enemies.

"Sometimes a deal with the devil is better than no deal at all," wrote novelist Lawrence Hill. This rings true. With Scarpa, Hoover cracked the case, LBJ put out his raging political fire, and not a word of this surfaced during their lifetimes. It was a very good deal for the men at the top. Not so much for the dozens of men at the bottom that Scarpa likely killed during his remaining decades of freedom.

6

Richard Nixon

"A THIEVERY BASIS"

I want this implemented on a thievery basis.

—Richard Nixon on how he wanted Vietnam files to be retrieved
from the Brookings Institution

As with his nemeses, the Kennedys, Richard Nixon's dance with the mob had mind-boggling paradoxes. He both cozied up to mob-connected characters, namely the Teamsters' Jimmy Hoffa and Frank Fitzsimmons, and prosecuted them vigorously. H. R. Haldeman, Nixon's chief of staff, recorded in his notes the following order from the president to the attorney general: *Mitchell—no prosecutions whatever re Mafia or Italians until Nov.*

The note may have referred to an eventual deal where Nixon would commute the prison sentence of union boss Jimmy Hoffa in exchange for the Teamsters' support in the 1972 presidential election.

However, John Mitchell's biographer James Rosen cites the timing of Haldeman's notation as the best clue: Haldeman recorded it just before the November 1970 midterm elections. Accordingly, Nixon may have simply been trying not to antagonize Italian Americans and labor for primarily political purposes. Mitchell discouraged DOJ and FBI officials from using the terms "Mafia" and "La Cosa Nostra" during this time period. There is nothing illegal about being savvy about elections. Either way, the record compliments Nixon's reputation for clever machinations with a directive to the nation's chief law enforcement officer to lay off the Mafia.

It's a bad look—even though Mitchell didn't obey his boss and led a seminal program to prosecute organized crime and doubled the number of LCN strike forces, efforts Nixon backed enthusiastically. Haldeman himself admitted there were times he hadn't listened to Nixon's directives when he felt they had been motivated by his baser instincts.

It is now a core tenet of anything written or said about Richard Nixon that the catalyst for his rise was his targeting of those with Communist sympathies, real and imagined. What has been discussed less has been the role of organized crime in his anti-red crusade.

Nixon's longtime political strategist was attorney Murray Chotiner who had built his law practice defending underworld types. These were not one-offs; Chotiner worked hundreds of racket cases. Chotiner was friendly with arguably the most influential mob lawyer in American history, the Chicago Outfit's Sidney Korshak. Bobby Kennedy hauled Chotiner before the Senate Rackets Committee to question him about having represented mobsters, which seriously damaged Chotiner's standing with Nixon and the Republican National Committee. Columnist Drew Pearson "repeatedly connected the Chotiner-Nixon relationship to criminals," according to author and election analyst Irwin Gellman. One must wonder if Kennedy's motive had been to neutralize Chotiner as an effective Nixon advocate as the vice president and JFK's presidential prospects headed toward a likely showdown. (One must also wonder why super-lawyer Edward Bennett Williams, who represented Jimmy Hoffa and Frank Costello—but had also been a player in national Democratic politics—wasn't similarly investigated by the Rackets Committee.)

Chotiner had represented Philadelphia/South Jersey boss Marco Reginelli while Chotiner was an adviser to Vice President Nixon at the same time he was negotiating a deportation case that allowed Reginelli to remain in the United States. Nixon denied having contact with Chotiner during his vice presidency, which wasn't true, noting for the record, "It was a tragedy" that Chotiner "had to get involved in the kind of law business that does not mix with politics." Nixon had been very loyal to Chotiner, who had also represented Genovese capo Angelo "Gyp" DeCarlo and the Los Angeles Mickey Cohen mob. Cohen, who was Jewish, had taken over the L.A. rackets of Bugsy Siegel after Siegel's 1947 murder and had been in constant war with his Italian rivals, the Jack Dragna LCN family.

Cohen signed an affidavit in 1962 stating that he met Nixon, held a fundraiser for him with other mobsters, and raised $25,000 for Nixon's 1950 Senate campaign. Cohen said he:

> reserved the Banquet Room in the Hollywood Knickerbocker Hotel for a dinner meeting to which I invited approximately two hundred and fifty persons who were working for me in the gambling fraternity. . . . Everybody from around here that was on the pad naturally had to go to the dinner. It was all gamblers from Vegas, all gambling money; there wasn't a legitimate person in the room.

Cohen added that the fundraising goal for this dinner hadn't been met, so he got up and said, "Well, we're short for this quota and nobody's going home till this quota's met." Nixon briefly spoke, and it isn't clear whether he appreciated to whom he was speaking. Years later, Cohen admitted that he had done the fundraisers at the behest of "the proper

Los Angeles mobster Mickey Cohen held a fundraiser for Richard Nixon. Cohen said, "There wasn't a legitimate person in the room."
CSU Archives/Everett Collection

persons back east," meaning New York racket bosses. Chotiner was said to have been the broker of this arrangement, which he vehemently denied. Columnist Pearson had printed the rumor but was later forced to retract it.* Cohen claimed he had also helped raise money for Nixon's 1946 congressional race, giving the Nixon campaign a $5,000 check, the equivalent of $75,000 today.

Chotiner was famously the architect of Nixon's earliest campaigns for Congress and the Senate. Both successful campaigns, against Jerry Voorhis and Helen Gahagan Douglas, were anchored in efforts to paint these opponents as Communist sympathizers. In the Senate campaign against Douglas, charges surrounding her left-of-center voting history were printed on pink leaflets and circulated at political rallies, a not-so-subtle effort to link her with "red" causes.

If nothing else, the solid and dotted-line connections among Nixon, Chotiner, racketeers, and anti-Communists suggest a fertile environment for these relationships to flourish. The players were certainly ruthless and shameless enough to do it.

THE TEAMSTERS PLAY

Richard Nixon had been prepared to do good things for the Teamsters from the moment he was elected in 1968. He always remembered that Jimmy Hoffa had personally backed him in 1960 when the Teamsters organization decided against endorsing either Nixon or John F. Kennedy. Despite this, reported Dan Moldea, the Nixon campaign received a $500,000 cash "contribution" in September 1960 from Hoffa and New Orleans Cosa Nostra boss Carlos Marcello, according to a DOJ informant from the Teamsters, Ed Partin, who was found to be credible by a jury that convicted Hoffa of attempting to bribe a federal jury. "I was right there, listening to the conversation," said Partin to Moldea. "Marcello had a suitcase filled with five hundred thousand dollars cash, which was going to Nixon. . . . The other half was coming from the mob boys in

---

* A minor magazine ran an exposé about Chotiner called "Dick Nixon's Secret Link to the Underworld." It was later retracted, presumably because Chotiner was an attorney and it was lawful to represent controversial clients.

New Jersey and Florida." Partin was later used as a reliable witness against Hoffa in other cases.

Officially, the Teamsters contributed only $30,000 to the Nixon campaign in 1972. Still, those linked to the union likely gave much more, including Chicago Outfit associate and pension consultant Allen Dorfman who gave campaign chief John Mitchell $300,000. The ultimate disposition of the money has never been determined, and in 1977 the Watergate Special Prosecution Force found insufficient evidence that money had been paid for a pardon.

"There's a great deal of gold to be mined," Nixon said, referring to the Teamsters. Government informants had pointed to other large cash contributions from mobsters and Teamsters to Nixon campaigns. Wrote Dan Moldea in *The Hoffa Wars*, "Within a few weeks of the alleged payoff, Nixon managed to stop a Florida land fraud indictment against Hoffa." Years later, Nixon's DOJ indicted one of the witnesses who testified against Hoffa in his recent trial. The effort to swing the Teamsters from the Democrats to Republicans was beginning to pay dividends.

In addition to Chotiner, another engineer of Nixon's political strategy was White House attorney Charles "Chuck" Colson. Colson, who was Nixon's spiritual soulmate regarding dark maneuvers, thought that based on cultural trends, Nixon might win over blue-collar Democrats, especially those in labor and from the South. Thus the "Southern strategy" was born in the late 1960s and early 1970s.

Nixon knew that the Teamsters were capitalists at heart. Labor would succeed only if the business succeeded. In a recorded conversation, he asked colleagues, "Reuther [Walter Reuther, progressive labor leader] was always interested in the great social issues. The Teamsters were interested in more in terms of wages, right? . . . Reuther's a socialist, that's the difference, social economy." The Teamsters and their two million members were a crucial beachhead in Nixon's political strategy, especially since the union had historically leaned heavily toward Democrats.

Colson's scheme went like this: Nixon would commute the sentence of Teamsters boss Jimmy Hoffa to time served, but with a proviso preventing Hoffa from pursuing leadership of his union until 1980. Acting Teamsters boss Frank Fitzsimmons supported this because he wanted to solidify his union leadership without worrying about Hoffa challenging him—and Hoffa had been making noises about doing precisely that. Attorney General Mitchell said to Nixon in a recorded conversation, "And he [Fitzsimmons] wants Hoffa out of there and, uh, I think he's having substantial troubles with his union because he isn't outta there, for whatever reason."

One of those "troubles" was that LCN didn't like uncertainty, and they had begun to prefer the pliant Fitzsimmons to the oft-combative Hoffa for reasons we shall see. The political motives behind the commutation were confirmed on the audiotapes Nixon made in the White House, with Mitchell clarifying: "Well, it's not a complete pardon, but there is an executive clemency aspect of it, where you would reduce the sentence enough so that he could get out of the clink."

Fitzsimmons would give Nixon the Teamsters' endorsement in exchange for the commutation. This would ensure Nixon a windfall in votes, not to mention inroads with other unions and working-class Democrats. This is especially interesting because Fitzsimmons was able to offer input on wage controls, which Nixon wanted to freeze, and the unions wished to raise. The better things went for Hoffa, Fitzsimmons, and the Teamsters, the better things went for Nixon on multiple fronts. Said Colson, "Fitzsimmons is very happy with us at the moment."

Mitchell's successor, Richard Kleindienst, later admitted to Senate investigators that he had contacted Hoffa's attorney and said he would have Hoffa arrested if he attempted to violate his commutation agreement and seek the Teamsters' presidency again. Nixon had spoken about "the ability to keep him [Hoffa] restrained." Furthermore, according to author Don Fulsom: "In March 1973, obeying Nixon's orders to go easy on the Mafia and their Teamsters allies, Kleindienst refused to renew a 20-day extension of FBI wiretaps that were beginning to expose Teamsters complicity in a Mafia kickback scam involving Teamsters health and welfare benefits." This scheme involved West Coast and Chicago mob figures siphoning off 10 percent of the value of a $1 billion health plan.

If nothing else, Nixon and Hoffa had been cultural soulmates. The president and his advisers appeared enthusiastic about a plan to mobilize Teamsters to counterbalance antiwar and anti-Nixon protesters. After an aide tried to remember the name of the man who could be called upon to rough up the protesters, Nixon volunteered, "Fitzsimmons." One would have thought that after the massacre of students at Kent State by the Ohio National Guard the year before, there might have been more caution about using force against protesters, but apparently not.

THOSE WHO WERE BORN TOO LATE TO LIVE THROUGH THE "HOFFA WARS," as the dean of Hoffa journalists Dan Moldea tagged them, often wonder what all the fuss is about Jimmy Hoffa when they hear his name. A cursory summary is in order. Hoffa was among the most famous Americans in the late 1950s and 1960s. Bobby Kennedy had excoriated Hoffa during the Senate Rackets Committee hearings in 1957, where the labor leader invoked his Fifth Amendment rights against self-incrimination 140 times. The AFL-CIO voted to expel the Teamsters unless Hoffa was replaced. Hoffa wouldn't budge, so the Teamsters left the federation.

RFK formed a "Get Hoffa" squad at the DOJ and successfully prosecuted him for fraud and jury tampering. Hoffa even attempted to bribe the Senate committee. Despite these fireworks, Hoffa successfully brought all road truck drivers into the union and tried to get other transportation workers with uneven results. Hoffa remained popular with his union and won a third term as Teamsters boss despite multiple criminal convictions. After appeals, he began serving a federal prison sentence in 1967. The media couldn't get enough of Hoffa.

The mob and Hoffa were linked in a few ways. First, gangsters were historically able to ensure labor peace by threatening unions or management into doing whatever they wanted. Otherwise, people would get hurt,

Richard Nixon commuted the prison sentence of troublesome Teamsters boss Jimmy Hoffa at the behest of his mob-connected successor. This political move set in motion a chain of events that resulted in Hoffa's 1975 disappearance and presumed murder. *Hank Walker/ The LIFE Picture Collection/ Shutterstock*

property would be damaged, and business would be disrupted. Corporate bosses would have disruptions when the mob was helping the unions. If the mob was supporting management, however, the union would suffer if it didn't fall into line. There was no ideological principle at work here. It was about whatever paid the most money and gave the mob the most power.

Another union scam involved extorting kickbacks from everyday workers, a practice Hoffa deplored but could not always fight. Yet another mob scheme was stealing from the union by giving officials—sometimes LCN members—bloated salaries or expenses. They could also unite to extort companies into rewarding heavily padded work contracts. Mobsters also used brute force to ensure that a leader loyal to them would be elected. In other words, "Vote for Jimmy, or we'll kill you." For this, Hoffa and other leaders were indebted. In return, these leaders would allow the mob to pilfer the union. Once gangsters got their hooks into a union leader early in his career, that influence lasted forever.

Among the other benefits of union influence was the ability to provide mobsters with "no-show" jobs. In other words, if a loan shark needed to show legitimate income and get medical benefits, he could have a "job," on paper, with a union or construction company that he didn't have to show up for. He'd get all the benefits but not do the work. He could just continue being a loan shark and earn dirty money (and maybe get a leased car), along with the clean. Labor racketeers were often very popular—and harder to remove—within mob families because of the ability to provide these services.

THE VERY CONCEPT OF A PENSION IS BORING. IT MAKES PEOPLE THINK OF retirees opening envelopes in the mail containing documents filled with numbers. Boring was a good thing for the mob because not since Prohibition had they enjoyed the kind of criminal pillaging they came to have with the Teamsters' massive pension fund, the money set aside for members' retirements. Wrote Jeff Gerth in a 1974 exposé: "By 1969 the billion dollar Central States Pension Fund was considered the prime source of working capital for the mob, or as the Oakland Tribune labeled it, the 'bankroll for some of America's most sinister underworld figures.'"

Before (and after) gangsters lost their Cuban casinos, they bet heavily on Las Vegas. They wanted to own and control hotels and casinos there.

This required a great deal of investment. While they had the cash, dragging sacks of currency into the desert didn't look very good. Regulators asked questions. The construction enterprise had to appear respectable to be embraced as legitimate and licensed. How did legitimate people fund investments? They got loans. Mobsters couldn't get loans from banks because they were criminals. What bank was going to loan crooks millions of dollars? Very few. So, where would they get the money? The answer: Gangsters could use their influence with the Teamsters to get a loan from its pension fund, which is why they really loved Jimmy Hoffa.

The core problem remained that they were crooks, and not even the Teamsters' pension fund could justify giving money to crooks. Most union pension funds allotted 5 to 10 percent of their holdings to real estate, but at one point, the Teamsters held 70 percent of their funds in properties, most of them mob-controlled. Casino developers borrowed roughly $250 million from the Central States Pension, which would be several billion today.

The mobsters then identified "front men" or "fronts"—businesspeople with good reputations who would be the legal owners of Las Vegas casinos who would pass basic background checks. These fronts would enjoy some of the benefits of ownership, *but the mob wanted access to the cash in the casinos' counting rooms.* Given that the front legally owned the hotel and controlled security, they could order the guards to look the other way. At the same time, a mob courier walked freely into the casino, took bags filled with cash, walked out the door, and delivered the cash to the mobsters across the country. This cash was known as the "skim" because the legitimate earnings of the casinos were taken off the piles of cash collected. It was all about the skim.

Nixon's intimacy with rough customers manifested itself in the Hoffa pardon when he knew full well where the Teamsters' power came from, and he didn't care. On the infamous Watergate tapes, Nixon refers to a slush fund that could be tapped for paying "hush money" to the burglars, saying, "What I mean is you could get a million dollars . . . I know where it could be gotten. . . . We could get the money. There is no problem in that." White House counsel John Dean made a similar reference on the tapes.

For some time after this surfaced, there were questions about precisely what Nixon was referring to. According to a confidential FBI memo,

The Stardust Hotel and Casino
was among those built by
mobsters with funds from the
Teamsters pension.
Billy Stock/Alamy Stock Photo

the money may have involved a payoff from Teamsters leaders to ensure Nixon's commutation of Hoffa. An informant said that Genovese family heavyweight and New Jersey Teamsters official Anthony Provenzano indicated that Colson had requested the cash and that $500,000 had been given to a White House operative in Las Vegas. A Colson memo stated that "substantial sums of money, perhaps a quarter of a million dollars," might be located "if we could arrange to have James Hoffa released from prison." The thinking was that this money would come from the skim, money that didn't exist as far as the government could ever prove.

The FBI confirmed that Provenzano indeed had a courier in Las Vegas and that Colson and Fitzsimmons had spoken around that time. The theory is that the White House could have eventually used the cash for "hush money" for the Watergate burglars* who needed to pay for their lawyers and other expenses. Eerily, John Dean had once referenced the Mafia when discussing paying off the Watergate burglars: "It'll cost

---

* I spoke to G. Gordon Liddy, one of the key Watergate operatives during his years as a radio show host. The New Jersey native had a lot of knowledge about the mob and spoke warmly about Jewish mobsters he knew, which was surprising given his chronicled affection for the Third Reich.

money. It's dangerous. Nobody, nothing—people around here are not pros at this sort of thing. This is the sort of thing Mafia people can do: washing money, getting clean money."

JIMMY GETS PLAYED

Author and law professor Jack Goldsmith acknowledged that Hoffa was a "serial criminal" who nevertheless pushed back against organized crime whenever possible. Deeply committed to his members, Hoffa saw gangland cooperation as a means to an end to help his union. He reasoned that he had to give up something with the mob to get something. Gangsters knew they were accessing a gold mine with the Teamsters' pension, so even they could pull punches occasionally. Nixon had been recorded saying to Henry Kissinger, "What we're talking about, in the greatest of confidence, is we're going to give Hoffa an amnesty, but we're going to do it for a reason."

The year before the 1972 election, Nixon commuted Hoffa's sentence four months after the parole board had rejected his application for release. The commutation included the provision keeping Hoffa out of union leadership for almost a decade. They didn't want Hoffa, his criminal baggage, and his loose-cannon personality back. Nor did the mob really want Hoffa back out of any sense of personal affection; while they had greatly benefited from their relationship, their loyalty was to the money, not to one man. They felt they had found that man in his successor, Frank Fitzsimmons. Gangsters wanted Hoffa free enough to feel indebted but not so free that he could resume control over the Teamsters.

By that time, Nixon, Colson, and Mitchell reasoned, Fitzsimmons would have maneuvered sufficiently to render Hoffa irrelevant. Nixon and Hoffa's successor had known each other well. In fact, Nixon's first public appearance after his resignation was with Fitzsimmons at the labor leader's golf tournament to raise money for mentally disabled children. One of the other players was Anthony Provenzano, the Genovese family member considered the engineer of Jimmy Hoffa's murder. Provenzano was described in news coverage as a "Florida consultant." Also in attendance was the Chicago Outfit's union pension operative, Allen Dorfman. The event was held at the La Costa Resort in Carlsbad, California, which had been built with funds from the Teamsters' pension (some of the Watergate damage-control meetings had also been held at La Costa). The Teamsters endorsed Nixon for president in 1972, not his ultraliberal opponent George McGovern. Nixon won by a landslide. Nixon publicly said that Fitzsimmons was "welcome in my office any time; the door is always open to Frank Fitzsimmons."

Despite evidence to the contrary, Colson continued to deny that he had anything to do with the Hoffa commutation deal. Perhaps this was because after leaving the White House in 1973, he received a $100,000 annual consulting retainer from the Teamsters and was concerned about an appearance of impropriety. The following year, at the height of the Watergate scandal, Nixon claimed executive privilege to withhold White House documents related to the Hoffa clemency deal. If Colson would deny involvement, former mob lawyer Murray Chotiner openly took credit for facilitating Hoffa's pardon, saying he was "proud" of his role. He even tipped off Hoffa friend and elusive Washington operative I. Irving Davidson about the commutation, who in turn informed the Hoffa family of the good news.*

LCN had a big problem with Hoffa that was always bubbling beneath the surface: He knew too much. In fact, he knew everything, something he wasn't shy about pointing out during his failed comeback campaign. This was disconcerting, to say the least, to the Genovese family of New York, the Chicago Outfit, the Detroit Partnership, the Civellas of Kansas City, and other syndicates that didn't want Hoffa running his mouth on television or the witness stand.

It's worth noting that one of the other people whose prison sentence Nixon commuted was Genovese capo Angelo "Gyp" DeCarlo. This was done ostensibly for compassionate reasons, but the FBI said DeCarlo immediately went back to gangster business. DeCarlo died ten months

---

* Davidson represents another fascinating link between politics and organized crime. Among other things, he helped supply Cuban strongman Batista with weapons, guided Hoffa through the political aspects of RFK's crusade against him, facilitated Hoffa's backing of Richard Nixon over JFK in 1960, and supervised overseas investments for New Orleans LCN boss Carlos Marcello. Davidson was later convicted of fraud for his role in obtaining financing from the Teamsters' pension fund.

Nixon political adviser
Murray Chotiner
*Ed Clark/The LIFE Picture
Collection/Shutterstock*

later. FBI records contain a reference to Frank Sinatra having spoken to a high-ranking Nixon administration official, perhaps Vice President Spiro Agnew, about granting this commutation.

With Hoffa prohibited from running again, the mobsters achieved one of their objectives: control over the union through Fitzsimmons. Despite being freed from prison, rather than being grateful, Hoffa was furious about the ban on seeking office. He saw the union as being *his* and was not going to go gently into a lucrative retirement. Bad for the mob. Bad for Jimmy.

Nixon's commutation of Hoffa's sentence (he had been in prison for five years) set in motion a chain of events that ultimately led to Hoffa's demise. Hoffa began talking like a crime-busting crusader. He even wrote a treatment for a book with the author who had written one with Eliot Ness of *The Untouchables* fame. Shortly after Hoffa's 1975 disappearance, his sentiments and intentions were confirmed from the grave; his son held a news conference and shared quotes from the book Hoffa was about to publish. Among the more provocative quotations: "I charge Fitzsimmons with political influence peddling and conspiring with John Dean and Charles Colson of President Richard Nixon's 'Watergate staff' to prevent me from regaining my office. . . . I charge him with selling out to mobsters and letting known racketeers into the teamsters."

Nixon did plenty to cut mobsters and mob-connected people a break. In 1972, DOJ refused to move ahead with the prosecution for income tax evasion of Morris Shenker, an attorney who represented more gangland figures than any other lawyer of his time. Authorities determined that by the early 1970s Shenker was the biggest borrower from the Teamsters pension fund. Wrote reporter James Drinkhall, "The entire file on the Shenker case disappeared from Justice Department files in St. Louis." In subsequent administrations, the Department of Labor prevailed in its suit against Shenker for taking illicit loans from union pensions.

Nixon also granted Hoffa's predecessor, Dave Beck, a five-year delay on paying the $1.3 million he owed the IRS. FBI agents, concerned about Nixon's closeness with Fitzsimmons, leaked information about how his new attorney general, Richard Kleindienst, was pumping the brakes on an investigation of gangland looting of the Teamsters pension fund. Prior to Fitzsimmons's arrival in Los Angeles for a meeting with a mob-connected firm arranging a huge healthcare contract for the Teamsters, the FBI had bugged the office where the meeting was to be held. When the FBI applied for a wiretap to extend the bugging operation, it was denied by the Justice Department. According to criminologist William Chambliss, the halting of the bugging operation "came less than a month before Charles W. Colson, special counsel to the President, left the White House to join a Washington law firm to which Mr. Fitzsimmons had transferred the union's legal business."

Prior to its cessation, the bugging operation had corroborated that Fitzsimmons had been meeting with Chicago Outfit pension corruptor Allen Dorfman and West Coast LCN members. It also captured a discussion between a mob-connected physician and a Los Angeles mobster regarding the role of a front company called People's Industrial Consultant in skimming a large percentage of the Teamsters' healthcare contract.

The *Los Angeles Times* reported that Fitzsimmons had been meeting with a leading organized crime figure and then boarding Air Force One with Nixon. Nixon's Justice Department also abandoned a plan to prosecute Fitzsimmons's son for credit card fraud, prompting an FBI agent to say, "This whole thing of the Teamsters and the mob and the White House is one of the scariest things I've ever seen. It has demoralized the bureau. We don't know what to expect out of the Justice Department."

Under Fitzsimmons, multiple mob families dove into the pension. Chicago's Dorfman, whose lineage went way back with the Outfit through his father, inserted himself into the decision-making process for loans given out by the Central States Pension Funds. Like Hoffa, his days were numbered, too. In 1983, three days before he was to be sentenced for trying to bribe a U.S. senator, Dorfman was shot multiple times while walking in a Chicago-area hotel parking lot with a friend. Dorfman was killed. His friend was not hit. The Outfit had been concerned that its well-liked and long-standing executive would turn state's evidence at the last minute rather than go to prison.

THE FLORIDA MOB SWAMP

The Kennedys accurately assessed they could push things far. Nixon understood that he was not somebody who could get away with much. Michael Deaver, Ronald Reagan's "image-maker," once told me the story of how Nixon called him at the beginning of the Iran-Contra scandal and said, "Mike, here's what I think Ronnie ought to do: He should hold a press conference and say, 'I'm stupid' . . . and the whole thing will go away." Then Nixon sighed and said, "Now, dammit Mike, I could never have gotten away with that."

He wasn't wrong. Nixon deserved his downfall and his association with the dark underbelly of politics. Among the things that made him different from other presidents, however, was the intimacy with which he directed dirty tricks. He trusted no one else to make sure things were done right.

Nixon was so aware of his own penchant for dirty work that he suspected himself of it even when he may not have been complicit. The Kennedys had been far more responsible for anti-Castro efforts than Nixon was, but it was Nixon, as we shall see, who was acutely haunted by whatever early involvement he may have had.

If one thing dogged Nixon throughout his career, it was his need for money and his resentment of those who had a lot of it. From charges of having accepted gifts as vice president (leading to the famed "Checkers speech") to allegations of having not fully paid his income taxes while president (prompting him to utter the memetic "I am not a crook") to his brother Donald getting a large, never-returned "loan" from billionaire Howard Hughes, Nixon always appeared to be scrounging for cash. In 1952, the *New York Post* ran a story titled "Secret Rich Men's Trust Fund Keeps Nixon in Style Far Beyond His Salary." The story named wealthy California businessmen with interests in oil drilling and dairy products who helped fund Nixon's living expenses.

Then there is the byzantine story of grocery chain Winn-Dixie's attempt to acquire the mob-linked Las Vegas Tropicana Hotel and Casino,* the simplest version of which goes like this: Darius Davis, the president of Winn-Dixie, wanted to buy the Tropicana. Davis was close to Florida senator George Smathers, who had promulgated legislation that saved the company a fortune in taxes. In 1967, Smathers delivered $25,000 from the Davis family to Nixon's Cuban American friend Charles "Bebe" Rebozo to give to Nixon for use in the New Hampshire Republican primary. Wrote Jonathan Marshall:

> In 1969, Smathers intervened with Deputy Attorney General Richard Kleindienst and Rebozo to kill a criminal tax case against the Davis brothers for illegally deducting political contributions from their taxes. In April 1972, the two brothers contributed $50,000 in cash to Rebozo, their longtime family friend and banker, prompting further investigations by the Senate Watergate Committee and Special Prosecutor.

The Tropicana sale never went through, and it is unclear if Nixon did anything of value in exchange for the Davis contributions, but suspicion about Nixon and Rebozo's proximity to money from Florida's mob land remains—and continues. In 1968, Nixon vacationed in Paradise Island, Bahamas, and dedicated the opening of its Resorts International hotel and casino. Resorts had been frequently investigated for ties to organized crime. Rebozo persuaded the company's CEO, James Crosby, to give Nixon's campaign $100,000, which was delivered to the presidential

---

* After Frank Costello was shot in 1957, the police found a slip of paper under his hat with the Tropicana's revenues, amounting to $651,284 for its first few weeks in existence.

candidate's apartment in New York City. Resorts also loaned Nixon its yacht during the Republican convention in Miami Beach. Crosby maintained a large account at Rebozo's Key Biscayne Bank and Trust and hired one of Nixon's Secret Service agents to be his security chief.

In the desire to prove that Nixon was a crook, his detractors sometimes overshot the mark. Some of the mob allegations against Nixon are particularly suspect, especially notions that Rebozo and Nixon himself had conducted business with Meyer Lansky. Nixon was many things, but stupid wasn't one of them. He would have likely been more circumspect about anything that could be interpreted as being linked to a major organized crime figure as he pursued the presidency. Indeed, the investments and transactions we do know about are layered. A family member once broached Lansky's knowing Nixon and the mobster immediately responded, "Yes, I know him from the television." This is telling because Lansky hadn't hesitated to tell his family that he had met John F. Kennedy in Havana and that JFK had no interest in gambling; he just wanted the women. Said Lansky's wife, Teddy, in 1989, Meyer "told him where he could go for it [women]." Not a word about knowing Nixon.

Charges about Nixon and his relationship with Lansky were peddled by Lansky's most sensational biographer, Hank Messick, who rarely encountered a criminal scheme that Lansky hadn't masterminded. Messick hadn't been alone. One rumor that had begun to gain traction was that Nixon had been "comped" a room in Lansky's Hotel Nacional de Cuba and had run up a $50,000 debt that had been forgiven in exchange for some unspecified favor. This charge is not out of the question as it is known that Nixon had traveled to Cuba for vacations, including with his wife and Rebozo. Nixon had met with Cuban leader Fulgencio Batista as vice president in 1955. Nixon also had gone fishing with Miami Beach hotel owner Tatem "Chubby" Wofford, who served as a front for midwestern gangsters. Still, this falls well short of Nixon conducting extensive business with Lansky.

Nixon's administration via J. Edgar Hoover hounded Lansky so relentlessly that the mobster fled the country to settle in Israel. Initially, Prime Minister Golda Meir didn't understand what all the fuss was about Lansky. Raised in Milwaukee, where there was a very active Mafia family, she was persuaded when told (somewhat inaccurately) that Lansky was a leading figure in the Mafia. She snapped, "I don't want Mafia here."

According to family members, Lansky may have spent as much as $5 million during his attempt to settle in Israel under the Law of Return that allows Jews refuge there, a policy that grew out of the Holocaust. He was the first known exception made to this convention. The politicians and operatives that accepted money from Lansky were happy to reach into his pocket, deeply validating the distrust of public servants he had held since the 1932 U.S. presidential election when he backed FDR only to be double-crossed.* In a letter to a friend, Lansky wrote of politicians, "These bastards have been corrupted from the time they got out of knee pants. College wasn't a place for them for higher learning, they learned what their fathers liked most, money."

Among the chief reasons for turning its back on Lansky and one of its founding tenets was that Israel had been anticipating receipt of seventy-four Phantom fighter jets and Nixon's Justice Department wanted to prosecute Lansky in the United States and was hinting they might obstruct the deal. In another private note, Lansky wrote, "The Nixon powers at that time needed sacred goats to cover up their crimes. I was no one on the totem pole."

If the Nixon-Lansky connections were overhyped, Bebe Rebozo's connections to other racketeers were not. Rebozo owned property in Florida with an investor who also had ties to southern U.S. bosses Carlos Marcello and Santo Trafficante. Rebozo had also retained the construction firm of his friend Alfred "Big Al" Polizzi, a Cleveland LCN figure, to build one of his properties. The Federal Bureau of Narcotics called Polizzi "one of the most influential members of the underworld in the United States . . . associated with narcotics traffickers . . . and illicit gambling activities in the Miami area." The Genoveses' Jimmy Alo once quipped, "Everyone knew Rebozo would take a hot stove."

---

* According to sociologist William Chambliss, Lansky did contribute to other presidential campaigns, primarily to Democrats including Al Smith (1928), Franklin Roosevelt (1932), Harry Truman (1948), Lyndon Johnson (1960, 1964), and Hubert Humphrey (1968).

In the late 1950s, Rebozo developed oceanfront property with investors including Senator George Smathers and Vice President Nixon. The banker facilitating the deal had been associated with handling deposits from Havana casinos and illegal South Florida "carpet joint" casinos. Nixon unloaded his shares, doubling his money. Soon after this sale, Nixon promulgated legislation that would upgrade the Port of Miami, near where his investment property had been. It was likely a thank-you gesture to his erstwhile partners.

Nixon and Rebozo helped each other in other ways. When Rebozo opened a bank, Nixon dedicated it, an unusual gig for a national political figure. Nixon's Justice Department demurred when faced with prosecuting Rebozo for having used stolen IBM stock as collateral on a deal. The stock had been in the possession of an LCN gambling figure. Rebozo's wealth quadrupled during Nixon's presidency.

The atmospherics surrounding Nixon, Rebozo, and the South Florida mob swamp are disturbing, but the hard evidence suggests more adjacency than criminality. The head of the Nixon-Agnew Florida campaign had also been chairman of Miami National Bank in the early 1960s when racket links were at their apex, but this may say more about the marshes Nixon was slogging through than a discrete dirty deal. Still, when Miami Beach mayor Elliott Roosevelt, FDR's son, was asked if organized crime had influence in Miami Beach, he responded, "Hell, no. They own it."

THE OMNIPRESENT INVISIBILITY OF HOWARD HUGHES

To understand Nixon's mindset during Watergate, we need to consider the figure of Howard Hughes, who was also important in the trajectory of LCN in Las Vegas and America more broadly. Hughes was a transitional bridge between organized crime and corporate ownership of gambling establishments, not to mention a serious player in presidential politics, the defense industry, and, indirectly, the world of high-stakes spying. Much of his business success was anchored in his ability to influence political outcomes by paying for them, not always subtly. Among his most ham-fisted schemes was to provide Nixon's brother Donald with an enormous "loan" (never repaid) in 1956 that was widely assumed to have found its way into Richard's pockets. True or not, Nixon was never able to step out of the tar of bribery.

Hughes was a brilliant eccentric who first moved to Las Vegas in 1966. His entry into casino gambling was a ricochet from what was supposed to be a change of scene after his sale of the airline TWA. First, Hughes rented the top floor of Moe Dalitz's Desert Inn for a few weeks. Dalitz had been a major bootlegging figure in the Midwest who later transitioned into gambling. He was never able to shake his reputation of having been a mob figure despite his legal ownership of casinos and hotels.

Soon, Dalitz wanted Hughes to leave the hotel so that he could use the suite for high-rolling guests. Hughes resisted and put pressure on Dalitz through Jimmy Hoffa, who had facilitated real estate loans for Dalitz from the Teamsters' pension. Dalitz allowed Hughes to extend his stay, but only for a few weeks. When his time was almost up, the billionaire inquired about how much it might cost to *buy* the hotel. He was told the cost would be about $7 million. Hughes paid double that to remain at the Desert Inn.

There were some obstacles to Hughes's takeover, namely that he didn't have a casino license. In order to get one, state law required him to appear in person before the regulating commission. It was a nonstarter for the recluse: He had no intention of leaving his hotel room. He had also become agoraphobic, was addicted to prescription pain pills, had lost a great deal of weight, and his hair and fingernails had grown long. Nevada governor Paul Laxalt made a deal with Hughes: The mogul could have the license if he would contribute several hundred thousand dollars to the University of Nevada at Las Vegas each year for twenty years. In exchange, he wouldn't have to attend the hearing to get his license.

To avoid onerous taxation after the TWA sale, Hughes needed to reinvest the proceeds, which he did by buying additional Las Vegas properties, including the Sands, Castaways, the Frontier, and the Silver Slipper.

Howard Hughes
*UNLV Libraries Special
Collections & Archives*

To protect his investments, Hughes brought in executives in-cluding Robert Maheu and a group known as the Mormon Mafia. Hughes believed that Mormons would be more trustworthy because they didn't smoke, drink, or, ironically, even gamble (the Mormon executives justified their involvement in the casino business on the grounds that they never handled gambling accouterments such as dice, cash, and chips). Maheu and the Mormons also came with another benefit: They had strong connections with federal law en-forcement, which afforded Hughes a layer of protection in case the mob guys decided to get cute with him or his operations. Hughes had told his right-hand man, Maheu, on more than one occasion, "Bob, remember that there is no person in the world that I can't either buy or destroy." During this period, Governor Laxalt also grew closer to J. Edgar Hoover, who ran with RFK's strategy of driving racketeers out of Las Vegas by having richer and more powerful players buy them out.

Publicly traded corporations took note of Hughes's success and realized that the gaming industry need not be restricted to organized crime ownership. The laws were promptly changed, ushering in the blue-chip domination of Las Vegas that remains today—an economic juggernaut that the mob could never compete with. Wrote Lansky mournfully in his private records: "The lower Mafia or organized crime syndicate lack[s] the strength to break out of an eggshell. It is the upper organized crime syndicate [corporations] that the general population has to fear. They possess the facilities to enslave us and be at their command."

"THE BAY OF PIGS THING"

No discussion of Nixon and Watergate or the rackets can ignore the president's multiple references to "the Bay of Pigs thing" in the White House's secret recordings. The references have led to a suspicion that among the items the burglars may have been looking for at the Democratic National Headquarters were plans to link Nixon to the Castro assassination plots. Nixon had been briefed on the CIA's anti-Castro maneuvers involving LCN while serving as Eisenhower's vice president. These references have never been adequately explained and are the subject of furious debate.

One school of thought is that Nixon was *the* anti–Castro and Bay of Pigs–planning point man for Eisenhower. This has been accepted as an article of faith among many experts on the era. Nevertheless, both CIA reports and Nixon biographers have concluded that there is little credible evidence that Nixon ever played such a role. Nixon's national security assistant during his vice presidency (and later CIA official) was Robert Cushman, Jr., who said, "Only the good Lord knows whether President Ike knew about it [assassination plans] or whether Vice President Nixon knew about it. I would say the odds are he didn't know." Here we must evaluate the evidence and make a responsible assessment on what likely happened.

It is indisputable that the CIA program to depose Castro began during the Eisenhower administration and that these plans involved organized crime. Nixon had met with Castro and had received briefings from the CIA on Cuban developments. The Eisenhower playbook was titled "A Program of Covert Action Against the Castro Regime." What remains uncertain is the extent to which those briefings included details about assassination or invasion plans as opposed to propaganda and the recruitment of exiles.

There is little evidence that Eisenhower himself was enthusiastic about assassinating Castro or attacking Cuba militarily. By most accounts, the aging general was tired of war and its attendant machinery. Still, Eisenhower's national security advisor, Philip Corso said of Nixon, "He wanted to get rid of him [Castro]. He wanted him hit hard . . . when he was vice president." This makes sense because Nixon had the same obsessive quality Bobby Kennedy did, and one can see him viewing Castro as a Commie wiseass who had no business thumbing his nose at the mighty United States. And what did it say about American might that we couldn't get rid of a pissant? Nevertheless, the CIA's point man on the Castro program, Richard Bissell, said that Nixon had not been informed of the assassination element of the program.

We also know that as president, Nixon repeatedly hectored CIA chief Richard Helms during the Watergate cover-up about sharing files with him about the Bay of Pigs because he was concerned it could "blow" the Agency's (and theoretically Nixon's) involvement in the fiasco. Nixon claimed to have needed the information "for defensive reasons. . . . Is Eisenhower to blame? Is Johnson to blame? Is Kennedy to blame? Is Nixon to blame?" Nixon had been attempting to cite national security as a feint to obstruct investigations into the Watergate break-in, which involved the CIA's E. Howard Hunt and Agency-connected Cuban operatives. The notorious "smoking gun tape" that ended Nixon's presidency was about enlisting the CIA to dissuade the FBI from investigating Watergate.* Investigative reporter Lamar Waldron asked of Nixon's "obsession" with the files: "What was left to 'blow' about the whole 'Bay of Pigs thing' that involved Helms (and Nixon) except the CIA-Mafia plots?"

Nixon said to Helms: "I need to know what is necessary to protect, frankly, the intelligence gathering and Dirty Tricks Department, and I will protect it. Hey, listen, I have done more than my share of lying to protect you, and I believe it's totally right to do it."

There is a dual way to look at Nixon's importuning of Helms to deliver to the White House files related to anti-Castro efforts: It may have been Nixon's way of saying, *Look, pal, if all this stuff comes out about what went*

---

* One wonders if the Watergate break-in would have occurred had Hoover lived a little longer—he had died the month before. Nixon would have had in Hoover an asset who might have dampened the president's interest in tapping a band of looney tunes for such endeavors.

on in Cuba with the Mafia, it won't be good for you either so you might want to get the FBI to back off its Watergate investigation. Later in life, Helms acknowledged that Nixon had threatened him and that his methods had a "devious, hard-nosed smell." Haldeman wrote that Nixon's requests were "the president's way of reminding Helms, not so gently, of the cover-up of the CIA assassination attempts on the hero of the Bay of Pigs, Fidel Castro, a CIA operation that may have triggered the Kennedy tragedy and which Helms desperately wanted to hide."

Watergate and JFK journalist Jefferson Morley concluded, "Nixon just wanted to know how the Mafia plots relate to Kennedy's assassination."

The question about whether Helms tried to help impede the Watergate investigation is loaded with intrigue. On one hand, Watergate prosecutors found a memo where Helms claimed that he had asked FBI director L. Patrick Gray to tread lightly on aspects of the Watergate investigation that might "run afoul" of CIA operations. On other occasions Helms claimed righteousness; he had told Nixon and his top aides that he would do nothing to derail the FBI's investigation. Nixon had been known to play a similar game: Despite the "smoking gun" tape's directive to involve the CIA in the Watergate cover-up, Nixon had also told Gray to keep digging. This is a page from the guilty man's playbook of publicly "welcoming an investigation" while privately trying to scuttle it, the kind of charade deployed on the contemporaneous TV detective show, *Columbo*.

What catalyst besides the Watergate cover-up might have gotten Nixon so exercised? As we saw in the Kennedy chapter, in 1971, Washington investigative reporter Jack Anderson had begun publishing stories about the CIA's anti-Castro mischief. His source, Johnny Rosselli, had successfully blackmailed the CIA to intervene in his deportation case. What Nixon cared about was any potential link between himself and the violent failures in Cuba. His own aide John Ehrlichman wrote in his notes that Nixon demanded that the CIA hand over "*full* [Cuba] file or else; Nothing w/ held." Ehrlichman added that Nixon "was involved in the Bay of Pigs . . . deeply involved." Haldeman wrote, "Nixon knew more about the genesis of the Cuban invasion than almost anyone."

The word "genesis" is an important one because it is more likely that Nixon was there at the outset of the American misadventure in Cuba than he had been the manager of it in the way he was in the Watergate cover-up. While evidence of this remains contested, two things are not: E. Howard Hunt of CIA and Watergate fame definitely *was* involved in the Bay of Pigs, *and* it's impossible to ignore the overlap between the CIA's anti-Castro program and Watergate. Wrote journalist and historian James Rosen:

> No credible historian now questions that both Hunt and [James, Watergate burglar] McCord—though each officially retired from the CIA when they joined the Nixon White House and Committee to Re-elect the President, respectively—maintained direct contact with the agency's senior echelons, in ways that called their allegiances, and agendas, into question. Consequently, the role of the Central Intelligence Agency in Watergate is now widely understood as deeper—*more entrenched, controlling, and malign*—than was known in 1974.

The pathway to Nixon's anxiety that could have catalyzed Watergate may have evolved like this:

a. In 1968, in addition to his support for Nixon, billionaire Howard Hughes had made a significant contribution to the campaign of Nixon's opponent, Hubert Humphrey. It is routine for donors to hedge their bets like this, but Nixon was worried. In 1956, Hughes had given Nixon's brother Donald a $205,000 [$2.2 million in today's dollars] loan ostensibly to open a hamburger restaurant, a loan that was never repaid and was suspected to have gone to Nixon personally. This had become a major issue in the 1960 campaign, especially since Hughes, who hated paying taxes, had received an exemption from the Eisenhower-Nixon administration. This was granted after having twice been rejected. The Foundation technically owned Hughes's TWA and received tax-exempt benefits that added $36 million per year to the billionaire's pocket. Hughes had also recently made a $100,000 cash contribution to the Nixon campaign through the candidate's friend Bebe Rebozo. Some investigators suspect to this day that these funds went to Nixon personally.

b. Humphrey's 1968 campaign manager had been Lawrence O'Brien, who eventually became chairman of the Democratic National Committee prior to and during the Watergate scandal. It was O'Brien's Watergate office that had been broken into by a team of burglars, among them Cubans with CIA* and anti-Castro ties. One of the Cubans, Bernard Barker, had even been a member of the mob-partnered dictator Batista's secret police.

c. Hughes's long-standing executive and fixer was Robert Maheu, who also had the CIA as a client. As we've seen, the CIA had retained Maheu to coordinate the Mafia contract to kill Castro. And now, Hughes was in Las Vegas buying up mob properties.

d. O'Brien and Maheu knew each other through their mutual work for Hughes, O'Brien having been a lobbyist for the billionaire. *Nixon feared that Maheu, having bitterly left Hughes's employ, might pass along to O'Brien that Nixon had been involved with the campaign to remove Castro from power in Cuba, an effort that eventually involved the Mafia and CIA, which, according to Jack Anderson, had boomeranged into the murder of John F. Kennedy.*

It's hard to resist the temptation when looking at the facts and behaviors surrounding Watergate and the CIA/mob machinations to come up with a theory about the possible spark for the Watergate break-in:

Nixon was irrationally terrified of losing the 1972 election. His mind was spinning with scenarios of how Democrats might come at him. He was snakebit over anything associated with Hughes given the fallout from his loan to his brother Donald during the 1960 election. Plus, Hughes had recently given Nixon's campaign a lot of money, something O'Brien likely knew and may have wanted to exploit. Knowing of the Maheu-Hughes-O'Brien nexus, Nixon feared that his involvement—whatever the degree—in the early days

---

* Nixon was engaged in a power struggle with the CIA, the leadership of which resented attempts to use them as an arm of the Nixon White House. Some familiar with the investigation even speculate that CIA operatives tipped off the Washington, D.C., police about the break-in.

of anti-Castro planning would surface. This was particularly distressing considering the burgeoning JFK assassination theories about possible CIA and Mafia involvement in Kennedy's murder.

*Nixon, of course, had nothing to do with the Kennedy assassination. Nixon likely did not know the particulars of what had played out with Cuba, the CIA, and the mob—but he desperately wanted to find out because he had been aware of the broad brushes of a Castro offensive during its embryonic stages. Nixon either ordered his men to find out, or they knew he wanted to find out and went ahead and did it. His mindset was more important than the facts. Thus, the break-in involving Cuban operatives who might be uniquely qualified to know what to look for.**

The other thing Nixon understood was that what the media can prove is very different from what they can merchandize. The Kennedys' dirty plays in politics should have been of interest to the press. They hadn't been. Then there were JFK's sexual escapades. Nobody wanted to hear about that, either, at least not for a few years. But now that Kennedy had been martyred and the conspiracy industry began to boom, all of Nixon's enemies would be thrilled to play the media's favorite parlor game of JUST ASKIN'!: WAS NIXON INVOLVED WITH JFK'S MURDER? *JUST ASKIN'!*

Nixon had been very worried about Jack Anderson's tales of the Castro-Mafia plots and was horrified to see the Mafia plots publicized. The boomerang/turnaround theory, however dubious, had enormous emotional resonance, especially given some of the things Castro had said publicly, including this two months before JFK was killed: "Let Kennedy and his brother Robert take care of themselves since they, too, can be twice the victims of an attempt which will cause their death." Nixon understood political reality very clearly, mainly that the media detested him and would never give him the benefit of the doubt over any dark deeds,

---

* In most of the Watergate literature, there is general agreement that Nixon did not directly order the Watergate break-in. He certainly set the mood for such activity and his senior people were aware of the kinds of things he obsessed about. My crisis management career taught me that while most people suspect malfeasance to be vertical—top-down—it's actually horizonal with lower-level operatives anticipating the boss's priorities and taking action without line-item approval of each task.

be it the Mafia plots against Castro, the turnaround theory, or the Hughes loans and contributions, past and present.

After Anderson's 1971 column on the turnaround theory appeared, the Nixon White House saw an opportunity to turn it against the Kennedy-Camelot legend in advance of a 1972 presidential challenge by Senator Ted Kennedy. Every source that has written about Nixon makes the same baseline observation: *Nixon was not about to be rolled by the Kennedys in 1972 the way he had been in 1960.* Attorney General Mitchell arranged for Maheu to confirm and memorialize the Kennedy brothers' complicity in the kill-Castro plots and keep a record of it in the event of a challenge from Teddy, which never materialized, according to author Mark Feldstein.* The Maheu record also served a secondary purpose: to defang potential claims about Nixon's involvement in the early stages of the anti-Castro programs.

Nixon had yet another reason to feel burned by the Kennedys on the Cuba front. During the 1960 election, JFK had been accusing Nixon of helping to lead an administration that had been weak on Cuba. Nixon had to pull his punches in order not to betray that aggressive, if covert, action was being taken. Candidate Nixon called the White House to inquire about whether JFK had been briefed on the anti-Castro efforts. He *had* been briefed, and Kennedy was deliberately putting Nixon in the infuriating position on national television of having been soft on Communism, which was off brand for Nixon, to say the least.

Despite Nixon's reputation for paranoia, the word means an *irrational* fear of what one's enemies might do. Nixon was anything but irrational when it came to what the Kennedys were capable of. In addition to having illicitly obtained Nixon's psychiatric records, it was the Kennedys that had procured files on Donald Nixon's controversial 1956 "loan" from Howard Hughes. A lawyer for an accountant named Phillip Reiner, who had been involved as a financial "cutout" in the Hughes loan, had contacted Ted Kennedy about the existence of Hughes/Nixon files during the 1960 campaign. Soon after, the accountant's office was burglarized and the files were removed.

---

* Rosselli had also confirmed the Kennedys' involvement in the mob plots to Anderson, not for attribution.

Kennedy family attorney James McInerney, a former Justice Department official and friend of Bobby Kennedy who served as the 1960 campaign's "clandestine investigative arm" (according to Jack Anderson), packaged the Hughes/Nixon materials and shared them with targeted reporters. Anderson was strongly inclined to run with the story on the Hughes loan but believed it still fell short of ironclad proof. So, Anderson concocted a scheme, according to Mark Feldstein: The Nixon campaign would be told that Anderson was about to run with an explosive story; Nixon would overreact and release his own version of events; then, once there was enough in the public domain, Anderson would tweak his reporting and supplement it with what he had, and the story would be out.

This is exactly what happened. While the story about the Hughes loan hadn't been the blockbuster Anderson had hoped for, Nixon always believed it played a role in his narrow defeat to Kennedy in 1960.

A White House memo validated why there was so much concern about Robert Maheu: "Maheu's tentacles touch many extremely sensitive areas of government, each of which is fraught with potential for Jack Anderson–type exposure." In 1976, a *Rolling Stone* reporter, Howard Kohn, even tied current skullduggery to past skullduggery, suggesting that the present-day template of using tough guys to carry out sub-rosa programs had begun with Operation Underworld: "Both the Bay of Pigs affair and the Watergate scandal were rooted in the cynicism of a World War II alliance."

Intelligence operative
Robert Maheu
*UNLV Libraries Special
Collections & Archives*

A memorandum to Senator Sam Ervin who presided over the Senate Watergate Committee noted: "The significance of Anderson's column on January 18, 1971, was that *on the same day*, Haldeman requested [John] Dean to find out what he could about the Hughes–Maheu–O'Brien relationship." And:

> Therefore, the obsession of the Administration in keeping tabs on Larry O'Brien in 1971 and 1972 was in part motivated by a fear that Maheu would impart some of this sensitive information about the plot [to kill Castro] to O'Brien. . . . And these concerns could have been a possible motivation for the break-in at the offices of the DNC and Larry O'Brien by four Cuban-Americans on June 17, 1972, especially since their directions were to photograph any documents relating to the Cuban contributions or Cuban involvement in the 1972 Democratic campaign.

Most of those involved with investigating Watergate believe that O'Brien's files were specifically targeted before the burglars were caught mid-break-in. In an interview decades after Watergate, lead break-in conspirator G. Gordon Liddy confirmed this but said he didn't know if a particular subject matter had been of special interest. Getting O'Brien's files on "the Bay of Pigs thing"—if, in fact, he had any—is one theory of the possible motives.

THIS ASSESSMENT MAY BE TRUE; HOWEVER, HOW MANY INVESTIGATIVE reporters and voters would find this analysis comforting, especially coming from the CIA? It's the assassination version of Bill Clinton's telling voters that he had tried marijuana but "didn't inhale." Try this pitch for Nixon: *I was at some meetings about what kinds of actions might be taken against Castro in Cuba where I was briefed by the same people who were ultimately involved with Mafia assassination attempts on Castro and in the failed Bay of Pigs invasion, but even though I was the vice president of the United States who was running for president, I had no idea that these guys were going to take things that far.*

Scandal figures often act not upon what has surfaced but on what their imaginations tell them is "out there" that *could* surface. The true fear may or may not be rational but is of intense psychic importance to the protagonist. Accordingly, Nixon's preoccupation with "the Bay of Pigs thing" may well have been a projection of his uncertainty about a broad range of matters he had been involved with related to Cuba and/or Kennedy that had not yet surfaced and had the potential to snowball into a full-blown crisis.

ANOTHER BREAK-IN?

There is a hilarious, you-can't-make-this-stuff-up sideshow to Watergate and the Hoffa commutation that says something about how the mob, labor unions, and Nixon interacted at that time. During the weekend of March 24, 1972, bank thieves, considered by the FBI among the best in history, broke into the United California Bank in Laguna Niguel, California, a few miles away from Nixon's "western White House" in San Clemente. They were in search of cash they had been told by LCN associates in Ohio belonged to Richard Nixon for slush fund purposes. Indeed, Nixon had been caught on tape speaking about "shaking down" dairy producers to raise the price of milk. Two executives from the largest milk cooperative were convicted of making the payment.

The thieves were told the total was $30 million, which is likely preposterous, but in the planning stages they referred to the lucre as "milk money." Nevertheless, Jimmy Hoffa allegedly tipped off Ohio mobster Butchie Cisternino after he became angry about being forbidden to hold union office again. Hoffa was especially furious after having given $3 million* to Nixon's campaign. Said one of the thieves, Harry Barber, "What was Nixon going to say? They took the money from the milk scam I pulled?"

The burglars were led by Amil Dinsio, who held very strong feelings about taking money from banks: *Robberies* were stupid because the perpetrators never got away with it, and innocent people could get hurt. *Burglaries*—breaking in under cover of darkness without weapons—minimized risk and maximized gain. Dinsio was told that if he and his crew retrieved Nixon's purported cash and shared the wealth with the

---

* However much Hoffa gave Nixon, it was likely a lot less than $3 million, but why not aim high and see what you can get?

mobsters who gave them a tip, they could keep the lion's share of the booty. Among other things, Dinsio and his crew thought Nixon was a bigger crook than they were and were hoping they could really, really annoy him.

They ended up stealing $9 million (as best as anybody could figure). It was the most successful bank burglary in American history. The FBI immediately concluded that the thieves were heavy-hitting professionals, not a ragtag band of local opportunists. They had defeated multiple alarms, used explosives, and sliced through rebar. "They're the best who ever lived," said FBI agent Paul Chamberlain. Law enforcement estimated that before the California break-in, the mob-linked crew had stolen $20 million across thirty burglaries.

Given what we now know about Watergate and slush funds, aspects of this story are plausible, especially since the burglary provably occurred and the perpetrators walked away with a fortune. Further adding to its credibility is that Nixon friend Bebe Rebozo admitted that he had stashed a $100,000 cash contribution from billionaire Howard Hughes in a Florida safe deposit box (which may have been moved from California at some point). Rebozo had also acted as a courier and launderer of cash contributions for Nixon. Similarly, Attorney General Richard Kleindienst

Amil Dinsio was the lead burglar who went after cash allegedly belonging to Nixon that was stored in a California bank vault.
Courtesy of Amil Dinsio

admitted under oath to having refused a $100,000 cash bribe for Nixon's political campaign if the DOJ would drop its prosecution of specific organized crime figures.

Like many crooks, as good as the Dinsio crew was at stealing the money, they were less good at getting away. Dinsio decided to break into an Ohio bank about a month later using the same methods. The FBI thought it seemed familiar. Dinsio was a neighborhood legend, and his name came up quickly. Federal agents began showing his photo to taxicab drivers at Los Angeles International Airport until one remembered having received a $100 tip. Dinsio was famously generous with civilians.

One would have thought that Dinsio's gang may have been pinched earlier because when they blew the concrete roof of the bank using multiple sticks of dynamite, the entire beach town shook. Some passed it off as an earthquake, not an exotic experience in Southern California. No one investigated. Perhaps the best thing about this bank job was that the thieves didn't just break in once; they broke in three days in a row to steal as much as they could over a weekend.*

The burglars were captured and later convicted after fingerprints were found on the dishes of the town house they had rented as a headquarters while conducting the heist. As successful as the break-in had been, they had forgotten to turn on the dishwasher. They also used their names to book the flights between California and Ohio. Most of the cash was recovered. A few burglars later claimed that their haul had been light because Nixon had diversified his deposits between two banks. An FBI agent on the case disputes this and the Nixon people never acknowledged that a nickel of their money had been stolen.

Among the other factors lending credence to the Jimmy Hoffa connection in the heist is that an associate of the Teamsters leader, Harry Hall, a midwestern mob-linked swindler, attempted to launder $175,000 in securities taken from the United California Bank vault at a Chicago bank in April 1972. In addition, a week after the bank job, a tiny Las Vegas PR firm that had recently reported billings of only $20,000 "won" a $1.3 million contract from the Teamsters. That kind of money would

---

* Years later, Dinsio sued a North Carolina bank he attempted to steal from for understating the amount they had stored in their vault.

be a huge contract for a PR firm today; by 1972 standards, it was gargantuan. It turned out that Hall had been their business partner and that the contract was almost surely an attempt to launder some of the stolen cash.

NIXON, FRIEND OF THE MOB? NOT SO FAST

Nixon's foes will swear that there was no more mobbed-up president than he was. There are certainly disturbing links, but the notion that he was in the mob's pocket is wishful thinking.

While the spiritual father of the RICO law that decimated LCN was Bobby Kennedy, the actual author was Kennedy acolyte G. Robert Blakey—but it was Nixon who signed it into law. He did more than that. According to Blakey, "Nixon had recommended all of the major provisions that are in the Organized Crime Control Act."

While Blakey has said that much work still needs to be done to combat organized crime, the number of "made" members in America has been reduced from about five thousand at the height of LCN's power to roughly one thousand today. He likens fighting organized crime to garbage removal: Trash will never go away, but you can prevent it from piling up in the street.

A nascent Nixon administration advocated for significant legislation hostile to organized crime, including $61 million in mob-specific funding, a substantial sum in those days. Nixon also supported legislation that expanded racket-busting field offices from eight to twelve and adding one thousand agents to the Justice Department. His proposals, which were coordinated with Senator John McClellan, would also grant immunity to federal witnesses and assign serious punishments to primary gambling operations.

In April 1969, Nixon's DOJ summoned kingpins Anthony Accardo, Jimmy Alo, and Meyer Lansky to testify under oath to address charges that they had convened to discuss a successor to imprisoned mob chief Vito Genovese after his death. They were predictably unhelpful. In over a year, 117 gangsters had been indicted under Nixon's new regime.

THE RICO LAW WAS SIGNED BY RICHARD NIXON AND WENT INTO EFFECT on October 15, 1970. Nixon also began the National Council on Organized Crime that year. Prior to RICO, mobsters had to be prosecuted for individual crimes. Under RICO they could be charged for a pattern of crimes, including as little as two everyday state or federal offenses that took place within a ten-year time frame. Even associating with other criminals in a provably criminal way could be folded into a prosecution that could carry sentences that were greater than the sum of its parts. The *American Bar Association Journal* described the penalties as "draconian" and designed to outlaw the Mafia. Nevertheless, it took years before the feds really knew what to do with it. To some, it sounded strange: Convicting gangsters for getting involved with other gangsters seemed unsavory but not criminal.

In 1975, killing Jimmy Hoffa, once the most influential labor union leader in America, took guts—and said something about the mob's power and arrogance. Organized crime was arguably at the zenith of its power in the 1970s and could no longer be given short shrift. Nixon was so heavily favored to win the 1972 election that he probably hadn't needed the Teamsters' support, but Nixon did a lot of things that he didn't need to do that proved to be self-destructive. The deal he cut with Fitzsimmons to eject Hoffa was tawdry but shrewd. If, in fact, as many experts and investigative reporters believe, the Nixon campaign received cash bribes as an additional incentive to commute Hoffa's sentence, he never got caught, which disproves the post-Watergate canard that it's always the cover-up that gets you. In fact, cover-ups can work very well, but we never hear about successful ones—or punish the perpetrators—because they're cover-ups.

Fitzsimmons and the mob cut a fine deal, too. They got Hoffa out of power until the gangsters found a more permanent solution. Hoffa had been characteristically ungrateful for his freedom; he wanted his pre-1967 life back, and that wasn't what Nixon's action granted him. Nixon was a politician, not a genie. The Teamsters' rank and file may not have fared so well because Fitzsimmons agreed not to attack Nixon for freezing wages.

Nixon overestimated certain threats and maintained the ability to see himself as a law-and-order president by cracking down on the mob while breaking other kinds of laws from the Oval Office. In fact, the Nixon White House used the very tactics they were supposed to be deploying against LCN against their political adversaries.

It is an ironic coda to Nixon's story that the hero of Watergate, FBI honcho Mark Felt, Bob Woodward's secret source "Deep Throat," had himself been engaging in the same kind of "black bag jobs"—break-ins, illegal wiretapping—at roughly the same time he was meeting with Woodward in dark parking garages. He was later convicted for the offenses but wasn't identified as Deep Throat for more than thirty years.

The relationship between Nixon and organized crime was one of long-distance symbiosis rather than a tight quid pro quo. Nixon got help early on in his career from mob money and from a strategist, Chotiner, who had defended mobsters in court. Later, he was able to make deals with mobbed-up unions, but at a distance from criminals themselves. As we will continue to see, the politics-and-crime racket is all about natural mutuality and layering. Still, while LCN and its tentacles benefited from decisions Nixon made, Nixon felt secure enough in his position to come down hard.

Nixon's punishment for unholy alliances was having to perpetually hear the footsteps of his enemies, which caused him to take actions during Watergate that were disproportionate to the threat. Some of his fears had mob aspects, such as the anti-Castro efforts in which his role has been exaggerated. If we can give Nixon credit for something, we can acknowledge that he possessed the capacity for shame. This informed his restraint in the aftermath of his loss in the razor-thin 1960 election and later when he resigned from office during Watergate rather than put the country through an even more prolonged fight. The concepts of shame and respectability are ones we shall return to in the peculiar dance between pols and hoods.

Wrote Garry Wills in *Nixon Agonistes*:

> The tapes are the real man—mean, vindictive, panicky, striking first in anticipation of being struck, trying to lift his own friable self-esteem by shoving others down. [Political commentator] Murray Kempton said he wanted to leave no fingerprints, but he went about it in such a way as to leave his fingerprints all over his story. Nixon's real tragedy is that he never had the stature to be a tragic hero. He is the stuff of sad (almost heartbreaking) comedy.

7

Ronald Reagan

HOLLYWOOD FRIENDS

Stay clear of the press. No interviews. No panels.
No speeches. No comments. Stay out of the
spotlight. It fades your suit.

—Lew Wasserman

The dynamic of organized crime as threads in the broader tapestry of presidential politics continues with Ronald Reagan and those close to him. This chapter provokes daunting shake-the-hand-that-shook-the-hand questions about judging organized crime and presidencies. To what extent should we judge a politician whose mentor derived his power in part from organized crime? How much time must pass between when that politician benefited from the actions of that mentor and when we decide that the past is past and what's been done in the ensuing decades matters more? Ronald Reagan's presidency presents a particular difficulty here because while some of his close friends had deep mob-related origins, how much of this can be fairly pinned on Reagan himself?

Take Reagan's close friend Walter Annenberg (who also knew Richard Nixon well). Annenberg's media empire had been rooted in Chicago's newspaper distribution rackets of the early 1900s in which fourteen newspaper dealers were murdered and countless injured and maimed. These wars, which involved Walter's father, Moses ("Moe"), mobilizing thugs to distribute William Randolph Hearst's newspapers who were battling Colonel Robert McCormick's *Chicago Tribune*, eventually evolved into a national horse racing wire service, the *Daily Racing Form* newspaper, and a number of major newspapers and magazines throughout the country, including the *Philadelphia Inquirer* and *TV Guide*.

Hearst "circulation director" Moe Annenberg grew the racing wire service the same way he had used hoodlums on behalf of William Randolph Hearst: He teamed with mobsters to persuade local racing wires to sell out to or partner with him. The racing wire was rooted in the philosophy articulated by the Annenbergs' biographer Christopher Ogden: "You could gamble at a track, so why was offtrack gambling illegal? To Moses' thinking, there was a class factor involved, and something was inherently unfair about the entire system. Not everyone could visit a track. Millions of factory workers and day laborers could not get away from their jobs during the week or leave their families on a weekend."

Or, as Moe himself told Walter, "It isn't right to deprive the little people of a chance to be lucky."

Moe Annenberg didn't shy away from violence to help his fellow man. He bought his initial racing wire company after the owner agreed to sell after his office was firebombed. Sabotage and beatings had been the main tools of persuasion. Organized crime groups, including Chicago's Outfit and Lucky Luciano's gang in New York, facilitated distribution. One of Annenberg's leg breakers was Dion O'Banion, who was later killed during an internecine Chicago gangland turf war. Said Luciano, "I used to think of the Mirror as my paper . . . I always thought of Annenberg as my sort of guy."

Things began to turn south for the Annenbergs after their *Philadelphia Inquirer* consistently hammered President Franklin D. Roosevelt's New Deal policies. FDR didn't have to dig too deeply to figure out Moe Annenberg's business methods, but the RICO law was decades away and there were no torts prohibiting having mob ties. As FDR's predecessor figured out during the long hunt for Al Capone, there were laws against income tax evasion, so he sicced the Internal Revenue Service on the Annenbergs.

Moe and his son Walter were indicted; it was one of the largest tax cases in history. Moe took the fall for the entire enterprise, agreeing to pay $9.5 million in fines and back taxes. This deal allowed young Walter to escape conviction and prison. The same judge who sentenced Al Capone sentenced the senior Annenberg. Moe served three years in Lewisburg, stunned his sentence was that long. He died a month after his release, not even trying to salvage his ownership in the vicious wire service. This recalls the deleted scene in the original *Godfather* film when Michael Corleone confronts the Don about not seeking vengeance for the death of his brother Sonny, telling his father it will look like a sign of weakness. The Don bows his head and concedes, "It is a sign of weakness."

To the Annenbergs' ultimate good fortune, they were out of the race wire business. Benjamin (Bugsy) Siegel's partner, Allen Smiley, who had been on the sofa with him when he was shot to death, believed competition over the racing wire had been the catalyst for Siegel's murder. Some Siegel family members agreed, attributing the hit to the "spaghetti mafia," Chicago gangsters who wanted control over the wire. Smiley's daughter, Luellen, said that Smiley had been actively involved in trying to expand the TransAmerica wire service in the Southwest and had personally felt competitive pressure from representatives of the Chicago Outfit who had taken over the remnants of the Annenberg wire. Another wire service–related theory claims Siegel wanted a percentage of the Outfit's profits.

Media dynasty patriarch
Moses Annenberg
Bettmann Archive via Getty Images

Perhaps the Outfit felt they no longer needed Siegel's participation in the marketplace. Other news reports suggested that Smiley may also have been a target.

The Outfit's Continental Wire Service had been acquired in a manner that gave new meaning to "hostile takeover": They killed its hardheaded proprietor, James Ragan. When bullets failed to finish Ragan off, they poisoned him with mercury while he was recovering in the hospital. Siegel suggested to the Outfit that he'd be pleased to back off for a few million dollars. Luciano and Lansky had warned Siegel that he was poking a mighty big bear in Chicago, but Siegel was congenitally fearless and behaved this way in every facet of his life.

Siegel is understandably thought of as a New York mobster, but the Chicago Outfit had also been investors in early Las Vegas and had interests in Los Angeles, both of which grew as the twentieth century progressed. Given the racing wire's provenance in Chicago, the Outfit felt they had stolen it from Annenberg fair and square. New York believed they had a point. Siegel's murder has never been solved and multiple credible theories are hotly debated. While some true crime books and films have put the blame on Lansky because of Siegel's cost overruns at the Flamingo, sources close to Lansky indicated that he had been Siegel's most ardent defender. Siegel's death was one of the few subjects that could make Lansky emotional, and he wrote in his diary that had it been up to him his friend would "live as long as Methuselah." Siegel's family believed him. Lansky stood in for the slain Siegel at his daughter Millicent's wedding.

Companies such as Western Union and AT&T had supplied the wire services with the hardware necessary to transmit timely data to and from racetracks and bookies. While they were investigated, neither of these blue-chip companies nor their executives ever faced prosecution. Western Union's board of directors included none other than FDR's friend and spy chief Vincent Astor, not to mention a Harriman, Warburg, Vanderbilt, and Rockefeller. No, it was the ethnic immigrants such as Annenberg and an assortment of mob-connected bookies who ended up in the calaboose.

Walter Annenberg got the message loud and clear. He spent decades rebuilding the business, and it took years to dig out from under the massive back taxes and fines obligations. He paid the debt but never lost his antipathy for Roosevelt and Democrats. Walter Annenberg set out to befriend presidents and blue bloods, not be targeted by them. He also never fully abandoned his father's strong-arm tactics although he was somewhat savvier about it. Wrote Jack Shafer in *Slate*: "After purchasing the *Philadelphia Daily News*, Annenberg practically turned over local police coverage in the city to Police Commissioner Frank Rizzo, a brutalist who rose to mayor in large part thanks to Annenberg. Rizzo returned the favor by providing extraordinary protection when the Teamsters and Newspaper Guild struck the Inquirer."

Annenberg served as Nixon's ambassador to the U.K., creating controversy given the family's criminal past. Annenberg addressed his background candidly in confirmation hearings, referring to his father's criminal conviction as "a tragedy in the life of the family. There is no question that a tragedy of such magnitude will either destroy you or inspire you to overcome it, and drive you on to deeds of affirmative character."

Walter's wife, Leonore, became Chief of Protocol of the United States during the Reagan administration. Annenberg became one of the greatest philanthropists in history, once again raising the question: When are past bad acts forgiven?

"THE OCTOPUS" ORIGIN STORY

Any nexus between Reagan and organized crime reasonably begins with his relationship with what was once harmlessly called the Music Corporation of America. Founded in 1924 in Chicago by ophthalmologist Jules Stein as a band booking agency, it grew over the decades into a broader talent agency and movie studio with its ownership of Universal Pictures, a television production company, a major record label, and an amusement park company. In addition to Universal, other brands that have passed under the MCA umbrella over the years have included names like Revue Productions, Decca Records, G.P. Putnam's Sons, Motown Records, and Geffen Records, to name a few. MCA's aggressive expansion across multiple disciplines of show business inspired a menacing nickname for the company, "the Octopus."

The mob entered MCA's existence early since it booked bands during Prohibition in speakeasies run by Al Capone and the Outfit. Stein used Capone muscle to encourage recalcitrant clubs to schedule his bands to perform and gave Capone some percentage of ownership or profit-sharing for his services. Despite the back-alley feel to a business such as band-booking, from its earliest stages, MCA sought to cultivate the reputation as a serious enterprise instead of the "flesh peddler" patina that so many Hollywood agencies had. This mien only deepened when Stein hired as a talent agent a onetime movie usher, the tall, smooth Lew Wasserman from Cleveland, Ohio.

Wasserman began his career selling candy and serving as a cinema usher. When Stein hired him in 1936 to be his advertising and publicity manager, he handled advertising for the Mayfair Casino, a Cleveland supper club controlled by local racketeers. It was here that Wasserman learned that messages can be received without technically hearing them and sent without saying them.

Jules Stein had doubts about the gangly kid in his early twenties because he didn't have a college education and had been dressed in an old suit. It was a shortcoming Wasserman never forgot because appearance became an essential tenet of MCA agents' conduct. Dark suits and dark ties conveyed the ethic "Think Yiddish, dress British." Wasserman could pull it off, too, with his height, trim build, and thick head of hair that showed streaks of gray early. As he aged, he accessorized his look with oversized dark glasses contrasting with his white hair.

The Mayfair's owners wanted it to be a gambling casino, but the mayor nixed it. It was secretly owned by Morris "Moe" Dalitz, Sam Tucker, Lou Rothkopf, and Morris Kleinman. They had been the Jewish faction of the mob known as the Cleveland Syndicate that dominated bootlegging and gambling in the region. The men, especially Dalitz, were to become powerhouses in Las Vegas, Cuban casino gambling, and running illegal casinos in Ohio and Kentucky.

Wasserman's wife's family had a Dalitz connection, too. Her father, an attorney who had faced serious legal problems, including charges of arson, was a player in local Republican politics. The Cleveland political boss was one of Dalitz's business partners. One Hollywood figure interviewed said in confidence that he had lunch with Wasserman in the MCA commissary after the mogul had retired. Someone at the table brought up the name Moe Dalitz and Wasserman became furious and said he never wanted to hear that name again. When he calmed down, he told the younger Hollywood types that he'd tell them what went on in the old days when they "grew up."

SIDNEY

Wasserman became MCA's president in 1946. Ronald Reagan was an early film client whom he continued to represent even after his management responsibilities increased. They became friends and spent time together. Among those in their social circle was attorney Sidney Korshak, who may have been Wasserman's best friend. Korshak was never licensed to practice law in California, but most lawyers wouldn't see his "practice" as having much to do with jurisprudence anyway. In an interview with the *New York Times*, Wasserman said of Korshak, "He's a very well-respected lawyer. He's a man of his word and good company." Seymour Hersh and Jeff Gerth wrote in the *New York Times*, "To scores of federal, state, and local law enforcement figures, Mr. Korshak is the most important link between organized crime and legitimate business" in the United States.

California's Organized Crime Control Commission described Korshak as "an active labor lawyer, an attorney for Chicago organized crime figures and the key link between organized crime and big business." Indeed, Korshak's corporate clients included Gulf & Western, Max Factor, Diners Club (founded by Reagan friend Alfred Bloomingdale), Schenley Industries, Hilton and Hyatt Hotels and the Los Angeles Dodgers. Reported the *New York Times*, Korshak once told an associate, "I've been investigated by more Congressional committees than anybody, but nobody's got anything on me." So smoothly did Korshak navigate in legitimate society that he sat at the same table as J. Edgar Hoover at a Loyola University Medical School fundraiser in Chicago in 1964 despite the FBI having been wiretapping Korshak for years.

Korshak was the linchpin of the Chicago Outfit's stranglehold over Hollywood because by controlling the unions the mobsters made themselves indispensable because they had the power to shut down production. Many wrongly think of labor racketeers as exclusively extorting corporations, but there was another way to look at it that went back to Piker Ryan's list:

They were partners. For a steady fee (bribe), film and television production would continue. No fee, no entertainment. Studios had no choice but to pay. Nor did they bother to fight it to any great degree. In fact, some like MCA saw mob muscle as a valuable insurance policy and a warning to obstreperous union types not to get cute. Neither the entertainment companies nor the mob saw any reason to shake up an arrangement that was working.

Korshak and Reagan also became friends. The lawyer personally liked Reagan but ribbed him for his corny tendencies, once saying, "Ronnie says he's so pure. He's really a phony with this big moralistic platform—he and I used to be with hookers in the same bedroom!" when Reagan was between marriages.

Korshak played the role to the actual Chicago Outfit that the fictional German Irish Tom Hagen played to the Corleone family in *The Godfather*. He was an attorney when legal credentials were needed. He was an emissary to the legitimate world when the mob required an assimilated character to handle transactions that required a lighter touch than the knuckle-dragging bosses along Lake Michigan could conjure. Korshak likely never committed an act of violence in his life. Then again, Korshak never had to play rough personally. The subtext of his suave and understated presence was clear: *Sign here (the easy way) or we'll kill you and everyone you love.* The periodic savage murder by the Outfit was better than any brochure or credentials presentation. Korshak rarely used the telephone and maintained no records other than what he filed away in his brain.

Some mob authors and aficionados strictly equate ethnicity with degree of influence. They argue that given Korshak was not Italian and ineligible to be a "made" member of a Cosa Nostra, he should be dismissed as a major force. This overlooks an important point: Top-level mobsters are, at root, organized enterprise criminals—antisocial and violent businessmen. They respect money and those who reliably make it for them. Accordingly, the Chicago Outfit had non-Italian executives like Jake Guzik, Murray Humphreys, and Gus Alex, who held great power, as Meyer Lansky did as a partner with New York's Luciano-Costello-Genovese family. That these men didn't take a blood oath or burn the image of a saint was of little practical importance.

Some have argued that an Italian boss could order a Jewish boss killed if he wanted to and not the other way around, as if this were the ultimate arbiter of influence. Perhaps, but a defense contractor like Lockheed Martin *could* bomb a technology company like Microsoft, but why would they when they could be partners and make fortunes together?

So it came to pass that Korshak, loved like a son by long-standing Outfit boss Anthony "Joe Batters" Accardo, became a "labor consultant" for the boys back home for well over a half century. He delivered peace with unions to department store chains, hotel corporations like Hyatt, and manufacturers like Motorola. The unions knew that somewhere over Korshak's well-tailored shoulders there were men who would kill them as soon as look at them. The corporate clients knew it, too, and they didn't care, provided a horse's head never landed on their mattress.

There was nothing illegal about being a labor consultant. There was nothing illegal about receiving a fee for your counsel, especially if there was never a paper trail detailing the true nature of the transaction. Nor was there anything provably illegal about some of those checks finding their way back to Chicago as "finder's fees" for "consulting."

This was Sidney Korshak's world, allowing him to spend time with corporate and political leaders with a mutual sense of relief. After all, if

Los Angeles attorney
Sidney Korshak and client,
actress Debbie Reynolds
Courtesy Everett Collection

questioned, "honest" people could truthfully say (and they often did) that they "never saw Sidney with any criminals."*

My own Korshak lesson came when I got to know an author, private investigator, and all-around Dickensian figure named Ed Becker in the 1990s. Becker had become known years earlier for launching the rumor that New Orleans mob boss Carlos Marcello had told him of his desire— and intention—to kill Kennedy. Becker even gave federal officials his version of events. When I met him, Becker said he had worked for Gus Greenbaum, Ben Siegel's successor at the Flamingo. He also claimed to have done publicity work at the Flamingo for Siegel himself. Greenbaum and Becker later moved to the Riviera. Becker had also co-authored a biography about Johnny Rosselli and had been a researcher on *The Grim Reapers* about the mob by Ed Reid.

Becker remained scarred thirty-five years later about the murder of Greenbaum and his wife in 1958. He blamed the Chicago Outfit for the knife slayings and admonished me when I characterized Sidney Korshak (who was still alive) as an "attorney." Becker said viewing Korshak as a mobster in the Chicago Outfit was more accurate. He resented Korshak's ability to position himself as being respectable because of his law license, business contacts, and society presence when he had been backed by the most violent mob family in the country (I got the strong impression that Korshak may have threatened Becker in some way).

Regardless of who may or may not have "seen" Korshak with criminals, we cannot escape the kinds of criminals the Chicago Outfit was comprised of and the implied weapon Korshak wielded: When a loan shark was suspected of being a snitch (he wasn't), then boss Sam Giancana ordered William "Action" Jackson to be tortured, suspended by a meat hook in his rectum, and repeatedly zapped with an electric cattle prod. He was also stabbed and beaten with a baseball bat until he expired. The men who did it—ranking Outfit members—were recorded on FBI bugs laughing and saying things like, "We tossed water on him to give the prod a better charge and he's screamin'."

---

* His "direct report" was political boss the Greek Gus Alex, although he had personal contact with Accardo, too. Discreetly.

When Gus Greenbaum wanted to retire due to ill health, his sister-in-law was murdered. Greenbaum went back to work. For reasons ascribed alternately to skimming, drug addiction, or the Outfit's desire for a management transition, Greenbaum and his wife had their throats slit in their Arizona home, Gus nearly decapitated with a butcher's knife. After boss Accardo's home was burgled, evidently not by long-range strategic thinkers, he demanded that they be hunted down and dealt with. Five men were tracked, tortured, and killed, including one castrated, disemboweled, with his face burned off with a blowtorch.

Lew Wasserman badly needed Korshak's Teamsters connections when MCA moved into TV production. Everything seen on a film or TV set had to get there somehow, and that somehow was by trucks driven by Teamsters. Then there were the artists' unions like the Screen Actors Guild (SAG) or the American Federation of Television and Radio Artists (AFTRA), where Korshak was also connected.

According to an official from the International Alliance of Theatrical Stage Employees (IATSE), Wasserman had also taken loans from the Teamsters when MCA expanded into the TV production business, which was far more capital-intensive than talent representation. According to IATSE official Roy Brewer, who later teamed with Reagan to address Communist infiltration* in Hollywood, Korshak brokered the Teamsters loans. Harris Katleman, an MCA agent, said, "Lew and Sidney were joined at the hip in the fifties. Sidney did whatever Lew needed."

PREMATURE SUNSET

It was in this environment in the early 1950s that Ronald Reagan found himself with his film career winding down. The Warner studio had dumped him, his finances were teetering, he owed back taxes to the IRS, and, in his early forties, having just been remarried, he had a young family to care for.

Wasserman was in a transitional period as well, facing a civil war within MCA. The New York faction of the company felt Wasserman's

---

* It is a matter of public record that Reagan had been an FBI informant about Communist inroads in show business.

elevation to president was undeserved. Personal conflicts aside, the New Yorkers felt the future of television was in live production. Most shows at that time were indeed broadcast live. Wasserman was placing his bets in another direction, filmed entertainment, because he believed it could be produced in more of an assembly-line manner without the encumbrances and vulnerabilities associated with a live audience. To make this happen, however, Wasserman needed a bigger production pipeline.

Wasserman's idea was for MCA to be *both* a talent agency and a television producer. This was a conflict of interest because MCA would be in a unique position to secure its clients jobs on TV that wouldn't be available to its talent-peddling competitors.

Problem: Everybody knew this would be a conflict of interest, so SAG didn't allow talent agents to make movies. *Movies*, not TV shows. Television was a new medium so there were no such restrictions from SAG on production and Wasserman had no interest in a level playing field; what he wanted was an unfair advantage. To do that, MCA needed a bespoke waiver for its TV arm, Revue Productions. By this point, his client, Ronald Reagan, had become president of SAG and was able to help.

In any self-dealing business pitch, it's essential to find a peg to demonstrate that it's about more than personal benefit. Wasserman had a good one: MCA would be creating jobs in television production and, given that SAG members would be getting these jobs, it would allow them a competitive edge over rival union AFTRA.

In subsequent SAG meetings in July 1952, nearly all the actors were against the waiver concept. Said SAG official Chet Migden, "Indeed, the waiver was going down, Reagan didn't say anything, he was in the chair,

MCA's Lew Wasserman was Ronald Reagan's talent agent and Hollywood's first among equals for decades.
Photo by William Nation/ Sygma via Getty Images

he was presiding over the debate that was going on." Eventually, beloved actor Walter Pidgeon, one of the older actors there, asked, "Is anybody working?" He lamented his declining prospects and income flow, adding, "Somebody wants to create some work, what the hell is wrong with that?"

Wrote Wasserman biographer Connie Bruck, "During the next few months, in early 1952, Wasserman navigated this process in ways so characteristically deft and traceless that even FBI and grand jury investigations undertaken later would be unable to fully reconstruct it."

The waiver passed unanimously.

Reagan's July 23, 1952, letter read: "We agree that for a period commencing with the date hereof and expiring October 31, 1959, if any contract rule or regulation made by us prevents your engaging in both businesses we hereby give you waiver thereof for such period."

Wrote Bruck, "With the waiver won, Wasserman launched MCA into the TV production business." Wasserman began working on a new deal for Reagan shortly after. Concluded Dan Moldea, the lead chronicler of the Wasserman-Reagan relationship:

> As Justice Department records noted, "It was thought . . . that SAG might have purposely favored MCA for some illegal consideration." Although it may never be proven that Reagan or any other SAG official pushed through the SAG special arrangement with MCA and then received a suitcase filled with cash, it is clear that, within months of the deal, Reagan benefited personally, financially, professionally, and politically from his relationship with MCA.

A Reagan friend, SAG official Jack Dales, saw no grand conspiracy saying, "I think Ronnie did more or less what he thought he should—and then he was rewarded for it, with the GE job." An unidentified DOJ official was less kind: "Ronald Reagan is a complete slave of MCA who would do their bidding on anything."

COMEBACK

Reagan had gotten the GE gig that saved his career through MCA as a result of the waiver he pushed through because his agent found it easy to get Reagan a job at a TV production company he controlled. The new show, called *General Electric Theater*, began broadcasting with Reagan as its only host in 1954 (it had debuted earlier but in a different format). It represented MCA's landmark entry into the world of big-time TV production. It was an anthology series that broadcast entertainment derived from literature, plays, or films. It featured heavyweight stars including Bud Abbott, Fred Astaire, Anne Baxter, Jack Benny, Joan Crawford, Sammy Davis, Jr., Judy Garland, Louis Jourdan, Boris Karloff, Alan Ladd, Piper Laurie, Cloris Leachman, Art Linkletter, Fred MacMurray, E. G. Marshall, the Marx Brothers, Burgess Meredith, Jason Robards, Stella Stevens, Gene Tierney, and Natalie Wood.

General Electric Theater soon became the third best-rated show after *The Ed Sullivan Show* (which aired right before Reagan's show), and *I Love Lucy*. In addition to hosting the show, Reagan toured the country giving multiple speeches daily and rallying the company's employees, who were excited that a show about where they worked was becoming so popular—and they got to meet its star, Reagan. It was at G*eneral Electric Theater* that Reagan perfected his telegenic skills, altering his voice and facial expressions in accordance with the subject matter being presented. (It was a fascinating thing to watch as a young communications aide in his White House decades later.) Disliking air travel, he mostly toured the country by train and bus where he learned to interact with his audience. Many stars and politicians dislike engaging with everyday people, but Reagan enjoyed it. The new show also ended Reagan's financial problems, giving him $125,000 per year (about $1.3 million today) and perks like a new GE kitchen for the Reagan household. His salary continued to rise.

In 1960, Reagan helped resolve a strike in MCA's favor when SAG threatened to picket mostly over the issue of residual fees for actors. SAG settled with MCA and other select companies, but they could not reach a deal with the larger studios. Some SAG members questioned Reagan's priorities. Another union, IASTE, cried foul at the special arrangement. Among Reagan's supporters was Frank Sinatra, who owned his own production company. IATSE official Richard Walsh, reported Moldea, summarized the SAG machinations by attributing them to Reagan's relationship with Korshak, not to mention Korshak and Reagan's with Wasserman: "Reagan was a friend of, talked to Sidney Korshak, and it would all tie back together. That's the whole thing that was going on at the time you're talking about. . . . I know Sidney Korshak. I know where he comes from, what he is, and what he's done. He's a labor lawyer, as the term goes."

Opinions about the settlement diverged. SAG's chief negotiator cited favorable raises and a pension deal. Detractors included Bob Hope who felt the studios had taken advantage of the actors. Some cried hypocrisy and self-dealing, citing Reagan's GE deal where he was both host (actor and union member) and a producer (management). Reagan soon became a partner in an MCA production venture and resigned as SAG president.

A FEW FACTORS COLLIDED IN THE EARLY 1960S THAT IMPERILED REAGAN'S role at GE. Robert F. Kennedy's Justice Department impaneled a grand jury examining MCA's monopolistic status as talent agency and TV and film production studio. The company settled by shedding its talent management division, which was not especially difficult because while it reflected MCA's origins, it was the studio business—and later music production—that was going places.

In 1962, Reagan testified before a grand jury looking into MCA's anti-trust practices that he hadn't been a producer of *General Electric Theater* while serving as SAG president when, in fact, he had been.* Also, GE was recovering from an intense price-fixing scandal. Blue-chip GE could not have been comfortable dealing with the talent agency and studio that was also under fire for anticompetitive behavior, not to mention suspected of having mob connections.

Reagan had also been developing more conservative, anti-government political views that began seeping into his on-air performance. Reagan's anti-Communism, like Nixon's, was the animating element of his conservatism. His position was sincere; however, like other presidential

---

* Reagan could be slippery under questioning such as when he denied having informed to the FBI on any actors alleged to have Communist leanings while he was the head of SAG. FBI documents confirm that Reagan was a source of information of this nature. The concept of "informing," of course, could have multiple meanings depending on how the informer defined it. Had law enforcement been alerted? Were they told of criminal activity or just opinions about personal predilections? Were studio investigators notified? Congressional investigators?

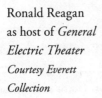

Ronald Reagan
as host of *General
Electric Theater*
*Courtesy Everett
Collection*

administrations before his, if resources and attention spans were finite and focused on the Cold War, it was harder to make a case that more needed to be done about the rackets.

It was the deeply held view in the Reagan household that Attorney General Kennedy had pressured GE to get rid of Reagan. There is no way to know what the final catalyst for the end of Reagan's run might have been, but it was over. Reagan had mastered radio as a sports announcer and film as an actor, but with *General Electric Theater*, he got the chance to perfect the medium that would play the essential role in his political career, television.

Reagan's hosting of *General Electric Theater* did for his political career what Donald Trump's competition program *The Apprentice* did to launch his. To be sure, these were very different shows. On *General Electric Theater*, Reagan was the genial host who traveled across the country to GE laboratories and factories to showcase the company's products while broadcasting adaptations of novels, short stories, and other literature. *The Apprentice* was a game show that presented a fantastic caricature of a brilliant, self-made businessman.

There is little question that Reagan and Wasserman benefited from a long-standing relationship and that the latter wouldn't have been the power that he became without his underworld contacts. It is hard to believe that Reagan didn't know how Wasserman had climbed to the pinnacle of Hollywood (or Frank Sinatra and the Annenbergs' gangland ties). The SAG waiver had aided MCA in the leap from flesh-peddler to conglomerate. Wasserman didn't keep pounding the pavement for his 10 percent anymore. But his challenges would return years later.

TRANSITION TEAM

In 1980, the Reagan team knew his presidential candidacy was vulnerable on the issue of labor as Reagan was openly pro-business. He was tagged with desiring only to make his rich friends richer. The Jedi mind trick became: *Was there a way to be both pro-business and pro-labor, making the argument that the more that free enterprise succeeded, the better it would be for workers?* The campaign was undoubtedly going to try.

According to sources familiar with Reagan's strategy, while organized labor might not have loved Reagan on policy there were cultural affinities. While labor favored Democrats, the movement had no love for President Jimmy Carter, Reagan's opponent. AFL-CIO boss George Meany openly called Carter a disappointment and a "conservative." Carter was aloof, didn't seem to understand the issues important to labor, and had no personal chemistry with labor leaders, not to mention the rank and file who didn't know what to make of the remote and brainy nuclear engineer and peanut farmer. It wasn't unusual to see cowboy hats and sidearms at Teamsters meetings. These folks instinctively felt they lived in Reagan Country, not Carterland.

Reagan found a cultural wedge to divide labor with the building-and-construction trades and the Teamsters who were largely white, hawks on foreign policy, skeptical of progressives, and accepting of gun culture. The labor movement, despite its origins in anti-corporate activity, was at a crossroads: Did labor embrace the progressive politics often associated with Marxism and United Auto Workers boss Walter Reuther, or did they, like Hoffa, rally behind dealmaking capitalism? Nixon had shown he could capture support from labor with the help of building-and-construction trade boss Peter Brennan (later his secretary of labor) and Reagan's approach was to demonstrate to those with whom he had cultural simpatico that he represented the best opportunity for them.

The Teamsters were a viable target for another reason: They were the bad boys of labor and most likely to give Reagan a chance. The Teamsters had been ejected from the AFL-CIO for not cooperating with a probe involving organized crime, and the Reagan camp thought the benefits of pursuing them outweighed the risks associated with their links to the rackets. Another appealing circumstance involved the critical swing state of Ohio, which Reagan deemed necessary to winning the 1980 general election.

Reagan found his target in Ohio Teamsters boss Jackie Presser. The nature of the Reagan campaign's interaction with Presser tells us a lot about how mob power in national politics works—and doesn't. The Reagan people, of course, were aware of the rumors about Presser's mob relationships but compartmentalized them as just rumors. Said one Reagan official, they never encountered anyone they even suspected of being a representative of organized crime. To them, Presser was a colorful union official and singularly pleasant to work with, utterly without menace or negotiation. Yes, the mob had likely been somewhere in Presser's food chain, but in the same spirit that the sandwich we're enjoying at some point involved an animal encountering a pneumatic bolt gun on the other side of the country. The dynamic was about prophylactic distance: There was no reason for a mobster ever to encounter a high-ranking politician, which is one reason why it's so challenging to accurately tag someone as having colluded with racketeers.

Said one Presser biographer of the Reagan political relationship, "It was an odd romance if one considered that the Teamsters had hated Reagan when he was governor of California." Reagan gave a speech to a large Teamsters group in Ohio in August 1980 and had a private meeting with Presser and national Teamsters leader Roy Williams. Shortly before this meeting, Williams testified before a Senate committee investigating organized crime and invoked his Fifth Amendment rights two dozen times.

The Teamsters endorsed Reagan in 1980 after a game of gin rummy between Washington tax attorney Myron Mintz and national Teamsters boss Frank Fitzsimmons. When speaking to the Teamsters board to gain their endorsement, Presser wasn't exactly subtle: "You Italians, listen up! More than anyone else in this room, you should be supporting Reagan! Reagan has agreed to lay off of us. The Justice Department will not be on our backs for once!"

Jackie Presser was quite a character. His father had been a Teamsters boss and jukebox proprietor and his maternal grandfather had been a bootlegger. Obese and perfectly rotund, the former auto thief looked like a mob boss albeit a lot more cheerful. It didn't hurt that Presser and his family were well-known in Ohio, a state Reagan especially needed to win given how poorly Republicans had fared there in the past.

A Mafia turncoat had concurrently testified before a federal grand jury that Presser had privately acknowledged taking orders from the Cleveland Cosa Nostra. There was another reason to believe this was true as it would later be learned that Presser had been a top-echelon FBI informant since 1972. Of course, one doesn't become an informant unless one has someone to inform *on*. Presser later told the government that LCN leaders had selected at least two Teamsters bosses. He also admitted to the FBI that LCN overlords demanded that anyone who wanted access to Presser go through their designated people, including Cleveland's Milton "Maishe" Rockman and John "Peanuts" Tronolone, according to Ron Fino, son of a Buffalo, New York, mob boss and later a law enforcement consultant.

It was difficult to believe that Presser was an LCN asset, said one source involved with the 1980 campaign. The union boss had been so likable, so concerned about his members, and utterly without aggression that he was simply confident that the Teamsters would get something in return for supporting Reagan. The campaign hadn't faced a single mob goon or hard negotiation. Reagan named Presser a "senior economic advisor" to his campaign. There were also reports of Teamster cash contributions made to Reagan's campaign. Presser had been under investigation for fraud at the time. In the 1980 campaign, in addition to political support, Presser mobilized the Teamsters' telephone banks on Reagan's behalf and was able to accomplish one of the greatest challenges in politics: swelling crowds for candidates. Presser also provided a modern portable stage and a sophisticated broadcast system that Reagan used on the road throughout his eight years in office.

A Reagan aide, former FBI agent Clarence Newton, raised a red flag to Ed Meese III, another top Reagan adviser (and future attorney general), about getting involved with Presser because of his deep mob entrenchment. Meese responded, "But Newt, he's never been indicted." Presser became an adviser to the Reagan campaign again in 1984. Years later, when Presser found himself in more trouble, Meese said of Presser's mob ties that "there was no such available evidence at the time." Such were the standards when trying to win an essential voting bloc. Ken Paff, head of the reform organization Teamsters for a Democratic Union, said of the Reagan-Presser relationship: "He doesn't represent the Teamsters, but if you want a spokesman for millionaires and organized crime, get Jackie."

During the 1980 campaign, Reagan challenged his opponent Jimmy Carter's policies on trucking deregulation and, according to Reagan historian Craig Shirley, vowed to alter Carter's approach if elected, which endeared him to the Teamsters who endorsed him. After Reagan won, Presser was rewarded with a position on the president-elect's transition team. Not the smoothest operator, Presser spoke publicly about his new powers, saying he'd be calling the shots on appointments such as labor and transportation secretaries. Presser spoke to his Ohio Teamsters: "President Reagan and his people, through our union, are now considering reviewing the deregulation issue, which will be a benefit to the Teamsters."

The Teamsters' Jackie Presser
Bettmann Archive via Getty Images

This provoked adversaries to come forward with claims that Presser, in addition to being under the influence of the Cleveland mob family, had also been known to give pension loans to New Jersey's DeCavalcante clan and the Patriarca family of New England. Senator Sam Nunn of Georgia asked, "Is it a violation of fundamental principles of government ethics for Mr. Presser to help organize the very department that has brought suit against him?"

Rather than jettison Presser, the 1980 Reagan transition team said it had been unfamiliar with such charges and, besides, the team's work was over anyway. When national leader Roy Williams was convicted for attempting to bribe a U.S. senator, Presser succeeded him. It turns out that one of the people informing on Williams had been Presser himself.

In return for the Teamsters' support, Reagan slow-rolled deregulation efforts and proposals to disband the Interstate Commerce Commission that the union supported. Presser publicly praised Reagan for lowering interest rates and pulled his punches when it came to criticizing Reagan on other deregulation initiatives. Wrote Presser's biographer James Neff of the Reagan-Presser alliance: "It was an odd romance if one considered that the Teamsters had hated Reagan when he was governor of California. . . . A free market advocate, Reagan didn't believe in tariffs, restrictions, and price setting regulation."

Reagan's own President's Commission on Organized Crime eventually took a position particularly hard on labor racketeering, including the Teamsters, Longshoremen, and hotel and restaurant employees, even blasting the White House for doing so much business with Presser: "The long delays in reaching a resolution of a Department of Justice investigation concerning . . . Presser have led to a similar concern— whether Presser's support of the administration in the 1980 and 1984 election campaigns influences the conduct of the investigation [into Presser for multiple crimes]."

Despite this scolding, some law enforcement sources acknowledged that it was easier for a Republican administration to hold labor to account than Democrats because labor has historically been a vital component of the party's more progressive base. With the Teamsters, Reagan embraced their support through Presser but hadn't hesitated to take mob-linked unions to task.

WAR ON THE MOB

As with other presidents, Reagan and his administration were capable of being alternatively permissive and prosecutorial when it came to organized crime. Wrote Moldea: "As President, Reagan watched as his Justice Department quashed major federal investigations of the Mafia's penetration of both MCA and the entire motion picture industry, which were being conducted by the Los Angeles office of the U.S. Strike Force Against Organized Crime."

When working on a new budget, Reagan cut back funding for investigating the mob by one-third, reduced staff and throttled back on undercover operations. One of the commissioners involved with the 1986 President's Commission on Organized Crime cried foul at hands-off treatment for Reagan's old friend, Sid Korshak. Reported Dan Moldea: "Leaving Korshak out of the final report was no accident. A conscious decision was made to leave out any reference to him, and we were told about it at that meeting. . . . I felt there was pressure to keep Korshak out. And where that pressure came from, well, your guess is as good as mine."

During a period when Korshak had been under increasing scrutiny from the news media and gaming officials (who had confronted Hilton Hotel leaders about having retained Korshak, whom they later fired), the Justice Department didn't pursue him. Wrote Moldea, "Although the President's Commission on Organized Crime scheduled hearings to be held in Los Angeles, where Korshak was sure to be a major target, the planned trip was aborted at the behest of the Justice Department." At best, Reagan's team may have intervened. At least, they demonstrated a remarkable lack of interest in taking a close look at West Coast rackets figures.

The subject of Reagan's friends being linked to organized crime surfaced again in the winter of 1981 when Frank Sinatra testified before the Nevada Gaming Board about his application to own a stake in a Las Vegas casino. The singer was grilled for hours about alleged mob contacts and smoothly differentiated between having met colorful people during his long career and having done business with them. The hearings were televised at great length, and the media broadcast them in part because of who was testifying and because Sinatra had just managed the entertainment component of Reagan's inauguration extravaganza. Interest waned somewhat when Sinatra was granted his casino license. A few weeks later, Reagan was seriously wounded when an assassin shot him in the chest as the president walked out of the Washington Hilton. The media were interested in nothing else.

Even if the shooting hadn't occurred, Reagan had weathered questions about Sinatra before and had been unfazed by them. During the 1980 campaign, he responded to a letter from a voter who had been concerned about the friendship with a characteristic shrug:

> I'm aware of the incidents, highly publicized, quarrels with photographers, nightclub scrapes, etcetera and admit it is a lifestyle I neither emulate nor approve. However, there is a less publicized side to Mr. Sinatra, which in simple justice must be recognized. . . . I know of no one who has done more in the field of charity than Frank Sinatra. A few years ago a small town in the Midwest had suffered a terrible calamity; he went there on his own and staged a benefit to raise funds. All expenses were paid out of his pocket. He'd be very upset if he knew I'd told you these things.

If Reagan's cops appeared to be going light on the rackets in California, they were showing no mercy to the boys in the East. "The attack on Cosa Nostra . . . reached its pinnacle during the Ronald Reagan Presidency," stated an analysis in the University of Chicago Press: Journals. Reagan's attack on organized crime was supplemented by the formation of his commission and congressional investigations led by Georgia senator Sam Nunn. Reagan himself said:

> I've always believed that government can break up the networks of tightly organized regional and national syndicates that make up organized crime. So I repeat, we're in this to win. There will be no negotiated settlements, no détente with the mob. It's a war to the end where they're concerned. . . . We mean to cripple their organization, dry up their profits and put their members behind bars where they belong.

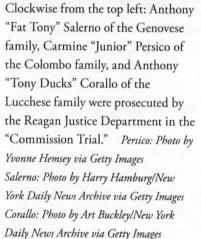

Clockwise from the top left: Anthony "Fat Tony" Salerno of the Genovese family, Carmine "Junior" Persico of the Colombo family, and Anthony "Tony Ducks" Corallo of the Lucchese family were prosecuted by the Reagan Justice Department in the "Commission Trial." *Persico: Photo by Yvonne Hemsey via Getty Images Salerno: Photo by Harry Hamburg/New York Daily News Archive via Getty Images Corallo: Photo by Art Buckley/New York Daily News Archive via Getty Images*

In 1986, the New York Mafia's own "Commission," which had settled disputes between the Five Families since the 1930s, went on trial in federal court. It resulted in the convictions of the heads of the Genovese, Colombo, and Lucchese families. The Bonannos had already been kicked off the New York Commission after it was infiltrated by FBI agent Joseph Pistone, who was known on the street as Donnie Brasco. Still, they were facing their own prosecutions.

The Gambino family boss, Paul Castellano, avoided a likely

conviction when he lost in a management reorganization at the curbside entrance to Sparks Steakhouse in Manhattan in December 1985. Among the catalysts contributing to his murder at the hands of John Gotti's crew were concerns about what might come out during Castellano's trial.*

Gotti's underboss Sammy "the Bull" Gravano recently said that he had told his associates, "Reagan is coming after us," adding, "They [Reagan's DOJ] killed us. They slaughtered us." Gravano turned state's evidence when George H. W. Bush was president, but he credited Reagan's Justice Department for his prosecution, adding "I was in jail for twenty-two years of my life."

All the New York mob bosses convicted at the time of the commission case died in prison, save the Bonanno boss, Philip Rastelli, who was granted compassionate release and died a few weeks later in 1991.

Despite Korshak's kid-glove treatment in Los Angeles, it is hard to say that there had been mutual back-scratching between a president and mob bosses. It was more targeted than that. Korshak's bosses in Chicago, Joseph Aiuppa and John Cerone, were convicted in a federal casino-skimming case the same year as the New York Commission convictions and spent most of the rest of their lives in prison. Four other mob figures pleaded guilty before the trial. The skimming scheme had been abetted by the Outfit's access to Teamsters pension loans, which gave them control over casino management. The head of the Chicago FBI, Edward Hegarty, assessed the case "as the most significant prosecution of organized crime figures in the history of the United States."

THE PRESIDENT-MOB POWER DYNAMIC

One of the most significant portals connecting organized crime to the presidency during the Reagan years fell open by accident. Federal prosecutor Marvin Rudnick had been conducting a routine pretrial interview of

* The main reason why Castellano was removed was because Gotti and his faction feared that the boss was going to kill them for violating his prohibition on drug dealing. The Gambinos, of course, were known to traffic in drugs but not as recklessly as Gotti's gang had been doing it, which underscored that the real violation was not drug dealing per se. Rather, Gotti's gang was guilty of being sloppy and getting caught.

a witness in Los Angeles. The case was a tax matter involving a Gambino family solider named Salvatore Pisello. When Rudnick asked the witness where Pisello could be reached, he casually said that Pisello was working at the entertainment colossus MCA.

A Mafia soldier with an office at a blue-chip company?

Enter Salvatore Pisello aka "Sal the Baker," aka "Sal the Swindler," alleged member of the Gambino Cosa Nostra family, and who indeed had been working out of MCA offices at points beginning in 1983. Pisello was specifically identified as being with the Aniello Dellacroce crew; Dellacroce, the underboss of the Gambinos, had been identified by NYPD investigator Joseph Coffey as "one of the scariest individuals I've ever met in my life."

Among the hodgepodge of schemes Pisello was suspected of working on within MCA was helping the company unload "cutouts," old records that are no longer part of a company's catalog. He had shipped sixty tractor-trailer loads containing millions of records to a contact who would distribute them. There is nothing necessarily illegal about selling cutouts, but the question became, "What is a soldier of the Gambino Cosa Nostra family who has no music background doing conducting business from MCA corporate headquarters?" This was not a question MCA was enthusiastic about answering, especially when pressed by board member former U.S. senator Howard Baker who famously asked during the Senate Watergate hearings, "What did the president know and when did he know it?"

Among the people to whom the cutout matter led back was the notorious music industry executive and Genovese family associate Morris Levy of Roulette Records. (The character Hesh Rabkin in *The Sopranos* was loosely based on Levy.) A Philadelphia area mob associate had been beaten within an inch of his life over the cutout deal. Prosecutors were also looking into MCA's relationship with the Teamsters, a major inconvenience given CEO Wasserman's long relationship with labor peacemaker Korshak, President Reagan's acquaintance with Korshak, as well as Reagan's political dealmaking with Teamsters boss Jackie Presser.

Pisello had been convicted of tax evasion for not reporting much of the income he earned from MCA. The full answer to the question of what a Gambino mobster was doing working at MCA may never be known because Reagan's Justice Department killed the probe. This happened while MCA was evaluating a sale of the company to the Japanese giant Matsushita. During the transaction, MCA had been very sensitive about reputation issues. The sale eventually went through.

The DOJ's interest in the Pisello investigation stalled not long after a grand jury had been impaneled. MCA put forth a very aggressive lobbying and legal campaign, which included alleging prosecutorial misconduct. This happened concurrently with Lew Wasserman becoming the most generous contributor to the planned Reagan Library, whose fundraising Wasserman had been working on with Reagan's attorney general, Ed Meese. Then MCA retained a partner of legendary Washington power lawyer Robert Strauss, an MCA board member. Rudnick, the U.S. attorney in charge of the investigation, was not persuaded that the MCA probe should cease. Rudnick was called to Washington and soon relieved of his duties despite having twice successfully convicted Pisello of tax fraud. According to the *American Lawyer*, Rudnick's boss "pointed to a photograph on his office wall. It was [William] Hundley, ex-chief of the [DOJ] mob section . . . and top man in the MCA effort. Margolis [Rudnick's boss] said, 'When this guy starts complaining about you, you've got real problems.'"

It's also possible that Justice was legitimately unconvinced that there was enough to pursue a case. The *American Lawyer* reported: "Troubling questions arise from the strange behavior at Justice. Was a credible inquiry into possible mob infiltration of an industry sabotaged by MCA pressure? If not, why did Justice—already reeling from allegations of influence peddling (under the stewardship of Attorney General Ed Meese)—call off the dogs?"

MCA president Sidney Sheinberg had a swaggering sense of impunity when asked by the *American Lawyer*'s Michael Orey about the presence of Pisello inside the company's corporate offices: "I don't know the answer to that question and, more importantly, I don't care about the answer to that question. How Pisello managed to get inside the company and basically con the company out of its money isn't a question we have decided needed investigating."

Other than the statements of former prosecutors, there is no proof Wasserman leveraged his friendship with Reagan to kill these investigations. A Justice Department official said, "None of my superiors have given me any direction or suggestions of any kind at any time regarding the disposition" of the investigation. Nevertheless, one thing that investigative reporters often get wrong is believing that players in an unholy arrangement always meet in back alleys to cut dirty deals. What happens more often—and why collusion is so hard to prove—is that participants in a bureaucracy often *intuit* what's in (or against) their best interests and make decisions without telling a soul or memorializing it in any way. This may well have been what happened when the investigation of MCA was quashed. Even if MCA was not provably complicit in all the schemes that were alleged, the company recognized the damage and disruption such probes would generate and had very good reason to want them stopped. In contemporary parlance, if nothing else, the "headline risk" was terrible.

Gus Russo reported that Bill Knoedelseder left his job at the *Los Angeles Times* "not long after being ordered to curtail his MCA coverage. At the same time, the paper's publisher was Tom Johnson, a former LBJ aide, who had obtained his *Times* position thanks to Lew Wasserman's kind intercession with the Chandler family [owners of the newspaper]."

Richard Stavin, a former member of the Justice Department's Organized Crime Strike Force in Los Angeles, said in an interview:

It's my belief that MCA and its involvement with Mafia individuals, Mafia-dominated companies and our inability to pursue those was not happenstance. I believe it was an organized, orchestrated effort on the part of certain individuals within Washington, D.C. to keep a hands-off policy towards MCA. . . . I would like to think that the people in the highest levels of this government were not protective of MCA. . . . But I'm not so sure about that. I was unable to fulfill the duties for which I took my sworn oath.

Stavin quit his position at Justice when he realized that his investigation, like Rudnick's, was being blocked. Years after the case, Rudnick was to learn, there "was a 1987 West Hollywood dinner meeting between MCA CEO Lew Wasserman and President Reagan. Two weeks later I was threatened by MCA's Beverly Hills lawyer Allen Susman who told me he 'had friends in the courthouse too.'"

DOJ had ignored Rudnick's report of the threat by MCA's attorney and the company's "friends" in the courthouse. Concurrently, Rudnick learned that "the FBI's secret wiretap at MCA incredibly was discovered, and therefore compromised." Rudnick said that thirty years after his MCA investigation was put on ice, an FBI agent involved with the case contacted him to express his lingering concerns about the "interference." Concluded Rudnick: "The background history of organized crime in this context arises from the relationship of Wasserman and Sidney Korshak, Chicago mob's lawyer in the movie business. The Strike Force court-authorized wiretap sought to pursue some of this. Did the U.S. Attorney and the Strike Force chiefs in DOJ know this when they shut down the investigation and fired me?"

RAYMOND DONOVAN AND THE THEATER OF "MOB TIES"

Raymond Donovan was President Reagan's secretary of labor. Donovan had been a construction executive in New Jersey who had raised a lot of money, about $600,000,* for Reagan's campaign and had been rewarded with a cabinet position. His relationship with unions was complex because labor's demands often conflicted with Reagan's free-market agenda.

Donovan hadn't been confirmed without a fight in the Senate. He was questioned about having paid corrupt union officials for labor peace. A government informant claimed to have personally witnessed Donovan at a meeting where a union official had been bribed. Donovan denied being at the meeting and even having ever been at the restaurant where it was alleged to have happened.

While Donovan was being investigated for his confirmation, a man named Fred Furino was found dead in his car in Manhattan, having been shot in the head. The FBI believed Furino had once been a courier for Genovese mobster Salvatore "Sally Bugs"

---

* This was serious money in politics in 1980.

Briguglio, a labor racketeer widely suspected of being the man who personally killed Jimmy Hoffa. A special prosecutor was twice appointed to investigate Donovan's mob ties and twice returned having declined to prosecute for lack of "sufficient credible evidence," a phrase Donovan said was in and of itself incriminating.

Additional violence erupted that was publicly tied to Donovan. According to a government informant, Genovese mobster Philip Buono sought permission from family leadership to murder thirty-one-year-old Nathan "Nat" Masselli. Masselli, who was affiliated with a subcontractor, Jo-Pel Construction & Trucking, which was partially owned by his father William ("Billy the Butcher"), a Genovese soldier. Buono feared that Nat, his godson, had been cooperating with a federal investigation into Donovan. Indeed, Masselli had apparently allowed federal investigators to monitor his telephone calls. Jo-Pel was suspected of defrauding the New York City government in a subway excavation project. Buono and the Genovese leadership in the form of boss Vincent Gigante and consigliere Louis "Bobby" Manna were concerned that Nat's testimony would draw scrutiny to Donovan and, by extension, to the Genoveses' dealings with Donovan's former company, Schiavone Construction.

Complicating matters was that William Masselli had been scheduled to testify before a grand jury examining the Donovan case. Nat visited William in prison—the father had been imprisoned on a narcotics and hijacking charge—on August 25, 1982. Later that evening, Nat was shot to death in his car while speaking to two Genovese men, one of them Buono. One theory is that by killing Nat, the Genoveses were dissuading his father from testifying against them in exchange for leniency in his current sentence.

A law enforcement source said, "The time sequence makes it very much look that way," referring to Nat Masselli being eliminated to prevent his testimony. The source added, "These people are so frequently into things where eliminating an individual is part of the operation." Indeed, a less popular theory of the crime was that Masselli had shortchanged his mob partners in several deals. Buono and another Genovese soldier were convicted of the murder where there were numerous witnesses who saw an obese shooter comically struggle to climb out of the back seat of the two-door death car and waddle to the getaway vehicle.

In October 1984, weeks before the presidential election, Donovan was indicted for having been a player in a scheme to pilfer $7.4 million from the New York City Transit Authority. Donovan resigned as labor secretary, the first incumbent cabinet member to have been indicted. Donovan and seven others were acquitted. Wrote the *New York Times*, "Several jurors said they had found the evidence sorely lacking and said the indictment should not have been brought."

After his acquittal, Donovan famously quipped, "Which office do I go to to get my reputation back?" Predictably, his enemies didn't believe he deserved his reputation back seeing his tarnished image as second-place prize for retribution after Donovan's acquittal.

If Donovan felt he had been defamed, why didn't he sue? The answer is that defamation lawsuits in the United States are stacked against the plaintiff. Donovan would have to have proven that there had been a conspiracy for the news media to knowingly use false information for the purpose of harming him. This standard is called "actual malice" and is extremely hard to prove because it is largely a state of mind on the part of the journalist.

Furthermore, Donovan had been tried in court and the media would have argued—successfully—that they were simply reporting on a legal case, which they are allowed to do without fear of being sued for defamation. Finally, in a defamation lawsuit, the plaintiff is on trial. Donovan would have to be questioned about extremely

Reagan Labor Secretary Raymond Donovan asked, "Which office do I go to to get my reputation back?" after acquittal in a trial involving mob ties.

AP Photo/Jeff Taylor

sensitive subjects that would have rehashed all the original allegations, and more. In other words, it wasn't worth it. There aren't many squeaky-clean people who could endure the kind of scrutiny a defamation suit would bear.

There is a serious problem with the whole concept of "mob ties." Exactly what qualifies someone as being "tied" to the mob? Is it mere personal acquaintance?

Does having "mob ties" mean that one has had contact with mobsters even if they do not participate in criminal activity? What if a car salesman sells a Toyota to a mobster? Or a journalist who has sources in the underworld that inform his stories? What about the entertainers who rubbed elbows with gangsters in Las Vegas or posed for photos with them? Then there are FBI agents who have informants—or even coaxed their targets into stings.

Perhaps the most pernicious problem with throwing around allegations of "mob ties" is that anyone can make them about anybody else with no constraints or repercussions. Concerned about the vagaries of potentially damaging labels, retired LCN unit chief at FBI headquarters Gary Klein wrote a memo to his unit chief in 1996 inquiring:

> In discussing the LCN, certain terminology is used. Some words, such as "LCN member," are easily defined. Other words, however, such as "associate" or "inactive member," are not so precise. When evaluating the presence of the LCN, it is important that the terms "associate" and "inactive member" are applied consistently. Failure to do so will make it difficult to monitor the progress of our organized crime initiatives. It is the writer's [Klein's] recommendation that criteria be established for use within the FBI to define the terms, "associate" and "inactive member."

As Klein suggested, such monikers have the potential to be arbitrarily assigned and create trouble in other venues.

The late New York governor Mario Cuomo was a case in point. Cuomo constantly battled suspicions that he had been connected to organized crime. In fact, Cuomo's mob ties were often stated as accepted fact. That he was a New Yorker of Italian heritage contributed to these pervasive rumors, none of which came close to being proven.

Mob informants in pursuit of leniency must constantly demonstrate their value to the authorities by identifying juicy targets. One way to do this is to make a claim that a successful figure in the legitimate world is dirty. Such scenarios have been known to turn up on mob organizational charts with dotted-line links.

The legal process only adjudicates one's freedom, not one's reputation. Donovan's case proves that one can both be acquitted and have charges be sufficiently weak as to not warrant prosecution *and* have one's reputation destroyed. Perhaps the whole mob ties trope is nature's way of discouraging us from getting *anywhere near* something potentially shameful. As Saul Bellow wrote, "A scandal is a service to the community."

Not all "mob ties" pursuits end in reputational damage. Through its spying campaign on student subversives, the FBI once warned Ronald Reagan prior to being elected governor of California that his son Michael had been friendly with the son of mob boss Joe Bonanno. Did this mean that Michael Reagan, a teenager then, had been at a party where the Bonanno son had also been present? Regardless, the charge never went anywhere. (The son in question, Joe Jr., had studied animal husbandry in college, perhaps used recreational drugs, and had gone into the animal care field, not exactly the pathway toward becoming a gang lord.)

There can be little doubt of Lew Wasserman and Reagan's transactional relationship and MCA's long history with gangland operative Korshak. But there is nothing in the way of Reagan having done anything illegal in this relationship. Perhaps this is either because Reagan is innocent of wrongdoing or Wasserman's sleight of hand was extraordinary. Reagan himself tiptoed deftly around the MCA waiver affair, and even this required no underworld contact. Nor should we cite the proof of conspiracy as being the lack of evidence, somehow demonstrating that the players were so clever that they covered it up perfectly. In the meantime, the Reagan-Wasserman association remains a fascinating study of how stratified connections play a role in power dynamics:

1. *Mostly* legitimate, small but ambitious business people solicit the help of small-time mobsters in order to advance early in their careers (Jules Stein and Wasserman);*
2. These businesspeople help out politicians and union leaders (Reagan) on the rise;
3. Businessmen, mobsters, and politicians progress in their careers;
4. After succeeding, the businesspeople and politicians become concerned about prestige, clean up their reputations, distance themselves from the mobsters, and identify intermediaries and prophylactic techniques to manage shady activity;
5. The legitimate people rise to the pinnacle where they can influence national policy, and they:
   a. don't need mobsters anymore because they now have overwhelming power;
   b. can use their power and respectability to buy distance from their origins;
   c. identify opportunities to punish select malefactors to demonstrate their law and order bona fides; and
   d. deny past associations or justify them through a combination of hazy memory or time passed. They can also create risk for less powerful functionaries (Reagan DOJ officials) who don't need to be told why it is not in their best interests to pursue certain lines of questioning.

We see this pattern emerge repeatedly (with some variations), which is why the absence of smoking gun proof of a Mafia boss tiptoeing across the White House South Lawn at midnight is beside the point. That's not how it works, nor does it need to be for the symbiosis to work.

---

* This model often applies to union leaders who get their start with the help of mobsters; however, they are rarely able to distance themselves from criminals during their rise.

Nevertheless, Wasserman's deal for Reagan for *General Electric Theater* had nothing to do with organized crime. The extent to which one believes the provenance of a career taints later achievements is a highly subjective one. Does Franklin Roosevelt's family's (Delanos) fortune from the opium trade sully his presidency? Should Reagan be blamed for capitalizing on a career opportunity offered up by a businessman whose company was abetted by the muscle of racketeers? Should the Kennedy brothers' political advancements be graded downward because their father was a stock swindler? And, for that matter, should we think anything less of Frank Sinatra's talent because he may have had some assistance early in his career from hoodlums who were looking out for him? There is also a difference between symbiosis and connivance; one can only inflate shake-the-hand-that-shook-the-hand adjacency to the level of a coconspirator to a certain point.

However, such attenuated, dotted-line links tell us something important: Crooks and politicians benefit each other, but any symbiosis is accomplished opportunistically and at a distance. None of this requires command-and-control orders being carried out from on high toward specific ends. It surely never occurred to Lew Wasserman early in his representation of Reagan that his client would one day head SAG, let alone become the leader of the free world.

David Chase, creator of *The Sopranos*, once said that he created the show with a line in mind from the Jean Renoir film *The Rules of the Game*: "The awful thing about life is this: Everybody has their reasons." What bonds organized crime to politics is that all the parties found a way to rationalize why they did what they did. The politicians could write off mob linkages to the necessary evils of realpolitik and the gang lords all believed they were no worse than the politicians. The layers and distances helped in these rationalizations.

With the next president examined here, Donald Trump, we won't need to hold chin-scratching debates about the vagaries of interactions with organized crime; we just need to listen to the man himself.

8

Donald Trump

"VERY NICE PEOPLE"

I've got to be the cleanest, I think I'm the most honest human being, perhaps, that God has ever created.

—Donald Trump

In the late summer of 1984, handsome Salvatore "Salvie" Testa had just been dubbed by the media the heir apparent as boss of the Philadelphia LCN when he entered the Something Sweet candy store. Lured to the South Philly location by a childhood friend, he was quickly shot behind the ear. After falling to the ground, the shooter, another boyhood pal, shot him behind the other ear. His body was soon found hog-tied on a road near the South Jersey Pine Barrens. His crime: getting more attention as a potential mob boss than the reigning crime lord, Nicky Scarfo.

Salvie Testa was the man whom the future president, the canny real estate developer Donald Trump, grossly overpaid for a plot of land to be used in the development of one of his Atlantic City hotel casinos. Why would Trump get involved with such characters? And why would the tough negotiator overpay?

To fully understand Donald Trump's gangland dealings and mob boss affectation, it helps to have grown up around the culture in which he thrived. Anyone who emerged from a community where racketeers sprang from the manholes will acknowledge that a segment of society admires these guys. This comes up in any discussion about why *The Godfather* remains so popular a half century after its release, when so many other movies of that vintage have dropped out of the public consciousness. Francis Ford Coppola has been known to say that the film's enduring popularity is because it's about family. I don't think that's it. It's way more primal and testosterone-driven.

Mobsters are like superheroes in the subconscious of many men, especially those who have had proximity to them. People like superheroes because they have power over a world in which mere mortals have very little. Is there anyone who hasn't fantasized about beating up a bully or committing some supernatural feat that inspires awe in witnesses or inflicts pain upon those who have hurt us? To quote *Pulp Fiction*'s Marsellus Wallace, haven't we all wanted to "get medieval" on somebody's ass? But few of us follow through because we are either unaccustomed to violence or want to continue to enjoy the benefits of leading a civil life.

We all know that Superman and Wonder Woman do not exist. We humans are not bulletproof. No golden lassoes allow us to entrap our enemies and toss them through a plateglass window. But mobsters? They exist, so there's hope!

Here's the mobster fantasy: In a world where we all suffer slights, indignities, and setbacks, mobsters don't. They've got what they like to call "respect," but it isn't respect; it's fear—the fear that they will physically harm those who don't comply with their demands. If you're a mobster, the fantasy is that you're never bullied, you're not cut off in traffic, you get the table you want at the restaurant without waiting, you're attractive to sexual interests, your spouse doesn't bark at you to take the trash out when you're exhausted, your kid will be accepted into the Ivy League school if you stare down the dean of admissions, you're unfettered by the law, and you're swimming in cash. And nobody can do a damned thing about it. You laugh to the end of a long life and die rich and in bed with your loyal family and friends all around you. The American Dream in its most unfettered form is getting whatever the hell you want, however the hell you can.

There was a time in the twentieth century when cultural anthropologists enjoyed contemplating "the myth of the American West," concluding that the cowboy was our greatest legend. That changed as the decades wore on and the cowboy was replaced with the gangster, especially as he was portrayed in entertainment by Marlon Brando, James Cagney, Robert De Niro, James Gandolfini, Al Pacino, Edward G. Robinson, and Richard Widmark. Cowboys and gangsters existed, of course, but not in the form they were presented in cinema. An FBI agent told me that prior to *The Godfather*, most mobsters greeted each other the way most American businessmen do, with a handshake. As the 1970s wore on, the hugs and kisses took off, because gangsters saw it in the movies. Colombo family mobsters were caught on listening devices debating which *Sopranos* character they were most like.

The reality is that mobsters are "messed with" all the time. Their enemies and, yes, friends are trying to kill them, and the government is gunning to put them in prison, and usually succeeds. The toll on their physical and mental health (and that of their families) is devastating. Their expenses are onerous, their finances dire, even at the highest levels. Every day they must get out of bed and figure out where they can make money illegally that they cannot show and not get caught or wind up dead, face down in a bowl of linguini puttanesca. Carlo Gambino, admired as the "boss of bosses" with his elfin smile and grandfatherly demeanor, was widely believed to have been cleverly faking a heart condition to avoid prosecution; he wasn't—the strain on him was withering and he spent much of his life believing every twitch in his chest would be the fatal heart attack. Finally, the most ironic aspect of mob life is that despite all the tough talk about snitches and rats, when the authorities come knocking, most hoodlums quickly become informants to stay out of prison.

Reality is not the currency we are trading in here. Fantasy is. And while it's considered unseemly to offer psychological profiles of people we do not personally know, the outlook and conduct that Donald Trump displays is easy to tag.

Donald Trump is the apotheosis of the phenomenon I've seen in action: the desire to overcome very human and deeply held anxieties about powerlessness and even the shame associated with weakness by adopting the qualities of a mob boss who controls his environment rather than letting it control him.

This phenomenon is especially true of men who have grown up in comfort and want others to believe they clawed their way up out of the gutter. Call it the "Reverse Gatsby," often suburban kids who want you to think they're John Gotti. Like his client, former Trump lawyer Michael Cohen exhibited this.

While most of us have impulses along these lines, few of us would be shameless enough—and have the inherited bankroll as everlasting insulation—to act on them in a manner that would cause us to take an embarrassing and irredeemable pratfall. Not so with Trump. If he wants to swagger and give orders like Gotti, he'll do it regardless of what you think. It is this kind of unrestrained bravado that helps explain Trump's success and we would do well not to dismiss it out of hand simply because it's boorish. The fact is it has worked steadily for the better part of eight decades.

NEW YORK REAL ESTATE: PAY TO PLAY

What makes Donald Trump's dance with organized crime different from other presidents' is that with others, dealing with hoodlums had been a means to an end, not to mention a *secret* means. With Trump, dealing with thugs has been an aspect of the end goal. He enjoys the whiff of gangsterism to the point of having adopted it as part of his branding. If you search the terms "Trump" and "Mafia" on the internet, you will find millions of references to him mimicking the style of a Mafia Don.

As he faced multiple criminal prosecutions, Trump not only compared himself to Jesus, but on several occasions referred to another indicted, New York–born defendant, Al Capone. Referring to Capone intimately as "Alphonse," Trump rallied an audience by observing of the gangster, "He was seriously tough, right?" He further praised Capone's toughness, warning, "If he had dinner with you, and he didn't like the smile on your face, and he thought you were mocking him by smiling, you would be dead before you got home and said hello to your wife."

Former FBI director James Comey, who had prosecuted racketeers, wrote about his encounter with Trump: "The demand was like Sammy the

Bull's Cosa Nostra induction ceremony," referring to Salvatore Gravano, the Gambino underboss who ended up cooperating with the government. Trump incorporated mob speak into everyday dialogue. When commenting about his former lawyer Michael Cohen's cooperation with the government, he said, "It's called flipping, and it almost ought to be illegal. It's not a fair thing, but that's why he did it. He made a very good deal." He also called Cohen a "rat." Alleged Philadelphia–South Jersey LCN boss Joseph "Skinny Joey" Merlino, who posed with Trump in a photo, agreed: "President Trump was right. They need to outlaw the flippers."

In a book, Trump bragged about being a very aggressive kid, stating, "In the second grade I actually gave a teacher a black eye—I punched my music teacher because I didn't think he knew anything about music and I almost got expelled." This is very similar to comments gangsters have made about their troubles in school. Luciano said that "school had nothing important to teach" him but outside the school windows he observed that "some people had money, some people didn't." But it was far more than the aura of gangsterdom—the loud talk, the overdecorated properties, the demands for loyalty, and the love of instilling fear and bullying that make one curious about Trump's ties to the mob—it is his actual business relationships.

As opposed to paper gangsters who talk big with toothpicks stabbing out the sides of their mouths but who have no meaningful ties to the rackets, Trump has dealt with mobsters to significant effect—and without shame or ramifications. The only thing worse for Trump than the reputational consequences of admitting links to the mob are the psychological consequences of denying them—and having people believe he *doesn't* know killers. Despite Trump's reputation for dishonesty, he has been capable of remarkable candor about dealing with the mob. Until, of course, he isn't.

* * *

Brushing up against the mob was a reality of being a real estate and casino developer in New York and Atlantic City. It wasn't as if Trump had been engaged in illegal gambling, prostitution, or narcotics smuggling; he was buying a service from Piker Ryan's list just to stay ahead of the competition. Trump did this with singular aplomb.

It began with Donald's father, Fred, who was no stranger to partnering with mob-connected figures to create his empire. In the late 1940s, he began building the Beach Haven apartment complex in Gravesend, Brooklyn. Fred didn't traditionally take on partners, but in this case, he did. His 25 percent partner was a little-known brick contractor named Willie Tomasello, according to investigative reporter Wayne Barrett. Fred Trump hadn't needed Tomasello's money, so what did Tomasello bring to the partnership?

It turns out that many of Tomasello's partners were members of the DiBono family, some of whom were part of the Gambino LCN clan. What Tomasello brought to the partnership were cheap labor and union and political contacts to assure that construction went smoothly, which is the greatest fear developers have once a project gets underway.

Vincent Impellitteri became the mayor of New York with the help of the savvy mob boss Tommy Lucchese. Fred Trump was delighted because he found himself an even more resourceful contact. Trump returned to Queens to undertake huge projects and also began lobbying to rezone parts of Coney Island for residential development. Barrett wrote that Fred's aggressiveness in the 1950s underscored how sure he was "that he could obtain the zoning approvals necessary to build housing where no one else had even been permitted." It was these early—and unglamorous—developments that have reliably served as the base of the Trump family fortune.

The relationship with racketeers was a template that Donald perfected thirty years later with the help of adviser, attorney and cutout Roy

Lawyer Roy Cohn (left) was Donald Trump's intermediary with mobsters, providing him with a layer of legal cover.
Photo by Sonia Moskowitz via Getty Images

Cohn. The benefit that Fred had, of course, is that he was able to build the bulk of his holdings in the years before significant scrutiny of such lowly companions.

Donald Trump's method was to manage mob interactions through the thoroughly corrupt Roy Cohn, who claimed that sometimes Trump called him twenty times a day. There was a simple brilliance to having Cohn as a fixer. For one thing, Cohn's name sent shivers through the bones of would-be adversaries as if the lawyer were Keyser Soze or Hannibal Lecter. A former Trump assistant spoke of how, when encountering frustration during complex negotiations, Trump had produced a small photo of Roy Cohn and identified him as his lawyer who would come after them. Given Cohn's notoriety as a mob lawyer, it was the closest thing to saying, "You saw what happened to Julius and Ethel Rosenberg, didn't you?" Trump once cooed that Cohn was willing to "brutalize" for him.

The attorney provided a measure of legal and psychological cover. Attorney-client discussions are privileged, meaning that no party can have access to this information unless a court orders it. The concept of privilege was designed to protect clients from things that would jeopardize their ability to have the best legal representation and protection.

The problem is that unethical attorneys like Cohn used privilege in order to protect criminal activities with the logic that if there were ever legal inquiries or lawsuits, the content of related discussions would be off-limits. At least in theory. So it came to pass that Cohn used his status as legal counsel to bring together clients like Donald Trump and Genovese kingpin Anthony "Fat Tony" Salerno, who could enjoy some modicum of protection beneath the cloak of privilege.

It's not hard to paper over various interactions as being privileged and force opposing parties to try to prove otherwise. The ploy often works. While most serious attorneys tread lightly in this area, Roy Cohn was never concerned about crossing lines. Donald Trump may have been, which is why he took pains to manage things in a technically legal way. "Sharp practice" strikes again.

Simply declaring something privileged doesn't make it so. However, the claim of privilege creates several hurdles that hostile parties need to clear before they can access information that could be problematic for somebody who's up to no good. This affects law enforcement, too, because if they saw someone like Salerno meeting with his attorney, there were legal obstacles to eavesdropping.

For Trump, there was also an element of protection in using Cohn. Like Moe Annenberg and Joe Kennedy, Trump knew the strategic and psychological importance of being seen as a legitimate businessman. Trump could attend a meeting with Cohn and maintain confidence that it was technically legal—and terrifying to his adversaries. *The degree of emotional protection provided to people walking on a thin legal or ethical line cannot be underestimated because the best con artists have themselves as their primary mark.* Lawyers like Cohn also provided clients with a layer of protection from media inquiries: An attorney could always argue that he couldn't discuss existing or potential litigation, which freed clients from having to answer uncomfortable questions.

At the root of Trump's dealings with racket-tied operators were union challenges, and it's worth revisiting what gangsters wanted from unions and vice versa. Mob families had a stranglehold over many trade unions, especially construction ones, for the better part of a century. They gained this control with violence or the threat of violence. There are a few reasons why they wanted this control. As we saw in the chapter on Nixon and Hoffa, unions had pension funds that gangsters wanted to access for loans they couldn't get from banks. Said Los Angeles LCN turncoat Jimmy "the Weasel" Fratianno: "You find out who controls the money. Then you see if you can make a deal. If that doesn't work, you try threats. And if all else fails, you break the guy's leg, or worse."

LCN also infiltrated unions because it allowed leverage over labor peace: *If you don't hire the construction company we designate, we will strike and throw the project into chaos.* Then, once the company was retained, it would charge an outrageous fee to complete the job. Another version of this was for mobsters to take an ownership interest in a company as a fee for ensuring labor peace. Unions also helped rig bids among companies so that the only options for those seeking construction services were obscenely expensive, creating a "mob tax" for doing business. Finally, union infiltration allowed gangsters access to commerce venues to steal goods.*

---

* Law enforcement has made extensive progress in scaling back mob influence in labor unions since the mid to late twentieth century.

The New York State Report concluded, "The construction industry in New York City has learned to live comfortably with pervasive corruption and racketeering." In other words, Donald Trump was not alone in his industry and others in dealing with the mob, which had become an integral part of the mosaic of New York commerce and civic life.

ALL ABOUT LABOR

In addition to representing Trump, Roy Cohn also had in his stable of clients the heads of three of the five New York Cosa Nostra families, including Salerno of the Genoveses, John Gotti of the Gambinos, and psychopathic Carmine "Lilo" Galante* of the Bonannos, who identified himself as a tomato gardener (an unlikely occupation that would lead gunmen to blast his eye out on a Brooklyn restaurant patio). In a sense, however, Galante was a gardener—of poppies—since he was one of the biggest players in the heroin business.

Salerno, however, was no garden-variety mobster; his stewardship of the Genoveses led law enforcement to dub them "the Ivy League" of the mob. He has been alternately named an underboss, acting boss, or "front boss" of the clan below the wily Vincent "The Chin" Gigante, who faked mental illness for thirty years to dodge prosecution. Regardless of his title, Salerno was no mere "front"; he had a considerable gangland portfolio and was one of the country's richest and most powerful Cosa Nostra leaders.

And he looked the part. Heavyset, medium height, and balding, Salerno was always photographed wearing a fedora, a thick cigar torpedoing out of his mouth. The mirror image of the other reigning boss of the era, the slick John Gotti, when a reporter asked Salerno after a court appearance if he had anything to say, he responded, "Go fuck yourself." When the reporter thanked him, Salerno, climbing into the back seat of a waiting sedan, politely croaked, "You're welcome."

Village Voice reporter Wayne Barrett noted that two witnesses had seen Trump meet with Salerno at Cohn's house. Cohn's strategy of using his home or office for gangland conclaves was confirmed by surveillance

---

*   Most law enforcement sources now believe Galante was in a power struggle to become the Bonanno boss, as opposed to being its official leader.

photos, including one of Cohn conferring with Salerno and Cleveland associate Maishe Rockman, partners in Teamsters pension fund activity. Wrote famed journalist Jimmy Breslin of Salerno, "Tony was the Tip O'Neill of the underworld and would reside forever in [then federal prosecutor] Rudy Giuliani's mind."

Indeed, one of the most surprising eventualities in the history of organized crime and the presidency is that Giuliani, one of the greatest mobbusters in American history, became the leading defender of Donald Trump, the most confessed mob-curious president the United States has ever had. While U.S. attorney, Giuliani indicted New York's mob bosses, resulting in the "Commission Trial" that decapitated the region's LCN. "Our approach is to wipe out the Five Families," Giuliani said. As mayor of New York, Giuliani debilitated LCN's stranglehold over the Fulton Fish Market and evicted wholesalers believed to be controlled by organized crime.

A few days after the 2020 presidential election, Giuliani spearheaded a tragicomical news conference to announce a legal challenge to the vote in Pennsylvania, where Joseph Biden was declared the winner. The event was held at the Four Seasons Total Landscaping service, adjacent to a sex paraphernalia shop and crematorium in a rough Northeast Philadelphia neighborhood. It was widely assumed that the media opportunity had been intended for the plush Four Seasons Hotel in Philadelphia, but ineptitude by Trump's team had landed the attorney in a richly deserved hellhole. In 2024, Giuliani was disbarred in New York and Washington, DC, over his role in contesting the 2020 election. Giuliani's troubles have spread overseas: The government of Ukraine has charged three of its officials with treason, specifically conspiring with Russian intelligence and Giuliani to link the Biden family to political corruption.

Some of the massive racketeering charges Salerno and others faced included inflating some concrete prices for Trump properties. Reported investigative journalist David Cay Johnston, "In 1986, Salerno and seven others, including the head of the concrete workers union, were convicted in a racketeering trial that included murder, payoffs, and inflated prices for concrete."

To build Trump Tower in the early 1980s, Trump bought ready-mix concrete from S&A Concrete, secretly owned by mob bosses Salerno and Castellano. Trump Tower was constructed with a disproportionate amount of concrete versus steel compared to other buildings. It was reported at the time to be the world's largest structure using this composition. It is also worth noting that there were only two concrete manufacturing plants for New York City, and both were controlled by LCN. Salerno's concrete firm had also been the beneficiary of a $7.8 million contract at the Trump Plaza apartments around the time he had met with Trump. (According to published reports, it is possible that the bid-rigging occurred without the knowledge of the developers.)

Said the Gambinos' "Sammy the Bull" Gravano in an interview with Diane Sawyer: "I literally marvel at the sight of Manhattan . . . because I controlled it. I literally controlled Manhattan. . . . I marvel . . . when I see the lights and everything about it. Donald Trump . . . couldn't have built a building if I didn't want him to build it."

Gravano's lesson in labor racketeering underscores the concept of businesspeople and mobsters being partners rather than adversaries per se. When accused of dodgy behavior, Trump has said things like, "That makes me smart." He makes a fair point. Given that some kind of arrangement with the mob was inevitable in his field, Trump did it with more savvy than others. By paying off the unions through gangsters, he gained a competitive advantage over other New York developers to keep his construction projects going.

Before building Trump Tower, Trump first demolished the landmark Bonwit Teller building. To do so, he used a Genovese family–linked company, Kaszycki & Sons, that heavily employed undocumented workers from Poland to handle the risky process, which included asbestos removal. According to Ron Fino, the crew was known as the "sneaker brigade" because of their stealthy methods. The sneaker brigade would quietly leave one construction site and go to the Bonwit site.

One of the men Trump contacted to try to smooth things over at the worksite was Daniel Sullivan. Sullivan was a six-foot-five, three-hundred-pound giant who was referred to as a "labor consultant." Sullivan, who had a criminal record and had been arrested on weapons charges, had been an associate of and fixer for Jimmy Hoffa. Like most shadowy players who stay out of prison, Sullivan was also an FBI informant who dished the dirt about the hoods and businessmen with whom he came into contact. Trump blamed the Bonwit demolition skullduggery on Sullivan.

Sullivan claimed he tried to persuade Trump that he couldn't treat the 150 to 200 Polish workers this way, but this may have been because their relationship soured. When the work was done, some union members sued Trump for not paying the pension and medical benefits that were due them in their contract. Trump, who enjoys boldly claiming that he never settled lawsuits, settled this one perhaps over concern about what might come out in discovery during prolonged litigation.

Trump also went into business with Sullivan by investing in a drywall company, Circle Industries. Reported by the *Washington Post*: "Circle was among the firms implicated in a racketeering scheme involving the carpenters' union and the Genovese crime family. One of those indicted was union president Theodore Maritas, who disappeared and was presumed murdered. As it happened, Trump's attorney, Roy Cohn, also represented Genovese leaders."

Trump eventually withdrew his investment in Circle but offered Sullivan a job as his company's main labor negotiator. He consulted with him while attempting to buy the *New York Daily News*, which went nowhere.

Wrote Johnston, "With Cohn as his fixer, Trump had no worries that the Mafia bosses would have the unions stop work on Trump Tower; Salerno and Castellano were Cohn's clients. Indeed, when the cement workers struck in the summer of 1982, the concrete continued to flow at Trump Tower" because Trump agreed to pay inflated prices as a "fee" for labor peace. Johnston's reporting was even more specific as he identified the union boss who gave the order, John Cody, of the Teamsters Local 282: "Cody, under indictment when he ordered the city-wide strike in 1982, directed that the concrete deliveries continue to Trump Tower." Cody said, "Donald liked to deal with me through Roy Cohn." Other sites across the city didn't have Trump's good fortune; *their* construction stopped cold. A Colombo family labor racketeer, Ralph Scopo, known as the boss of the "Concrete Club," told Fino that "the families benefit from everything that is used to construct his [Trump's] properties." Mobsters were later prosecuted for their Trump Tower scheme. Trump, of course, was not.

A construction executive on the wrong side of Trump's mob connections wasn't as lighthearted about his experiences. Irving Fischer testified that "a bunch of labor goons once stormed into our office and held the switchboard operator at knifepoint," demanding no-show jobs at Trump Tower. Such were the "very nice people" Trump told David Letterman he knew when asked about mob contacts.

One thing that has immunized Trump against the consequences of having such deep mob ties is his blatant honesty, whereby he commingles lies with admissions that are so true and offensive that they are disarming on a reptilian level. Over the years, Trump has alternatively denied dealing with mob companies and praising them without compunction. In a 2007 deposition for a libel suit, his response to a question about having dealt with mobsters was, "Not that I know of." Two years earlier he had bragged to the very reporter he was suing that one of his associates was the mob character who "killed Jimmy Hoffa."

Trump told the *Wall Street Journal* in 2015: "Virtually every building that was built was built with these companies. These guys were excellent contractors. They were phenomenal. They could do three floors a week in concrete. Nobody else in the world could do three floors a week."

Union chief Cody may have had other reasons for hoping construction went well at Trump Tower. Verina Hixon, a friend of Cody's, decided to buy three apartments in Trump Tower valued at $10 million. Hixon had little means of support and could not by any reasonable measure afford the properties. When she didn't get the loan, Trump arranged a mortgage that didn't require Hixon to share information about her finances. Cody later went to prison for racketeering in a case unrelated to the Trump transactions. Not enjoying his time away from the streets, Cody plotted with another inmate to kill his successor at the union, Robert Sasso. The inmate had been wired with a listening device, and the men discussed the merits and drawbacks of using explosives or firearms. Cody was convicted of attempted murder. Hixon was later evicted from the apartments when she couldn't pay. When asked in a deposition how she made a living, her response was, "That's a good question!"

There were also mob links involving Trump's development of the Grand Hyatt in Manhattan. The demolition company he used was operated by one Biff Halloran, who was later convicted for participating in a mob-run cartel that had been inflating project prices. The carpentry firm was linked to the Genovese family and was also in a price-fixing scheme. According to Fino, some of the asbestos removed from Trump's Grand

Hyatt project was dumped by a Genovese-linked company into the New York City sewer system and carted unprotected and dumped illegally in New Jersey, a storyline that found its way into *The Sopranos.*

Trump has a unique, if not bizarre, history with asbestos. As president, Trump eased regulations on asbestos use and disposal and stated that the material was being defamed by none other than the Mafia because they would get the contracts for its removal. A Russian asbestos company, Uralasbest, appears to have been grateful: It put Trump's image on its product containers with a stamp reading: "Approved by Donald Trump, 45th president of the United States." (There is no reason to believe Trump approved this.)

Trump also had a profitable relationship with Vito Pitta, an officer of the Hotel Employees and Restaurant Employees International Union's (HEREIU) New York local. The Roy Cohn–connected Pitta, linked in an indictment to the Colombo family, cut a side deal with Trump in 1985 so that his properties would not be affected by an impending strike. Wrote Wayne Barrett: "Donald eagerly broke ranks with the city's Hotel Association on the eve of a 1985 strike by Pitta's union to sign this agreement, pleasing Pitta so much that he called the Scarfo crime family overlords running Local 54 in Atlantic City on Trump's behalf, telling them that Donald 'would be no problem for the local there.'"

DO NOT PASS GO, DO NOT COLLECT $200

In 1982, as Trump's ambition to take over the Monopoly Board of Atlantic City, he bought a nightclub, Le Bistro, that was owned by Philadelphia Mafia prince Salvatore "Salvie" Testa, the supremely violent son of recently slain boss Philip "Chicken Man" Testa, the latter who was memorialized that same year in the Bruce Springsteen song, "Atlantic City." Phil Testa had been blown to bits by a nail bomb when he stepped onto his South Philadelphia porch. Trump paid Salvie $1.1 million for the property, a premium price for a building that would be torn down and used for a casino parking lot. It had sold several years earlier for $195,000.

Why would a shrewd real estate developer like Trump pay multiples of the value of a piece of property? One possibility is that the developer wanted to wrap up the deal as soon as possible and had the cash to do it.

Another is that the developer was looking to compensate a mobster for an unspecified service and do it through a mundane, perfectly legal real estate transaction. (There must have been some foreknowledge that Trump was dealing with colorful characters because the purchase was made in the name of a secretary for one of Trump's attorneys.)

Sources close to Atlantic City racketeers told me that going back to the 1980s, Trump knew how to leverage mobsters without necessarily breaking the law. Purchasing property from Salvie Testa was a possible example because by overpaying for the property, what Trump was likely doing was purchasing a service such as labor peace. If he happened to pay too high a price, well, oops.

Kenneth Shapiro, described as a scrap metal dealer, testified before a federal grand jury that he had made covert contributions to the mayor of Atlantic City, Michael Matthews, at Trump's behest. As the operator of casinos, Trump was prohibited from contributing to anyone who regulated gambling properties within the city limits. Shapiro was a Scarfo agent whose purpose was to interact with the mayor because Scarfo couldn't do so directly. In other words, Shapiro was a bagman. New Jersey state authorities observed traffic in and out of Shapiro's office, which included visitors such as Scarfo and Trump. Matthews became

Maniacal Philadelphia mob boss Nicodemo "Little Nicky" Scarfo testifying before Congress
Teresa Zabala/New York Times

receptive to Trump's entreaties for construction concessions and air rights. Matthews eventually was convicted of crimes related to his dealings with the Scarfo mob. Shapiro was given immunity and became an unindicted coconspirator. Trump has never been charged for any crime related to his casino dealings.

Shapiro had teamed with labor consultant Dan Sullivan to lease property to Trump so that he could build the Trump Plaza Hotel and Casino. Sullivan served as Trump's liaison to the mob-connected unions handling the various construction projects within the renovation of the Grand Hyatt in Manhattan. The New Jersey Casino Control Commission became concerned about Shapiro and Sullivan's mob links and ordered Trump to *buy* the land outright to avoid any perception that he had on-going business with organized crime. Said Trump about these men in a book, "I don't think there is anything wrong about these people. Most of them have been in Atlantic City for many, many years and I think they are well thought of." When asked about his relationship with Shapiro and Sullivan, Trump later said, "I'd go by the lowest bid and I'd go by their track record, but I didn't do a personal history of who they are."

It is a source of astonishment to those who cover organized crime and politics that Trump's activities and relationships didn't trigger more investigations or public outrage. In 1987, when Trump attempted to de-velop a casino in Sydney, Australia, the New South Wales Police Board rejected his application saying, "Atlantic City would be a dubious model for Sydney and, in our judgment, the Trump Mafia connections should exclude the Kern/Trump consortium." None of these relationships, of course, were disclosed to the Casino Control Commission in New Jersey.

In addition to being opaque with the authorities, Trump must also have been, as usual, lucky because certain explosive data points failed to make it into the New Jersey Division of Gaming Enforcement's (DGE) analysis of his business dealings. Wrote Barrett:

[Kenny] Shapiro's mob associations were so well known to authori-ties that two weeks *after* Trump won his casino license in 1982, the state police began a twenty-four-hour watch on his Atlantic City office, noting that Nicky Scarfo, as well as other mobsters from all across the state visited him, as had Donald and Robert Trump. . . .

This . . . made their business relationship a clearly appropriate subject for DGE review when considering a license for Trump.

Further testimony about Trump's dealings with organized crime in Atlantic City recently surfaced from retired Northeastern Pennsylvania LCN boss, William "Big Billy" D'Elia. D'Elia told investigative journalist Matt Birkbeck that "Trump, when he did deals, he didn't want his lawyers doing it.* He didn't want anyone else doing it, he did it himself, and he did it with gangsters," says Birkbeck.

D'Elia met with Trump and Shapiro (along with Shapiro's brother Barry) to purchase property for the Trump Plaza Hotel and Casino. Trump, according to D'Elia, had agreed to pay $8 million for the property but showed up to the meeting saying he wouldn't pay that amount. Trump agreed to flip a coin and if he won, he would pay the lesser amount of $7 million. Trump won, of course. Said D'Elia, "(He's) just like he's on TV now, arrogant. He don't keep his word." Barry Shapiro confirmed D'Elia's version, adding, "We gave him a fifteen-year mortgage and he paid it off." The Trump campaign denied Trump had participated in such a deal.

Birkbeck also reported that Trump would pressure partners to buy copies of his books in bulk, which would improve his standing on best-seller lists. "They used to give out these rewards and gifts to timeshare people, and one of the gifts would be a copy of the book, only Billy had to buy the book. He had to buy 5,000 or 10,000 copies of the book which would raise the book up the best-seller charts. Basically, Billy would have had to put up $100,000."

It's important to point out that even if true, none of this would have been illegal. In fact, by taking advantage of crooks, it could serve to confirm Trump's long-standing contention that he's every bit as clever and as tough as he often claims he is.

Trump, of course, understood that the FBI found someone of his high profile to be of interest. They would have been foolish not to. According to an FBI internal memo: "TRUMP advised that he wished to cooperate

---

* Meaning that Trump preferred to negotiate the deals before passing along the "deal sheet" to be finalized by attorneys.

with the FBI if he did decide to build a casino. . . . TRUMP stated in order to show that he was willing to fully cooperate with the FBI, he suggested that they use undercover AGENTS within the casino."

Even though Trump worked with mobsters, he was comfortable helping the feds, too. According to Ronald Goldstock, former chief of New York State's Organized Crime Task Force, Trump offered his assistance: "After we issued our interim report and we were considering various way of reforming and restructuring the industry, Trump offered to be of whatever help he could and we did take him up on his offer and we talked from time to time and he provided insights into the industry and construction process."

"All the construction unions were mobbed up," former FBI special agent Mark Rossini said. "How did he [Trump] deal with the mob all these years and never appear before a grand jury?" Former FBI special agent Myron Fuller believes that "Trump was an informant for someone in the FBI New York office." An internal FBI memo acknowledged that Trump and his brother Robert "are aware that this is a very rough business" and that some of the people they would have to deal with "may be unsavory by the simple nature of the business." The government has never confirmed nor denied that Trump was a confidential informant.

MORE OF THE USUAL SUSPECTS

Any examination of Trump and organized crime wouldn't be complete without a look at Felix Sater, who is more a figure out of Elmore Leonard than Mario Puzo. The Moscow-born Sater, reported to be the son of a Russian underworld figure, served as a "Senior Adviser to Donald Trump," according to his business card. His office was two floors below Trump's in Trump Tower. Sater played a vital role in the financing of the Trump Soho hotel and condominium through a real estate investment firm called Bayrock, where he was a partner. The deal was that Trump would give his name to the property without investing any money in exchange for 18 percent of the profits.

Sater was also a long-standing FBI informant. Reported Bloomberg, "According to federal prosecutors, Sater and his team set about laundering money for the mob and fleecing about $40 million from unwitting and largely elderly investors, a number of whom were Holocaust survivors."

His cooperation led to the prosecution of Cosa Nostra figures who had been engaged in "pump and dump" security schemes in the 1990s. The *Washington Post* reported that it was "a concerted effort by organized crime to make inroads on Wall Street." During the lead-up to Trump's presidency, Sater sent a grandiose pitch to Trump's attorney Michael Cohen: "I will get Putin on this program and we will get Donald elected . . . our boy can become president and we can engineer it."

Well.

Sater was referring to a proposed idea for Trump Tower Moscow. It never went anywhere but may explain what was widely interpreted as evidence of collusion with Russia when it may have been proof of sophomoric chutzpah. Trump had tried five times to build in Moscow since 1987. This was some big talk from Sater, who had served time for slashing a man's neck with a martini glass in a bar fight. In Sater, Trump had dug up the George Costanza of Shadowland for a leader who prided himself in dealing with "the best people" when doing business with shady players. At some level, he knew it, too: Trump once walked out of a BBC interview when asked about Sater and his mob ties.

If Sater was Costanza, then Robert LiButti was the Danny DeVito character of Trump's carnival. A degenerate gambler and racehorse trader, LiButti referred to Gambino chief John Gotti as his "boss." LiButti racked

Trump associate Felix Sater
Photo by Mark Wilson via Getty Images

up $11 million in losses at Trump casinos in Atlantic City in the 1980s and early 1990s, all the while shocking employees with racist and sexist remarks. Trump was fined $200,000 for not permitting Black employees to work near LiButti, who was imprisoned for tax fraud.

Trump, who as a casino owner was forbidden to give gifts, was fined for giving $1.65 million in "comps" (some estimates were as high as $3.5 million), including cars, to LiButti, who converted them into cash. Trump, of course, denied knowing LiButti despite being photographed with him at VIP casino events, including LiButti's daughter's birthday party. LiButti's daughter said her father had been specifically—and repeatedly—invited to Trump casinos by the casino owner. LiButti was banned in 1990 for his alleged ties to Gotti.

Then there was the Long Island car dealer, John Staluppi, identified in the media as a member of the Colombo LCN family who regularly met with the family boss, the lethal Carmine Persico. Trump acquired twenty limousines from Staluppi for his casinos and later claimed not to know Staluppi's affiliations. Trump also used a helicopter business that Staluppi owned.

Another helicopter vendor Trump employed was Joseph Weichselbaum, a convicted cocaine trafficker. Trump also rented Weichselbaum one of his apartments in Trump Plaza. When Weichselbaum asked for a change of venue in a cocaine case, the new judge was Maryanne Trump Barry, Trump's sister. She wisely handed the case off to another judge. Trump wrote a letter on Weichselbaum's behalf asking for leniency in sentencing. In the letter, Trump described him as "conscientious, forthright, diligent in his business dealings and a credit to the community."

Weichselbaum was eventually banned from Atlantic City for having links to organized crime. He was sentenced to three years in prison but served only eighteen months. Weichselbaum informed his parole board that he intended to work for Trump upon his release, according to one report. While his case was making its way through the courts, he continued to pay rent for his Trump apartment through in-kind services, presumably the ones his helicopter services provided Trump's casinos. When he did get out, Weichselbaum moved into a Trump Tower apartment his girlfriend bought, according to the Smoking Gun.

Another mob-linked character, Lucchese family associate Robert

Hopkins, was arrested in his Trump Tower condominium in 1986 on charges that he had a gambling racket rival murdered. Manhattan district attorney Robert Morgenthau said Hopkins had been operating an illegal hundred-location gambling ring from his Trump Tower headquarters. Donald Trump attended Hopkins's condominium sale closing and personally counted the $200,000 in cash Hopkins delivered as part of his down payment on two properties in the building. A New York mob-tied mortgage broker who managed the $1.7 million financing of the transaction was subsequently convicted on two unrelated federal fraud charges.

IN NOVEMBER 2013, DONALD TRUMP WAS EXPERIENCING NIRVANA. HE, not the cavalcade of beautiful women trailing him, was the star of the Miss Universe pageant taking place in Moscow. He had high hopes for the event, tweeting in advance, "Do you think Putin will be going to The Miss Universe Pageant in November in Moscow—if so, will he become my new best friend?" He surely hoped so because he had big ambitions in Russia. Putin didn't show, but oligarchs and alleged crime lords did, including Alimzhan Tokhtakhounov, who was characterized by the Justice Department as a "vor," or top-level mobster.

Several months before, federal agents had raided a Trump Tower apartment and arrested twenty-nine operatives in a gambling ring they hoped would include its boss, Tokhtakhounov, but he was nowhere to be found. Tokhtakhounov did, however, show up on the red carpet of the Miss Universe pageant along with moguls such as Aras Agalarov, a Putin crony, with whom Trump had hoped to build a Trump Tower in Moscow. According to an indictment, Tokhtakhounov used "explicit threats of violence and economic harm" to run his illegal gambling empire.

The Miss Universe event, where Trump posed for photos with his trademark finger-point and open-mouthed shout expression, underscores a theme that repeats in many examinations of Trump's career: the impulse to conflate loutishness with criminality. Former Colombo family capo Michael Franzese has spoken of buying condominiums in Trump Tower with cash in the early 1980s but differentiates between Trump having accepted mob money and being involved with organized crime. Franzese added that there was no way Trump could have been a developer in New York and Atlantic City without having dealt with LCN (through

Roy Cohn), but this made him one of many consumers of mob services versus a participant in organized crime. The mixing of brutishness and criminality has led to overwrought media coverage of Trump and expectations of legal sanctions that have often overshot the mark. Still, national political officials are held to a different standard of scrutiny, and several outstanding questions remain about Trump and his underworld dealings, especially as they involve Russians, where gangsters, oligarchs, and government leaders blend.

If the American LCN's talent for money laundering has been exaggerated, Russian mobsters and oligarchs are a whole other story. Wrote Craig Unger in the *New Republic*, "The public records make clear that Trump built his business empire in no small part with a lot of shady Russians—including the dirtiest and most feared of them all." Wrote Adam Davidson in the *New Yorker*, "But a simple fact remains: we have no idea who gave our President hundreds of millions of dollars and what he might owe in return. We have a right to know."

In one transaction, Trump spent $41 million on a Palm Beach property and sold it to a Russian magnate four years later for $95 million, a profit far exceeding the appreciation rate in that region. The sale occurred immediately before the 2008 crash in markets worldwide. When a reporter asked Trump if a Russian bought the property, Trump barked, "Don't say Russian."

Why would a shrewd businessman pay so much? Said Jonathan Winer, a State Department official in the Clinton administration:

> During the '80s and '90s, we in the U.S. government repeatedly saw a pattern by which criminals would use condos and high-rises to launder money. . . . It didn't matter that you paid too much, because the real estate values would rise, and it was a way of turning dirty money into clean money. It was done very systematically, and it explained why there are so many high-rises where the units were sold but no one is living in them.

One of those who bought condos at premium prices in Trump Tower in the 1980s was David Bogatin, a Russian mobster and former partner in a gasoline tax scam of the onetime Colombo family capo Michael

Franzese. The Justice Department seized Bogatin's assets during an investigation of the massive fraud, the government declaring that Bogatin used them to "launder money, to shelter and hide assets." The 1980s were the Golden Age of the Russian partnership with LCN. Reported Craig Unger:

> Over the past three decades, at least 13 people with known or alleged links to Russian mobsters or oligarchs have owned, lived in, and even run criminal activities out of Trump Tower and other Trump properties. Many used his apartments and casinos to launder untold millions in dirty money. Some ran a worldwide high-stakes gambling ring out of Trump Tower—in a unit directly below one owned by Trump.

For a Miami-area Trump property, one real estate agent estimates that one-third of the five hundred purchasers of condos for sale were Russian. Trump's son, Donald Jr., admitted as much at a conference in 2008: "Russians make up a pretty disproportionate cross-section of a lot of our assets. . . . We see a lot of money pouring in from Russia."

A frequent visitor to Trump's Taj Mahal in Atlantic City was Vyacheslav Ivankov, a leading figure in money laundering for Russian racketeers. This is noteworthy because one method of laundering money is to gamble at a casino and receive whatever remains of your money in the form of a check, which may be legally deposited into an American bank and taxed. Shortly before Trump's 2016 presidential run, the Trump Taj Mahal paid "the highest penalty ever levied by the feds against a casino—and admitted to having 'willfully violated' anti-money-laundering regulations for years." According to operative Fino, Taj Mahal chief operating officer Dennis Gomes left the hotel casino because "he wanted a ten percent ownership and told Donald Trump he wanted the mob out of the Taj Mahal." Fino said Gomes was tired of the Philadelphia and New York mobs "muscling" the hotel casino and demanding "no-show" jobs. Trump noted that Gomes had been fired.

Kenneth McCallion, a U.S. attorney in the Reagan Justice Department who had investigated Trump's mob ties, said, "They [Russians] saved his bacon" when Trump was scrambling to stay afloat after bankruptcies. At the depth of his financial troubles, Trump was in debt for $4 billion, with $800 million personally guaranteed.

It was not illegal for Trump to accept money from someone who may have earned it illegally any more than it is for a cashier at McDonald's to take a five-dollar bill from a drug dealer buying a hamburger. Still, the question must be asked, *If Trump was getting all this money from Russians tied to foreign mobsters and the American LCN, what was he giving?*

The answer may range from nothing at all to goodwill to pulling punches on sanctions during his presidency. Neither media investigations nor legal inquiries have provided definitive answers at this writing—and many have ended in embarrassment for having set expectations of criminality much too high.

BUCKWHEATS

As Trump pursued the crime boss aura, real gangsters like Meyer Lansky and Frank Costello sought respectability, albeit in different ways. Lansky had been a straight-A student who privately hired tutors. Costello consulted a psychiatrist who, in therapy, tried to steer him toward a better class of people.

The word "respect" is one tossed about regularly in gangland. Its meaning, however, is misconstrued. In that world "respect" means "fear," which is not what the smarter racketeers (and others seeking to advance) were going for; they wanted acceptance among a higher class of people, but the closest they could get was to have others show deference because they were afraid of being harmed.

This gets to the broader theme of respectability woven into the history of presidents and the mob. Did a rich man's son like Trump want to be respected by Manhattan elites, or did he want to be a gangster accepted by real gangsters? Likely both. Trump was an Outer Borough kid who was laughed at by the Park Avenue crowd. He wanted to be one of them, but he couldn't, so he did the next best thing: Like Rodney Dangerfield's flatulent Al Czervik in *Caddyshack*, he deliberately grossed them out. Trump supporters took this to mean that he "didn't care what people thought of him." But he *did* care; he was so angry that he both was rejected by his societal betters and was unable to justify his brash style as the consequence of having clawed his way out of the gutter, like John Gotti, that he deliberately offended them. This mirrors a larger pattern in American politics where each wing of the political spectrum seeks little more than to enrage the other by taking positions that will best provoke an extreme reaction.

Lyndon Johnson did things like this in front of the snobbish Kennedys, once purposely mispronouncing "hors d'oeuvres" as "horse dove-rees." Richard Nixon told this story, laughing, as a compliment to LBJ. Poor Nixon, who, in a futile attempt to be Kennedyesque, once walked along the beach in his black wingtip shoes. While no one ever suggested that John Gotti sought acceptance on Park Avenue, FBI sources have spoken about how much he enjoyed driving crazy the uptight agents wearing cheap suits by wearing his $1,800 hand-painted ties and Giorgio Armani suits. More cultivated gangsters like Costello and Lansky were famously polite, dressed conservatively, and attempted in their ways to better themselves.

Trump has always wanted to have things both ways—tough guy "street cred" and Wall Street respectability. Consider what Trump has repeatedly stated about not paying taxes and outfoxing and outfighting regulators: "It shows I'm smart." Now Lucky Luciano: "Everybody's got larceny in 'em, only most of 'em don't have the guts to do nothin' about it. That's the big difference between us and the guys who call themselves honest. We got the guts to do what they'd like to do only they're too scared to."

At an Iowa rally, Trump said, "If you see somebody getting ready to throw a tomato, knock the crap out of them, would you?" And in 2022, he said he would deal with Russia by putting "the Chinese flag" on American aircraft and "bomb the shit" out of Russia. "And then we say, China did it, we didn't do it, China did it, and then they start fighting with each other, and we sit back and watch." During his New York fraud trial, Trump posted online, "If you go after me, I'm coming after you!"* and challenged (regarding New York's top law enforcement officer), "You should go after this attorney general."

During the 2020 unrest after police officers suffocated George Floyd

---

*   Compare this to Vito Corleone's admonition to a supplicant, "If by chance an honest man like yourself should make enemies, then they would become my enemies. And then they would fear you."

while arresting him, then president Trump said, "When the looting starts, the shooting starts." Trump admitted to having sued reporter Tim O'Brien for underestimating his wealth just "to make his life miserable." In Mafia terms, making victims suffer and demonstrating your power over them is known as "buckwheats."

Wrote Johnston, "No other candidate for the White House has anything close to Trump's record of repeated social and business dealings with mobsters, swindlers, and other crooks." The question then becomes, So what? Why does it matter that Trump had mob ties before he became president? After all, no one has suggested that heirs to Fat Tony and Big Paul were kicking back in the Lincoln Sitting Room being handed government contracts.

Americans have traditionally been concerned with the backgrounds of their presidential contenders, especially during an era of withering scrutiny and transparency. It wasn't that long ago that New York governor Mario Cuomo demurred from pursuing the presidency after being dogged by *false* allegations of having links to organized crime. If, in fact, the electorate no longer cares about presidential candidates dealing with racketeers, this will be good to factor into our new reality.

Trump's associations didn't stop him from anchoring his 2016 presidential run on the alleged criminality of his opponent, Hillary Clinton. With any other candidate under any other conditions, that contender would not have survived the primaries, but despite extensive—and admitted—mob links, either such relationships no longer matter or no longer matter as they apply to Trump.

With the other presidents being explored here, the pre-presidential links to organized crime were: (1) so stratified and attenuated as to make a line of attack unfruitful (Reagan); (2) largely unknown until after the presidency (Kennedy); or (3) part of a mishmash of corruption allegations whereby mob ties in and of themselves weren't strong enough to resonate (Truman). With Trump, however, Americans elected him knowing much of what was reported here. If he wanted to be embraced in the spirit of a mob boss, there were prosecutors waiting in the wings to indulge him. At this writing, Trump faces prosecution on ninety-one criminal charges, some of them under the RICO Act alleging that he led a criminal enterprise (none related to LCN). In May 2024, he was convicted of thirty-four

294 WISEGUYS AND THE WHITE HOUSE

counts of fraud in his trial to conceal "hush money" payments to porn star Stormy Daniels.

Much of what becomes a scandal is specific to the individuals in question and the circumstances in which they became public figures. Trump entered the fray during intense tribalism, where the only thing that mattered was identity, as opposed to "the issues" per se. As we saw in the Kennedy chapter, those with an evangelical faith in JFK are disinterested in the possibility that he could have benefited from organized crime while also prosecuting them. Similarly, those who believed Trump was saving the country, including religious conservatives who, in theory, should have been repulsed by him, dismissed any notion of his corruption. When we don't like you, jaywalking is on par with child abuse; when we do like you, your venality gets lost in a boys-will-be-boys miasma.

By the time Trump reached the White House, LCN was on its last legs. Trump and the mob's mutually beneficial relationship was ancient history. He owed them nothing anymore, and they couldn't touch him. He had "walked," in mob parlance, and made it to the top.

9

Joe Biden

COLORFUL ANCESTORS

They were people nobody would mess with.

—Teamster Frank Sheeran

Most of us have a unique relative or two, but Joe Biden had picaresque characters with underworld links—quite literally, as his dad was into a shady grave vault racket. At this writing, there is intense media coverage surrounding the Biden family and alleged criminal activity. It's safe to say that members of the Biden family earned multiple millions in a variety of business deals. It is unclear how much of this money, if any, reached Joe Biden personally and whether this income was earned illegally. (A House Oversight Committee report indicated a $1,380 monthly direct deposit from a Hunter Biden business into Joe's bank account.)

At the very least, the income of Hunter Biden, President Biden's son, has been extensive and unconventional, and he merchandized his family name to win business. Hunter was on the board of the private equity fund, BHR, based in China between 2013 and 2020. The company invests in Chinese state-owned enterprises, among others. Given that China is an adversary of the United States known for aggressively conducting surveillance, this relationship could have placed Hunter and his father in compromising positions, although there is no evidence that it did. Hunter also received a $1 million payment in 2018 from an executive at a Chinese company who has since been prosecuted for unrelated bribery charges.

Hunter Biden was on the board of the Ukrainian holding company Burisma where he earned tens of thousands of dollars per month as an attorney. Critics charged that, because his father was then vice president, he was able to influence U.S. policy. The most damaging claim, later dismissed upon investigation, was that Hunter got his father to call off the prosecution of Burisma in the Ukraine. What cannot be in doubt is that Hunter Biden leveraged his family name and occasional telephone calls with his father to impress his foreign clientele. Illegal? Not necessarily. Improper? Definitely. Nor do we have proof that Hunter was able to deliver anything tangible in return to his contacts, which would have been the whole idea. Foreign officials have been criminally charged with colluding with Trump associates for trying to damage the Bidens.

Nevertheless, in June 2023, Hunter pleaded guilty to income tax evasion and was later indicted on additional tax felonies. These charges alleged that Hunter enjoyed more than $7 million in income in a four-year period and a lifestyle including drugs, escort services, and high-end cars and clothing. A trial on illegal gun possession charges has yet to be scheduled.

What cannot be disputed is that Hunter Biden, and Joe Biden's brother, Jim, are wildly inept at business and would not have received the staggering opportunities and loans they have were it not for their ties to Joe. Jim Biden, to drum up support for a venture fund, said, "Don't worry about investors. We've got people all around the world who want to invest in Joe Biden." Indeed, brother Jim became famous for pushing what became known as the Biden "brand." When Joe Biden's son, Beau, who was running for attorney general of Delaware, heard about the pitch, he was appalled, telling Uncle Jim, "I will have nothing to do with this." Financier Charles Provini, who was asked by Hunter and Jim to run a hedge fund they took over, explained the Bidens' model: "The story was that they had relationships with different unions and that they would anticipate being able to get union funding or union investments into the fund" given their proximity to Joe.

According to public records, Americore Health loaned Jim Biden $600,000 "based upon representations that his last name, 'Biden,' could 'open doors' and that he could obtain a large investment from the Middle East based upon his political connections." The investment never came through, but Jim paid Joe back for a $200,000 loan in 2018, the same day he received some of the Americore money.

In 2005, a lobbyist who had once been a Senate aide to Biden bought Virgin Islands property from Jim Biden for a hefty amount. According to *Politico*, the lobbyist's "clients benefited from Biden's support and appropriations requests." News reports claim that Biden's youngest brother, Frank, would frequently disrupt meetings at the manufacturing firm that employs him to announce he had to take a call from "the big guy." During the 2020 campaign, Joe admonished Frank, "For Christ's sake, watch yourself!" Frank Biden only recently began paying his obligations after decades of evasion to the family of a California man, Michael Albano, who was killed in a traffic accident involving Biden.

In the 1990s, plaintiff's lawyer Richard "Dickie" Scruggs paid Jim Biden's consulting firm Lion Hall $100,000 for advice on how to get Biden's senator brother to support his litigation against tobacco companies. "I probably wouldn't have hired him if he wasn't the senator's brother," said Scruggs. "Biden had gone from being one of its [the tobacco settlement's] biggest critics to becoming one of its leading defenders," reported the *Washington Post*. Joe eventually befriended Scruggs and used his airplane for campaign travel.

It is commonplace, and distasteful, when a politician rises to the top, that people around him will seek to exploit that relationship. For his part, Joe certainly joined telephone calls and made appearances that facilitated a lot of income for his extended family—and he has been less than forthcoming about these things as evidenced by photographs and White House logs from when he was vice president. Subpoenas are flying in the investigations of Hunter and Frank. Nevertheless, there remains a difference between disorganized slime and organized crime, the evidence currently falling short of warranting the moniker of the "Biden crime family" that is tossed around by adversaries. More like the "sharp practice" we've seen with other presidents—and a mind-boggling volume of shady attempts by the Biden family to grab loans and exploit its name, from setting up nightclubs to law firms.

FOR A MAN WHO TRAFFICS IN TALES OF WORKING-CLASS HUMILITY, IT AP-
pears that the Biden antecedents had higher aspirations that were fleetingly
achieved with the help of scoundrels, some of whom were mob-connected.
They were more chiselers than lethal gang lords. However, Biden received
support early in his career from a noteworthy mob figure projected into
the national consciousness through the 2019 Martin Scorsese epic, *The
Irishman.*

President Biden's father, Joseph R. Biden, Sr., was very close to his
uncle, William Sheene, Sr., who went into business with a gangland-
linked bootlegger, Arthur Briscoe, who was a menacing figure. Sheene
and Briscoe founded the Asphalt Grave Vault Company, which boasted
in the 1920s that its products could protect graves from the elements for
hundreds of years. Among the deceased who benefited from these miracle
entombments were Presidents William H. Taft and Warren G. Harding.

Biden Sr. lived high on the hog from his uncle Bill Sheene for whom
he worked. Their lifestyle included mansions and yachts. Among other
things, Sheene was mentally unstable, and it turned out that the grave
business was a racket. According to a *New Yorker* exposé, the vaults were
"neither 'waterproof' nor 'airtight.' Some of them didn't even contain
asphalt." The Federal Trade Commission went after the company, and
Sheene and Briscoe, Biden Sr.'s employers, settled with them.

Sheene and Briscoe, with Biden Sr. as a top executive, started a new
company to manufacture a product called "plastic armor" for soldiers
during World War II. This company incorporated asphalt from the
sketchy grave company. The military wasn't so sure about the Sheene–
Briscoe–Biden Sr. trio. The government learned about the grave racket
and a violent arrest involving Sheene in its due diligence. They also learned
that the bootlegger Briscoe had spent time in a psychiatric institution.
Despite these demerits, the company got the go-ahead to begin putting
plastic armor on ships. The Maritime Welding & Repair Company made
a fortune.

Trouble came when the homicidal mobster Albert Anastasia tried to
unionize Maritime's personnel. The workers stopped working. Business
suffered. Briscoe approached Frank Costello, the Luciano crime family
leader, and legendary political and labor fixer. Costello regretted informing Briscoe, "Well, we may have to break a few heads" to bring the strike to

a halt. The respectability-seeking Briscoe, who was sensitive to the fragility of government contracts, wanted to avoid violence, so he paid Costello extra to reach a deal with the union so Maritime could get back to business.

It's important to note that despite their very different styles, Anastasia and Costello were friends and associates. Briscoe's actress mistress had known Costello and had introduced the two men. Anastasia probably created the strike mess in cahoots with Costello knowing that Briscoe would ultimately run to Costello for help. The scheme worked perfectly. Problem created, problem solved. The hundreds of thousands of dollars Maritime kept in its vaults for expenses—in the 1940s, no less—had gone to good use.

Briscoe and his actress girlfriend, the hoodlum-friendly Marie Gaffney, were quite a pair. Briscoe married Gaffney. After the married Briscoe met her, his wife died after being scalded in her bathtub. An investigation ruled out foul play.

During this period, the Bidens were much more than working class. They lived in a mansion near Boston, used expensive china when they dined, and flew in the Sheenes' private plane. Biden Sr. had some involvement with a yacht that had been used in an insurance scam. The yacht burned up apparently during a brief excursion with Biden Sr. and Sheene's son, who was accompanied by "two unmarried women." No one was injured.

Frank Costello helped resolve a labor strike at a business where Joe Biden's father was a senior executive.
Leonard McCombe/The LIFE Picture Collection/Shutterstock

Maritime, like Asphalt Grave Vault, soon ran into trouble. The company had been paying huge salaries and was heavily fined. Whether these salaries had been padded to accommodate kickbacks for the racketeers who resolved the strike is unknown. Wrote Adam Entous in the *New Yorker*:

> The stage was set for another investigation. War contractors were expected to limit their profits, and in the middle of the war the average profit on a naval contract was about eight percent. The Maritime Commission began looking into whether the Sheenes and Briscoe might have taken a larger cut, and it found that, on average, the men's businesses made a twenty-three-per-cent profit. In the case of the Asphalt Grave Vault Company, which was part of the plastic-armor outfit, the pretax profit was an egregious forty-eight percent.

The Biden family's fortunes greatly suffered. The government demanded that Maritime return "two-thirds of its profits." There were other business misadventures, and the Biden family finally became working class, but the man who became president never lost his taste for big houses. Nor was the World War II crisis to be the last time a Biden had been the downstream beneficiary of organized crime.

THE 1972 ELECTION

The elections of 1972 took place during a time of ongoing civil unrest. The Vietnam War raged on with no end in sight, and the protest culture was the backdrop against which most political coverage was being framed. There were thousands of bombings annually in the early 1970s within U.S. borders. The FBI counted about five domestic bombings per day in 1971 and 1972. While few of these were lethal, they were emotionally resonant. Journalist Bryan Burrough characterized the bombings as "exploding press releases." Richard Nixon was the Republican nominee, and the Democrats had tilted to the left in response to events foreign and domestic; they had selected liberal South Dakota senator George McGovern as their nominee.

Joe Biden running for U.S. Senate in 1972
AP Photo/Henry Griffin

Joseph R. Biden, Jr., was a young attorney representing New Castle County, Delaware, that year. He was twenty-nine years old, too young to be a U.S. senator, but if elected, he could serve because he turned thirty two weeks after the election before being sworn into office. His election had a pipe dream feel because his opponent was a two-term Republican, Senator J. Caleb "Cale" Boggs, who had been contemplating retirement at sixty-three. President Nixon, concerned about a destructive primary battle, encouraged Boggs to run again. The consensus was that given his stature, Boggs would easily be reelected.

Biden ran the kind of campaign one might expect from a kid with limited experience and funds. His campaign manager was his sister, Valerie. The campaign staff consisted of members of his immediate family. Mainly, his outreach consisted of personal appearances supported by position papers distributed as leaflets. Advertising was minimal because funds were scarce, and Biden couldn't take advantage of the slick, highly produced television ads coming into fashion.

Biden had been faring poorly against Boggs throughout the summer, trailing by 30 percentage points. A week before the November 7 election, Teamsters official Frank Sheeran was approached by an attorney (who has never been identified) who needed assistance for an aspect of Biden's campaign. Sheeran was president of Teamsters Local 326 based in New Castle, Delaware. He was also a mob associate close to Teamsters boss Jimmy Hoffa, not to mention Cosa Nostra bosses Angelo Bruno of Philadelphia, whose territory included Delaware, and Russell Bufalino of Northeastern Pennsylvania, where Biden was originally from.

Bufalino was also influential with New York's Genovese family, the primary powerhouse behind the Teamsters at that time, specifically North Jersey's Anthony Provenzano. There is no evidence that Biden knew any of these men.

The mystery lawyer's request involved an anticipated advertisement that Boggs was planning to run in newspapers in Delaware that was critical of Biden. Specifically, the ads would demonstrate how Biden had distorted Boggs's voting record. The Biden camp, of course, didn't want the ad to drop so close to the election, and the Teamsters, seeking to endear themselves to Biden's campaign, believed they could help.

They could. And they did.

According to Sheeran, he organized a work stoppage so that the Teamsters, who distributed newspapers, could not circulate the ads that Boggs's campaign had prepared. The ads were to run in the *Morning News* and *Evening Journal*, published by the same entity. They were heavily circulated in the northern part of Delaware, where the state's population was densest. Said Sheeran: "I told him [the Biden-linked lawyer] I would hire some people and put them on the picket line for him. They were people nobody would mess with. . . . I told him that once we put up the picket line I would see to it that no truck driver crossed the picket line."

Sheeran claims to have met Biden during the 1972 campaign. Boggs had asked to speak to the Teamsters but was declined because he was too pro-business, which he denied. Biden approached the Teamsters and was invited to speak. Sheeran said: "He gave a really good pro-labor speech to the rank and file at that membership meeting. He took questions from the floor and handled himself like someone many years older. He said his door would always be open to the Teamsters."

Sheeran was an imperfect source, but his election assistance is one of his more credible claims as it would have been a logical aspect of his Teamsters' work. Portrayed by Robert De Niro in Martin Scorsese's *The Irishman*, Sheeran was an important figure in Teamsters' history. He was close to Hoffa, but his role in Hoffa's murder depicted in the film has been sharply contested. But Sheeran was known to be accurate about less dramatic events, and a *New York Times* article published several days before the election validates his version of the Biden election caper: "*The Morning News*, struck by a union representing drivers who deliver newspapers, did not publish a Friday edition. Members of other unions, such as pressmen, printers and newspapers, would not cross the picket lines set up at 6 PM today by the 21 drivers. They are members of Local 10, American Newspaper Guild of Greater Philadelphia."

Wilmington is a twenty-minute drive from Philadelphia and well within the sphere of influence of Sheeran's associate Angelo Bruno.

Biden won the election in an upset, defeating Boggs by just over 3,000 votes. It was the tightest Senate election of 1972. On the other hand, McGovern was destroyed in the Delaware election, losing to Nixon by 20 points.

The big question is whether the intervention of the mobbed-up Teamster Sheeran's actions a week before the 1972 election played a role in Biden's squeaker victory. The best we can say is that given Biden's early poor showing, it didn't hurt to have a hostile advertisement neutralized before it reached hundreds of thousands of Delawareans. Sheeran said: "The Republicans say that if those newspaper inserts from the Boggs side got delivered inside the newspapers, it would have made Joe Biden look very bad. The Boggs ads coming as they almost did that last week there would have been no time for Biden to repair the damage."

Concluded Sheeran, "I do know that when he became the U.S. Senator, the man stuck by his word he gave to the membership. You could reach out for him, and he would listen."

Teamsters heavyweight Frank Sheeran made sure that newspaper advertisements hostile to the 1972 Biden Senate campaign never got delivered.
AP Photo/Jon Falk

While the Sheeran story retains credibility, another Delaware Valley mob story associated with Biden that arose almost fifty years later does not. Shortly after the 2020 election, an online news site found to have a pattern of spreading fake news reported that alleged Philadelphia Cosa Nostra boss Joseph "Skinny Joey" Merlino was paid $3 million to unload boxes of counterfeit ballots for Joe Biden at a central vote-counting location. The *Buffalo Chronicle* website claimed Merlino had forged 300,000 votes and planned to turn the state's evidence against Biden over the fraud. No such thing had ever happened, and the *Chronicle* was exposed for circulating disinformation about liberal-leaning politicians. When asked about his alleged role in the vote-counting fraud, Merlino said, "If I fixed the election, Trump would have won. . . . I hate Biden."

Nevertheless, disinformation about the rigging was shared on Facebook seventeen thousand times and reached about three million viewers. While the Trump campaign declared that Biden had stolen the election from him by fraud, the *Chronicle* deception was unlikely planted by Trump's campaign. Even mob-busting Trump lawyer Rudolph Giuliani expressed skepticism that Merlino had had anything to do with the fraud in Philadelphia or anywhere. Still, a "Stop the Steal" campaign had been encouraged by the Trump team even if elements of it were executed independently at a grassroots level.

Despite the falsity of the Merlino hoax, its existence is a testament to the Mafia's lasting hold over popular culture: There is always somebody out there who will devour and circulate even the most outrageous tidbit of Mafia news that validates the meme of far-reaching and nefarious influence.

President Biden himself was far removed from any of his ancestors' sketchy activities. However, his youthful lifestyle was financed by business scams, some of which were run by mob-linked characters. The notoriously corrupt Teamsters had abetted his career-making election to the U.S. Senate in 1972. Nevertheless, Biden's support of the unions would have been a natural extension of his existing politics, as opposed to anything that an unseemly backroom deal would have needed to accomplish.

10

"That License"

In most cases, people, even wicked people, are far more naive and simple-hearted than one generally assumes. And so are we.

—Fyodor Dostoyevsky, *The Brothers Karamazov*

From the beginning, this book begs the question, "So what?"

We've come a long way from hoods like Piker Ryan, Owney the Killer, Dopey Benny, and Kid Dropper roaming the Five Points. Still, we must reflect precisely the distance traveled from the nineteenth century back alleys to the White House; what has changed, what hasn't, and, more importantly, what it means. Some shady characters made some dirty deals with ambitious politicians. Shocking? After all, it wasn't as if mob bosses were calling shots from the Situation Room.

There are a few reasons we should care. *The most important is the sheer frequency and presence of the mob in the American power structure.* These were not aberrations; organized crime was steady in presidential politics, indirectly and directly, close and from a distance. In several presidential and pre-presidential environments, people with major mob connections were close to those in the orbit of once, present, and future presidents. Not only were criminals playing a role when presidents were on the way up, but they were also mobilized on some occasions when they were in office.

Another point of interest is the nature of the interactions between presidential politicians and organized crime because similar dynamics were at work across the board. The mob contacts were never between the mob figure and the president or candidate. There were always layers in between in the form of operatives, which demonstrates a desire to keep some distance for obvious ethical, legal, and political reasons.

In most—but not all—cases, the president knew that mob-connected figures were being used. FDR almost surely knew about Operation Underworld. Truman knew that his patron, Pendergast, was mobbed-up to his gills. JFK knew about Operation Mongoose, including the Mafia plot against Castro, and Richard Nixon knew that Hoffa and the Teamsters were mob controlled. Donald Trump openly bragged on television about working with gangsters.

Dealings with big-time politicians and mobsters were short-term interactions of convenience and mutual benefit instead of far-ranging strategic partnerships. Any relationships that existed between gangsters and presidential politicians were ephemeral. There can be little doubt that the Kennedys leveraged mobsters to their benefit, but attorney general Robert F. Kennedy also hunted them down. Richard Nixon, described by several melodramatic writers as a front for the mob, promulgated the legislation that destroyed them.

The businesspeople who quietly used the mob also found ways to do most of their business "legitimately" (Annenberg, Kennedy, Wasserman, Trump) and profited far more than the mobsters who snickered that they controlled the businessmen. Ultimately, those who did the dirty work paid a greater price than those who kept their distance.

The story of wiseguys and the White House is replete with paradoxes and hypocrisies. Consider these:

1. The government engineered Operation Underworld, then denied it, punishing those who were most responsible for whatever success it had.

2. Two of our most mob-relevant presidents (Truman and Trump) were the most open about having had such connections.

3. A presidency (Kennedy) that benefited significantly from mob assets also tormented the mobsters who helped it (Giancana).

4. The president widely regarded as having been the most corrupt (Nixon) and his attorney general, who was convicted of a felony (Mitchell), developed and implemented the law that decimated the mob (RICO).

5. A president whose career mentor built his conglomerate with the help of mob muscle unleashed the most crippling LCN prosecutions in history (Reagan).

6. The mob's greatest nemesis, Rudy Giuliani, who famously leveraged the RICO law to prosecute mobsters, became a leading apologist for the only president who was boastful about dealing with mobsters and whose contacts with crime figures have been heavily documented. He was indicted under the RICO statute for attempting to overturn the results of the 2020 election in Georgia.

7. Leaders of aristocratic bearing (Roosevelt, Kennedy, and Patton in Sicily) benefited from the dirty work of gangsters.

8. Some of the greatest gangland beneficiaries of their major political connections ended up in prison, exiled, dead by violence, or mercilessly hunted by the feds (Giancana, Lansky, Lanza, Luciano, Rosselli).

To decide how much organized crime impacted a president or presidency, we must address things like the amount of time passed since there were gangland ties, how direct those ties were, and the degree to which a leader moved past shady connections to accomplish good things. Given these considerations, I have summarized below where the presidents explored here rank in terms of being affected by organized crime. *This is not an evaluation of the full scope of their presidencies, just an imperfect and narrow assessment of the mob's impact on their presidential careers.* The scale, again:

5 Wouldn't have been president without mob
4 Career significantly affected by mob
3 Mob involvement relevant to aspects of presidency
2 Mob links not very impactful to overall presidency and career
1 Tangential mob links at best

Franklin Delano Roosevelt

FDR authorized wartime measures under conditions of great peril. He was likely aware of mob involvement in one intelligence aspect of national defense in World War II, but it was a risk worth taking.

Mob-impacted: 2

Harry Truman

Truman was the president with the active involvement of the LCN-partnered political machine that he continued protecting when he was president. Few believe he greatly benefited in the material sense, but he saw dealing with racket-connected people as a necessary evil and advanced accordingly.

Mob-impacted: 5

John F. Kennedy

Kennedy benefited from racketeers' involvement in his presidential career; his father sought it, and he and his brother either knew or should have known. The extent to which mob influence impacted the 1960 election result is rightly a subject for debate, but there is little question that Joe Kennedy pursued and received help. While Jack and Bobby likely didn't know details, they *chose* not to learn and had the luxury of not knowing how their father was pursuing power and glory for them. The brothers also knew that gangsters had been involved in the Castro assassination plots even if they had not directed the mob component of the Castro campaign. Given what they knew about other elements of Operation Mongoose, there is a hairsplitting aspect to whether they were involved with mobilizing one band of murderers versus another. Still, the Cuban campaign can be debatably ascribed to national security. While the brothers played a significant role in going after the mob, it's hard to allow this to cancel out the other things we now know.

Mob-impacted: 4

Lyndon B. Johnson

Johnson ordered the FBI to do what was necessary to determine what happened to the missing civil rights workers. There is no evidence he knew of mob involvement, and personal gain was not the main cause driving him despite the vicious character Scarpa ultimately retained for the job.

Mob-impacted: 2

Richard Nixon

Nixon knew precisely who the Teamsters were and how they got their power. He made shrewd calculations to advance personally. He likely used or seriously considered using mobsters to abet aspects of the Watergate scandal, and given what we now know about Nixon, it's hard to give him the benefit of the doubt.

Mob-impacted: 4

Ronald Reagan

Reagan's career resurrection was due to his relationship with Lew Wasserman and MCA, which had multiple gangland links that allowed the company to prosper. Much of MCA's power came from mob muscle, which helped give Wasserman the leverage to provide Reagan with career-saving support. Nor does the absence of a smoking gun on the SAG waiver mean that a suspicious deal did not occur. The mob, however, did not play a direct or decisive role in the events that allowed Reagan to advance.

Mob-impacted: 3

Donald Trump

Trump was the beneficiary of too many mob links to keep track of. He openly admits to having dealt with gangsters. While his career as a developer is replete with such contacts and transactions, they didn't materially translate to his presidency.

Mob-impacted: 4

Joe Biden

Biden's family had colorful connections, but the mob links were attenuated. He likely benefited from an underhanded ploy in his original 1972 Senate campaign, but there is no evidence of a pattern or major impact.

Mob-impacted: 1

THE MOB'S PATH TO PRESIDENTIAL RELEVANCE

When thinking about the impact of the rackets on the presidency, it helps to revisit whence the mob came. Even though labor racketeering came first, Prohibition was the taproot of American organized crime. The corruption associated with bootlegging occurred nationwide but manifested on the local level. When the labor movement found its national footing, organized crime got its clutches into presidential politics. Labor was fused into American business's everyday give-and-take. FDR needed labor influence at the wartime docks from Luciano and Lansky and for political muscle with union chief Sidney Hillman. Truman benefited from labor support during his political career from Hillman and Pendergast. The Kennedys received help from the Outfit's Giancana and Humphreys in the 1960 election. Nixon's gangland benefactors and beneficiaries were Hoffa, Fitzsimmons, and the Teamsters. The success of Reagan's mentor, Lew Wasserman, was built with the help of union thuggery through Sid Korshak and the Outfit—and in turn, Wasserman's MCA received Reagan's support from the SAG union. Later, Reagan enjoyed the backing of the Teamsters under Jackie Presser. Much of Trump and his family's real estate success was rooted in deals from mobbed-up unions via Roy Cohn, and even Joe Biden got an early push from the Teamsters in his first Senate race.

Organized crime has persevered for so long because it was decentralized. It was not one monolithic corporation united in carrying out a particular agenda. Yes, they made money illegally, but they were always a loose confederacy, each clan making its own decisions and picking its fights. To hunt one was not to hunt them all, and to enable one was not to allow them all.

In Cuba, different families had interests in discrete operations. The New York contingent headed by Lansky "crapped out" in Havana while the Cleveland group got out in time. When Chicago mobsters Sam Giancana and John Rosselli joined with Tampa's Santo Trafficante to coordinate with the CIA to kill Castro, they were doing so individually. Later in life, Lansky and his partner Jimmy Alo told people they hadn't known about Operation Mongoose then, but when they found out, they thought it was idiotic and a scam. They had known the mob's Cuban jig was up in 1959.

To the extent that the mob had power in presidential politics, it was mainly localized. Operation Underworld was primarily a New York Luciano (Genovese) family operation. Truman's origins were with the Kansas City rackets, and his administration's parole scandal involved the Chicago Outfit. The Kennedys' mob games concentrated mainly on Chicago. Lyndon Johnson's civil rights posse consisted of one brutal New York mobster. Nixon's Teamsters efforts ultimately affected the Chicago Outfit and the New York/New Jersey Genovese clans. MCA's hidden muscle was out of Chicago and Los Angeles. Donald Trump's links were with New York and Philadelphia mob families, and Joe Biden benefited from a Teamsters mix from Pennsylvania and Delaware.

Despite the mob's disunity, they had help from the federal government along the way. This was not the grand conspiracy that many believe but rather a gift of climate and serendipity: The rise of the American mob coincided with the rise of Communism.

J. EDGAR HOOVER AND THE GIFT OF COMMUNISM

Prohibition catalyzed the mob, and labor racketeering institutionalized American gangsterism. Still, something bigger allowed it to grow practically unchecked into the behemoth it became: the diversion of resources by the federal government and especially the FBI toward catching suspected Communists versus enterprise criminals.

Going after Communists was a low-risk/high-reward endeavor, especially for men like Nixon and Hoover. Nixon had built his career on the foundation of anti-Communism, which was very effective. Hoover kept his job for almost a half century by pivoting from catching bank robbers to nailing Communists while building the world's most advanced law enforcement organization.

Communism was the best thing to have happened to the mob after Prohibition ended. Hoover's natural mindset, strategic outlook, and bureaucratic instincts were the reasons he had given the Mafia short shrift. It was a by-product, not a conspiracy, on Hoover's part. He is the one individual who runs through many of the presidents addressed in this book. To understand why the mob flourished during the Hoover years, it's essential to understand that Hoover's pursuit of Communists was rooted in genuine concern about threats to the United States as opposed to a subjective fetish.

In a peculiar sideshow during the mid to late 1960s, Hoover tried to use the mob to harass Communists through a scheme called Operation Hoodwink. The gist was to convince mobsters that Communists were a threat to their labor rackets so the gangsters would disrupt their activities. These Philadelphia-focused efforts were accomplished by forging letters purportedly from CPUSA officials to mob-connected labor leaders threatening to turn them in to law enforcement. Hoodwink was disbanded in 1968 for lack of tangible results.

One of the Soviets' most remarkable achievements was propaganda, especially turning a new generation of Americans against their government by fanning racial divisions and publicizing the U.S. government's abuses. A brilliant subset of this effort was persuading many that the very suggestion that there was a Communist influence in our government and culture was irrational and, perhaps worse, culturally uncool.

There had been justifiable strategic reasons for Hoover to pursue Communists even if he overestimated the threat and his tactics were overzealous and, in some cases, criminal. Furthermore, his anticommunist views were in the mainstream of American political thought and embraced by multiple presidents.

What these leaders had in common as the twentieth century wore on was a terror of nuclear war. In research for a previous book, the one thing that FBI, CIA, and KGB agents interviewed agreed upon was that the spy game was driven by fear of a nuclear exchange. Hoover's concern was that a bomb would be smuggled into the United States by a Communist fellow traveler and planted in a major city. He and other officials believed these comrades would come in the form of American radicals such as

Julius and Ethel Rosenberg in the early days of the Cold War and, later, activist Angela Davis, who received an honorary doctorate from Moscow State University, won the Lenin Peace Prize, and openly praised the Soviet Union. These views intensified with the rise of Martin Luther King, Jr., and the civil rights movement. FBI honcho William Sullivan disturbingly wrote of Martin Luther King, Jr., "We must mark him now, if we have not done so before, as the most dangerous Negro of the future in this Nation from the standpoint of communism, the Negro and national security."

During Hoover's reign, his FBI discovered and prosecuted espionage rings that had been passing along nuclear secrets to the Soviets, including the Rosenbergs and Ethel's brother David Greenglass, and physicists Klaus Fuchs and Theodore Hall. In the late 1930s and early 1940s, the FBI captured and helped convict two German spy rings (not including the Long Island and Florida Nazi submarine spies addressed in the Roosevelt chapter). In concert with the Army Signal Corps, the FBI helped identify 350 operatives in the United States who were providing the Soviets with valuable intelligence. It is believed that the FBI was able to eliminate most Soviet moles within the government through the mid-1950s.

No less than a vice president of the United States, secretary of commerce, and secretary of agriculture in the form of Henry Wallace had been a Soviet asset. Even ultraliberal writer and critic Dorothy Parker thought Wallace a Soviet stooge. Historian John Lewis Gaddis wrote, "There is Soviet documentation that Wallace was regularly reporting to the Kremlin in 1945 and 1946 while he was in the Truman Administration."

Ohio senator Robert Taft said: "The greatest Kremlin asset in our history has been the pro-communist group in the State Department who surrendered to every demand of Russia at Yalta and Potsdam, and promoted at every opportunity the communist cause in China until today communism threatens to take over all of Asia."

The *New York Times* journalist Walter Duranty, one of the most influential reporters of his era, was a pro-Soviet propagandist. He consistently downplayed Joseph Stalin's genocidal methodology and orchestrated famines.

Hoover authorized break-ins at Soviet and Eastern Bloc offices based in U.S. cities, efforts that presidents and attorneys general approved. He provided Senator Joseph McCarthy with reports on suspected Communists, which McCarthy cited, with creative flourishes. In 1958, Hoover published a ghostwritten book, *Masters of Deceit*, which became a bestseller and focused on the Communist threat to America. *Deceit* earned today's equivalent of $500,000, which Hoover kept personally.

There had been a spiritual component to Hoover's zeal. He told a reporter: "I've been studying [Communism] since 1919. It is really not so much a political creed as an insane kind of fanaticism, a fanaticism that is basically atheistic—anti-God, if you like—and against the concept of any supreme being."*

According to the FBI:

> In the six years following World War II, the Bureau had moved from having a shadowy perception of the Soviet intelligence threat to having a clear picture of the extent of Soviet penetration of the U.S. government and the damage that its agents had done to America's interests.
>
> With this vastly clearer image of the threat we faced, the FBI was able to move from a reactive counterintelligence policy to a proactive one. . . . By October 1951, the Bureau had initiated a program of intensive coverage of Soviet and Satellite personnel and establishments to thwart Soviet intelligence efforts and those by its allies . . . this program included intensive electronic surveillance, a long-term effort to develop double agents within hostile intelligence establishments, and an effort to develop other double agents to flush out hostile intelligence personnel.

No less than Vladimir Putin has bragged that Soviet agents stole nuclear secrets from U.S. scientists. Said Putin to the Itar-Tass news service: "You know, when the States already had nuclear weapons and the Soviet Union was only building them, we got a significant amount of information through Soviet foreign intelligence channels. . . . It was the cream of the scientific world that was gathered in America, and I personally have

---

*   Indeed, Communism was not just the obsession of federal operatives like Hoover but of evangelical leaders such as the Reverend Billy Graham, who grew his flock on radio and television in part by relentlessly hammering the idea that Communism was the work of Satan and could only be countermanded by the Christian faith. All self-justifying entities need a hardened villain.

gotten the impression that they consciously gave us information on the atom bomb."

THE SUBVERSION DIVERSION

It's telling that in the late 1950s, at the height of the Cold War, the New York office of the FBI had four hundred agents hunting Communists and other "subversives" and four keeping an eye on the rackets, the latter because Hoover believed gangsters were the purview of the New York Police Department. Beginning in the late 1950s, Hoover's COINTELPRO (counterintelligence program) effort to disrupt Communist sympathizers ran more than twenty-three hundred operations against suspected subversives. It was here that Hoover's efforts lost their bearings. He had 300,000 pages of files on likely homosexuals because he believed they were uniquely vulnerable to Communist influence.

The FBI collected files on college students making observations ranging from "an inveterate Marxist revolutionist" to an "average liberal-minded student." The FBI would show these files to university leaders with the hope that they would crack down on campus free speech. The FBI also arranged for the Internal Revenue Service to audit specific targets and forged correspondence to turn cell leaders against one another. It didn't work.

Yet organized crime galloped on apace until the FBI began taking it seriously, the efforts catalyzing after Hoover's death.

Going light on organized crime was a by-product of a diversion of focus and resources, not corruption. This worked out beautifully for the mob, but only a tiny portion of this outcome had anything to do with their cleverness. Hoover and American political leaders had written off organized crime as a local priority. Hoover had linked the civil rights movement to *national* Communist infiltration, whipping up racial unrest as a desire to tear the country apart from within. There was an element of Soviet "active measures" at work, but this ignores the real injustices animating the push for civil rights.

Nevertheless, Hoover should have recognized earlier that there had been national implications to gangland's reach and that the FBI had the greatest capability to have met this challenge. The by-product was to unfetter a network of enterprise criminals who ran operations that did billions of dollars in business annually. One can only wonder what the impact would have been had the FBI directed its wrath against organized crime sooner. Qualified sociologist Daniel Bell: "Unfortunately for a good story—and the existence of the Mafia would be a whale of a story—neither the Senate Crime Committee in its testimony nor Kefauver in his book presented any real evidence that the Mafia exists as a functioning organization."

TECHNICALLY, HOOVER HADN'T BEEN WRONG TO SEE ORGANIZED CRIME AS a local phenomenon. There were twenty-four local mobs. Gangsters liked this model because had they been perceived as a national enterprise, they would have become attractive to the feds, and the last thing they wanted was to be interesting. When LCN oozed onto the national radar, bosses admonished their hoods not to cross state lines or perform bank robberies, a federal crime, because they hadn't wanted to awaken Washington. They were sensitive to the investigative power of national agencies (besides the FBI) hunting down narcotics, tax evaders, and counterfeiters and had been prosecuting LCN members since the early 1900s. Many in Congress shared Hoover's view that federal budgeting hadn't been needed for local crimes. An FBI agent put it somewhat differently, stating that the bureau could only investigate under the laws that existed, not the laws it wanted to exist.

LCN could coordinate with multiple cities when needed, primarily to defuse conflicts. The problem was proving it, an endeavor promising too little investment return. This was complicated by another fortuitous reason the mob got a break after Bobby Kennedy died: His successor, Ramsay Clark, disapproved of electronic surveillance, believing it was a slippery slope toward a mass violation of civil liberties.

Yet another bureaucratic development may have slowed Hoover's pursuit of the mob. As attorney general, Bobby Kennedy had proposed the formation of a crime commission to supplement the FBI's efforts. Hoover hadn't wanted the competition. Then there was Kefauver, whom Hoover had little interest in helping. For Hoover to retain power, he needed to be the only national crime czar. Kennedy's commission idea quickly faded. Said biographer Gage: "Whatever was said at the meeting [between RFK and Hoover], in the following weeks Bobby's enthusiasm for the commission dropped markedly, while his public praise of Hoover notably increased."

While it had been shrewd of Hoover to duck the mob, it was against the country's best interests to allow the rackets to go unchallenged for so long. Wrote organized crime expert Thomas Reppetto, "It [the FBI] could have argued that the activities of the Mafia constituted a clear and present danger to national security, citing, for example the Teamsters' ability to paralyze transportation."

Hoover only accelerated his war on the mob after the disastrous Apalachin conference in 1957, when he had to. A document unearthed decades after his death confirms that Hoover eventually realized he had been wrong about not having devoted more to the mob than he had. In 1970, a colleague was circulating a new book by Ed Reid called *The Grim Reapers*. As organized crime legal scholar Alex Hortis reported, Hoover sent back the cover note that came with the book with a scrawl reading: "I have in mind that I was originally advised by Rosen that the Mafia or anything like it in character never existed in this country. I have been plagued ever since for having denied its existence."

Hortis concluded that Hoover "simply may have underestimated the Mafia. Ironically, the FBI came to understand organized crime better than any agency."

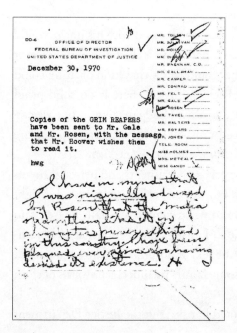

J. Edgar Hoover, in a handwritten note, regretted not taking the Mafia more seriously.

Federal Bureau of Investigation

THE HOOVER BLACKMAIL THEORY

There have been claims by conspiracy theorists that Hoover was in the mob's pocket and even received horse racing tips about fixed races from Frank Costello. In reality, Costello feared Hoover, having called him a "professional blackmailer." This theory, of course, is a lot of fun. Still, outside of internet obsessives and sensational authors, there's no evidence that it's true.

The most sensational Hoover theory was that the FBI director was gay and that Meyer Lansky, the mastermind of first resort, kept a photo of Hoover in a compromising position in his well-guarded private records. There are a few problems with this theory. First, the primary source for this was an unstable, bitter divorcée who had been paid for her testimony and had served time in prison for perjury. She was the estranged wife of liquor mogul Lewis Rosenstiel and claimed to have seen Hoover at a cocktail party wearing a fluffy dress, identifying himself as "Mary." Hilarious and vivid but preposterous. Wrote historian David K. Johnson (no relation to Trump chronicler David Cay Johnston): "Given the near hysteria in 1950s Washington about the threat posed to national security by homosexuals in high government office, the existence of so much evidence of Hoover's sexuality would have led to his ouster."

Even if Hoover had been gay, a man so obsessed with his image would not be parading around Georgetown parties in a chiffon gown, however stunning he may have looked. One would think that kind of thing could get around. As journalist Frank Rich opined, "There is no solid proof for the transvestism charges leveled against J. Edgar Hoover, but we can dream, can't we?" Hoover's alleged cross-dressing remains pop-culture gold, featured in TV shows like *Seinfeld* and *Saturday Night Live.*

I have reviewed Lansky's most private documents and personal financial records, and there was nary a Hoover centerfold to be found. Might Lansky not have leveraged this photo when Hoover virtually chased him out of the country in 1970? Wouldn't Lansky's family, some acutely cash-strapped after his death, have put the sexy Hoover pic on the open market in the last half century? After all, some family members sell swaths of cloth from Lansky's suits online.

Hoover's FBI not only prosecuted Lansky, but the Justice Department that employed him formed the only one-man-target strike force at that time, Project Financier. Hoover even called for a "crash investigation" of Lansky, according to FBI records. Lansky had his version of a last laugh, observing to an Israeli official, "Attorney General Mitchell who since then has been convicted of a felony, is at present in jail" and in an interview, "I'm free, but look who's in jail now. Mitchell."

Lansky's partner Jimmy Alo put it best when asked about the Hoover photo: "There was never no such picture. If there was, I'd have known about it, being so close to Meyer." Approaching a century of life, with Hoover dead for decades, Alo had no reason to lie.

Still, lesser mobsters than Alo cherish the Hoover-in-a-dress meme because it's a cheap and self-aggrandizing proxy battle: *See what happens when you mess with us! We even control the federal government!* As the 1960s wore on, Hoover *stepped up* surveillance, not to mention outright harassment of key mob figures, whether he had the goods on them or not.

IN *THE GODFATHER*, WHEN THE AGING DON SPEAKS TO MICHAEL IN THE garden about their failure to have become senators and governors, Michael scoffs, "Another *pezzonovante*," which roughly means "big shot." Almost everyone misses this critical point of the movie: *Even Don Corleone didn't think he had become a big shot, thus the obsessive push toward legitimacy with "the move to Nevada."*

Discreet and bookish
Genovese family legend
Vincent "Jimmy Blue
Eyes" Alo
*AP Photo/Anthony
Camerano*

Some of the smarter retired mobsters combine nostalgia with re-markable candor and insight. Sammy Gravano shared a story about John Gotti's suggestion while incarcerated about bribing President Bill Clinton to pardon them. Gravano was dumbfounded by Gotti's brainstorm and suggested that breaking out of their eleventh-floor prison cell was a better idea because that was something they, as criminals, might know how to do: "He's the President of the United States! He wants $5 million, he needs it from us? And he's gonna release me and you for multiple murders, give us a pardon for what reason? 'Cause we gave him $5 million? He's not gonna make that public. That's insane. I'm goin' out the window. You can bribe the president. I wish you all the luck in the world."

For all its bad-boy mystique, the Mafia thrived during earlier times be-cause it knew its place in the shadows. In addition to not provoking the federal government, they preferred not to stir trouble with other groups. Someone close to my family once owned the heavyweight boxer Sonny Liston's contract. I asked him if LCN ever got it hands on Muhammad Ali, who lived in our town. He said, "Hell, no, we didn't want to tangle with the bow ties," meaning the Nation of Islam, which guided Ali's career.

THE POLS AND LEGIT MOGULS OUTPLAYED THE MOB

The politicians ultimately got the better end of their deal with the mob because they *used* the mobsters, as did later respectable businesspeople who got rich off mob muscle. Said Lucky Luciano of Roosevelt, "I never knew that a guy who was gonna be President would stick a knife in your back when you wasn't looking. I never knew his word was no better than a lot of racket guys." In referring to a politician who hadn't come through for him, Giancana said: "He's like Kennedy. He'll get what he wants out of ya', but you won't get anything out of him."

It is no surprise, therefore, that politicians would make promises and renege as events warranted because that's what politicians do. Wrote William Howard Moore in his analysis of the Kefauver hearings: "While the Kefauver group stressed the gamblers' political power, the evidence suggests that the politicians used the gamblers, their funds, and their organization more frequently than the gamblers used the politicians."

The idea of the mob getting outfoxed—or having limited power—goes against everything we desperately want to believe. It ruins the fantasy of malefactors who run the world from the shadows and get the last laugh. Presidents could use the mob with impunity because they knew who had the power in the end. There is no grand moral principle at work here besides opportunistic self-interest. There never was a single hand on the tiller.

The only thing the mob could sustain was their criminal activities. Racketeers lost the booze business to legal manufacturers adept at straddling the proverbial line when Prohibition ended. Large, heavily regulated corporations chased the mob out of casino gambling and turned it into a legal industry worth hundreds of billions—the best the gangsters could do was rob them through skimming. For a while. Noted Lansky in his private records: "About the year of 1957 the gambling commission of Las Vegas declared a ruling not permitting holders of a gambling license to indulge in gambling in any other State of [the] Country. This also excluded the operators of Hotels. How come the Hilton Corporation wasn't obliged to sever their gambling holdings in other areas?"

The corporations argued that they never had to get violent to build their businesses. This may be true, but they didn't have to build the *gambling* business from the ground up and had no conception of what was required. The companies weren't offended enough by the immorality of gambling not to swoop in after the mobsters created it and buy it cheaply. Wrote Lansky in his private notes of blue-chip corporations: "They never had the courage to explore Las Vegas or a few other places but when they saw the gambling business was very profitable then they got the machinery working to oust the people who sweated to make it profitable."

Lansky also wrote to a friend, "After a taste of the profits in it they spray the holy water (by legalizing) and all is forgiven. It is now moral." He was right: Gambling is still a destructive endeavor, but it's booming now that it's regulated by the government and sanitized by corporations.

Nor can we conclude that "crime doesn't pay." It's more accurate to figure that large-scale malfeasance pays big if you are shrewd enough to keep it on the margins of lawful conduct and invest heavily in the shibboleths of respectability. Law enforcement understood this. Said the Justice Department's Jay Waldman in a 1976 interview: "Organized crime is no longer a bunch of characters hanging around ethnic neighborhoods. If you're talking about what the feds should be doing, it's going after the big-time criminals who are operating like most legitimate businessmen."

HOW THE FEDS WON

Everything you need to know about who has the power in the Wiseguy–White House nexus lies with RICO. RICO gave the feds a broader spectrum of offenses to charge targets. It was one thing to be caught stealing; it was another if that theft was part of a more comprehensive criminal enterprise. If that were the case, a crook could get ten instead of a four-year sentence. It was easy to be brave about facing a four-year sentence. Thirty years? Not so much. RICO made it easier to indict mobsters and get them to turn state's evidence against their associates (it recently ensnared a former president). Mob bosses lost the insulation that had protected them for generations, because prosecutors now had a broader standard with which to convict them. Making things even harder for the mob was the Witness Security Program, which was authorized in 1970 to protect those who testified against organized crime and were guarded by the U.S. Marshals Service.

All of this has put pressure on gangsters that they could not handle. Contrary to the tough talk we are told about their hatred of rats and love of omertà, it's hard to be tough when the feds kick down your door at four in the morning and throw your family on the cold floor with semiautomatic weapons pointed at your heads. A vast majority "flip" pronto when presented with reasonable cooperation deals. One FBI agent on a New York LCN squad marveled that they had more informants than agents.

Moreover, it turns out that some of the most prominent mob-world people in history who remained free men and died of natural causes had been informants for decades.* Las Vegas gambling boss Frank "Lefty" Rosenthal of *Casino* fame comes to mind. As Tony Soprano told his shrink, "Guys

---

*   There have also been credible reports that Sidney Korshak was a "dry snitch," meaning that he could point law enforcement in the right direction without directly naming names and giving details. Specifically, Korshak shared information with Las Vegas sheriff Ralph Lamb, who happened to be his wife's cousin, who in turn told the FBI. This horse trading continues regularly despite fanciful notions that gangsters were always discreet.

today have no room for the penal experience." Or, as an analysis published by the University of Chicago summarized, "A few important prosecutions were brought in the 1970s, followed by a torrent in the 1980s. Practically every Cosa Nostra boss, and usually their successors, were convicted."

PERHAPS ONE REASON JOHN F. KENNEDY WAS SO RECKLESS ABOUT HIS links to mob-connected types was that his status and respectability didn't keep him up at night the way they had Nixon. Kennedy was careless because he could be. Doors had been swinging open for him from the day he was born. Whereas Ben Bradlee's newspaper, the *Washington Post*, justifiably helped end Nixon's career, Bradlee was his fellow Harvardian's best friend and had no interest in publicizing Kennedy's dark side.

Nixon and Kennedy's life stories illustrate the unfairness of class and thuggery in America. Nixon White House aide Bryce Harlow said, "Richard Nixon went up the walls of life with his claws." The star-crossed Nixon scratched his way out of the gutter, and no matter high he climbed, he retained his hustler's whiff, five o'clock shadow and all. JFK had a scoundrel father who did all the rough stuff so his son(s) could operate charmingly in the right circles without scrutiny. The distance from original sins matters. Meanwhile, Kennedy's tan was due to a disease of the adrenal glands, yet it was spun as "youth" and "vigor."

Crime pays bigger for those who try to play the system rather than beat it. I hearken back to the childhood story I was told about "Uncle Vince" being in the car with Vito Genovese at Apalachin and the level of disgrace Genovese felt, not only because he looked foolish in front of his friends but because he was tagged as a gangster before his neighbors. The desire to have things both ways—grab the money and the power while avoiding shame—never ceases. There is a reason why many mob leaders cover their faces when they're booked.

Why would Donald Trump admit to knowing mobsters when someone like Joseph P. Kennedy worked so hard to distance himself? It's a question of what kind of status each was seeking. Trump admired gangsters and sought to emulate their style of flouting convention, demanding loyalty, and punishing enemies. Whereas Joe Kennedy wanted to be embraced by the Eastern Protestant elite, Trump coped with his outer-borough rejection by deliberately offending them. Said former Trump press secretary

Stephanie Grisham of Trump's feelings toward Vladimir Putin: "I also think he admired him, greatly, I think he wanted to be able to kill whoever spoke out against him. . . . In my experience with him, he loved the dictators, he loved the people who could kill anyone, including the press."

Nevertheless, the *New York Times'* Maggie Haberman describes Trump as a "credentialist" desperate for respect from legacy institutions such as the Ivy League or the *Times.* If Trump's modus operandi was to act like Rodney Dangerfield's crass developer Al Czervik in *Caddyshack,* Joe Kennedy's was the nuanced and ruthless poseur Tom Ripley in *The Talented Mr. Ripley,* creeping his way into higher society by adopting the persona of those who had been born there. Joe Kennedy didn't want to punish the press; he tried to schmooze them. His sons never had to think about such things.

Whereas Trump slathered his properties with gold, the Kennedy homes were furnished with Brahmin understatement, and the siblings often dressed in the kind of well-worn clothes one might expect from New England preppies with inherited wealth. Trump referred to "the best people" publicly, while Joe Kennedy used the precise term privately because he knew that to do otherwise would appear grasping.

GETTING IN AT THE END

Contrary to the cliché that it's the cover-up, not the crime, that gets you, it's clear that cover-ups have worked nicely for the mob and presidents. Operation Underworld was kept quiet for many years—and the official report didn't become public for decades—and hasn't hurt FDR's reputation. The Kennedy mob links took a decade and a half after the actual events to surface, and it didn't put a nick on his reputation during his lifetime. Whatever was done to tamp down the Reagan administration's abandonment of investigations into MCA was a nonissue during his presidency despite journalistic attention from the most intrepid in the business. Even though there was coverage of Trump's ties to organized crime contemporaneous with his political career, these relationships haven't been sufficient to cause him the slightest setback, let alone legal jeopardy.

The mob has never made or controlled a president in the sense that occurs in pulp thrillers. As we've seen, racketeers have sometimes been helpful to legitimate businesses and political and government figures. Organized crime, however, was an omnipresent combination of gear and invisible lubricant in the engine of capitalism and democracy. Perhaps Bill Bonanno, son of LCN family founder Joseph Bonanno, put it best: "My tradition—the tradition of my fathers—allowed a small group of men operating in secret, often against the law and convention, not only to survive but also to thrive. The Mafia for a long time was part of the power structure of the country itself. No history of the United States from 1930 on that doesn't take that into account will be a false history."

THE OVAL OFFICE IS DISARMINGLY SMALL, NOT MUCH BIGGER THAN A two-car garage. I was surprised when I first saw it. It reminded me of a Fabergé egg; it feels vulnerable. The room is surprisingly cozy except for the high curved ceiling rising to the Great Seal of the United States. The photos the public often sees are taken with a lens that portrays a more cavernous space. It made me think of *The Wizard of Oz* and how "the great and powerful Oz" was just a little man from Kansas winging it on a much larger stage.

I remember studying the Oval Office from the open door to the hallway on an August Friday afternoon, where the left turn is made to go to the press office. It was perfectly quiet, just a Secret Service agent, my boss and friend Doug Elmets, and me. I wondered why people wanted to be president. I don't doubt that all the presidents who occupied this office hoped to do good, but the *personal* reason that drove these men of self-esteem is that the presidency is the ultimate symbol of having made it in America. It is a certification of transcendence—we tell children, *"If you work hard, Bobby/Sally, someday you can be president!"*

After leaving work, I drove to see my family in Margate, New Jersey, a beach town south of Atlantic City. We went to the Greenhouse Restaurant, and in walked the 1980s Cosa Nostra boss of Philadelphia and South Jersey, the hair-triggered Nicky Scarfo, with his entourage. Very much in the spirit of contemporary America, these gangsters wanted to be seen and feared. Unlike Uncle Vince and the others at Apalachin, these men were not ashamed. They were either proud to be outlaws or refracting the desperate state of their lives through bravado because, in a few short years, they would *all* be murdered, incarcerated, or in witness protection.

Scarfo's reptilian eyes darted around for recognition as servers bowed. He was a fidgety, immaculate, and diminutive man who appeared as if he might explode if a breadcrumb landed on his lap. I wondered why some criminals wanted so badly to be on display. I figured that this is what we do in America: We equate achievement with visibility, regardless of what we had done to get noticed. We constantly wrestle with the big dreams of who we can be and the small realities of who we are. Bob Dylan sang, "Even the president of the United States sometimes must have to stand naked." Scarfo and his crew wanted to feel big, powerful, and masters of a world mortals could not control. That is before they were killed on the street or imprisoned. No, this crew wouldn't be influencing presidents.

Controlling a shakedown racket of Jersey shore unions doesn't compare with commanding the United States military, but for a time in this country, it must have seemed that way. The American rackets *had influenced* events above their station until those who resided in that realm turned on them when they didn't need them anymore. What's more, there would be nothing the gangsters could do about it: compensate with swagger or hide in their shabby social clubs and pray they hadn't been bugged.

Meyer Lansky probably never said, "We're bigger than U.S. Steel," but he did hire private tutors in economics and history. Not long after Meyer's wife, Teddy, died, I felt a twinge of sadness as I paged through his copy of Benjamin Graham's *Security Analysis*, the same book that inspired a young Warren Buffett and saw the handwritten notes the underworld pioneer had made in pencil. Marlon Brando's *Godfather* rasp was stuck in my head: *"I thought that when it was your time, you would be the one to hold the strings . . . Senator Corleone, Governor Corleone."* It was what Meyer hadn't written that haunted me most about his journey: why he had chosen July 4 as his birthdate after his real records vanished into the wilderness of immigration, what America had promised, and who else he might have become.

Author's Note and Acknowledgments

This book has been a lifelong endeavor. I have been collecting stories about organized crime since I found out who some of the people were who made appearances in the lives of those of us who grew up near Philadelphia and Southern New Jersey/Atlantic City. I didn't know until I committed to writing books that I'd have use for these memories and data points. Nor did I understand the degree to which some of these characters and stories I was told would stake a disproportionate claim on my mental real estate.

Then there are the presidents. The first book I remember ordering as a child was about the presidents. Nixon was in office and was the most recent president featured. My mother and I picked it up at a bookstore at the Cherry Hill Mall. For a time, I considered a political career and wanted, at the very least, to work in the orbit of a presidency, which I ended up doing. I became a collector of books and facts about the presidency; the more arcane, the better. I don't know much about Constitutional theory, but I can tell you how high the Oval Office ceiling is (eighteen feet six inches). My point is that sometimes you don't know what an accretion of fact-collecting will ultimately get you, but whether the subject matter is organized crime or the presidency, sometimes it gets you somewhere.

One of the strange things about sifting through so much information on a singular subject was the contradictions in the information I found. There are very different versions of the same events, excellent sources that provide dubious information, and questionable sources that provide valuable insights. There have been a few things stated as fact in scholarship on organized crime that I'm embarrassed to say I once believed, including that J. Edgar Hoover refused to testify before the Kefauver Committee (he did testify) and that Sam Giancana and Santo Trafficante were on the FBI's 10 Most Wanted List (they weren't). It's also possible to agree with some of the data other fine journalists report but draw different conclusions. When it comes to organized crime and national politics, I continue to be surprised by some of the things that have been accepted as fact and the credibility assigned to rumors that have compounded over the years.

In my first career in the crisis management business, I had to be a clinician more than an academic—it wasn't enough to understand the complex facts of the matter; I had to decide what they meant and recommend actions that must be taken. As an author, I have a similar tendency: I reach practical conclusions based on what most likely occurred, given the available data. Accordingly, in *Wiseguys and the White House* I haven't shied away from telling the reader what I think happened.

When I had to judge what I believed when it came from a mobster's lips (or those of their families, friends, and associates), the questions I asked included: Were they under oath? Were their statements blatantly self-serving? Can what they said be corroborated? Was it consistent with other information? Did it square with what I've learned or concluded?

To this end, another challenge in writing about organized crime is that many people lie, which begs the question, "How can you tell if somebody's lying?" There are no foolproof "tells." However, as a rule, I don't trust those who appear to know how everything went down. Put differently, I'm encouraged when a source knows a lot about one thing and then knows nothing about another. I've also been skeptical of highly centralized conspiracy theories involving masterminds and stories people appeared to need to believe a little too much.

Cynthia Duncan, the granddaughter of Teddy and Meyer Lansky, gave me access to Meyer's personal records over many years, which provided texture to the man we thought we knew more than a writer could dream of. I reviewed private records, diaries, personal correspondence, legal documents, travel papers, financial papers, and notes made on newspaper clippings and in books. Meyer's nephew, Mark Lansky, also shared noteworthy stories. Thanks also to Cynthia's partner, the great artist Julio Blanco. There were others in the Lansky orbit who were also helpful who preferred not to be cited. Thanks to Meyer and Teddy from one of those little kids running around a pool on Collins Avenue.

Presidential and law enforcement archives have become more accessible in recent years, and I benefited from these in my research. The FBI has been particularly assertive in making more of its files available to journalists and authors, including some that don't always portray the bureau's past in the most flattering light, which is to their credit. People in law enforcement, those who cooperated with investigations, and even informants were discreetly generous with their time, records, and insights. Given the subject matter, not everyone wanted to be quoted or acknowledged, so I have been careful about respecting ground rules, including using pseudonyms in some cases.

Some of my friends squeamishly asked me if I intended to write a chapter on Ronald Reagan in this book, given that I had been a young aide in his White House. The answer was that I couldn't *not* include him, not because he was unique in the context of this book—he wasn't—but because not having the MCA story would be a conspicuous oversight. Some old friends aren't pleased that I included Reagan, but sadly we're in that tribal age where in politics there are only friends or foes. Thanks to former prosecutor Marvin Rudnick for his insights into Justice Department investigations of MCA.

My friend and editor Sean Desmond catalyzed this book, and without him, I would never have been an author. I could have gone a thousand lifetimes without finding someone like him. My literary agent Kris Dahl has stood by me from the beginning of my wild ride. Thanks also to Josie Freedman of CAA and David Howe and Jackie Quaranto at HarperCollins.

I am blessed to have Gus Russo and Dan Moldea as friends and colleagues, whose pioneering organized crime journalism I tapped into and whose guidance I sought in researching this book. Their investigative skills and adventures exceed and predate my own, and I have proudly cited their work even though we sometimes have affectionate authors' quarrels over the conclusions we've reached. I hope I have credited them properly, as they deserve it (and I'd be mortified if I failed them).

Larry Gragg has done exceptional work on Las Vegas, Ben Siegel, and the racing wire service and was patient with helping me refine and clarify a few essential points. Thanks to Jack Farrell, who gave me valuable direction on the JFK and Nixon chapters. James Rosen also provided a unique perspective on Watergate.

Larry Leamer's depth of knowledge on the Kennedy family gave me greater confidence in my skepticism of commonly held misperceptions, especially about Joe Kennedy's alleged bootlegging and mob connections, which existed but have been vastly exaggerated.

Gary Klein gave me historical insight into the FBI's organized crime work and related statistics. Gary spent the majority of his twenty-five-year FBI career working organized crime investigations, many with the Organized Crime Strike Force, while assigned to FBI offices throughout the country, to include Phoenix, Cleveland, Newark, and New York City. He also served as the unit chief of the La Cosa Nostra/Italian Organized Crime/Labor Racketeering Unit while assigned to FBI Headquarters. For decades, Gary has allowed me to pretend I'm an FBI agent without rolling his eyes too often. While the FBI has been accused of not addressing the mob soon enough, Gary's generation of agents and leaders took the threat very seriously, which yielded extraordinary results. I hope I have captured these achievements accurately and respectfully.

Dr. John Fox, the FBI's historian, was generous with his time and, as always, was candid about the FBI's adventures over its long history. He set me straight on a few issues that hopefully contributed to this book's accuracy. The FBI is lucky to have someone who is both helpful to writers and candid enough not to shy away from inconvenient history. I appreciate the information I received from my former colleague Darren Tromblay, now a historian at the FBI focusing on counterintelligence.

My other author friends have been resourceful touchstones during my moments of self-doubt, including Marty Bell, Peter Cozzens, Paul Dickson, Ed Grosvenor, Virginia Hume, Ron Kessler, Ed Leamer, Jane Leavy, Nancy Lubin, Gene Meyer, Mark Obenhaus, Mark Olshaker, Ira Shapiro, Craig Shirley, David Stewart, Joel Swerdlow, and Stuart Taylor.

Alex Hortis has done exceptional research into novel aspects of organized crime and was very generous in sharing sources that put some of my research into perspective. His work on J. Edgar Hoover's philosophy and actions on LCN will be the ones that stand the test of time.

Mark Feldstein is always the best source for how journalists cover sensitive issues, and I used some of the examples he provided to make my case.

Howard Willens, a staff member of the Warren Commission to investigate the assassination of President Kennedy, was generous with his time in discussing the near certainty that organized crime played no role in the tragedy.

Philip Angell, Jennifer Avellino, Bob Bates, Ann Haldeman Coppe, Frank Donatelli, Doug (one of my White House bosses) and Pam Elmets, Matt Mosk, Bill Novelli, Bruce Ochsman, Norm Ornstein, Sam Potolicchio, Serge Samoilenko, Sally Satel, Bill Taylor, Frankie Trull, and Marc Wassermann cheered me on. My sherpa-to-the-mountaintop Cary Bernstein is always a touchstone.

Micaela Quinn's research skills allowed me to access databases with news reports and government archives. Jessica Lacher-Feldman at the University of Rochester was of great assistance with the private records of Thomas E. Dewey and his role in the commutation of Lucky Luciano's prison sentence and deportment.

If it were not for Casey Hebert, I would not have been able to access this implement known as a "computer," which I'm told many people are using these days. I predict these things are going to be big (I am still convinced my use of Grammarly software secretly did something hideous to my manuscript that is going to get me into huge trouble).

Former Watergate prosecutor and member of the 911 Commission Richard Ben-Veniste gave me perspectives on the Watergate scandal that sent me in directions I hadn't considered, especially since there is so little new besides compendiums. I focused on the narrow passageways between organized crime and the Watergate affair. I am responsible for any conclusions reached here about Watergate, wise or foolish.

I am grateful to Carole Russo, niece of Vincent "Jimmy Blue Eyes" Alo, for her insight into the myths and realities of her uncle Jim's life over the years. Even the little anecdotes help animate one of the Cosa Nostra giants who remained a ghost to many. Uncle Jim was indeed "the last gentleman gangster." Thanks also to Carole's son Kevin Russo.

Luellen Smiley had terrific stories about her dad, Allen, and his business partners Benjamin "Bugsy" Siegel and Johnny Rosselli. She brought these colorful characters back to life in our discussions and in her writing.

Thanks to Geoff Schumacher of The Mob Museum in Las Vegas and authors J. Michael Niotta and Rick Warner, who pointed me in directions I would not have otherwise known about. Robert De Niro has graciously taken an interest in some of the organized crime research I've got going.

E.B. shared her experiences with the Black Panthers in the 1960s and observations about the organization's interactions with law enforcement and organized crime groups in Philadelphia.

I am always grateful to my businesss partners and colleagues at Dezenhall Resources, Ltd., Maya Shackley, Steven Schlein, Josh Culling, Anne Marie Malecha, and Jennifer Hirshon for their support for my writing endeavors.

I appreciate the anecdotes I heard from friends and relatives from New Jersey and Philadelphia who shared colorful stories with me that I never imagined being able to use in a book. Still, many of these things were the kind of firsthand accounts one could never find in archives.

As always, my thanks to my family who had to overhear me on the phone talking about this book during its research and writing stages: Donna, Stuart, Eliza, Nate, Meghan, Lincoln, Jayme, Oliver, my sister Susan and her merry band including Kayla Seidman and Maggie Barson, not to mention our collection of dogs, cats, and alpacas.

Sally Rosenthal curated the photos that appear on the pages. I have no idea how she found some of them but am very appreciative.

Thanks, finally, to Taylor Swift. I don't know her but by putting her in the acknowledgments, maybe a new generation of readers will think I do.

Given the sheer volume of data I had to review, not to mention contradictory versions of events and imperfect sources, I have very likely made some mistakes or oversights, and I'm sure I'll hear about them. These are my fault alone, and I'll keep trying to get things right. My work adds threads to the broader mosaic and doesn't claim to be the final word on my subject matter.

Selected Bibliography

Abadinsky, Howard. *Organized Crime*. Chicago: Nelson-Hall, 1994.

Asbury, Herbert. *The Gangs of New York: An Informal History of the Underworld*. New York: Alfred A. Knopf, 1928.

Baime, A. J. *The Accidental President*. New York: Hughton Mifflin Harcourt, 2017.

Barrett, Wayne. *Trump: The Deals and the Downfall*. New York: HarperCollins, 1992.

Bell, Daniel. *The End of Ideology*. Cambridge, MA: Harvard University Press, 1960.

Benson, Michael. *Gangsters vs. Nazis*. New York: Citadel Press, 2022.

Birkbeck, Matt. *The Life We Chose*. New York: William Morrow, 2023.

Black, Matthew. *Operation Underworld*. New York: Citadel Press, 2023.

Blakey, G. Robert, and Richard Billings. *The Plot to Kill the President*. New York: Times Books, 1981.

Blum, Howard. *Dark Invasion*. New York: HarperCollins, 2014.

Brandt, Charles. *I Heard You Paint Houses: The Inside Story of the Mafia, the Teamsters and the Last Ride of Jimmy Hoffa*. Hanover, NH: Steerforth Press, 2004.

Bruck, Connie. *When Hollywood Had a King*. New York: Random House, 2003.

Bugliosi, Vincent. *Reclaiming History*. New York: W. W. Norton, 2007.

Burrough, Bryan. *Days of Rage*. New York: Penguin Press, 2015.

Campbell, Rodney. *The Luciano Project: The Secret Wartime Collaboration of the Mafia and the U.S. Navy*. New York: McGraw-Hill, 1977.

Caro, Robert. *The Passage of Power*. New York: Alfred A. Knopf, 2012.

Chambliss, William J. *On the Take: From Petty Crooks to Presidents*. Bloomington: Indiana University Press, 1978.

CIA Targets Fidel: The Secret 1967 Inspector General's Report on Plots to Assassinate Fidel Castro. Melbourne, Victoria: Ocean Press, 1996.

Cockayne, James. *Hidden Power: The Strategic Logic of Organized Crime.* New York: Oxford University Press, 2016.

Collier, Peter, and David Horowitz. *The Kennedys: An American Drama.* New York: Warner Books, 1985.

Costanzo, Elio. *The Mafia and the Allies.* New York: Enigma Books, 2007.

Cowles, Virginia. *The Astors.* London: Alfred A. Knopf, 1979.

Cressey, Donald R. *Theft of the Nation.* New York: Harper & Row, 1969.

Dasch, George. *Eight Spies Against America.* New York: Robert M. McBride, 1959.

David, William C. *The Pirates Lafitte: The Treacherous World of the Corsairs of the Gulf.* New York: Houghton Mifflin, 2005.

De Toledo, Zali. *They Called Him a Gangster.* eBook-Pro.com, 2020.

Deitche, Scott. *The Silent Don.* Fort Lee, NJ: Barricade Books, 2007.

Denton, Sally, and Roger Morris. *The Money and the Power: The Making of Las Vegas and Its Hold on America.* New York: Alfred A. Knopf, 2001.

DeVecchio, Lin. *We're Going to Win This Thing.* New York: Berkley Books, 2011.

Dillard, W. O. *Clear Burning: Civil Rights, Civil Wrongs.* Jackson, MS: Persimmon Press, 1992.

Drosnan, Michael. *Citizen Hughes.* New York: Broadway Books, 1985.

English, T. J. *Paddy Whacked: The Untold Story of the Irish American Gangster.* New York: William Morrow, 2005.

Evans, M. Stanton. *Blacklisted by History.* New York: Three Rivers Press, 2007.

Farrell, John A. *Nixon: The Life.* New York: Doubleday, 2017.

Feder, Sid, and Joachim Joesten. *The Luciano Story.* New York: Da Capo Press, 1994.

Feldstein, Mark. *Poisoning the Press.* New York: Farrar, Straus and Giroux, 2010.

Ferrell, Robert H. *Truman and Pendergast.* Columbia: University of Missouri Press, 1999.

Fino, Ronald, and Michael Rizzo. *Mr. Undercover.* Washington, D.C.: Triangle Exit, 2013.

Fox, Stephen. *Blood and Power.* New York: William Morrow, 1989.

Fraser, Steven. *Labor Will Rule.* Ithaca, NY: Cornell University Press, 1991.

Fulsom, Don. *The Mafia's President.* New York: Thomas Dunne Books, 2017.

Gabler, Neal. *Winchell: Gossip, Power and the Culture of Celebrity.* New York: Alfred A. Knopf, 1994.

Gage, Beverly. *J. Edgar Hoover and the Making of the American Century.* New York: Viking, 2022.

Gannon, Michael. *Operation Drumbeat: The Dramatic True Story of Germany's First U-boat Attacks Along the American Coast in World War II*. New York: Harper & Row, 1990.

Gellman, Irwin F. *Campaign of the Century*. New Haven, CT: Yale University Press, 2021.

Giancana, Antoinette. *Mafia Princess*. New York: William Morrow, 1984.

Glushakow, H. B. *Mafia Don: Trump's 40 Years of Mob Ties*. Self-published, 2016.

Gragg, Larry. *Bugsy's Shadow*. Albuquerque, NM: High Road Books, 2023.

Grover, Warren. *Nazis in Newark*. New Brunswick, NJ: Transaction Publishers, 2003.

Haldeman, H. R. *The Haldeman Diaries: Inside the Nixon White House*. New York: G. P. Putnam's Sons, 1994.

Haldeman, Jo. *In the Shadow of the White House*. Los Angeles: Vireo Books, 2017.

Harmon, Sandra. *Mafia Son*. New York: St. Martin's Press, 2009.

Hersh, Seymour. *The Dark Side of Camelot*. New York: Little, Brown, 1997.

Hickham, Jr., Homer. *Torpedo Junction*. New York: Dell, 1989.

Hortis, Alexander C. *The Mob and the City*. Amherst, NY: Prometheus, 2014.

Hougan, Jim. *Secret Agenda: Watergate, Deep Throat and the CIA*. New York: Open Road, 1984.

Jacobs, James. *Mobsters, Unions and Feds*. New York: New York University Press, 2006.

Johnson, David Alan. *Betrayal*. New York: Hippocrene Books, 2007.

Johnston, David Cay. *The Making of Donald Trump*. Brooklyn, NY: Melville House, 2016.

Kaplan, James. *Sinatra: The Chairman*. New York: Doubleday, 2015.

Katz, Leonard. *Uncle Frank: The Biography of Frank Costello*. New York: Drake Publishers, 1973.

Kavieff, Paul. *The Life and Times of Lepke Buchalter*. New York: Barricade Books, 2006.

Kelley, Kitty. *His Way: The Unauthorized Biography of Frank Sinatra*. New York: Bantam Books, 1986.

Kessler, Ronald. *The Secrets of the FBI*. New York: Crown Forum, 2011.

———. *Sins of the Father*. New York: Grand Central Publishing, 1996.

Knoedelseder, William. *Stiffed: A True Story of MCA, the Music Business, and the Mafia*. New York: HarperCollins, 1993.

Knott, Stephen F. *Coming to Terms with John F. Kennedy*. Lawrence: University Press of Kansas, 2022.

Kuntz, Tom, and Phil Kuntz. *The Sinatra Files*. New York: Three Rivers Press, 2000.

Lacey, Robert. *Little Man: Meyer Lansky and the Gangster Life.* New York: Little, Brown, 1991.

Lance, Peter. *Cover Up.* New York: Regan Books, 2004.

———. *Deal with the Devil: The FBI's Secret Thirty-Year Relationship with a Mafia Killer.* New York: William Morrow, 2013.

Lemann III, Arthur. *Hail to the Dragon Slayer.* New Orleans: Vetter Communications, 1998.

Litwin, Fred. *I Was a Teenage JFK Conspiracy Freak.* Ottawa: NorthernBlues Books, 2018.

Maier, Thomas. *Mafia Spies: The Inside Story of the CIA, Gangsters, JFK, and Castro.* New York: Skyhorse Publishing, 2019.

Marshall, Jonathan. *Dark Quadrant: Organized Crime, Big Business, and the Corruption of American Democracy.* Lanham, MD: Rowman & Littlefield, 2021.

McCullough, David. *Truman.* New York: Simon & Schuster, 1992.

McDougal, Dennis. *The Last Mogul.* New York: Crown, 1998.

Moldea, Dan. *Dark Victory: Ronald Reagan, MCA, and the Mob.* New York: Viking, 1986.

———. *The Hoffa Wars: The Rise and Fall of Jimmy Hoffa.* London: Paddington Press, 1978.

Morley, Jefferson. *Scorpion's Dance: The President, the Spymaster, and Watergate.* New York: St. Martin's Press, 2022.

Navasky, Victor S. *Kennedy Justice.* New York: Open Road, 1971.

Neff, James. *Mobbed Up.* New York: Open Road, 1989.

———. *Vendetta: Bobby Kennedy vs. Jimmy Hoffa.* New York: Little, Brown, 2015.

Newark, Tim. *Lucky Luciano: The Real and the Fake Gangster.* New York: Thomas Dunne, 2010.

———. *Mafia Allies: The True Story of America's Secret Alliance with the Mob in World War II.* St. Paul, MN: Zenith Press, 2007.

Newton, Michael. *Mr. Mob: The Life and Crimes of Moe Dalitz.* Jefferson, NC: McFarland, 2007.

Nixon, Richard. *Six Crises.* New York: Simon & Schuster, 1962.

Ogden, Christopher. *Legacy: A Biography of Moses and Walter Annenberg.* New York: Little, Brown, 1999.

Ouseley, William. *Open City.* Kansas City, MO: The Covington Group, 2008.

Persico, Joseph E. *Roosevelt's Secret War, FDR and World War II Espionage.* New York: Random House, 2001.

Peterson, Virgil W. *The Mob: 200 Years of Organized Crime in New York*. Ottawa, IL: Green Hill Publishers, 1983.

Poulsen, Ellen. *The Case Against Lucky Luciano*. Oakland Gardens, NY: Clinton Cook, 2007.

Ragano, Frank, and Selwyn Raab. *Mob Lawyer*. New York: Scribners, 1994.

Rappleye, Charles, and Ed Becker. *All American Mafioso*. New York: Doubleday, 1991.

Reppetto, Thomas. *Shadows over the White House*. New York: Enigma Books, 2015.

Reynolds, Nicholas. *Need to Know*. New York: Mariner Books, 2022.

Risen, James. *The Last Honest Man*. New York: Little, Brown, 2023.

Robb, David. *The Gumshoe and the Shrink*. Santa Monica, CA: Santa Monica Press, 2012.

Russo, Carole Cortland. *Me and Jimmy Blue Eyes*. Bellerose Village, NY: Red Penguin Books, 2020.

Russo, Gus. *Live by the Sword*. Baltimore: Bancroft Press, 1998.

———. *The Outfit: The Role of Chicago's Underworld in the Shaping of Modern America*. New York: Bloomsbury Press, 2001.

———. *Supermob: How Sidney Korshak and His Criminal Associates Became America's Hidden Power Brokers*. New York: Bloomsbury Press, 2006.

Schumacher, Geoff. *Howard Hughes*. Reno: University of Nevada Press, 2008.

Scott, Peter Dale. *Deep Politics and the Death of JFK*. Los Angeles: University of California Press, 1993.

Server, Lee. *Handsome Johnny*. New York: St. Martin's Press, 2018.

Shirley, Craig. *December 1941*. Nashville: Nelson Books, 2013.

———. *Rendezvous with Destiny*. Wilmington, DE: ISI Books, 2009.

Smiley, Luellen. *Cradle of Crime*. Self-published, 2016.

Snow, Richard. *A Measureless Peril: America in the Fight for the Atlantic, the Longest Battle of World War II*. New York: Scribner, 2010.

Stanford, Phil. *White House Call Girl*. Port Townsend, WA: Feral House, 2013.

Summers, Anthony. *The Arrogance of Power*. New York: Viking, 2000.

Tosches, Nick. *The Nick Tosches Reader*. New York: Da Capo Press, 2000.

Valentine, Douglas. *The Strength of the Wolf*. New York: Verso, 2004.

Villano, Anthony. *Brick Agent*. New York: The New York Times Book Company, 1977.

Vizzini, Sal. *Vizzini*. New York: Arbor House, 1972.

Waldron, Lamar. *Watergate: The Hidden History*. New York: Counterpoint, 2013.

Ward, Nathan. *Dark Harbor: The War for the New York Waterfront*. New York: Picador, 2010.

Weiner, Tim. *Legacy of Ashes*. New York: Random House, 2007.

Whalen, Richard J. *The Founding Father: The Story of Joseph P. Kennedy*. Washington, DC: Regnery, 1964.

Wilkinson, Rupert. *American Social Character*. New York: HarperCollins, 1992.

Willens, Howard P. *History Will Prove Us Right*. New York: Overlook Press, 2013.

Wills, Garry. *Nixon Agonistes*. New York: Houghton Mifflin, 1970.

Witcover, Jules. *Sabotage at Black Tom*. Chapel Hill, NC: Algonquin Books, 1989.

Witwer, David. *Corruption and Reform in the Teamsters Union*. Chicago: University of Illinois Press, 2008.

———. *Shadow Racketeer*. Chicago: University of Illinois Press, 2009.

Wojculewski, Stan. *Danger, Drugs & Dirty Work: The George Hunter White Story*. Self-published, 2013.

Zacks, Richard. *Island of Vice*. New York: Doubleday, 2012.

Index

About the Author

ERIC DEZENHALL is an award-winning author of twelve books of fiction and nonfiction, including *Best of Enemies: The Last Great Spy Story of the Cold War* (with Gus Russo), which is being made into a feature film. He founded one of the nation's first crisis management firms and worked in the White House, where President Reagan once called him "Derek." His organizational skills were deemed insufficient for membership in organized crime, but he's really trying.